retrohell

BY THE EDITORS OF **Ben Is Dead** MAGAZINE

retrohell

Life in the '70s and '80s, from Afros to Zotz

LITTLE, BROWN AND COMPANY   Boston   New York   Toronto   London

First Edition

Image credits appear on page 260.

LIBRARY OF CONGRESS CATALOGING-IN-PUBLICATION DATA

Retro Hell: Life in the '70s and '80s, from afros to zotz / by the
    editors of Ben Is Dead magazine. — 1st ed.
            p.   cm.
        Includes index.
        ISBN 0–316–10282–2
        1. Popular culture — United States — History — 20th century —
    Dictionaries.   2. United States — Social Life and Customs — 1971– —
    Dictionaries.   I. Ben Is Dead.
    E169.02.R48   1997
    306'.0973'03 — dc21   97-28089

    10 9 8 7 6 5 4 3 2 1

    MV—NY

Published simultaneously in Canada by Little, Brown & Company (Canada) Limited
Printed in the United States of America

BOOK DESIGN BY JULIA SEDYKH

LAYOUT BY MARY REILLY

THIS BOOK IS DEADICATED TO **Bobby**,

FOR ALL YOUR INSPIRATION.

MAY WE NEVER FORGET THE EXTENT OF OUR SUBJUGATION.

author's note

Information in this book is based upon sources and recollections of several people who helped with the preparation of this book about persons, events, and things that existed during the '70s and '80s. Many things mentioned in this book aren't around anymore or aren't produced in the same form. We hope that this book will amuse and encourage you to reminisce about people, events, and things of another era. In dredging up these memories, we may have exaggerated or fallen victim to hyperbole, so please read the entries with the gloss of your own version of the truth.

*"Every time you learn
something new
it pushes something old
out of your brain."*

— HOMER SIMPSON

obligatory enlightenment from your editress

We started work on this Retro Hell A–Z in 1994 for a small-press magazine entitled *Ben Is Dead*. The idea was to rid ourselves of our entertaining yet otherwise useless and decaying childhood memories by documenting the key people, events, concepts, objects, and artifacts that influenced our childhoods — roughly the period from 1970 to 1990. We wanted to get down the facts, but we also wanted to express what it felt like to *live* through this time. So we racked our brains for our personal perspectives and utilized reference materials to verify the information and remind us of the things we'd blocked out.

These memories are often distorted though, which is part of what makes them, and the whole retro phenomenon, so appealing. Many experiences can take on a different shade when the subconscious works its magic on them, often turning them into modern-day myths. But you can't really trust your own retrospections, and as in a good game of Operator, fact can be light-years away from what the person on the end of the line is hearing. (Consider this a disclaimer!)

Since we began this book, a disturbing number of these people, things, fashions, et cetera, have made mainstream comebacks — giving them a new life in the '90s, the decade we have officially deemed Retro Hell. We have left most of these entries in, acknowledging their comeback status with a koala symbol 🐨 (think of those insidious fuzzy clip-on koalas, or even the whole Aussie *Crocodile Dundee* outburst of the late '80s).

Retro Hell, which started off so capriciously in revival and camp, now seems to hold us entrenched in the past, like driving with your eyes glued on the rear-view mirror. This journey back has shown us that the past never stops and that no matter how hard you try you just can't keep up with retro. Even though we have completely exhausted our memories (and ourselves) on our trip through Retro Hell, we realize our research is by no means exhaustive.

This massive collection can be used as a reference guide, a map, or, if you want to do yourself some permanent damage, it can be read like a long, long story. It is our ultimate goal to have included enough memories here so that you don't need to waste your precious time and energy trying to recollect your own. Perhaps after this overwhelming indulgence you can finally get on with living life in the present. But in the meantime . . . enjoy. — darby

Jane, stop this crazy thing!

—GEORGE JETSON

introduction
by Bruce Elliott

Retroactive: A Brief History

Are you old enough to remember the Future? Remember all those moving sidewalks, picture phones, and moon rockets? Do you remember the '50s, all those great songs, big cars, and bigger hair? How about the '60s, all the cool clothes, great bands, and groovy drugs?

Even if you were not alive during any of these eras, chances are that you still have some memory of them. But can anyone have memories from before their birth? Or of a future that never came? Yet on a deep level, you do recall them, sort of. Why is this? The reason you "remember" them is retro. From fashion to food, the latest thing is now usually something old. How did this idea come about? How could a society's seemingly innocent flirtation with the past grow to where it now threatens its present and future? Since the retro ideal is that all answers lie in the past, we should look there, into retro's own history, for our answers.

The idea of retro has been with us as long as our memories. The ancient myths like the Garden of Eden or the *Odyssey* were always set in some distant, and presumably superior age. The same could be said for every tale that begins with "Once upon a time. . . ." However, it took the Industrial Revolution to truly produce retro. Before then, life was stable, predictable, and short — the same as one's parents', and their parents' parents' parents' (give or take the occasional mania for powdered wigs). The Industrial Revolution changed all this by giving rise to the notion of Progress. Progress held that social and technological changes were not only preferable but inevitable. Life would no longer be predictable or stable.

By the 1890s, this idea was being questioned by those with leisure time. Writers and thinkers began to extol the virtues of a bucolic past that was more fantasy than fact. They coined a new word to describe their mood: *nostalgia*. The word itself was a reworking of something old. It was derived from a combination of ancient Greek words: *nostos* (or "homecoming") and *algos* ("pain").

At first, nostalgia was a term suggesting a longing for a lost era. But it soon found a more popular meaning, that of a particular sadness common to the very old. It sprang from the heart instead of the mind and confined itself to living memory. As the new century dawned, poems and songs looked backward, praising the olden days of farms and family. By midcentury, progress had given us cars, airplanes, and atom bombs. America's victory in World War II had brought an uncertain new world order. In the late 1940s, the future didn't look bright, but somehow the past did. That seemingly innocent 1890s (now dubbed the Gay '90s) held a new appeal. What was formerly condemned was now considered the olden days. Songs, movies, and even fashions began looking back to a time of sing-alongs, swooning, and endless ice cream socials. Forgotten were the tenements, sweatshops, and manure-filled streets. The Gay '90s became a good place to hide from postwar realities like shortages, the Iron Curtain, and Senator McCarthy. This backward impulse went further still, all the way to Daniel Boone and his clean-shaven frontiersmen crossing the black and white West to a loud lush tune. Television's new window on the world looked backward, seeing mostly the cowboy, the cavalry, and the caboose. Cold Warriors in buckskin had arrived to keep the world safe from reality.

Then a *Sputnik* shudder ran down the nation's sturdy spine. It looked up and now saw the stars to grab. Brains were needed to match the brawn, and eggheads were lured into Big Science with a tantalizing taste of the future. The vision was tail-fin sharp and martini clear. It was atom-powered, with sprawling lunar suburbs. Contemporary, modern, and futuristic all melted into a single tangible now. Suddenly it was 1960, and there was little time for the past or anything old. It cherished the new, the big, and the bold. It would reach for the Moon. New frontiers and new adventures would all be part of this great big beautiful tomorrow. But by decade's end, there were many who doubted whether such a tomorrow should ever dawn. Progress had given them television and jumbo jets, but it came with napalm and pollution. Egged on by rambunctious youth, pundits called for an end to progress, an end to capitalism, and a return to nature.

In all this social tumult, the older generation felt lost. Again, the past looked brighter than the present. Even the Great Depression and World War II began to look good. This time, they were able to return to a past that moved, talked, and sang. A black-and-white world of Fred and Ginger beckoned, featuring the Andrews Sisters and a chorus line of USO dancers. Old films leaped from the late show to the revival house. Forgotten musicals returned to Broadway while television ads hawked compilations of old songs. The smell of mothballs gave way to that of money. Soon even the young would want in on this sort of fun, and the future began to slip away.

By the mid-'70s, progress itself seemed like a memory, and the great big beautiful tomorrow seemed only like yesterday. Today was in crisis, while tomorrow seemed just a nightmare away. In the middle stood those who'd been too old to march and were too young to retire. They found themselves with G-rated souls in an R-rated culture. Adrift and alienated, they too longed for escape to a simpler time, to recall their own happy days.

The stage was set for the return of the '50s, perhaps the most influential social movement on the '70s. Just as the Gay '90s were not the real 1890s, the '50s of the '70s was not the real 1950s. In the '50s there were no bomb shelters, only bobby sox; no polio, only Presley; no McCarthy, only Marilyn. These '50s weren't authentic, they were fun! In time, they sprayed *American Graffiti* across the walls of our minds, smeared *Grease* down Broadway, and reunited rock with roll. George Carlin observed that any future nostalgia for the '70s would have to include the '50s, or be found lacking. Before long, most baby boomers who grew up in the 1950s remembered only the '50s and embraced this phony past as their own.

Nostalgia's triumph over history was now total, and the idea of retro was born. Everything would return in time. The answers to today's problems would be found in the past. The retro idea spread and dimmed the wit of an entire nation. It was a social disease with a dismal prognosis. In the early stages, society began to ignore the future and its needs. Later, the present and its potential were degraded and even seemed deranged. In the final stage, the past and all its lessons became distorted beyond recognition. A light shone through the wrong end of time's telescope, and as the '80s dawned, it was clear it would be anything but a new age.

Having transformed popular culture, retro now caught on in higher circles. Politics became either conservative or cautious. Architecture was now postmodern, a nostalgic pastiche of all that went before. Even history itself went revisionist. Those who did proclaim a new age simply spoke of rediscovering long-lost ancient wisdom. Religion and politics seemed to merge as both spoke of a return to tradition, evoking an age as mythic as Eden's.

An odd transformation had occurred. America had become a graying nation, with its faded glory, crumbling cities, rising poverty, and yawning rift between its classes. By decade's end, there were even retro-themed restaurants, where you could dine amid visions of a midcentury that never was. Then came retro-themed cars and motorcycles. Ads promised they would "reach the '60s in seconds." But the 1960s didn't return, it was the '60s. Almost on cue, they were back with a vengeance, an attitude, and a marketing plan.

Nostalgia's turf of living memory had gotten as short as our attention span. Where it once meant sad old-timers looking back four decades, now it was about sullen thirtysomethings looking back fewer than twenty years. They wanted to escape their stagnant, polarized world and recall their own wonder years. Raised in a retro world, they had never known a future. Pop culture for them was a scavenger hunt through fashion's attic, breathlessly awaiting the newest rediscoveries. If the children of 1969 had swooned over Frankie and worn zoot suits, many would have thought something was profoundly wrong. Yet the summer of 1989 was filled with pot smoke and the Doors, while tie-dye came back like the taste of a bad hot dog. The '60s were no longer about power, they were about paisley. What lessons could they teach us now? Simply that memories were the market, and the market was the message. Meanwhile the Berlin Wall tumbled, along with the bodies in Tiananmen Square, and the world moved on.

We say we live in the '90s now, because we don't know what else to call them. A new kind of progress has given us the Woodstock Web page, the Kennedy assassination CD-ROM, and *Jurassic Park* (even dinosaurs are back!). The '70s returned as well, not out of anyone's desire for them, but just to complete the set. The clothing on our backs are often thrift-store hand-me-downs or overpriced reproductions of something older. A culture that long ago forsook wisdom for knowledge now simply settles for information.

Today, retro, like AIDS, has become a fact of life. Fashion already forecasts the '80s revival, while twentysomethings look back fondly to their adolescence. Once there was a time to put aside childish things, to shut them away in the box of memory, and get on with life's journey. But our childish things are no longer easily set aside. No longer fleeting and ephemeral, our memories are frozen on the screen, seemingly permanent. Captivated by them, we stare deeper and find it is we who are frozen, caught in the grip of retro's cold hell. The past literally in our face. How will we get on with life's journey? Will the millennium ever occur? Does the future belong to us? Or to retro?

ABC Afterschool Specials These were thought up in the heady early '70s, when people actually believed in educational TV for kids (of course, a federal mandate that the networks produce such shows also helped). One of the first ones shown, circa 1973, was titled "Last of the Curlews." A rather sad animated hour about a bird becoming extinct. The shows originally aired monthly and were a mixed bag of animation and live action. Other episodes included "Santiago's Ark," "The Incredible Cosmic Awareness of Duffy Moon," "It Must Be Love — Because I Feel So Dumb," and "Follow the North Star." Some productions were light entertainments, while others could be utter downers. As the '70s wore on, they all became live-action domestic dramas, and depressing. (bruce) ❧ Especially memorable was the marijuana one where Scott Baio pigs out on chocolate ice cream before almost murdering his brother with an oar while rowing on a lake; "Pinballs," starring Kristy McNichol and her awesome shag haircut; the death-in-the-family one where Melissa Sue Anderson argues with her little sister, who promptly falls out of a tree, breaking her neck. Melissa must cope with the subsequent funeral, her parents' depression, and a bunch of T-shirts her sister used to wear, with her name ironed on the front. This was a traumatic episode; I don't think they ever ran it again. (lisa m) ❧ I always liked watching things on fucked-up youth and these usually obliged. They're on again sporadically today, warning kids against being bad through their P.C. meanderings. (ju-ji) ❧ And a good excuse to make movies out of many of my favorite Y.A. novels. (gwynne) (See also CHACHI, *THE LITTLEST ANGEL*, PBS, and THE SHAG)

A&W Root Beer Stands One of my few good childhood memories is riding in an Oldsmobile Ninety-Eight convertible to the A&W root beer stand in the middle of some cornfield town in Bumfuck, Illinois. Mom and Dad in the front seat, me and Sis in the back, we'd pull up to the drive-in restaurant and roll down the windows so the waitress could attach the tray on the door of the car (like in the *Flintstones* intro). There were also pumped-in oldies through a thing like at the drive-in movies. Everyone would order brown cows, which was vanilla ice cream and root beer in a big frosty A&W mug. This was living! (jes) ❧ The one chain of real '50s drive-ins that survived into modern times. How can you not like a place that sells root beer on tap, by the gallon! Their hamburgers were named for family members and came in neat foil pouches with happy '50s people on them. My favorite was the teenburger — its pouch showed a cool-looking teenager with a hilarious crew cut. For the littlest kids, they served root beer in tiny mugs, which everyone's dad stole to use as novelty shot glasses at home. (bruce) ❧ The first time I saw the Ramones was not at a concert or on a video, but at an A&W in Tempe, Arizona, on an August afternoon in 1977. If you know anything at all about the lovely Arizona climate, then you know that in August, the temperature can get up to 130° . . . 120° in the shade.

There were the Ramones, standing there sipping root beers in the 125°+ glare, looking cool as hell, and *wearing their fucking leather jackets!!* I was one très impressed little punk rocker. "Now that," I remember thinking as I got up the nerve to get Joey's autograph, "is dedication!" (don)

Acid You'd plan out this amazing trip scenario with some of your friends, that hit of Window Pane burning a hole in your cigarette cellophane (I actually knew a guy who put a hit of Window Pane in his eye, and twenty years later he still has a tiny brown square in the white part). Finally, it's Friday night, and you ingest the sacrament about an hour before you go off to the guy's house who doesn't live with his parents, where you can just hang out and listen to weird music and be psychedelic all night. Without warning, Mom decides that it's high time you stayed home for once, because you've been "going out far too much lately." She's made reservations at this horrible restaurant where she always makes you eat steak so that anyone who might be paying attention will be way impressed that this woman's child is eating *steak*, so therefore she must have more class than the rest of the tarted-up white trash at the other tables. Since by now you're completely frying, all you can do is draw incomprehensible weirdnesses on the placemat and try not to look at the slab of dead stuff in front of you that the glowing maggots are crawling out of. Finally back home, Mom thankfully goes to bed, but not until she's made sure the house is deadbolted shut so the only way you can escape would be to smash a window. Luckily she's so plastered she hasn't a clue that you're, to put it mildly, in a "separate reality." I don't know what Carlos Castaneda would have done in this situation, but I just turned on the TV and watched a couple of late-night movies that changed my life (in what manner exactly I'm still not sure): *Jason and the Argonauts,* with the truly psychedelic claymation scene where the Hydra's teeth all come alive as reanimated skeletons and have sword fights with the Argo boys; and that indescribably demented classic of black 'n' white zombie-noir, *Carnival of Souls!* (don) ❁ I had this wild-girl girlfriend who used to beg me to turn her on to drugs, acid in particular. The only problem was that she was insane. I mean, she used to see the Virgin Mary driving westbound on Pico and stuff like that. Of course that kind of craziness can have its charm, but I was afraid that giving her drugs would lead to her becoming really crazy, and I didn't want that kind of responsibility. But she kept begging and begging for acid and making a real pest out of herself, so finally I had an idea: I took some Bayer aspirins and held them under the faucet until the big Bs rubbed off, then I put them in a zip-lock bag and gave them to her. Of course she hallucinated all night long, and I thought my problem was solved, but unfortunately a few years later she ended up doing lap dances in San Francisco and losing a couple of pregnancies to heroin. I guess you could say I ruined her life by placebo. (stymie) (See also DRUGS and PARANOIA)

Action Figures

Action Figures I had ongoing sagas with well-developed characters, not just meaningless shoot 'em up battles. The *Star Wars* figures were the foundation of any action figure collection. Micronauts had translucent plastic bodies and featured metal joints at the elbows and knees. There's nothing like the smell of a new action figure. (dave) (See also BIG JIM, G.I. JOE, and *STAR WARS*)

Adam Ant This character harkens back to a time when people used to go to extremes to entertain: Adam Ant decked out in his Nu-Ro pirate gear, androgynous god-child Boy George, even Madonna at the time. It's not that they *completely* relied on these images, but the effort they made to not just wear T-shirts and jeans was appreciated. Can't wait to see it happen again: Cutesy and simple is *out!* Adam tried for a comeback. I hope that hair-replacement stuff works for him. (ju-ji) ❧ His backing band left for Malcolm and Bow Wow Wow, but Adam Ant continued to utilize the tribal thump in his swashbuckling weightless pop punk escapades. Despite a slew of fun and fresh hits, the bombs were *bad*. Adam went on to become a decent actor, even appearing on one of my favorite '80s *Death Wish*/Bernhard Goetz–inspired TV shows, *The Equalizer!* (darby) (See also *DARK SHADOWS*, MALCOLM McLAREN, and NEW ROMANTICS)

The Adventures of Buckaroo Banzai Across the Eighth Dimension
This should have been a watershed and was planned as such. A great deal of tie-in merchandise went unsold and is now hyper-collectible. I still have the Viewmaster for it. I'd like to see someone restore the missing forty minutes, including all the flashbacks — then the film might make sense. (bruce) (See also VIEWMASTERS)

Aerobics Aerobics word association: Lycra, spandex, headbands, striped outfits, jiggling flab, perky overenthusiastic instructors, sports bras, bike

Adam Ant
sans Nu-Ro pirate gear

shorts, butts, bad music, *Perfect* (John Travolta and Jamie Lee Curtis), Richard Simmons, the beginning of the Evian/water bottle phenomenon . . . (darby) (See also *FLASHDANCE*, LEGWARMERS, RICHARD SIMMONS, and TENNIS SHOES AND SNEAKERS BECOME "ATHLETIC FOOTWEAR")

Afros I love the way it moves when you walk. I love how it just like — *boom!* — explodes and leaves your smooth shoulders bare. And I love the way it tells me, as only it can, that you are bigger and better *naturally*. Come here, Super Fly, and let me find all the secrets you got hiding in there. You are so on fire and I am melting. Ohhhhh, I wanna die with my face buried deep in your afro, sugar. (nina) ❧ QUIZ: Who had the biggest 'fro? (A) Christie Love, (B) Cleopatra Jones, (C) Angela Davis, (D) Link from the *Mod Squad*, (E) the John 3:16 guy at NFL games? (bruce) ❧ White People with Afros: Bernie from *Room 222* (a precursor to Carrot Top); the Bradys, Barbra Streisand in *A Star Is Born* and *The Main Event;* Linda Blair sported one (a really long one) in several of her films, including *Roller Boogie* and *Stranger in the House,* where her visiting cousin from the Ozarks turned out to be a witch; and let's not forget a '70s Ken (Barbie's boyfriend). (lisa m.)

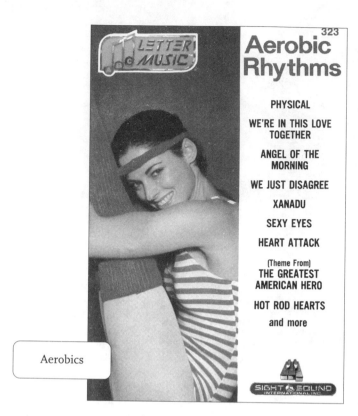

Aerobics

Aids The most significant disease of the '80s and '90s, for its novelty and social significance if not the number of people it killed. First noticed in 1981 as a slew of mostly gay young men in big cities began coming down with a disproportionate number of diseases like pneumocystis pneumonia and Kaposi's sarcoma, and called GRID (for Gay Related Immune Deficiency). By 1984, the disease was called AIDS, and Reagan's Secretary of Health and Human Services, Margaret Heckler, announced that they had identified the cause — a retrovirus now named HIV, or human immunodeficiency virus — and would try to find a cure posthaste. The latter promise is still unfulfilled, and lots of people have raised convincing doubts about the first proposition as well. Still, the disease has become an inescapable public emblem, even if the early scare stories that the epidemic would rapidly burst out of what were identified early as high-risk groups (gays, IV drug users, transfusion recipients) haven't quite panned out yet. AIDS changed sex, romance, and passion for a whole generation. In my world, by the mid-'80s, condomless sex, or sex without lots of questions to answer first, was a rare

and precious commodity indeed. While it rapidly came true that almost everyone at least knew someone with the disease, what got underemphasized, especially as the '90s progressed, was that the spread of the disease was actually slowing down. (brian) (See also UNPROTECTED SEX WITH STRANGERS)

Airbrush When coupled with denim and sparkles and the word *Rodeo* it was at the apex of its glory. (wendy)

Air Hockey Became pretty big in the '70s — every family with a playroom had it. The fan blowing through the holes of the table was supposed to make the puck all slippery. What it did was make the puck airborne if hit at the right angle. (katy) ❀ The truly cool places had them under black lights, with playing pieces made of fluorescent orange plastic. The official story was that the pucks could move at up to 200 mph, so this made for some pretty trippy trails, man! (bruce) ❀ My favorite arcade sport besides skee-ball. We had a little miniature version we played on the floor when I was younger. Its pivotal career move was in the *Bad News Bears* with sassy Tatum kickin' Kelly Leak's ass at air hockey, thereby forcing him to play on the retard team. (darby)

Airplane Rules and Regulations have changed a lot. You used to be able to walk right out to the plane in open air. It gave you a chance to check out the landing gear for yourself. And the days are long gone when a nervous traveler can calm her nerves by lighting up in the smoking section far in the back of the plane. You can't even smoke in most airports anymore. What the hell are those FAA guys trying to do anyway, kill us? Guaranteed torture for those who hate to fly. (jes) ❀ When I'm dictator, there will be special Babies and Non-Babies section-son airplanes, as well as in every public establishment. (gwynne) (See also DISASTER MOVIES)

Alarm Clocks with Flipping Numbers

Provided hours of amusement as we sat in front of them and tried to synch up and guess the exact moment the little metallic card would flip. We felt particularly lucky if we were around when the whole clock flipped to a new hour. More recently the flip clock had an important role in the movie *Groundhog Day*. (darby/don) ✢ The type you describe were originally known as "Sepdigital Clocks," as their numbers were made of actual separate digits. We forget today just how much noise those flipping metal tabs made, especially late at night. (bruce)

Alligator Shirts/Izods

For the record, we never called these "Lacoste" when we were kids. Around '78 there was some weird unspoken contest between my friends and me to own the most colors. The richer ones won out and then, a year or two later, moved up to Polo, which my mom wouldn't buy me — far too expensive. When they started wearing two at a time in different colors and folding up the sleeves and putting one collar up higher than the other, I passed. OTHER VERSIONS INCLUDE: Le Tigre (sorta okay for guys), Hunter's Run (a horse/The Limited), Jordache (another horse), Gloria Vanderbilt (a swan), Britannia (a flag), J. C. Penney (the fox), and the classic penguin for those old golfers. . . . Noël even recalls seeing a dog and a dragon. And now Don is saying that *National Lampoon* had one with a legless frog, but we should stop here. (darby)

All in the Family

The original idea of *All in the Family* was that this main character, Archie Bunker, was a stupid racist pig-headed old fuck with bad thoughts and a bad attitude. But after the first season or two, people started identifying with him — much to the chagrin of socialist actor Carroll O'Connor — and the show became more about poor Archie dealing with the modern world (the meatheads), instead of poor Mike and Gloria dealing with this horrible guy. There were books (*The Wit and Wisdom of Archie Bunker*) and posters, and his chair was donated to the Smithsonian — where I believe it still resides in the Television Room. Produced by Mr. Sitcom, Norman Lear (who bought the U.S. rights to a British sitcom called *Till Death Do Us Part*, which the show is based on), and following his request, it was one of the first U.S. sitcoms ever filmed before a live audience. Its blue-collar spin-offs included *Maude, Good Times, The Jeffersons, Gloria*, and *Archie Bunker's Place*. (bruce)

"Alternative"

Today we have "alternative music" (which doesn't mean anything), but back in the '70s they were starting up alternative everything: alternative stores, alternative schools, alternative technology, alternative medicine, alternative energy, alternative theater, alternative protein sources. Hippest of all: an "alternative lifestyle," which pretty much meant doing anything that square old Mom and Dad didn't do, whether it was engaging in orgies or washing the dishes only every other day. (candi)

V.C. Andrews

Creator of a gnarly incestual sicko freak scene read by every preteen girl I hung out with, and if parents only knew what those books were about, even the libertarian ones would have participated in the book-burning session. And they thought punk rock was a bad influence. This was a long-running series but books one (*Flowers in the Attic*) and two (*Petals in the Wind*) were the best. And the movie version was an absolute disgrace compared to the heights of horror the books reached. (darby) ✢ V.C. Andrews died in 1989, but the legacy of the novels continues — a new "V.C. Andrews" novel is released about every six months or so, "creating additional stories inspired by her wonderful storytelling genius!" (riley)

Angel

This '80s movie was about a really good girl who lived alone and had to become a prostitute to support herself so she could still go to school. And to spice up the already guaranteed winner of a plot, a psychopathic killer was after her. Ironically, all of the school scenes were filmed at the Harvard School for Boys in Coldwater Canyon. It's since become a classic. Don't confuse it with its asinine Western sequel, *Avenging Angel*, with the very hot Betsy Russell. (jon)

Anorexia/Bulimia   The secretive world of bulimia and anorexia was exposed through the tragic death of Karen Carpenter. It slowly crept into mainstream culture until every skinny girl was tortured by teachers and family worrying over her obvious eating disorder, and "fat girls" (i.e., any girl who looked like she was turning into a woman) explored the secrets of the binge and purge — usually with a best friend or even in pig-out slumber party–type settings. Famous folks were outed as anorexics or bulimics (similar to gay outings), until they too decided it was just easier ("healthier") and even decent publicity to go public themselves. Portrayed in TV movies (there was an especially noteworthy one starring Jennifer Jason Leigh, who got her weight down to eighty-six pounds for the role) and later by real-life *People* magazine cover girl Tracey Gold (the once *sorta* chubby kid on *Growing Pains* and regular guest on *Oprah* specials). (darby) (See also *Safe* director Todd Haynes's 1988 short *Superstar: The Karen Carpenter Story*, an underground cult classic, which tells this tragic tale through a star-studded cast of Barbies.)

Annie   Many a budding starlet sang the lovely songs of this Broadway musical, much to the chagrin of any within auditory range. Each song seemed to have a sticky, pathetic quality: "Toooomorrow, toooomorow, I love ya, toooomorow, you're always a daaaay aaaaaa-waaaaaaaaaaay!" Get me and my sister in a car for more than a few hours together, and in between fighting we'll sing a mean duet rendition of this puppy. (darby)

The Annie Hall Look   Yuck, yuck, yuck! Diane Keaton's character ripped off *Horses*-era Patti Smith but looked a lot worse because of all that earth-toned peasant damage left over from the hippie days. I was grateful for it; it was the one high-fashion look my mother hated enough to not try to force me to wear, and at ninth-grade dances it was ridiculously easy to be the girl with the sexiest outfit. (gwynne)

Aqua Net Hairspray   Definitely the hardest, crunchiest, slickest brand of aerosol hairspray, in tall bright-colored cans that fit perfectly in your palm. The biggest '80s hair (not to mention a pleasant fume-induced head rush) could be achieved with a continuous spray and a blow-dryer. The reign of Aqua Net came to a tearful close in the late '80s when a correlation between aerosol and the depletion of the ozone layer was discovered. (lorraine)

Army Gear   For a brief period people looked like ex-Vietnam freaks. Movies like *Private Benjamin* and *Stripes* made it cool in the early '80s. Camp Beverly Hills had pseudo-army fashion jackets, and the early punk bands wore the stuff as well. Petered out around the time of the *Rambo* backlash and came back in vogue when Punky Brewster began wearing Doc Martens. (howard) ❖ I wore my absolutely-skin-tight-to-the-ankles army pants, an army-green tight T-shirt that said "M*A*S*H," a ceramic whistle on a satin cord necklace that said "Army," high-heeled black pumps, and black sunglasses to the Police concert at the Big A. (riley) ❖ A designer brand who made fashion cammies was UFO. (laurel)

Art/Posters   The simplistic colored-pencil map of a New Yorker's view of the world (soon they had one for every major city); the bagels with red, white, and blue cream cheese; Patrick Nagel (whose art you still see in faux art galleries in Venice Beach); those half-inked '70s women in soft natural colors utilizing lots of negative white space; airbrush mania; Leroy Neiman '76 Olympics; Peter Max; the nude photo of Nastassja Kinski with a snake wrapped around her; Farrah all foxy in the swimsuit (already in her late twenties by then); Basquiat; Julian Schnabel; Keith Haring (an essential part of the legitimation of graffiti as art and of hip-hop as multiculturalism); Mark Kostabi; Neville Brody's industrial-influenced typography and design; Peter Rocha's paintings of President Reagan made with Jelly Belly jelly beans (each portrait contains about 10,000 beans!). ❖ It seems to me that the '80s marked a time when cheap mass-produced art got hip. Prior to this, it was more of the dogs-playing-poker variety, which is why I guess Aquarian-age hipsters opted for posters instead. (bruce) ❧ Life-size beefcake poster of Mark Spitz (wearing nothing but a tiny stars-and-stripes swimsuit, his Olympic gold medals, and a smile), Tolkien posters, stupid Day-Glo posters (like the one showing a couple in a different sexual position for each astrological sign). ❧ Real art: Judy Chicago's art project "The Dinner Party," a sort of banquet table with embroidered symbolic tablecloths and plates with vaginal motifs. (candi) ❧ Animal posters: Also refered to as "Secretary Posters." Free posters from Book-of-the-Month Club with little hanging kittens that said "Hang in There!" or chimps with phrases like "I've Gone Bananas Over You!" I really hated them. (wendy) ❧ Velvet paintings: I went to art school, so I know how expensive canvas can get; besides, portraits of Elvis, nude women, dogs playing poker, bullfighters, and scary clowns look so much more regal when done in this medium. Show me one couch that wouldn't look better with such a masterpiece hanging above. (lorraine) ❧ Neon: Cool for art but otherwise a geek thing. (jaz) ❧ Great moments in art include: Jeff Koons's giant Hummelware Michael Jackson, Chris Burden crucifying himself to a Volkswagen, Andy Warhol on *The Love Boat*, and Genesis P-Orridge giving himself blood, milk, and urine enemas. (howard) (See also JELLY BELLYS, GIRLY POSTERS, TRASH AS ART, and ANDY WARHOL)

Arts and Crafts Oh my! There were so many strange things to make and do back then. Is it just because we were young or was it the times? My life ran from one project to another, with barely time to bake a loaf of bread or attend an Ella Jenkins concert. If we weren't melting crayons and gluing sticks together with paste or making colored bath soap to write on the tile walls with, we were setting up for spin art or preparing to tie-dye. Fancier vacation projects included sand candles. We'd buy paraffin, line holes in the beach with shells and pretty polished glass, dump the melted wax in, wait awhile, and . . . voilà! Gorgeous candle, but what about the wick?

Other times, we'd dip bent hangers in awful-smelling, probably toxic, colored stuff and make a sort of stained glass–like thing. Really pretty, and great for mobiles or sun-catchers. (lisa aa) ❧ Assorted and frightening arts and crafts: macaroni art with gold paint and yarn, decoupage (wood plaques lacquered with burnt-paper images), rubber stamps made out of potato, playing with (dried) white glue, beading T-shirts, stained glass, colored rock art, string art with nails (usually of a boat scene), and the infamous god's eyes (made from yarn and two Popsicle sticks). . . . (bobby) (See also LANYARDS and MACRAMÉ)

Aspartame Sold under the brand name of NutraSweet, the champion sweetener of the regulatory age. After the FDA tried to ban saccharin, because it was linked to certain types of cancer in rats, the way was paved for aspartame to win the hearts and minds of a new generation of diet-conscious sweet fanatics. It was invented in 1965 and approved by the U.S. Food and Drug Administration for widespread use in food in 1981. If the artificial is the emblem of our age, NutraSweet, next to plastic, is the flagship molecule of our time. And despite suspicions, and the occasional published scientific paper trying to prove the opposite, it doesn't seem to be permanently harming anyone! (brian)

Astrology, Horoscopes, Zodiacs, Biorhythms The only pre-Judeo-Christian religious/superstitious belief widely acknowledged and generally believed — after all, there are astrology forecast columns in all the major newspapers and magazines — in this Bible-sucking country of ours. In the '70s and in '70s retro, a fashion statement and fecund source of cheesy pickup lines. (gwynne) ❧ Any possibly useful information that could be derived from these techniques is almost thoroughly discounted due for the most part to '70s culture, and second, to the equally pukable New Agers today. That's fine though, some of life's most useful tools are so socialized and beyond mainstream status that it's a trick to ignore that and rediscover their unique uses without being a part of the fanatical b.s. Of course biorhythms *should* be relegated forever to House of Pancakes status. (darby) (See also NEW AGE and SUN SIGNS) 🐛

Asymmetrical Haircuts Hello? What was up with this? I remember Emily Colburn got one in seventh grade, and even though I was cooler (because I was in eighth grade) I still thought it was fantabulous. It was spiky on the left side and like a blunt cut/bob on the other. You would laugh and point at someone on the street with hair like that today, but we were in the '80s. (morgan and ferris) ♣ I got voted "Wildest Haircut" in seventh grade for such an asymmetrical 'do. (noël) (See also TAILS)

Atari *"The fun is back, oh yessirree, It's the 2600 system from A-tar-i! Now under 50 bucks, but wait, there's more! There's a pack of new games at your video store! A real hip joystick controls the screen, Solaris is hot, and Midnight Magic's mean. One more thing: It's got a special low price — Under 50 Bucks. '50 bucks?!' Now isn't that nice. The fun is back, oh yes-sir-ee. It's the 2600 from A-tar-i."* Atari. Sheesh, just the thought of it makes me chuckle. There was a time when it was just plain king; at least it was for me. Who could imagine today that four-bit graphics and sixteen colors could have ever amounted to so much damage? Even with its display of shockingly rudimentary, retarded graphics, Atari was light-years ahead of the competition, opening up a brave new world of cathode rays to the delight of pasty spoiled brats everywhere (eclipsing the rise of the Sex Pistols and *Star Wars*). I guess the timing could not have been more perfect, even though there was nothing remotely punk rock about Atari (they were part of the Warner Bros. entertainment conglomerate), but it made that significant leap from the doldrum of Pong to the intergalactic madness of Space Invaders. This was, of course, a time when a score of 2,000 still meant something and pinball was still in vogue. But all of that was about to change. Oh sure, Atari had its share of competition. Nerdish types found pleasure in Magnavox's Odyssey 2 system, which featured a built-in keyboard for strategic word games and such, but it faded into obscurity. There was the Commodore VIC-20 that actually had more juice than Atari but failed to push the slowly developing gonads of prepubescent kids.

And who can forget Mattel's plunge into video-game history with Intellevision? Perhaps the only system at that time that gave Atari a run for its money, Intellevision instantly appealed to sports enthusiasts with its catalogue of games like Football, Baseball, and Basketball. I, too, was caught up in all the hype, asking poor old Santa Claus for one (which I never got). But when push came to shove, the only games that I liked on that system were Burgertime and SNAFU, evidence of my lack of patience with games that required any extensive reading. On top of that, in some god-awful attempt to not duplicate Atari, they developed these stupid disc-shaped controllers for their system that made life difficult. If they only realized the power of the *joystick*. Atari had a clear advantage over the competition. Besides having tons of wonderful press coverage touting it as the greatest thing on earth, they had the support of numerous third-party software developers. The fine people at Activision, Imagic, and Parker Brothers, among others, were responsible for some of my personal faves, like Pitfall, Demon Attack, Frogger, and Dragon's Lair. If that wasn't enough muscle to flex, Atari boasted the exclusive rights to some of the most popular arcade video games around, among them Asteroids, Space Invaders, Defender, and Berzerk. Most important, kids, they had the rights to the bossest game around: Pac-Man. (noël) (See also PAC-MAN FEVER and VIDEO GAMES)

The A-Team We saw them film this near my home near where the Renaissance Pleasure Faire used to be. It was very depressing watching them switch from the stars to their doubles every couple of seconds during the fighting scenes. I was disenchanted with filmmaking from then on. (darby) ♣ They were predictable but always top-notch entertainers. I had a crush on Murdock. (wendy) ♣ When I was a wee lass I lived in a city with a girls' school that was a favorite location for TV show and movie shoots. I had a twisted obsession with Murdock, I wanted him to adopt me, and bless my lucky stars, *The A-Team* came one day to shoot. I walked up behind the man and tapped him on the shoulder. He turned around, and I jumped on his feet and hugged him and wouldn't let go. He was so sweet, he let me stay with him all day while he fed me doughnuts and walked around the set. I corresponded with him for a few years, but finally my obsession waned. A very sweet guy. This story has since made a number of slightly geeky people slightly jealous. (skylaire) (See also MR. T)

ATMs Before automated teller machines were everywhere, you had to get your cash from a large building with human tellers and lines. It was called a bank and was only open during business hours. People went there on payday, waited in line, made their deposits, and kept some cash for themselves. If they needed more, they had to go back to the bank and wait in line again. Sure, some people had checks and credit cards, but you couldn't buy beer at your local liquor store with those. The rest of us actually had to pay attention to how much cash we had, because it was pretty hard to get some more if you ran out. People really did stay home on Sundays, not out of picty, but because they were often out of cash, and there was no way to get more until the bank reopened on Monday morning. If you were traveling, your vacation money was what you had in your wallet, period. Sounds primitive, doesn't it? I'm not talking about the Depression, or the '50s, I'm talking about America circa 1980. ATMs had been around since 1974, but it took several years for them to fully enter our lives. First they were yet another convenience for the credit card class, then they showed up in chronically cash-starved college towns. By 1985 they were in every bank. By 1990, you could buy fast food with your ATM card. Everyone now understood the term *cash flow*. Soon, everything became an impulse purchase, life got simpler, more casual, and expensive. Fifteen years after ATMs arrived, nobody seemed to live within his means or have any kind of savings. America was suddenly a debtor nation. How did that happen? Look no further than that friendly glowing screen at the 7-Eleven. (bruce)

Attack of the Killer Tomatoes
The films I liked in the '70s . . . when you watch them twenty years later you see how stupid they were — so you realize how stupid you were. I just prefer to remember the good scenes from these movies. For instance: One of the characters is wearing a tomato disguise, and he's sitting around the campfire with a bunch of killer tomatoes eating steak or something, and he accidentally asks them to pass the ketchup . . . so of course they realize he's not really a tomato and kill him. (dad)

Autograph Hounds Like an autograph book except in the form of a dachshund. Mine was white vinyl with red ears and tail. I got Gramma's and Grandpa's and Mom's and Dad's and Cousin's and Aunt's and Uncle's and Teacher's and Neighbor's and maybe a few of my geeky friends', but nobody famous ever gave up their John Hancock for me (of course I faked their signatures like a true hound). (jes) ✿ I had a pink patchwork fabric autograph pig. My best friend Kimmie's was blue and they were both named "Soueee," as per the tags on their butts. We were in unspoken competition to see who could get the most signatures and of course it was Kimmie because she was more popular than I was. (jen g.)

Avon/Avon Ladies In addition to their newfangled line of cosmeticare products, Avon had catalogues full of jewelry, especially tacky plastic brooches that opened up to reveal stinky tubs of lip gloss and waxy perfumed lotions. They also had seasonal editions of said goop packaged in glass bottles shaped like cars, women, kangaroos, household objects, et cetera, that for some reason antique dealers seem to think are worth something today. As if that weren't enough, these fine products were sold door to door by bored housewives. God bless American entrepreneurialism. (lorraine)

b

Babies In a 1961 poll, it was found that most young women wanted four or five children. But after 1957 the birthrate began to fall, plunging with the '60s youth rebellion and reaching a low of zero population growth in the mid-'70s. According to the book *For Her Own Good*, "Hospitals began to close their obstetrical wards, suburban schools were shut down, and some manufacturers of infant formulas . . . transplanted their promotional campaign to the baby-rich countries of the Third World. The moral excuse for childlessness was the population explosion discovered by demographers and futurists in the mid-'60s, but the real reason, for most young couples, was that children just didn't fit into the lifestyle they had become accustomed to as singles." Some even hinted that drug use enlightened them to the detrimental effects of childbearing — that children steal your energy and suckle from you (realistically, symbolically, spiritually) until your death. The decision was made easier by the advent of the Pill, along with women's desire to work and the lack of day care. Coincidentally it was the zenith of evil child movies, including *Rosemary's Baby, The Exorcist, The Omen,* and *Audrey Rose*. Children became merely an option — and not the most appealing option at that. The infamous '70s book *The Joy of Sex* observed, "Children can limit the sex play of adults by being around." In 1973, NON, the National Organization of Nonparenthood, appeared on the scene with 2,000 members, including actress Shirley MacLaine and philanthropist Stewart Mott, to combat what they described as the "pervasive pronatalism" of American society. "People do not deserve honor and respect simply for having a baby," according to a psychiatrist who spoke at the 1975 NON convention. "Children are not that perfect — or likable either." Now that's a trend that is well due for a comeback. (darby)

Baby Alive If I remember correctly, this was the first doll that ate almost real food, would pee, and seemed truly babylike. I wonder if the friends of mine who actually wanted this devil-inspired creation are the ones cursed with kids today. (darby) ✿ The greatest doll in the world (next to my *Wizard of Oz* figurines). You bought Baby Alive's food in packages, added water, and shoved it into her tiny puckered pink lips that were caked with old dried food. All she did was eat, wet, and shit the food out her butt. She was real! (jes) ✿ The eating version of Baby Tender Love. My sister finally fed hers Comet and it died. (riley) (See also DOLLS)

Baby On Board! Yuppified rear-window car signs. Became in the late '80s what the rear-window rainbow sticker was in the late '70s. As if we cared *why* you were such a shitty driver! (darby)

Back of the Bus The only place the big kids sat on the bus to and from school. As a little kid, I spent an awful lot of time sitting backward in my seat peering back there hoping to get a glimpse of the big-kid life. But when I finally got to be one of the big kids, it wasn't really all that fun — except that I was able to make the little kids think it was. (jes) ✿

Where the cool kids on the bus sat, where we'd play Truth or Dare in fifth grade with the sixth-grade boys, and our rad bus driver would play KHJ on the radio if we were being good, and we'd all sing to it. (riley) ✿ If you're younger or just moved into the neighborhood, you'd have to earn your way to the back. I did when this conehead kid, who liked to tease me and who I'd usually ignore, spit a loogie on me but missed and hit my geek umbrella (that had my name all over it in script). Instead of ignoring it I wiped it back on him. From then on the back of the bus was no problem. (darby)

Bad Ronald In the early to mid-'70s, Scott Jacoby was being groomed for teen stardom. Back then (only slightly different than now) this was done by first establishing cute young boys as stars on TV. Then, a movie role. Then, the requisite pop-lite album. You may remember this ploy being used with John Travolta, Scott Baio, and others. It didn't work so well on the young Jacoby lad. With his nonstunning but comfortable Jewish-boy-next-door looks, warming smile, and soft Matthew Modine–esque voice, he hovered for a while before drowning in a sea of reruns. His high point began with the ultra-too-cool-for-TV movie *Bad Ronald,* where he played a dysfunctional family mama's boy who accidentally kills a neighborhood kid. His mother hides him by stashing him in a wall. Shortly thereafter she dies, leaving him inside the wall for the next family. After developing a raging jones for the young daughter, he goes totally wack-ass. His only other notable role was as the polite but slightly crippled Mario the Magician in the Jodie Foster chiller *The Little Girl Who Lives Down the Lane.* This time he gets the girl without having to resort to peeping through holes in the wall. If you feel compelled, try to find his one and only album. It looks all soft-focus and woodsy, like most pop-lite vehicles of its day. (kevin)

Baking Soda Started showing up in everything in the mid-'70s. Peak toothpaste started it off, when the back-to-nature movement had finally reached our teeth. Some genius at Arm & Hammer figured out that you could leave baking soda in the refrigerator and eliminate odor. This move doubled the company's sales overnight and became one of the most legendary stories of modern marketing. After that, baking soda showed up in laundry detergent, deodorants, shampoos, and anything that stank. It was America's last great love affair with things white — unless you count cocaine. (bruce) (See also DRUGS)

Bald Eagles The bald eagle nearly became extinct because their eggshells were too thin and broke when they sat on them. It was soon linked with the pesticide DDT. The banning of DDT was one of the main rallying points of the '70s eco-movement. (paul)

Bananas The big brother to *Dynamite* magazine. (katy) ✿ For some reason, bananas became funny to people in the early '70s. Anything having to do with bananas indicated madcap mirth. The best example of this would be the phrase "go bananas," which meant to go crazy. There were banana-shaped phones, pillows, hats, slippers, you name it. Where did this come from? Was it that LP cover that Warhol did for Velvet Underground? Bic came out with a pen called "The Banana"; it was supposed to give your writing a wacky edge. See also the Woody Allen film of the same period. (bruce)

The Banana Splits This wild musical bunch of nameless guys in costumes of scruffy, unidentifiable creatures ran around Saturday morning TV way too fast as if to offer final proof that *everyone* who was *anyone* on TV in the '70s had to be a *rock star* or at the very least pretend to be. Now all you have to do to impress TV viewers under seven years old is kill people. Who says life doesn't get simpler? "*One banana, two banana, three banana, four . . .*" (nina) ❖ That they inspired the Dickies version of the *Banana Splits* song was worthwhile enough. (jaz) ❖ Featured four guys in suits with dubbed dialogue. They went by the names of Fleegle (a kind of dog), Bingo (a gorilla), Drooper (a sort of lion), and Snorky (a baby elephant that never spoke). They jumped around, played tricks on each other, and had a good time. They would also film segments of them running around in those little six-wheeled recreational vehicles so popular at the time. And naturally, they had a rock band. During the dreadful songs, we'd be treated to some proto-MTV-style video editing, which mostly featured them running around an amusement park. The show also featured a separate adventure segment called "Danger Island," featuring Jan Michael Vincent, which introduced the short-lived catch phrase "Oh-oh Chongo." (bruce) ❖ The album is amazing, and why not? Participants on it include Al Kooper, Gene Pitney, and Barry White. About ten years ago, the band I was in covered and recorded "Gonna Find a Cave." In addition to their album, the Banana Splits released two 7" EPs and a couple of cereal-box-cutaway cardboard singles. (gwynne)

Banana Clips These long, toothy hair accessories made your skimpy little ponytail look long 'n' layered — *very* popular in early to mid-'80s and still available in 99¢ stores. (pleasant)

Bangs There was this period in the early '80s where, regardless of the scene (death rock, metal, val, Nu-Ro), you had to have some form of bangs in your face. (darby) (See also WISPIES)

Baretta's Cockatoo and Other TV Cop Accessories The real unsolved mystery about '70s–'80s detective shows is whether or not anyone would have watched them if the cops had been deprived of their pets and quirks. A few accessories to TV crime: Fred the cockatoo on *Baretta* ('75–'78); Telly Savalas's lollipop on *Kojak* ('73–'78); Peter Falk's trench coat on *Columbo* ('71–'77); Huggy Bear, the pimp informant on *Starsky and Hutch* ('75–'78); Freeway, the mutt dog on *Hart to Hart* ('79–'84); KITT, the computer in David Hasselhoff's Trans Am on *Knight Rider* ('82–'86); and Tom Selleck's mustache on *Magnum P.I.* ('80–'88). (nina/claire/angela) (See also MIAMI VICE)

Toni Basil In 1981, an infectious and innocuous cheerleading song called "Mickey" turned up with lead singer Toni Basil. Little did Martha Quinn and MTV know that this peppy cheerleader was perilously close to forty. She had been a go-go dancer (with Teri Garr) back in the days of *The T.A.M.I. Show* (1964). She also made a brief appearance in Dennis Hopper's *Easy Rider* as a New Orleans prostitute. After this inexplicable hit came the even more innocuous "Shopping A–Z." Then she went back to choreographing David Bowie. ¿Dónde estás? She was last seen on MTV's "It Came from the '80s" retrospective. (bruce)

Bathroom/Shower Items There was a whole slew of items invented just to make bathing more fun. The regular old Water Pik Shower Massage was especially groundbreaking, promising a shower that worked as a massage as well. Can you imagine! Soap on a Rope became the hip gag gift for the rest of the world for a while. It was shaped as a phallic microphone (stimulus for inspiring singers). The only problem was that after you used it for a while the microphone would slide off the rope and you'd have this cheap, weird-shaped soap that you'd have to bend over to pick up (oooooooh). While they worked they went great with the new waterproof shower radios. (darby) ❖ Schick Electric Hot Lather Dispenser —

who wanted or needed this device, which took a can of aerosol shave cream and made it squirt out as warm foam? Maybe it provided a marginally better shaving experience, but what this product *really* provided was a new answer to the question "What the heck do we buy Dad for Christmas this year?" (candi) ❧ I got one. (dad) ❧ The Skin Machine — A battery-powered spinning little brush to wash and scrub your face with, which all the girls had alongside their Buf Pufs, loofahs, Phisoderm, and Apricot Facial Scrub. (riley) (See also BRUSHING YOUR TEETH)

Battle of the Network Stars

ABC-sponsored spectacle in which stars from various sports competed in obstacle courses, rowing races, running races, weightlifting competitions, et cetera. Highlight: Watching Lou "The Incredible Hulk" Ferrigno drop from exhaustion in a 400-yard dash. Further proof that God has now left the universe. (bobby) ❧ I don't know what these celebs were amped on to make them need to show off as *the best* star tennis player or tug-of-war jock around, but they always had these goofy contests on TV. Uh, I actually went to one at Pepperdine University with my pal Jill Wahl and the memory really disturbs me. (darby)

Battleship

"B-11" "Shhhh . . ." "A-3" "You sunk my battleship!" Pseudo-electronic two-player war game that Daddy would never buy me. Classic commercial is with Vincent Price as a teller in an old-time bank where they're so involved in the game they ignore all their customers. (darby)

Battlestar Galactica

Low-budget outer space show starring pre-cancer Dirk Benedict and pre-dead Lorne Greene (though some seem to want to argue the latter). Really cool dog robot and also the evil robots the Cylons. Along with *Buck Rogers* formed the late '70s/early '80s sci-fi block, which has now been replaced with the new *Star Trek* shows, and, uh, *Babylon 5*. (It's strange when you grow up to find out things you thought were real big hits were actually "duds.") (darby) ❧ After the success of *Star Wars*, ABC blew the dust off the space-opera concept they had lying about and pulled out all the stops. The series was produced at the then unheard-of cost of $1,000,000 per episode! Its premiere episode was three hours long! (Later released in theaters, it became the last movie released domestically in Sensurround.) The official name of the dog robot was Muffett II, but the kid, Boxey, always called it Muffy. As for *Buck Rogers,* its pilot was also released theatrically, but before the series even aired. (bruce) (See also *BUCK ROGERS IN THE 25TH CENTURY,* STAR TREK-KIES, and *STAR WARS*)

Beatlemania

Not the Beatles but an *incredible simulation.* I went to *Beatlemania* with my temple youth group. I was just staring at this cute boy from a rival youth group the whole time and couldn't care

I knew we should have taken a left at Albuquerque.

78 ABC, Inc.

much about the silly show. The thing most interesting about this mega-popular event was that the Beatles had only been broken up seven years when *Beatlemania* first occurred. (darby) (See also TRIBUTE BANDS)

Bed-Wetting I never really had a bed-wetting problem in the traditional sense. Actually, I was such a pathetic, insomniac child that once I pretended to wet my bed (using water) in order to have an excuse to wake up my parents in the middle of the night to get attention (they still don't know this). (jen d.) ❀ Arnold Drummond did the same thing in an episode of *Diff'rent Strokes*. (noël) ❀ There was a movie called *The Loneliest Runner* (1976), written, directed, and produced by Michael Landon, about a teenage bed wetter (played by Lance Kerwin of *James at 15* fame) who goes on to become an Olympic runner. He got lots of practice because he would run home every day after school to hide the wet bedsheet, which his mom would inevitably have hanging outside, from the other school kids. Whew! (allison) (See also *JAMES AT 15*)

The Bee Gees Is there anybody who hasn't heard the bizarre bleating falsettos of "Stayin' Alive," "Nights on Broadway," or "Night Fever"? Who wouldn't recognize these satin-clad, open-shirted, bearded 'n' blow-dried "Children of the World"? What a ridiculous '70s relic, these Bee Gees; can they really be as worthless and silly as the films with which their name has become irrevocably connected (*Saturday Night Fever, Sgt. Pepper's Lonely Hearts Club Band,* and *Grease,* whose title song they wrote)? Well, silly, yes; but worthless? In a word, *nofuckin'waydude!!* The Bee Gees were so incredible in the '60s, I cannot adequately convey their bitchenness in mere printed words! As appalling as their disco-era crapola was, I think they should be granted a presidential pardon, or at least a papal dispensation, for the amazing amount of quality material they recorded back in their psychedelic-pop-ballad heyday. The first album alone contains some of the most psychotic Beatle-esque string-driven anomalies ever committed to vinyl; "Red Chair Fade Away" is as catchy and lysergically ethereal as anything on *Magical Mystery Tour,* with lines like "I can feel the speaking sky"; "Every Christian Lion-Hearted Man Will Show You" is one of the most obtuse pop songs *ever,* period. Besides the weird psych-lite fare, there were the Abysmally Depressing Pop Ballads: "Holiday," "New York Mining Disaster 1941," nearly all their other pre-disco work; the Abysmally Depressing Faux R&B Songs: "To Love Somebody," "I Can't See Nobody"; the then obligatory Silly English Songs: "Craise Finton Kirk Royal Academy of Arts" and "Cucumber Castle," which was still kind of morbid-sounding; and a few Fake Beatles Songs: "In My Own

The Brothers Gibb

Time." It must have taken a whole lot of grief to drive a person to off themselves back in those happier times, although anyone subjected to large doses of their later output might think otherwise. The Bee Gees sounded so completely, utterly miserable that Joy Division and Nirvana seem positively gleeful by comparison. I'll bet if modern teen rockers Silverchair had to deal with the combined stress of their workaholic taskmaster dad acting as their manager and the hard-core speed/psychedelics/alcohol/downer abuse that was the teenaged Gibb Bros.' only solace, there would be one less tiny-toon Pearl Jam clone for Kennedy to gush over. (don) Fact note: The Bee Gees shocked the music world recently when they were inducted into the Rock and Roll Hall of Fame. Yes! (See also ANDY GIBB)

Barbi Benton

Being Eaten Alive A persistent fear we humans harbor is that of being eaten alive, particularly by some kind of beast. Once the stuff of Mutual of Omaha's *Wild Kingdom,* these fears were exacerbated by a number of lame movies that involved great white sharks, piranhas, alligators, and even ants carrying out God's will. Not only are such fears unfounded, but they completely ignore the fact that we humans slaughter billions of animals every year in the name of Nike shoes, fur coats, and pork rinds. (noël) ✣ Bring on those flesh-eating bacteria movies! (darby) (See also DISASTER MOVIES and *JAWS*)

Belt Buckles A throwback to the golden age of bong-hit stadium rock, when high school kids donned faux-hologram ovular buckles sporting killer band logos such as Styx, Supertramp, and Kiss. As a variation on the band-theme belt buckles, beer company logos became very popular. A relic from an era in which people actually tucked in their shirts. For a more recent reference, check out the film *Dazed and Confused.* (cliff) (See also STADIUM ROCK and TUCKING IN ONE'S SHIRT)

The Benny Hill Show From the land of fish and chips and Page Three Girls waddled this cherubic, dimple-faced clown. Benny Hill's half-hour variety show was always a late-night treat for a ten-year-old like me. Filled with disgusting old men who were invariably subjects of derision and scantily clad young lovelies bouncing about in poorly orchestrated — but sometimes hilarious — comedy skits, the show gave me the sneaking suspicion that there was something completely wrong with it all. Of course, I felt pretty creepy staying up late, dealing with Hill's none-too-clever limericks and cheesy perversions, just to see a little boobage. (noël) ✣ Another in a long line of dead Bens. (jaz)

Barbi Benton Barbi was never married to Hef, although a lot of people think she was, and she was never a Playmate, although a lot of people think that too. But she did pose for *Playboy* many times — she had that smoldering All-American-Girl look. If you look at her pictorials, she is gorgeous, a cute, sexy sprite. She appeared on four covers (Pam Anderson has the record with six). (chip) ✣ It seemed like she was on every other episode of *Love Boat* and *Fantasy*

Island. She was hot and always played the same character. And Adrienne Barbeau seemed to be on the other half of those shows. Benton's been playing clubs in L.A. lately. They both promoted the natural-big-boob look. (jes/darby) ♣ Others who ended up on *Love Boat* and *Fantasy Island* included Charo, Debralee Scott, Morgan Fairchild, Cheryl Ladd, Shelley Winters, Eric Estrada, Susan Anton, and Robert Reed. (lindsey a.) (See also *FANTASY ISLAND* and *PLAYBOY*)

Bermuda Triangle There was always some TV special on the Triangle, which had foggy reenactment footage of planes vanishing in thin air. It always freaked me out that my parents went to Bermuda on their honeymoon, and I thought them very daring because of it. (darby)

The Best Friend This is a very youthful phenomenon where people are going to be friends *forever!* No matter what. (darby) ♣ It's 1981. I have fallen in love with my best friend, Susan. She is in eighth grade also and this is kind of cool, 'cause in eighth grade your best friend is fucking God. We lie on her bed and discuss what color Vans we want and how we're gonna kill ourselves if we can't be together. (nancy)

Bestselling (Or Just Essential Retro) Books To name a few: *All I Really Need to Know I Learned in Kindergarten; All the President's Men; The Big Book; Bill Cosby: Fatherhood; The Mammoth Hunters* (Watergate); *The Amityville Horror; The Anarchists Cookbook; And Ladies of the Club; Andromeda Strain; Angels: God's Secret Agents* (Billy Graham); *Bonfire of the Vanities, The Electric Koolaid Acid Test, The Right Stuff* (Tom Wolfe); *Real Men Don't Eat Quiche; The World According to Garp; The Book of Lists; The Man, The Prize, The Word* (Irving Wallace); *The Carpetbaggers; Carrie, The Shining, The Stand, The Talisman, It, The Tommyknockers* (Stephen King); *Centennial; Chez Panisse Cookbook* (birth of California cuisine); *Coma; The Covenant; Dianetics* (L. Ron Hubbard); *Demon Child, Invasion, A Werewolf Among Us* (Dean R. Koontz); *Dune* (Frank Herbert); *The Drama of the Gifted Child; E.T. Storybook; Fear and Loathing in Las Vegas* (Hunter S. Thompson); *Fear of Flying* (and the Erica Jong "zipless fuck"); *The Female Eunuch; Be*

Here Now (Ram Dass); *The Firm, Pelican Brief* (John Grisham); *The Godfather* (Mario Puzo); *Hollywood Wives, Hollywood Husbands* (Jackie Collins); *Helter Skelter; Iacocca: An Autobiography; I'm with the Band* (Pamela Des Barres); *In Cold Blood* (Truman Capote); *In Search of Excellence; Interview with a Vampire* (Anne Rice); *Jaws;* a few unknown titles by Leo Buscaglia (the hug guy); *Less Than Zero* (Bret Easton Ellis); *The Living Bible; Looking for Mr. Goodbar; Love Machine; Love Story; Money* (Martin Amis); *Ms. Piggy's Guide to Life; Myra Breckinridge, Myron* (Gore Vidal); *Noble House; Patriot Games* (Tom Clancy); *The Peter Pan Syndrome; Working* (Studs Terkel); *Portnoy's Complaint* (Philip Roth); *Power, Success* (Michael Korda); *Presumed Innocent; Princess Daisy, Scruples* (Judith Krantz); *Ragtime; The Road Not Taken* (Scott Peck); *Roots* (Haley); *Return of the Jedi Storybook; Rubyfruit Jungle* (Rita Mae Brown — first black lesbian novel); *The Satanic Verses; The Sensual Man* (by "M"); *The Silmarillion; Sophie's Choice; Star* (Danielle Steel); *The Teachings of Don Juan,* et cetera (Carlos Castaneda); *Thornbirds; Time Flies; The Total Woman; Trinity; The Unbearable Lightness of Being; Vanna Speaks!* (Vanna White); *Valley of the Dolls; What Really Happened to the Class of '65; Wheels; Winning by Intimidation.* (amy/darby/natalie) (See also V. C. ANDREWS; *BLADE RUNNER;* JUDY BLUME; ERMA BOMBECK; BOOKS; *BRIGHT LIGHTS, BIG CITY; JONATHAN LIVINGSTON SEAGULL;* SELF-HELP BOOKS; and *SHOGUN*)

Bic Lighters Especially on cords, worn around your neck. Check out Cherie Currie in *Foxes.* (allison) ♣ Don't forget Cricket lighters — another cheap disposable '70s thing. The environmental movement of the '70s was concerned with air pollution, not landfills. (dad) (See also ROCKY HORROR PICTURE SHOW and STADIUM ROCK)

Bicentennial The Spirit of '76 took over the nation. Glory, glory, hallelujah, America is two hundred years old! The buzz swept all across the country and everyone was wearing red, white, and blue bellbottoms and stars-and-stripes hankies in their back pockets. It was the biggest and the best Fourth of July ever, with plumper watermelons, juicier corn on the cob, more sparklers, and a fuck of a lot more firecrackers than any year before or any year since. (jes) ❧ In response to all the hype, "Residents of Lake City, Pennsylvania, decided they'd rather look forward two hundred years than look back to the past, so the town dedicated a landing pad for UFOs" (from the book *The '70s*). ❧ There were the quarters, the half-dollar, *and* the Eisenhower dollar. Ike had been on the big dollar coin for a few years, but the Bicentennial version had a different back image. It showed the moon being eclipsed by the Liberty Bell! (bruce)

Bicycles A big status symbol for kids (besides action figures and how many trading cards they possessed) was the most obvious, their bicycle. Bike varieties drove parents crazy as much as fashion did, changing from extremities such as tassels at the end of handle bars to Oakley grips. And who could forget that useless foam padding across your Schwinn Cruiser's handlebars, which inevitably got torn or rotten after a couple of months. Other bike accessories included banana seats to ride tandem, personalized plates, the fold-up pegs that you could put on your front or back wheels so your friend could stand on and ride with you. If you were the destructive type you had Mag Wheels, whereas if you were the acrobatic BMX star you generally had alloy rims (which were much lighter but somewhat weaker). For the BMX connoisseur, you just weren't happening unless you had a Red Line, Mongoose, Powerlite, Cook Brothers, Race Inc., Hutch, PK Ripper, or GT. For the less rambunctious, the Schwinn Cruiser was the flavor, invariably the Cadillac of bicycles. By this point 10-speeds were considered useless and dropped considerably in value. If you were really spoiled, your parents bought you a Schwinn Crate bicycle, which was the Harley-Davidson of the pedal-pusher scene. It consisted of five speeds, springer forks, sissy bars on front and back, a stick shift "gear shifter," and countless useless accessories that would make any kid on any block green with envy. Now these are extreme collector's items, as you would guess, and can garner sums up

to $2,000 in good condition. (mike) ❧ Another accessory was the number plate, which enabled BMX dweebs to pretend they were pro; often adorned with plenty of stickers, my favorite being the rainbow prism sticker of that buck-toothed fuzzy creature flipping you the bird, with the phrase "This one's for you." (noël) ❧ Don't forget baseball or Wacky Pack cards in the spokes, the McDonald's Bike Flags, and the bell-bottoms getting caught in the gears. And how *no one* but hemophiliacs, Mormons, and mama's boys wore bike helmets! (ju-ji) (See also WACKY PACKAGES)

Big (fashion statement of the early to mid-'80s) The opposite of the '70s flat look and the other end of the '90s loose/baggy idea, the earlier '80s were all about structured bigness. Of course, everyone needed bigger muscles, bigger tits, bigger hair, and bigger budgets to pull the whole thing off. Think Brooke Shields's and George Michael's bushy eyebrows, *Flashdance*-inspired big sweaters with widened necks, *Talking Heads* front man David Byrne-esque shoulder-padded blazers, and huge legwarmers or socks ballooning at the ankle. This "big" aesthetic was indeed a scary fashion nightmare that we woke up from around 1992 when the whole waif/grunge thing happened — which in Retro Hell years is just about long enough to see it all happen again. Don't look now, but is that a shoulder pad creeping up behind you? (nina) (See also LEG-WARMERS and WHAM!)

Big Jim Nobody remembers Big Jim. He was like G.I. Joe, but smaller and cheaper so I could afford him on my newspaper delivery boy's salary. Jim had this button in his back that when you pressed it made his arm karate chop. He also had very well crafted thigh muscles. I had a Big Jim ambulance, a Big Jim Corvette (with laser guns that popped up from the hood), and a rugged rescue truck with a tow rope for rescuing other Big Jims that fell over cliffs and were hurt really bad in the canyon. Things started going downhill when I asked my dad to build me a tiny fort and I insisted there be a bedroom so Jim could seduce

Barbie in his cardboard-and-felt bed. Soon after, I discovered other interests and willed my dolls to my bro, who promptly tortured Big Jim and broke his limbs off. If he ever becomes a serial killer, I'll tell the media about that. (chip) ✿ Remember the muscle band that he could pop by flexing his arm? (steven) (See also ACTION FIGURES and G.I. JOE)

Big Wheels When the Green Machine came along, Big Wheels were considered low-tech in comparison. A few years later some of my most spoiled friends had motorized minicars that invoked jealousy and an I-don't-care-Big-Wheels-are-better devotion to the original hot transport for kids. (wendy) ✿ Never thought of them the same way after seeing *The Shining*. (gwynne) ✿ They're still around even though its original maker, Marx Toys, is gone. (bruce) ✿ Also, don't forget the Wiz-Wheel. A big orange round thing where you sat in the middle and used your arms to crank two big wheels, sort of like a wheelchair for kids. (jaz)

Bike Shorts A fashion interpretation of the actual padded biking shorts worn by bicyclists, bike shorts were basically Lycra-enhanced leggings that kept getting shorter and shorter until they went from just above the knee to barely over the butt. In the aerobicized '80s, when all time was broken down into either pre- or après-workout, they were ubiquitous. Also very popular with the early hip-hop girls. Think of JJ Fad rocking the mike in supersonic tight spandex shorts with K-Swiss kicks, with big ol' baggy socks, a satin Nike sweat jacket, and reams of gold jewelry. Fresh! (nina)

Binaca Around for a while, Binaca became an essential accessory for men in the '70s, which is when the mini-spray version came out. (ju-ji)

Bionics Why as an eight-year-old I thought I could catch up to people on the playground by running *slower* is beyond me — wasn't that the most ingenious part of *The Six Million Dollar Man* and *The Bionic Woman*? I mean, they knew little kids would be trying to run faster than the bad guy's car and smashing into signposts and stuff and getting hurt, so they made him appear to run super *slow* to signify running super *fast*. And those sound effects! You really felt like you were strong when you made that metallic *dader-daderdader* sound with your tongue. I stayed up late to watch the episode where Jaime Somers got into that parachute accident, and she and Steve Austin had been in love but then she didn't remember their love! But she did get to become bionic. I cried myself to sleep, longing for something I did not understand. I was also too young to wonder if Steve had a bionic penis, but now I do. (chip) ✿ My sister hit me right above my eye with a heavy flashlight once when we were camping, and when my mom yelled at her for almost putting my eye out, she said, "She can just get a new one." They didn't let her watch *The Six Million Dollar Man* after that. (riley) ✿ Don't forget Luke Skywalker fixing up his chopped-up hand with a new bionic one. It was so easy that he just installed it himself with the hand he still had left. (darby) (See also *THE SIX MILLION DOLLAR MAN*)

Bionic Woman Jaime Somers and her bionic German shepherd used to be able to run faster than the cars on the freeway, and somehow, now, actress Lindsay Wagner ✿ has ended up pitching Fords on TV commercials, screaming because the guy's driving too fast! (jes) ✿ She was too strong to have a boyfriend, so she just tore up phone books in front of them, made them horny, and led them on. (mike) ✿ In the original episode, she died from a reaction to the bionics. This provided Lee Majors with a pensive and memorable moment: Steve Austin leaves the hospital, stares off into space, and has slo-mo footage of Jaime superimposed over his face, while in voice-over he *sings* something like, "Oh Jaime, I love-a-you. . . ." It was so horrid that my sisters and I would sing it to each other for years to come whenever we wanted to annoy one another. (bruce) ✿ My favorite episode by far was the fem-bot one! These lovely, bionic wannabes were no match for the

Lindsay Wagner

as part of keeping up their outlaw image. Bisexuality was momentarily something to boast about in the late '70s, because it implied you were free of taboos, experimental, in touch with both your male and female sides, and therefore potentially a better lover. (candi) ♣ Bisexual Chic came along around the time of Bowie, Mick Ronson, and Marc Bolan. The glitter rock scene seemed to promote bisexuality, at least among men. Actually, the British music scene has always brought sexual deviance (yuck, what a word) to the news. For instance, Marianne Faithfull and the Mars Bar, the lesbian scene in *Performance,* Bowie stating that he met his wife because they were dating the same person. Androgyne and feminine clothing for men came out during the early days of the Stones (Jagger himself a bisexual), flourished, and carried over to the days of Boy George. American musicians, on the other hand, have always been a big sex-and-fashion yawn. Oh yeah, we had Morrison and Hendrix. (patty) (See also GLITTER/GLAM ROCK) 🐾

Bitch Originally a female dog or an unfriendly woman. In the '70s, a Rolling Stones song or a proud proclamation worn as a fashion statement in the form of a gold medallion or glittered T-shirt logo. In the '80s, a difficult task (as in "Life's a bitch and then you die") or a terrible, short-lived heavy metal band from Encino. (gwynne) ♣ And a nag, as in "bitching." (mike) ♣ "A bitch is a dog. A dog barked. Bark is on a tree. A tree is nature. Nature is beauty. Thanks for the compliment." (howard) ♣ Stay sweet and have a totally bitchin' summer! (lorraine) (See also SAYINGS/SLANG)

power of Jaime Somers! I loved how she freaked out after she tore their faces off. (morgan) (See also *THE SIX MILLION DOLLAR MAN)*

Birth Control People used to think this was a good idea. What the hell happened? (gwynne) (See also AIRPLANE RULES AND REGULATIONS, BABIES, THE PILL, and SCANDALS)

Birthstone Rings Really cheap imitation rings that were adjustable in the back. Most had two faux diamonds on either side of your "gem." (katy) ♣ As important as knowing your sign. (jaz)

Bisexual Chic During the sexually liberated '60s and '70s, when the new rule of thumb was "if it feels good, do it," gay sexuality seemed a lot less taboo than before. Rock stars camped it up, or pretended to,

Bill Bixby Besides being our favorite Martian, Bixby was everyone's favorite father figure. From *The Courtship of Eddie's Father* to *The Incredible Hulk* (really!) and finally to the '90s, where he directed the smart and sassy *Blossom*, everyone loved Bill and we're sad he's gone. (See also TEEN IDOL FREAK-OUT)

The Black Hole The Stephen Hawking crowd had long understood the concept of a stellar body so dense that it even sucked in light, allowing nothing to escape. By the late '70s, everybody else got it too, sorta. Leave it to America's favorite stargazer, Dr. Carl Sagan, to find a wormhole in the credibility gap and bring theoretical astrophysics to the masses. In his book *The Cosmic Connection* (book titles don't get more '70s than that), the brainiac moptop explained all about black holes and "theorized" about how they might actually be portals to alternate universes, where they became "white holes" that spewed out star-stuff faster than a freshman at a Cornell kegger party. This highly questionable theory started showing up in sci-fi, where it became a catchall plot device. It all reached its zenith with Walt Disney's stupid film *The Black Hole,* which featured several collapsed stars in the cast. Eventually both the phrase and concept ended up in common usage. But to the masses, a black hole no longer referred to a dark star or a hyperspace portal; instead it usually meant a twelve-year-old's room or any waste of time. (bruce) ❧ There was a short-lived newspaper strip based on the movie, with artwork by the late great Jack Kirby. (martin) ❧ William James Sidis, a man who had one of the most advanced minds of our time, wrote an unpublished manuscript called *The Finite and the Infinite,* where he describes the concept of black holes. What makes this so strange is that the manuscript was discovered in the '70s and Sidis died in the '40s. (steven)

Blade Runner The 1982 Ridley Scott film, based on the Philip Dick novel *Do Androids Dream of Electric Sheep?,* presented a glittering, shiny, yet grimy vision of an L.A. future, which downtown now seems to be trying eagerly to live up to. The dirty secret of this tale of hunting replicants: It was pretty boring, despite being a classic, providing the basic feel for the future, and being adopted by the modern hipster sci-fi cyberpunk movement. (brian) ❧ *Blade Runner* is unforgettable! The concept that replicants don't even know they aren't real humans, and that their memories aren't their own, but programmed, strikes a chord so similar to our own Retro-Helled lives. It's horrifying! Philip K. Dick rocks the world and beyond! (nina)

Linda Blair Devil's advocate and child actor, Linda Blair levitated to stardom in the 1973 classic *The Exorcist,* and descended into Retro Hell with its terrifyingly bad sequel, *The Exorcist II: The Heretic* ('77). Her performance as a preteen possessed by Satan who spews green vomit and blasphemous profanities as naturally as she violates her holiness with a big ol' crucifix turned a few heads (including her own) and sentenced her to an acting career as the bad seed victim of bad circumstance. Memorable moments of masochism included *Born Innocent* ('74), in which little Linda is raped with a broomstick by her fellow juvie inmates; *Sweet Hostage* ('75), in which the dispossessed darling is seduced into evil by Martin Sheen; and *Roller Boogie* ('79), in which Boogie-oogie Blair is humiliated and debased by the demonic roller-disco craze. Along her road to acting ruin, Linda has strengthened her alliance with various beasts by designing otherworldly costumes for her rock star friends in Lynyrd Skynyrd and Molly Hatchet, as well as politicking mercilessly for animal rights. (nina) (See also *SARA T. — PORTRAIT OF A TEENAGE ALCOHOLIC*)

Mel Blanc We think he's the voice for God, too. (jaz)

Blaxploitation After the previous decade's civil rights victory, '70s America realized how hip, how happenin', and especially how highly marketable (and therefore exploitable) was the image of the "blacks." Hollywood saw major dollar signs, so a machine was quickly invented which churned out movies that showcased the style, rhythm, and badness which Whitey could never hope to possess but could view from a distance at the cineplex. The more noble production execs claimed that these flix were geared to appeal to black audiences, which were fast becoming a viable faction of the consumer market to be catered to. Starring predominantly black casts (with a token honky to play one of the bad guys or some hot chick that the black male star casts aside) and featuring soundtracks dripping with wah-wah pedal, a whole new genre of film was created. *Dolomite, Superfly, Shaft, Foxy Brown, Car Wash*, and *The Avenging Disco Godfather* are a few of the more well known. Television Land was quick to follow suit with sitcoms such as *Good Times, The Jeffersons*, and *What's Happening!* (lorraine) (See also BREAKDANCING)

Blazers I don't know if this was a movement of some kind, but in the early '80s we (girls) all had these corduroy or wool ones in earth tones (usually browns), which we'd wear to temple with our lace blouses and calf-length wool skirts. Very attractive. (darby) ❖ In the late '80s, boys had *Miami Vice*–style white blazers that were all the rage for bar mitzvahs. I can't remember if I ever had a crush on a boy as a result of his looking real sporty in one of those; maybe I thought he'd need stubble like Don Johnson rather than peach fuzz. (wendy) ❖ They were perfect for the '70s guy, casual yet formal. The later *Miami Vice*–type were known as "unconstructed," as they had no real form, and they looked as good (or bad) on Don Johnson as they do on the homeless who wear them today. (bruce) (See also GUNNE SAX and *MIAMI VICE*)

Bloody Mary A "game" that still scares me to this day. Go into the bathroom, shut the door, shut the lights, face the mirror, and with your eyes closed scream "Bloody Mary" thirteen times, and then open your eyes to the horrors (which should include lots of blood and gore, obviously). I've been brave enough to do it — but only when there are other people at home, and I usually run out of the bathroom screaming. (darby) ❖ Also the drink as a retro hangover cure. (ju-ji)

Blue Chip Trading Stamps If it weren't for that *Brady Bunch* episode (the one where they have the contest building the house of cards), absolutely no one would have any idea what these were all about. I'm still not sure I do. (gwynne) ❖ There were also S&H trading stamps, which were green. I'm not at all sure how they worked, but basically, one got these stamps when making purchases and stuck them into a book. Once the book was full, it could be exchanged for an item in a catalogue, or at a licensed store. They were phased out right about the time the *Brady Bunch* episode was made, hence the *tragic radio news* where all the trading stamp collection stores were closing their doors. I do recall that anything of value took dozens of books, and that it was only popular among the very old and kids with no disposable income. (bruce) ❖ These, or some variation thereof, are still around today, in various obscure locations around the U.S. Just beware. (jaz)

Blue Velvet David Lynch's *Blue Velvet* ('86) changed my life. Not that it was the best film I'd ever seen, but even more than with *Eraserhead*, David Lynch managed to inject a subliminal dose of strangeness into the film that filtered into my unconscious and continues to work me over. To this day, I have an image seared into my brain of Dean Stockwell as the "fuckin' suave" Ben, lip-synching "Candy-Colored Clown" to an enraptured Dennis Hopper as Frank. Not to mention a stark-naked Isabella Rossellini as Dorothy "I have you inside of me" Vallens hysterically sobbing on Kyle MacLachlan's, aka Jeffrey "The Neighbor"'s, front lawn. Three of my close friends at the time and I took on these roles; not that we actually acted out scenes or anything, we just transformed into these characters. Almost ten years later, I found myself interviewing Dennis Hopper for a Japanese TV show on *Waterworld* and told him of my *Blue Velvet* obsession; he laughed so hard all he did was make heavy sex references to every question I attempted to ask until I finally gave up and the world slipped away into ten minutes of straight laughter. I surfaced to find myself fired from a majorly cherry freelance gig. Of course, it was totally worth it. (nina) ❖ I swear this is a true story. I took a date to see *Blue Velvet* when it came out. When the scene came on where Isabella Rossellini held a knife to Kyle

MacLachlan's neck and told him to touch her breasts . . . I came in my pants. Spontaneously. Just like that. Boom! I wasn't touching myself or anything, I just came. I looked at my date, who didn't seem to notice, and excused myself and cleaned up in the bathroom. This has never happened to me before or since. (howard)

Judy Blume

Otherwise Known as Sheila the Great, Starring Sally J. Freedman as Herself, Tales of a Fourth-Grade Nothing, Superfudge, Iggie's House, Deenie, Are You There God? It's Me Margaret, It's Not the End of the World, and one of my favorite books, *Blubber.* Judy was one of the essential young-adult authors to help introduce innocent young girls to wet dreams, religion, bras, periods, spine diseases, boys, masturbation, and eventually sex (in *Forever*) and finally *Wifey* (her adult book, which you could always find hidden in your mother's underwear drawer). Best-ever cover blurb: "Wifey is tired of chicken on Wednesdays and sex on Saturdays. This morning a mysterious motorcyclist flashed and revealed himself to Wifey and brought her frustrations into rigid focus! Wifey sees her wildest fantasies taking flight, and Wifey has an itching and uncontrollable urge to catch up to them!" Sheesh! (darby)

Bodybuilding (otherwise known as Pumping Iron!)

Jack La Lanne and Charles Atlas had been around for decades, but it wasn't until the 1974 documentary *Stay Hungry* (featuring Arnold) that bodybuilding itself became a sport. It was only then that one heard of people "going to the gym." (bruce)

Erma Bombeck

"If life is a bowl of cherries, why am I always in the pits?" Goyische people are really boring, so I guess anything a little bit odd is funny to them. (dad) ❧ The last generation of American women who had enough leisure to be bored over such things. Erma filled hundreds of pages with this sort of middle-aged deadpan wit. It was all very funny to the kind of people who watched the *Carol Burnett Show.* Erma became the Art Buchwald of the kitchen. Innocuous housewife humor, a lost field of literature. (bruce)

Books (Kid/Young Adult)

Uh, just a few of our favorites: *The Adventures of a Two-Minute Werewolf; All-of-a-Kind-Family; . . . And I Don't Want to Live This Life; Animal Farm; Anne of Green Gables; Babar; Bloom County; Blubber; Bunicula; By the Shores of Silver Lake;* the *Castle Rock* series; *The Cat Ate My Gymsuit; Catcher in the Rye; Celery Stalks at Midnight; Charlotte's Web; The Chocolate War; The Diary of Anne Frank; Dicey's Song; Dinky Hocker Shoots Smack; Ever After; Fatmen from Space; 500 Hats of Bartholomew Cubbins; One Fish, Two Fish, Red Fish, Blue Fish* and *The Sneetches* (and all Dr. Seuss); *Flowers in the Attic; The Girl with the Silver Eyes; The Great Brain; The Great Gilly Hopkins; The Guinness Book of World Records; Half Magic; Harriet the Spy; The Hobbit; Hubert: The Caterpillar Who Thought He Was a Mustache; I Am the Cheese* (which was made into a bad movie starring Robert Naughton, the weird older brother in *E.T.*); *I Never Loved Your Mind, Jay's Journal; Knight's Castle; My Darling, My Hamburger* and *Pardon Me You're Stepping on My Eyeball* (Paul Zindel); *Lisa Bright and Dark;* the Little House series; *Lizard Music; The Long Secret;* Nancy Drew/Hardy Boys series; the *Oz* series; *The Phantom Tollbooth; The Pinballs; Pippi Longstocking;* the Ramona series; *Ribsy; Rumble Fish; Runaway Ralph* (motorcycle mouse) series; *Sheila Levine Is Dead and Living in New York; The Shrinking of Treehorn; A Solitary Blue; Sounder; The Story of Ick* (by Munster Fred Gwynne!); *Stuart Little; The Tale of Mrs. Tiggy-Winkle, There's a Monster at the End of This Book* (and the Golden Books series); *A Wrinkle in Time.* . . . (darby, dave, skylaire) ❧ Interactive Books: "Choose Your Own Adventure" books that let you decide how the story would go by choosing from different options and turning to different pages. Each read could be a whole new experience — very "interactive" for way back when. (darby) ❧ Pop-Up Books: The history of pop-ups — those rudimentary 3-D/interactive books — goes back even further than the 20th century, but there was certainly an upsurge during the '70s. Considering that they are all handmade, and that there are now only a few companies left that create them (mostly shipping off all the slave labor to Third World countries), it's interesting to note they've been working their own minor comeback. (jaz) (See also V. C. ANDREWS, JUDY BLUME, *CHRONICLES OF NARNIA*, ROALD DAHL, *GO ASK ALICE*, HARDY BOYS/NANCY DREW, and DANIEL PINKWATER)

The Boogie Board Tom Morey created the Boogie Board in 1971. As a surfer his goal was to make wave-riding more accessible and user-friendly, and so, with his wife's iron and some polyethylene foam, he shaped the first board. When they went into mass production a few years later (though always handmade), they came in lots of nature-type colors — I've got an old one that's orange with a tacky rainbow leash and that old-school groovy black plastic handle. Today they come in every color and a multitude of shapes, have a cool slick bottom so the thing doesn't snap in two and actually moves faster, and are called "bodyboards." Fuck that! What happened to the boogie? People too cool to boogie? I still call them boogie boards in a sort of homage to their creation. Anyhow, I'm sure some surfers today still curse Morey's name as they fight with the masses of boogie boarders for the waves. (darby)

Boom Boxes The bigger the better. And if there were multicolored lights that went on in time with the beat, you were *king* of your block. (darby) Panasonic TV spot, circa 1978: An enormous *Close Encounters*–size boom box flies low over a mostly "urban"-looking neighborhood. The giant radio lands in the street, its immense cassette door opens amid much music and smoke. Out emerges the band Earth, Wind & Fire, all members jauntily carrying the latest Panasonic street models. It was the high-water mark for big radios with little sounds. (bruce)

Debby Boone We all thought that "You Light Up My Life" was this sappy love song until we found out that she was a devout Christian. (riley) Pat Boone's daughter, which would also make her a descendant of Daniel Boone. Where is she now, and will she stay there? (bruce)

Boone's Farm (Strawberry Hill) You know your tolerance for toxic substances was higher when you were younger because you could actually keep this stuff down. Okay, it wasn't that bad. As a matter of fact, it tasted just like candy. An amazingly cheap and effective potion to get the chicks drunk off, which was an important selling point. I'd wear my dad's extra-large coat and walk out of the convenience store with a bottle stashed under each arm (only got caught once). Then we'd pull all-nighters out on the golf course, wwoooooooweeeeeeee! (darby) Once most states lowered their drinking age to eighteen, something like this was inevitable. The market exploded with cheap, sweet "pop" wines, and some pretty bad things got put in bottles. Companies who were used to catering to the white-port-and-lemon crowd geared up to produce these elixirs. Would-be sophisticates tried to gulp these things and got sick doing it. Once they tried a real wine, they moved on. Eventually, all those bottles of Annie Green Springs wound up in the hands of stupid adolescents, like myself. Soon even we tossed the stuff in the gutter, where it is enjoyed to this day. (bruce)

Boy in a Plastic Bubble Mr. Travolta (🕺) strikes again. . . . We now have to agree that he rules all things '70s. Probably one of Barbarino's most tender and sensitive roles. (jes) Made in 1976, this TV movie-of-the-week co-starred Travolta's then girlfriend Diana Hyland, who later died of cancer. (bruce) There was a hard-core remake of this movie made in the early '80s starring the guy who played Bruno on the *Fame* TV series. This version features a goofy scene in which the bubble boy and his girlfriend get naked and simulate sex by rubbing up against each other through the plastic bubble. (dave)

Boynton "Hippo Birdie Two Ewe," Chocoholic books, "Don't Let the Turkeys Get You Down." Very trendy '80s cute-core stationery. (ju-ji)

b

Braces It's weird to think I had these things on my teeth for *five years!* I had the new cemented version, not the band-around-the teeth version, and not the rich-kids-wanting-to-be-actors clear plastic or behind-the-teeth variety. I also had a headgear, neckgear, a few retainers . . . Alas, I had dreams of growing up and becoming a kinder, gentler orthodontist. And nightmares of meeting the cutest boy in the world and having chunks of food caught between my teeth and the metal. Definitely a test for the self-conscious youth. (darby) ❖ Thanks to aggressive dental care, braces became for '70s kids what tonsils were to those of the '50s. By the time I was strapped in, it was a bit strange if you didn't have them. (bruce) (See also BUMMERS, and the character Jaws in the Bond movie *For Your Eyes Only*)

The Brat Pack Anthony Michael Hall: The thin, geeky, pre-steroid version in *Sixteen Candles, Weird Science, The Breakfast Club.* His new buffness later shocked us in *Johnny Be Good* and *Edward Scissorhands.* Little-known fact: his real name is Michael, but there was already a Michael Hall and a Michael Anthony Hall in the Screen Actors Guild. Also, in *The Breakfast Club,* when his mother dropped him off for detention, that was his real mom and sister in the car. Emilio Estevez: *Repo Man,* yes. *The Mighty Ducks,* yawn. Charlie Sheen: We have absolutely nothing to say about him, except his name now makes one think of Heidi Fleiss instead of some of the good flicks he was in (*Platoon* and . . . oh, I can't think of any others). He was only a Brat Packer by association anyway; as was Demi Moore, for her appearance in the B.P.-related *St. Elmo's Fire.* She started out a boobless but likable sassy chick on *General Hospital* and *somehow* became one of the highest-paid and biggest-breasted things in Hollywood. Judd Nelson: Hot Rod in *Transformers: The Movie.* He wasn't *really* a failure till he shacked up with Shannen Doherty, but luckily the era of the retro comebacks helped him score on Brooke Shields's *Suddenly Susan.* My pal Lisa "Suckdog" Carver and I saw him driving Pacific Coast Highway in a big sport-utility vehicle recently, but I guess he's not much of a star 'cause we didn't follow him. Molly Ringwald: Would she have gotten fat, too, if she'd stayed on *The Facts of Life?* Molly was really *the girl* of the pack, but once Hughes pulled out, she sorta just faded from the limelight with the help of some poor movie choices (picture bad Alan Alda jokes). She starred in some French flicks in the meantime until her recent move back to the States to try again. Rob Lowe: Had a bad rep around Malibu for fucking high school girls — which grew into a bad rep worldwide after his hotel sex video fiasco. Starred in the disturbing *Hotel New Hampshire,* but got the Brat Pack image for playing the slutty bachelor in *About Last Night.* Ally Sheedy: So cute as Matthew Broderick's girlfriend in *WarGames,* so cool as the screwed-up pale chick in black in *The Breakfast Club,* but then *that was it!* Some blame the tailspin on her marriage to rocker Richie Sambora. Recently her career has revolved more around writing, with a few bestselling poetry books under her belt. Last seen in *Red Shoe Diaries 4: Auto Erotica.* Sad . . . but we still love her. Mare Winningham: A minor Brat Packer since she wasn't too pretty or cool (or stupid), who more recently starred in the Oscar-nominated *Georgia* with Jennifer Jason Leigh, but we liked her best in 1989's *Miracle Mile.* And lest we forget, Andrew McCarthy, a sort of forgettable member who, after finally seeing *Less Than Zero* all the way through, I can admit to liking, in a pukey kinda way. (darby with katy/stymie) (See also JOHN HUGHES, *REPO MAN,* and *WEIRD SCIENCE*)

Breakdancing A major component of the budding hip-hop culture of the early '80s, breakdancing was a physically demanding youth-oriented dance activity that involved complex, improvisational maneuvers that were like bizarre gymnastic floor exercises. As the story goes, it evolved from the street corners of urban areas like New York City. Ideally, it was a creative expression that allowed gangs to let off some steam and avoid fisticuffs (as depicted in Michael Jackson's "Beat It" video), which doesn't mean that fights didn't occur. All you needed was a smooth floor, or — for portability — a large piece of cardboard (more fortunate kids had rolls of linoleum), a dope pair of sneakers, a nice set of colorful threads (from Adidas active wear to sweat jackets to parachute pants), a few bandannas around your leg, and, preferably, not too much honkiness in your blood, and you were ready to roll. From Popping to Locking (Fred Berry, better known as Rerun on *What's Happening!!*, was a visible proponent of this) to Backspins to Moonwalks to Windmills, breakdancing was the shit. It was victim to greedy opportunists who made poor feature-length films like *Breakin'* and *Breakin' 2: Electric Boogaloo*. I will still maintain that *Beat Street*, *sans* the Harry Belafonte music, was a damn good film. Breaking still exists, just not on TV. (noël) ❖ Fred Berry had gotten his start as the star of a popular urban dance group know as the Lockers. They were all the rage on mid-'70s TV. There was something about watching Merv Griffin introduce a gang of seemingly happy young black men in silly nonthreatening clothes to dance for our pleasure that clicked with Gerald Ford's America. (bruce) (See also BOOM BOXES and *THE GONG SHOW*, and check out the book *Breakdancing: Mr. Fresh with the Supreme Rockers*)

Breakin' Moves Floor Rock (old-style breakdancing), the Handglide or Flow (horizontal spinning of body while balanced on one elbow stuck between hips, legs bent and spread), Backspin, Headspin, Windmill (spinning of body on shoulders and upper back), Suicide (no-hands forward flip where you land flat on your back), Freeze (the final position of breaking routine), Lofting (diving in air and landing on hands with body in air, back arched, legs high), Uprock (dance fighting), Electric Boogie: the Wave (movement that gives illusion of a wave going, which has found its home in stadium sporting events, and which the hip-hop pop girl band Luscious Jackson parodies on stage during their live shows), the Tick (hard snapping of any part of body that makes it look like body is snapping apart), the Mannequin (mechanical dance that imitates way a mannequin might move if it could dance), King Tut (dancing like an ancient Egyptian), the Pop (popping of different parts of body by tensing the muscles), the Lock It (dancing laugh), the Floats (illusions created by using legs and feet that make it appear you are floating across floor), the Toe-Heel Walk (side walk done by spinning on the toes of one foot and the heel of the other), the Bicycle (forward walk in imitation of the motion of riding a bicycle), the Smurf Walk (walk done reversing the usual order of heel-toe), the Collapse (feet wide apart, knees touching, and standing on the inside of your shoes), the Lean (half Collapse, where one side of body leans over left leg), the Heartbeat (put hand on chest, Pop chest forward with the beat of music, and step forward). Freestyle (using traditional breakdancing and Electric Boogie and adding a lot of own moves — Freestyle Electric Boogie looks like jazz or modern dancing done to breakdancing music. Freestyle breaking is more like traditional gymnastics).

Bright Lights, Big City by Jay McInerney — You are a painfully dated 1984 novel. You are about the coke-fueled nightlife of emotionally dead New York fact checkers. You inspire an embarrassingly moronic Michael J. Fox film in 1988. (You can at least be thankful you aren't *Doc Hollywood*). You are written in the rare and annoying second-person present narrative form. Your author, along with all his fellow hip New York novelists in the mid-'80s (Bret Easton Ellis, Tama Janowitz . . .), might as well have been abducted by aliens around the turn of the decade, even though they all still churn out novels. You silently hope that '90s hypes like Douglas Copeland and David Foster Wallace suffer a similar fate from some smartass "encyclopedia" in the year 2008. (brian)

Mel Brooks This king of Jewish comedy who made such masterpieces as *Young Frankenstein, Silent Movie, Blazing Saddles, The Producers, History of the World — Part 1,* and my fave, *High Anxiety,* is all but forgotten today. Mel and friends (Gene Wilder, Marty Feldman, Madeline Kahn, Cloris Leachman, Teri Garr, Bernadette Peters, Harvey Korman, Dom DeLuise, Kenneth Mars) were America's Monty Python. His burnout period of the mid- to late '80s was hard to take though, like a friend you were embarrassed to know, as he lost his spunk and just regurgitated merely likable duds, including *Robin Hood: Men in Tights* and *Space Balls.* (darby) ❖ The pinnacle of the man's career for me is definitely the "2000-Year-Old Man" records he did with Carl Reiner. They've been released as a CD box set that I highly, highly recommend. It's funnier than (almost) any of his movies, and it's all pretty much improvised — no script, no nothing, just Carl Reiner trying to paint Mel Brooks into a corner with random questions and Mel trying to wriggle his way out. (jesse g) (See also MONTY PYTHON)

Brown vs. White The '60s/'70s counterculture even managed to create a generation gap in the category of food: They rejected their parents' white foods (bleached, bland, textureless, flavorless, artificial, instant, factory-made, dead) in favor of brown foods (earthy, natural, chewy, raw, whole, live). Toss out the white sugar and white flour; head for the health-food store or food co-op to buy whole-grain bread, brown rice, honey and molasses, whole wheat pasta, beans and lentils, and jugs of that murky unfiltered cider. (candi) ❖ Miscellaneous health quirks: organic, ecological, nostalgic, political, economic, survivalist paranoia, rational consumerism, macrobiotics, fruit fasting. (See also HIPPIE FOOD GOES MAINSTREAM)

Brushing Your Teeth Do you brush up and down or side to side? And who the fuck flosses these days? After all that work brainwashing us kids into brushing properly and flossing after every meal you wonder why it didn't work. The best were those red tabs you'd chew to see how well you brushed (in the '70s we had much fun with red dye) and the Snoopy Doghouse electric toothbrush. (darby) (See also CAVITY CREEPS, SCANDALS, and WATER PICS)

Bubble Gum I remember when Bubble Yum came out (what *did* we chew before?) — it was like living *Willy Wonka,* for real this time. Big wads — I always chewed two at a time. After having to grow up with Mom's Trident it was an awesome experience to blow those kinds of bubbles. Bubbalicious (not as good as Bubble Yum) was soon to follow, and eventually Hubba Bubba. It had even more softener in it for a slimier feel. Another gum eventually ruined by gum softeners was Bazooka Joe, which rewarded you with redeemable points for mail-order prizes. Well, I guess since kids have got the cigarette prizes today they're not into Bazooka Joe's 'cause they don't offer them anymore; though you still get your stupid fortune told. Razzles (🍬) — "It's a candy! It's a gum!" (Remember the contest they forever advertised on the back of the wrapper asking for you to decide which it actually was?) — was recently brought back with new packaging. Though I never quite figured out how to enjoy it as a candy without chewing it up into gum immediately (I liked to shave them with my teeth). It was good for movies or school assemblies 'cause you could keep popping more into your mouth until you had the whole bag shoved in there. There were also the rocklike clumps of gum in those cloth pouches that were made to look like little bags of gold, called Gold Dust; the shredded variety in the tobacco-like pouch, called Big League Chew; and Asteroids Bubble Gum, in the little box with hundreds of tiny rock-shaped gum pieces in assorted colors. Freshen-Up (i.e., "Cum Gum") was a *very* big deal when it came out. I remember being on the bus for camp and the driver stopping at Gelson's for something and sternly telling us to stay put. But that unstable-kid candy force *made* me run off the bus, into the store, and buy a pack of Freshen-Up, which had *just* come out on the market. It had fucking juice filling! It doesn't sound important today, but compare it to the invention of that rad super-sour gum that's around now and you'll sorta get the gist of it. Chewels were the sugar-free version of Freshen-Up and a much better chew. Their cinnamon was my gum-o'-choice for many years. (darby) ❖ There was also Double Bubble, a dense, dusty knob, with a faint rubbery taste, usually only seen in the Halloween bowls of spooky, impoverished old ladies; Fruit Stripe gum; and a 1973 fad for Ice Cream–Flavored Gum — the chocolate flavor was gross. (bruce) ❖ And the miniature album gum,

Chu-Bops, that came in a small version of your favorite record sleeve (Blondie, Rolling Stones, et cetera). Now they have bubble gum CDs — environmentally incorrect, but who's to say they're more wasteful than most real CDs. (ju-ji) (See also CANDY CIGARETTES)

Bubble Gum Cards   They used to be called bubble gum cards because there was bubble gum inside the pack. Now they don't use gum because these nerd collectors don't want it ruining the cards and spoiling their value, so they're referred to as trading cards instead — some people are so boring. (ju-ji)

✿ In addition to featuring ballplayers, cards of the late '60s began to feature crappy bands that appealed to adolescents. This is how their music became known as "Bubble Gum Rock." Of course, names like "the 1910 Fruitgum Company" didn't help either. (bruce) (See also GARBAGE PAIL KIDS, TRADING CARDS, and WACKY PACKAGES)

Buck Rogers in the 25th Century

Starring Gil Gerard and Erin Gray. Buck was frozen in time — leaving the twentieth century as an astronaut, I guess, and waking up in the twenty-fifth so we as members of the twentieth century could relate to the dilemmas he was going through in the future. It had two of the best robot characters, Twiki ("Eat lead, sucker, bidibidibidi," which was the voice of Mel Blanc) and Dr. Theopholis (an intellectual computer-

Bubble Gum Belts

It's been a long time, I know. You sorta remember the concept but you haven't been able to recall the necessary, pertinent information to put it all together. No more bubble gum–wrapper bracelets, belts, or even headbands . . . poor you. But now, here it is. The forgotten is now resurrected. Take this golden information and run, you lucky, lucky soul. (Memories graciously given up by lisa aa.)

1. Okay, step one. Get yourself a few megapacks of stick gum. I used pink Carefree bubble gum because it's the prettiest. Note: Some of the old flavors that used to look good have gone cheapo and have white wrappers now.

2. So then you take the wrapper, fold it in half, and tear it on the crease.

3. Now you follow the instructions with both pieces of the wrapper. Take them and fold them in half.

4. Then fold them in half again.

5. Then you fold them in half in the other direction.

6. Using the crease as a guide, fold the wrapper in half from each edge to the middle.

7. After you've completed both pieces of the wrapper, you can then start the link, sliding one half into the other.

8. As the wrappers start taking form, and your obsessive-compulsive nature gets stirred, you can spend a multitude of hours creating your personal line of bubble gum wear. Have fun!

ized necklace charm that hung around Twiki's neck). Leonard Maltin says: "The legendary space hero returns, decked out in contemporary glibness, trying to prove he's not in league with intergalactic pirates. Much of the hardware and gadgetry (along with some footage) is from TV's expensive dud *Battlestar Galactica*." (jon/darby) (See also *BATTLESTAR GALACTICA*)

Jimmy Buffett For a while in the mid-'70s he seemed on his way to soft-rock stardom, but then the music got hard, and he didn't. Instead, the unflappable Mr. Jimmy simply sailed off in search of another audience. Although he ceased to be a factor in the big-time music business, Jimmy Buffett took his mellow sound, tropical image, and Banana Republic clothes on endless tours of snowbound midwestern colleges. Here he packed arenas and developed a devoted, almost cult following, who dubbed themselves Parrotheads. Many people first tasted Corona and margaritas at a Jimmy Buffett show. In the middle of winter, his breezy presence was as warm as a tropical breeze. For many years, he was the Martin Denny of mellow. Today he writes Caribbean detective novels and just does his thing. His safari-style hat became his trademark and it soon turned up on the head of every cool, balding hipster wannabe. (bruce)

Bummers Sometime in the '70s, *Dynamite* magazine came out with a Book of Bummers that was just terrific. I can scarcely conceive of what such a thing would be worth today and don't have the courage to go digging for it for fear that, in all probability, Mom saw fit to toss it eons ago. Just replace the word *sucks* in your vocabulary with the word *bummer* and you will be able to grasp the significance of its use and meaning to your average eleven-year-old of the time. For me, bummers would have been (1) **Braces**. The popular Kristy McNichol had made them look cool when she had 'em, but headgear? Major bummer. (2) **Glasses**. Before I got contact lenses or the cool specs I now sport, I had to suffer the indignity of really ugly glasses. I can still remember that the place my mom had to take me to because our insurance would cover it had absolutely *no* selection in the Hip Young Girl department and I was forced to walk out of the store wearing a pair of dopey pale-pink transparent frames with those lenses that turned into shades when you got out into the sun. Total bummer, man. (Karrin) Don't forget its adjective version, "bummed out." (bruce) (See also SAYINGS/SLANG and SCHLEPROCK)

Bumper Stickers I Found It; I Threw It Away; Marriage Encounter; ♡ with devil tail/Dodge ad campaign; I'd Rather Be . . . ; My Other Car Is a . . . ; I ♡ . . . ; I Brake for . . . ; Happiness Is . . . ; Rolling Stones tongue; Too Hip; No Fat Chicks; Keep On Truckin'; Keep On Keepin' On; Jesus Saves; Jesus Is Lord; Honk If You Love Jesus; Honk If You're Horny; Have a Nice Day; Protected by Smith & Wesson; If You Can Read This, You're Too Damn Close; If Handguns Are Outlawed, Only Outlaws Will Have Handguns; Go for It; Just Trippin'; Native; Free the Weed; hemp leaf (image); Ass, Gas, or Grass — Nobody Rides for Free; A Friend with Weed Is a Friend Indeed!!; No Butt, No Putt (for motorcycles); If This Van's a Rockin', Don't Bother Knockin'; Harley symbol; Grateful Dead; Stealyerface (image); Who Are the Grateful Dead and Why Do They Keep Following Me?; Black Power; Confederate flag (image); Shine It On; Forget Hell; Yer Dern Tooten I'm a Rebel; If You Value Your Life as Much as I Value My Shit, Don't Fuck with It; Move It or Lose It; Spirit of '76; Watch My Rear End, Not Hers!; Made in the U.S.A.; America, Love It or Leave It; P.O.W./M.I.A.: You Are Not Forgotten; Give Peace a Chance; Warning: The Police Are Armed & Dangerous; War Is Not Healthy for Children & Other Living Things; My Child Is an Honor Student at . . . Elementary School; Have You Hugged Your Kid Today?; Hang Ten; Let the Good Times Roll; Good Vibrations; Take It Easy; Easy Does It; Party Naked; American Pie; The Boss (Springsteen); I'm the Boss; Hang Loose (hand sign); Feelin' Groovy; Cruisin'; Eat My Dust; Happy Trails; Hot Stuff; Brown Sugar; Born Free; Don't Tread on Me; Sit on It; Sit on a Happy

Face; Females Wanted, Inquire Within; Free Mustache Rides; American and Proud of It; Buy American; One Nuclear Bomb Can Ruin Your Whole Day; My Country, Right or Wrong; Bicentennial comemmorative sticker with Liberty Bell; Make Love, Not War; Make Babies, Not Bombs; Eat S——t & Die; Power to the People; "Beep Beep" Your Ass! (Wile E. Coyote & Roadrunner); Born to Be Wild; Highway to Hell; Disco Fever; Disco Duck; Disco Sucks!; Save the Whales; Save Water — Shower with a Friend; Save a Tree — Eat a Beaver; Saturday Night Fever; I'm O.K., You're So-So; Party Animal; T.G.I.F; In God We Trust — All Others Pay in Cash; Live Fast, Die Young; Mafia Staff Car; Whip Me, Beat Me, Make Me Write Bad Checks; Southern Comfort; Beach Bum; Love Hurts; Life Stinks; Life's a Bitch and Then You Die. (karrin/jaz)

Busch Gardens As in Anheuser-Busch, this was another delightfully wrong idea for a theme park right up there with Lion Country Safari. Drunk parents and kids on speeding water rides that swoosh in and out of beer gardens. Instead of shaking hands with Mickey Mouse you threw back some brews with the flying Bud Man. (nina) ☘ We used to be taken here for school field trips. I'm not certain what it was we were supposed to be learning. They had a pretty good flume ride. (darby)

Bussing Bussing was created so that you'd hate your life as a child more because you had to be on a bus for an hour and a half to get to and from a school where most of your friends weren't and you'd blame it on other races. Is that the race relations they were striving for? This was a big boon for private schools and beyond-suburbia towns (and a great example for kids to learn that if you're rich enough you can escape life's tortures). (darby) ☘ The really ironic thing was that once the kids were bussed to a different school, they'd just clique around with the people from their own 'hood anyway, and who could blame them? And, of course, for all that money the city could have just as easily improved the still-existing inner-city schools. There must have been a more practical way of assuaging wealthy honky guilt. (gwynne)

Butterfly Glasses Mommies from Encino and Beverly Hills had no shame concerning their sunglasses. Butterflies and diamonds and . . . all shaded and above all *tacky*. Gilda Radner, as Rhonda Weiss, always wore a big pair when she did imitations of rich New York JAPs. (darby) (See also *SATURDAY NIGHT LIVE*)

C

C&C Cola   A very retro soft drink that is notable for its carbonation that was capable of producing a burp, watering eyes, and nasal gas all at the same time — and for its low price. The sound of a Harpo Marx horn was long a fixture of its television ad campaign. (cliff)

Cabbage Patch Kids   I recently noticed a tree in downtown L.A. that was the home of a number of homeless Cabbage Patch Kids — they were all tied up in it. It was raining and they stared at me with their sad eyes as I drove on by. I wanted to stop, I just couldn't. (darby) ✿ There was a shortage of these ugly things during the Christmas of their popularity. Opportunists snatched as many as they could and sold them on the black market for inflated prices, similar to the holiday experience a few years back with the Power Rangers White Tigerzord. Someone shoot me for knowing that. (noël) ✿ "If you don't remember what Cabbage Patch Kids are, they are those lovable little blubber-faced balls of nylon and plastic that people went crazy for in the early '80s. Everyone wanted one and people were more than willing to die for them. If you remember, each of these evil Chucky-like dolls were sold presuffocated and wrapped in plastic along with adoption forms that showed they were in fact born at Babyland General, in the mountains of northern Georgia, taken from the womb of a big (and apparently irresponsible slut of a) cabbage. Owing to their great popularity and the fact that each one was supposedly given a different name, you ended up with dead little bald babies with names like Jobad Kitty Pops" (from zine *Crime Wave U.S.A.*). ✿ There was that rumor that Cabbage Patch dolls had death certificates in their heads. (zoë) ✿ At the post-Christmas peak of Cabbage Patch mania, a small church in Middle America announced it would host a special Sunday ceremony for little girls who wanted their dolls baptized. Of course, it was simply an insidious ploy to lure innocent children into a church service. However, the whole thing backfired when the little church found itself deluged with more than a hundred pushy adults wanting their $60 Cabbage Patch Kids baptized. When it was explained to them that the ceremony was for little girls, a dozen adults became irate, resulting in a near riot that had to be broken up by police. (bruce) ✿ Once the hubbub died down, nothing was really heard about this doll for over a decade, until the Christmas '96 model, Snacktime Cabbage Patch Kids (they could chew plastic food with the aid of batteries), started to munch on children's fingers or attach themselves to ponytails and chomp. (lorraine)

Calculators   I was always fascinated by electronic gadgetry, and this could have been the start of it. I'd go regularly to the local Thrifty's to check out the new calculator stock, in awe at how small they were getting. At the time we could only afford the bulkier models, but I kept my eye on them and watched as they got littler and littler and cheaper and cheaper. By the time they had an affordable wristwatch version, I was already skipping my high school math classes and therefore terribly depressed that I couldn't utilize such technology in my devoted cheating techniques. (darby) ❧ Three years after Texas Instruments invented the silicon chip, the four-function (add, subtract, multiply, divide) calculators were introduced as a $100 mass-market item. Prices dropped quickly and many new designs were introduced. Casio was the leader in creating innovative calculators, pioneering the marketing of small devices with clocks and stopwatches in 1977. Sharp, Hewlett-Packard, and Texas Instruments introduced calculators specially designed for business analysis, scientific applications, and schoolwork. Credit card–sized calculators appeared in the late '70s, with pressure-sensitive pads replacing buttons on the keyboard. Manufacturers enhanced their products by adding musical notes to each key, alarm clock circuits, and ultra-flat or ultra-miniature formats. Some enterprising game inventors even created books full of games that could be played on calculators, trying to ignite a fad that never quite took off (facts stolen from some geek book). ❧ "I am the operator of my pocket calculator." (kraftwerk)

Calf-Length Pants Part of the retro-'50s look (à la Laverne and Shirley), the retro-sailor look for girls, and the retro-baseball look (just kidding). Some punks and skins utilized this style as well, depending on how high their boots were. (ju-ji) (See also DR. MARTENS)

Cameltoes You had to have your pants as tight as possible. This meant waiting until the last possible minute before school to put them on (so they wouldn't stretch out). You had to lie down on the bed and be careful not to zip your tummy flesh! After school, if you were going out and didn't have a fresh pair to wear, you had to spray them with water and put them in the dryer to reshrink. While you waited, you might look down and notice that they had imprinted your body with red lines where the seams were, and occasionally a welt around your waist. When you put them back on you knew they were tight enough if you could see the outline of your pussy, which, with the seam going up the crotch, made it sorta bulge on each side, vaguely reminding one of a camel's toe. (mikki) (See also DITTOS)

Calculator Games

Kids got much fun out of those newfangled pocket calculators by typing in certain numbers, holding the calculator upside down, and spelling a very limited number of words and sayings.

BOOBS — 58008

HELL — 7734

HELLO — 07734

BOBSLED — 0375808

GO TO HELL — 7734 2 09

SHELL OIL — 710 77345

C

Little Darlings

And they weren't even functional: people never actually lit these fad candles, because burning them would spoil their shape! Other candle fads: carved candles, made by craftspersons with booths in low-rent shopping malls, who used warm knives to peel down curls of wax and expose multicolored layers within; UnCandles, a Pyrex-glass cylinder with floating wick that burned oil instead of wax. (candi) ❧ There were loads of specialty shops that would carry one specific type of hippie item; in this case Wicks 'n' Sticks was the main mall version of the all-candles, all-the-time store. And for us poor folk, the favorite was the tall glass religious candles you can still pick up for 99¢ in most 7-Elevens and grocery stores. (jaz) 🐾 (See also LEIF GARRETT)

Camp Movies Movies about going to camp! *Little Darlings, Meatballs, Piranha,* and something with Michael J. Fox and JoBeth Williams. (wendy) ❧ The original *Meatballs* was, for many years, the most successful Canadian film of all time. (bruce) ❧ *Little Darlings* was about this contest between two girl campers (Tatum O'Neal and Kristy McNichol) to see which girl would lose her virginity first, and the other camper girls placed bets on who would win. Both characters lied — the one who did it said she didn't, and the one who didn't said she did. I only remember this line: "Take ginseng, it'll make you sexy!" (riley) ❧ Horror movies made summer camp a fine place to be brutally murdered by your resident psychopath. See *Friday the 13th, Sleepaway Camp,* and any number of other rip-offs. Also see the exceptionally fine film *Meatballs 4,* which won many awards at the Cannes and Venice film festivals. (howard) (See also KRISTY McNICHOL and JOHN WATERS)

Candles Buying these made '70s people feel all warm and natural and nostalgic inside, as if wise old pre-electrical Granny had hand-dipped each one from beeswax melted in a big iron kettle. Ha! Often, these candles were mass-produced, mass-marketed, made from petroleum byproducts, artistically scented with some overpowering artificial fruit smell, and molded to look like a giant green apple or a hot-fudge sundae.

Candy Besides some of the totally obvious choices, these candies were around in the '70s/'80s and either don't exist today or were just especially popular at the time: anything Willy Wonka (Gobstoppers, Bottle Caps, Nerds, Dinosaur Eggs), Smarties, Sprees, Pez, Lemonheads, Tiny Tarts, Fun Dip, Abba-Zabas, Reese's Pieces (*E.T.*), Clark Bars, Carnation Breakfast Bars, Tiger's Milk original, $100,000 Bar, Charleston Chew, Sweet-tarts that came in coffins and gym lockers, rope licorice, Pop Rocks, Necco Wafers, Astro Pops, Go Ahead Bars, Toffefay ("It's too good for kids, but not too good for you!"), Whatchamacallit, Jolly Rancher's Sticks. ❧ Jewelry/Toy Candy: Whistle pops, windmill with candy balls, wax candy (wax teeth and bottles filled with a weird juice), ring pops, candy bracelets, candy necklaces with candy charms. (See also BUBBLE GUM, MARATHON BARS, THE MUNCHIES, and ZOTZ)

Candy Cigarettes Sort of a stale, minty, chalky taste. The ends were pink for that "lit" effect. Also available in gum version. (morgan and ferris) ♣ I remember going into the gas station/liquor store and making my mom (or my friend's mom) buy these for me. The gum was good for about five or six chews, but if you puffed out lightly, some of the "smoke" would come out and you could be cool like the big kids. I preferred the Lucky Strike brand. (e.c. cotterman) ♣ Cigars made of gum were also standard. You'd wear the band around your finger as a ring. (darby)

Canopy Beds Do people have these anymore? Very big in the late '70s. (katy) ♣ I wanted one with a pink Holly Hobbie canopy but my parents said no way. (jen g.) ♣ We used to drape blankets around the sides and play covered wagon, no doubt inspired by the TV show *Little House on the Prairie*. (riley) ♣ I hated my canopy. I made little nooses and hung all my stuffed animals from the crossbeams. Finally I took that fucking thing down once and for all and stuck it in a closet for good. (gwynne) ♣ There were race-car beds for the boys. A gas-tank hole would've been good for bed wetters. (mike) (See also HOLLY HOBBIE)

Carl's Jr. French Fries This might actually be my most missed food. One day, as I routinely ordered some french fries from this scary corporate establishment, I was handed these standard-order Mickey D's–style fries, instead of their usual ridged, crispy, hearty fries. It took years before it sunk in that the old fries were gone forever. I still don't understand why they got rid of them (were they real food?), and I continue to this day to judge all fries by those awesome creations. If I could pick one food to make its retro comeback. . . . The closest we've found is at Del Taco, when they do them right. (darby) ♣ My first post–high school job was as the Guy Who Made the Fries at Carl's Jr. Basically, the fries were made of something called Frispo pellets. The Frispo was poured into a special device that added steaming hot water to the pellets, compressed them, then extruded the now putty-like substance through a special wedge-cut french fry mold (in the manner of those Play-Doh Fun Factories). The individual fries were cut by a metal wire as the potato putty oozed out of the mold. The fries would then fall into a basket, which was then dropped into hot oil. Fun facts: If you didn't shake the basket right away the molded fries would all clump together into a giant fused french fry mutant lump. Also, if you didn't sell the fries within five minutes, they would begin to devolve into a shapeless greasy mass. Yum. (scott s.)

Cars Camero, Trans Am, Corvette, AMC Pacer, Gremlin, Renault's Le Car, the Volkswagen Rabbit, and the "Thing," the forgotten Chevy Vega (GM's butt-ugly answer to the Pinto). There were also the first Mazda cars, with the revolutionary Wankel rotary engine — just three moving parts! (bruce) ♣ And don't forget the VW Bug of the late '80s, the Suzuki Samurai — a mini Jeep for poor folk. (jaz) ♣ My favorite car invention of the '80s was the electronic combo code lock that you can still see on some ugly variety of American leisure cars. (ju-ji) ♣ Also the name of a New Wave band with a lead singer so ugly he'd have busted the tubes in your TV if it wasn't for those Varnets he kept glued to his face most the time. Today Ric Ocasek is often seen cruisin' about L.A. with his billboard pal Angelyne in her pink convertible. (darby) (See also MODELS, MUSCLE CARS, and VAN CONVERSIONS)

Car Signs This was a hand-held plastic device with white cards (7" x 5", Rolodex style) that had messages printed on them. When driving about town you would hold them up to other drivers to bridge that communication gap. Simple, cute things like "Hello" and "What's Your Sign?" Of course, today's options would be more along the lines of "Too Ill," "HIV+," and "Please Don't Shoot." They did have some blank cards so you could write your own messages. *Retro*

Hell contributor Riley has the original version of these, called Toot 'n' Talk. I had it in my car the other day when I went out with my crazy seventy-eight-year-old grandma. She held up the one that said "Single" to any decent man that we passed and had a laugh riot. (darby)

LET'S DATE! NICE CAR ✓ BLINKER ✓ LOAD

Cartoons *Addams Family; Archies; Atom Ant; Bad Cat, Baggy Pants and the Nitwits, Banana Splits; Battle of the Planets; Beany and Cecil; Beverly Hills Teens; (Fat Albert's) The Brown Hornet; Brady Kids; Broomhilda,* Bugs Bunny / Roadrunner Hour; *Captain America;* Care Bears; Centurions; Charlie Brown specials, *Chilly Willy; Courageous Cat and Minute Mouse; Defenders of the Earth;* Donkey Kong; Dr. Seuss specials: *The Grinch Who Stole Christmas, Cat In the Hat; Droopy;* Dungeons and Dragons; *Dynaman; Ewoks; Fantastic Four, Far Out Space Nuts; Felix; The Flintstones; Pebbles and Bamm Bamm; Captain Caveman and the Teen Angels; Funky Phantom; Galaxy Rangers; Garfield; Gary Coleman Show; Get Along Gang;* Ghostbusters; G.I. Joe; GoBots; Godzilla; *Grape Ape; Groovie Ghoulies: Sabrina, Wacky and Packy, The New Adventures of Waldo Kitty, Lassie, etc.; Happy Days in Space;* Harlem Globetrotters; Heckle and Jeckle; *He-Man and the Masters of the Universe; Hercules; Herself the Elf; Hong Kong Fooey; Huckleberry Hound; Inch High, Private Eye;* Inspector Gadget; *Isis; Jabberjaw; Jem; Jesus; Jetsons;* Kid Super Power Hour; *Kimba; Laff-A-Limpics; Lippy the Lion & Har Dee Har Har; The Littles; Mad Monster Party; Magilla Gorilla; Mighty Heroes; Mighty Man;* (Ralph Bakshi's) *Mighty Mouse; Monchichis;* Mr. Magoo; Mr. T; Muppet Babies; *My Little Pony; New Shmoo; The Osmonds;* Pac-Man; *Pink Panther; Pole Position;* Popeye; *Possible Possum; Punky Brewster;* Q*bert; *Quickdraw McGraw, Richie Rich; Robotech; The Rocky and Bullwinkle Show; Dudley Do-right; Tom Slick; George of the Jungle; Super Chicken; Commander McBragg; Sherman and Mr. Peabody;*

Fractured Fairy Tales; Wacky Races; Catch That Pigeon; Roman Holidays; Rubik; Schoolhouse Rock; Scooby-Doo; *Secret Squirrel;* She-Ra; *The Shirt Tales; Skrewy Squirrel; The Smurfs; Snagglepuss;* Snorks; *Space Ghost; Speed Racer; Spider-Man and His Amazing Friends; Squiggly Diddly;* Star Trek; *Strawberry Shortcake; Sub Mariner; The Superfriends:* Dyno Mutt and Blue Falcon, Wonder Twins, Aquaman, Superman, Wonder Woman; *Super Adventures: The Fantastic Four, Bird Man, Herculoids, et cetera; Tennessee Tuxedo; The Tarzan / Lone Ranger Adventure Hour;* Thor; Thundercats; Tom and Jerry; *Top Cat;* Transformers; Underdog; Voltron; *Wally Gator;* Woody Woodpecker; *Yogi Bear;* Zorro. Also Claymation: *Davey and Goliath,* Gumby, *Mr. Bill,* and *Rudolph.* (howard/mike v./darby/dave) (See also *EMERGENCY PLUS FOUR, FAT ALBERT, JEM, JOHNNY QUEST, JOSIE AND THE PUSSYCATS, KAZOO,* MR. BILL, *ROGER RAMJET, SCHLEPROCK, SISSY VS. MACHO CARTOONS, WAIT 'TIL YOUR FATHER GETS HOME,* and *ZIGGY* — and watch the Cartoon Network)

Cavity Creeps "We make holes in teeth!" Cavity creeps were fuckin' scary. I really brushed after I saw those nasty critters hacking away at somebody's teeth with a pickax. I think that Crest should drop their new, nice-tasting, sparkly toothpastes and go back to their original ploy for selling the regular stuff — intimidation and fear. (wendy) ✿ Can't forget about *Yuck-Mouth* — another edu-cartoon short using gross-out tactics to teach dental hygiene. Me and my friend Jack used to go around singing "I'm a Yuk-Butt, 'cause I don't wipe." (jon)

CB Radio Phenomenon Citizen's band radios had been around for years, yet few people knew about them. Twenty-three channels of two-way communication, inhabited only by curious techno-geeks, lost hikers, and truckers. Before they became homo-erotic heartthrobs, truckers were seen by many Americans as the last of the cowboys (this is before cowboys also became homo-erotic heartthrobs). A potent working-class myth arose of the trucker as a proud and independent tobacco-chewing smartass who was both his own boss and King of the Road. Of course this myth never collided with the redneck reality of indentured speed freaks loose on the nation's highways. The only way these men stood a chance of getting ahead was to drive as fast as their heart rates. When the media made it known that truckers routinely used CB radios to get around the hated 55 mph speed limit, the country went wild for the things. While only 1 million people had gotten CB licenses in the years between 1958 and 1973, more than 2 million licenses were issued in 1974 alone. Soon every freeway-cruising Winnebago had to have one, and everyone was on the prowl for "Smokey." A lot of fun was found in ripping off "the man" and driving as fast as you liked. But there was also the tremendous appeal that came in talking that crazy trucker talk. Phrases like "Breaker, breaker" and "That's a big 10-4, good buddy" crept into conversations, and people who should have known better began swapping their CB names, or handles. Betty Ford even got one — "First Mama." Eventually, there were so many fools fouling the ether that more channels were needed. The forty-channel models came out, leaving the twenty-three crowd in the dust. CB songs rode the charts and trucker films and TV shows did well. Americans everywhere demonstrated their talent for talking a lot and saying little. By 1980, the fad had died. Perhaps we got used to 55, or the rebel cruisers had all joined militias. But I tend to think people simply got tired of tuning into tedious talk of trivia. No one wants to interact when there is no action. Take heed, Internet! (bruce) (See also TRUCKIN' MOVIES)

Chachi Chachi used to go to the skateboard park in La Crecentia, which my parents owned. He used to pull up to the skateboard park in his limo and sit in there; we guessed he was too scared to get out of the car. He used to do it all the time. Ricky Schroder was a member as well, but he'd actually get out of the car and skate. (gree) ❧ Okay, so he grew up, but who can resist calling him Chachi? Certainly not the guys from *Monk* magazine. When we were hanging out with them in L.A., we spotted Mr. Baio eating with his parents at Astro Burger on Melrose, and Jim, the Mad Monk, popped out of his chair as they were leaving, jumped in his face, and said, "Hey, you're Chachi." "It's Scott," he said back. Ignoring him, Mr. Monk repeated, "You're Chachi, right?" "Scott, my name is Scott!" At that point Jim didn't torture Chachi — I mean Scott — anymore and soon won him over with his charm. Jim asked him what he was doing there. And Chachi said, "Where?" "Uh, Astro Burger," Jim replied. And Chachi, confused, repeated himself, "Where?" Then his dad cut in, "Oh, we're visiting the studio today [referring to Paramount]." Chachi seemed to be in a fog though. (darby) ❧ You'd just never imagine, that day when he arrived on *Happy Days*, a total hunk of a kid, that he would end up being such a loser as *Charles in Charge*, with that other former teen idol, Willie Aames. (ju-ji) ❧ Don't forget: Joanie Loves Chachi (jaz) (See also FONZIE and *HAPPY DAYS*)

Chain Letters "This chain letter was started in 1972 by a man in Saskatoon, Saskatchewan, who was completely broke. In less than one year, he became extremely wealthy . . . *all because of the letter!* If you want to be rich as well, write five copies of this letter and send them to five of your friends. Don't break the chain! The last person who did had his penis severed by an electric drill and almost died." (howard)

C

Challenger Explosion/Christa McAuliffe Jokes "What's this button here do?" ✿ "I meant a Bud Light." ✿ (Q) What did she tell her husband before she left? (A) You feed the kids, and I'll feed the fish. ✿ (Q) What color were her eyes? (A) Blue; one blew this way, and one blew that way. ✿ (Q) What does NASA stand for? (A) *Need Another Seven Astronauts*. ✿ (Q) Why did they have Pepsi on the shuttle? (A) Because they couldn't get 7-Up. (all) (See also SCANDALS)

Jackie Chan There were certain things in life that most young girls without big brothers missed out on. I mean, a karate movie just never sounded appealing to me, and I had no reason to go out of my way to see one before. But when the local art theater had a Jackie Chan film festival recently my friend asked me to go, and I agreed to only because I wanted to hang out with him — I thought I'd be bored with the movies. It was a double feature, with *Project A* and *Wheels on Meals* — the biggest hormonal freakout I've ever experienced on the big screen. Arnold Swarzenwho? Rambimbo? Jackie Chan and friends do all their own stunts (blow yer mind), and Jackie Chan writes and directs as well! To top that he is a master of slapstick in a way Hollywood action stars will never grasp. (I know you all know this, but let me bask in my newfound fun.) "Action adventure" won't be the same for me again. *Project A* is one of the best movies I've ever seen — and his new ones are great too. (darby) ✿

CDs Win Over Vinyl

This was one of the quickest and bloodiest consumer technology routs in historical memory, turning the dominant format of commercial music of the previous three decades, the 12-inch vinyl long-playing record, into so much quarter parking-lot sale trash (and the occasional ridiculously big-ticket collector's item).

Enter the compact disc, that shiny 5-inch (12-centimeter) aluminum and plastic disc. Early prototypes first surfaced in 1979, and the full-on modern version was wheeled out in 1982. Early players cost as much as $1,000, but you can now get a decent CD boom box for less than 10% of that. By the late '80s the shiny demon spawn that reduced sound to digital bits was skunking the LP, which had itself ruled the recorded sound roost since being introduced some forty years before. Vinyl was showing signs of age even before the CD came along — the Walkman helped push cassette sales above vinyl sales for the first time in 1983. By the end of the '80s, total CD sales amounted to $2.1 billion yearly versus vinyl's 0.53 billion, and some big national retail chains stopped carrying vinyl altogether as major labels began releasing CDs and cassettes only.

CDs had smaller, less attractive covers, suffered from what the fussiest of stereo mavens liked to call a "sterile" sound, and were more expensive to boot. Still, consumers went wild for them. Of course, the extinction of the LP was shoved along by certain decisions made by big record labels, like in 1991 when a few of the biggest record companies stopped taking vinyl returns from retailers, effectively destroying any hope for the format's continued commercial health. Shockingly, most reliable figures indicate that more American houses still have more functioning turntables than CD players, for what that's worth, which is apparently nothing.

You will hear now and again from newspaper feature writers desperate for copy of a vinyl revival, triggered by such blips as vinyl sales almost doubling from 1993 to 1995, from 1.2 million a year to 2.2 million a year. As someone in the business of trying to sell vinyl-only releases, I can assure you, you shouldn't believe it. Look at the money: $25 million spent on vinyl in 1995 versus $9 billion on compact discs. The shellac 78 can't wait to torment the long-playing vinyl LP, which killed it, in hell. The CD is also finally surpassing its stronger competitor, the cassette tape (also a Philips invention, introduced in 1963), which thrived on the corpse of the 8-track, which it had pretty much eliminated by the end of the '70s. But the CD may be joining its former competitors in the graveyard if the forces of technical innovation have their way with the latest format innovations with which they are bedeviling the music-buying public. Enter the digital compact cassette and the mini disc. It is of such consumer technology innovations that retro nostalgia is made. But for many, love of vinyl is still a real, everyday part of our lives. I still have more than 2,000 vinyl LPs, am buying more every week, and will use them as long as needles and turntables are still being manufactured. (brian)

Suzie, the ultimate American ski bunny

Suzie Chapstick Née Suzie Chaffee, the former Olympic skier who hawked Chapstick on TV. Her image of the All-American Girl donning a virginal all-white ski suit was second only to the sight of her smearing lip balm over her sexy mouth. Chapped lips never looked as appealing. (cliff) (See also SKIING)

C

Bosley and the Angels wait for their next assignment from Charlie

big bad bull dyke at the health club [where she pretends to be an aerobics instructor] with lots of sexual innuendoes — *wooah!* Dang, lots of scary shit went down in those health clubs back then). Anyway, *The Seventies* book describes it best: "That was the little adventure in which the Angels were captured while investigating a southern prison farm, chained together, stripped, forced into a shower, and sprayed with disinfectants. Twenty thousand letters poured into ABC after that episode, asking for more of the same — which viewers got. But despite predictable howls from feminists, the majority of viewers were women." (ju-ji) (See also FARRAH FAWCETT-MAJORS)

Charlie "There's a new fragrance that's coming to town and they call it . . ." Also a wisecracking fish spokesman for Star-kist Tuna, a slang term for the Viet Cong, the kid who won a trip to Willy Wonka's chocolate factory, and the first name for that '60s cult leader who had Sharon Tate murdered. (howard) ♣ Charlie Brown was the biggest loser on the planet, next to Ziggy. (noël) (See also PERFUME AND COLOGNE)

Charlie's Angels They're the ones who started the two-hands-on-a-pistol thing. After the criminal was lying on the ground unconscious, the three of them would whip out their .38s, spread their legs, put two hands on their gun in a sort of *V* to their body and point it at the unconscious criminal. And since then, I've never seen women shooting a gun except in that position. The problem is when you shoot a .38 you fall back; you're suppose to brace your firing hand with your other hand. Anyway it may look good, it's just not the way to shoot a gun, that's all. (dad) ♣ "Angel's in Chains" was the most horrifying *Charlie's Angels* episode ever (though the one when Kris freaks out 'cause she's shot someone was awesome, as well as the one where she is forced to get a massage/steaming with hot towels from some

Charmkins Little plastic dolls with attachments on their heads so you could wear them as charms. Also what we used to call the dorky '60s-revival fanatics who hung out at the Cavern Club in Hollywood circa 1986. I was later told the term was coined because of the Charmkin-like bowl haircuts they all sported. I always thought it was because the post-mods were so antiseptic and regimented, the safest form of rebellion at the time. (gwynne)

Charms Every girl had one, usually more, around her neck. The more spoiled had a charm holder, which was a larger gold charm with a U-shaped hook which then held the other charms on it. Some may have included these popular designs: razor blade; pot leaf; lightning bolt; Kiss; cornucopia (also called: horn of plenty or Italian horn); happy face; horse; unicorn; Pegasus; #1; #1 dad/mom/grandma etc.; I ♡ you; the best friends mitzvah charm (each gets a half); *chai;* Torah; hamsa (the hand that keeps away the evil eye); Jewish star; the cross; Go Fuck Yourself (upside

down and looking like it's in Hebrew script). (darby)
✿ I think the Tiffany heart started it all. It was this lopsided heart outline that you put your S chain through. (riley) (See also #1 and BEST FRIENDS)

Charo The coochie-coochie girl may not be on TV much these days, but Charo is still as active as ever, making her flamenco records and teaching guitar. I thought she made a pact with the devil to never age, but in actuality she had her age legally lowered by ten years — the amount of time she was married to bandleader Xavier Cugat — so it all makes sense. (darby)

Cheech and Chong Following their early '70s albums of drug-related humor, Cheech Marin and Thomas Chong began to make movies. First was *Up in Smoke,* their best, which was followed by *Next Movie, Things Are Tough All Over, Nice Dreams,* and then some real turds like *The Corsican Brothers.* They had bad dopey jokes, stupid songs, and were much funnier if you were *really* stoned when you watched them. It all ended when Cheech sold his immortal soul to Satan, Lucifer, Beelzebub, and Bea Arthur and

became a regular on *The Golden Palace,* the short-lived spin-off of *The Golden Girls.* (howard) ✿ Their records were great, but their movies never lived up to them. The character Chong would be so desperate to get a hit that he would roll up his dirty sock into a joint and smoke it. Very funny. (dad) ✿ Also had that silly MTV video hit "Born in East L.A.," with Cheech and hundreds of other Hispanics sneaking into L.A. through the sewers. (ju-ji) ✿ Cheech Marin was a draft dodger from East L.A., who'd made his way to Vancouver. Tommy Chong was a third-generation Chinese-Canadian hippie with a flair for stand-up. It was in a seedy Vancouver nightclub that Cheech first met Chong. The pair began playing hip coffeehouses and opening for trippy bands. Once the draft was over, the duo came stateside and began to record a series of historic comedy albums. There were a few misses before they hit upon the personas of Pedro and Man, a brilliant comedy duo without a straight man.

Cereals

I rarely eat breakfast now, save for those hungover Sunday morning get-togethers with friends, although these are more of a social nature and devoid of the kind of emotional excitement I used to derive from breakfast as a kid. It's amazing that when I review those glory days in my mind's eye, there's no table littered with pancakes, hash browns, eggs, or any of the standard breakfast fare, but rather a large bowl, a spoon, and a brightly colored box containing enough refined sugar to send the average gourmand into diabetic shock.

The prospect of ingesting a couple of bowls of Cocoa Puffs was all the incentive I needed to wipe the sleep from my eyes and climb out of bed. However, the breakfast ritual usually began much earlier than this. It began on grocery night. This was the night that I accompanied Mom to the store to aid in the all-important decision-making process. In other words, if you didn't go along, you risked enduring an entire week of Special K, Shredded Wheat, Grape Nuts, Raisin Bran, some type of granola, oatmeal, or other such vapid commodity that Mom chose in your absence. Once in the cereal aisle, the standard four hours of daily television viewing helped facilitate the selection of "the most important meal of the day." In the current manufacturer's TV ad campaign you learned that Count Chocula was offering Dracula fangs, BooBerry had the glow-in-the-dark goblin stickers, Apple Jacks had the 3-D glasses deal, Honeycombs the baseball cards, and Alpha Bits had the slide rule. Occasionally some of the prizes advertised on TV were for some reason not to be found in the stock on the shelves, so you had to be careful to check. The next step was to inspect the boxes of your finalists, since the pictures on the box were always a more honest barometer of prize quality. There was nothing more disappointing than when the slick drag-racing car you'd seen on TV turned out to be some one-toned nonfunctional waste of good plastic.

Certain cereals had substantially more entertainment value, while others relied on originality of flavor for their consumer's satisfaction. Of the former group, Lucky Charms was the pinnacle. There was a certain etiquette of its consumption that had to be followed. Along with the more healthy brown wheat pieces, you were allowed to choose one other accompanying colorful sugar ornament — either a blue star, a pink heart, a yellow moon, or a green clover (Note: there were no purple horseshoes!). However, you couldn't start on a new ornament until all the previous ones had been systematically eliminated from the bowl. Everyone seemed to have his own Alpha Bit bylaws. Personally I found the Scrabble route the most satisfying. This was the method whereby you had to put a word together in every spoonful until there were no vowels left. I remember a historical time when Cap'n Crunch had been perfected upon with the advent of Crunchberries, and you had to have at least a couple of Crunchberries in each spoonful. Often this entailed pouring more cereal in to reproportion the berry-to-crunch ratio, and it was not uncommon to polish off an entire box in one sitting as a result of this.

As far as the pure palate-satisfaction cereals (those with little entertainment value) there was Froot Loops. Froot Loops are the O.G. of kid's cereals, with the flavor crystals on each potent loop packing a powerful whallop. Count Chocula, Frankenberry, and BooBerry all worked their inimitable magic by turning the milk brown, blue, and red, respectively, leaving you a colorful display of sucrose and mucous membrane to empty down your pipe. Cookie Crisps, those little pseudo chocolate chip cookies, were a blessing as well by integrating the cookie into the cereal market, thereby allowing children to get away with eating cookies and milk for breakfast — what a scam!

The propaganda campaign propounded by the big three food magnates (General Mills, Post, Kellogg's) was entertainment in and of itself, and Cereal commercials in particular seemed to exhibit an extreme amount of violence and addiction. For example, the Rabbit dressing incognito, in vain, to cop a bowl of cereal, and ending up with hernias from overexertion due to his need for this cereal, which was never satisfied, ultimately being met with a chorus of "Silly Rabbit! Trix are for kids!" Surly men were always busting through the kids' Honeycomb Hideout. The Honeycomb Kids would then give them Honeycomb cereal and make them nice. Then of course

Sonny the Bird had to be kept away from Cocoa Puffs by small children for his own good, otherwise he'd fall into a hyperactive, sugar-induced stupor. That humble-looking thug bear from the Super Sugar Crisp commercials was always punching people's lights out. And the frog from Sugar Smacks — if you gave him a "smack," he would "smack you back." The very paranoid Lucky the Leprechaun would excitedly itemize all the ingredients contained in Lucky Charms and try to keep them away from the frenzied kids. Obviously, Toucan Sam with his multicolored beak advising all to "Follow your nose, it always knows." The two Paleolithic cavemen Kel and Og hawked the boxed bliss of Cocoa Crispies. And Fred and Barney in the recurring scenario where Barney tries to scam a bowl of Cocoa or Fruity Pebbles from Fred, which for some reason Fred doesn't want to give him; inevitably he chases him in haste to get it back ("Barney!"). On the lighter side there were Snap, Crackle, and Pop, forever bending their ears to the bowl for a little sonic fury. Ultimately though, when I look back on my cereal-consuming youth, I can't seem to escape a sentiment put forth repeatedly by the kingpin himself — "They're grrrrrreat!" (cliff thurber) (see also MR. T)

Instead one laughed at just how differently stupid each one was. Thus the genre of stoner humor was born. George Carlin and others were then filling sides of vinyl with their own observations on life. They would talk about drugs before a whooping college audience, record the whole thing, and simply put it out as an album. Cheech and Chong were different: they didn't just talk about being stoned, they *were* stoned! In the early '70s, no big brother's record collection was complete without at least one Cheech and Chong album. Each LP was rumored to come with rolling papers or blotter acid, take your pick. They tried to negotiate a comeback deal in the early '90s, but it just didn't work out. Cheech wanted to try new things, and Chong wanted bigger hits off the past. Today Cheech has become Hollywood's favorite Latino wise guy and even does voices for Disney movies. Meanwhile, Chong mostly bad-mouths Cheech, holds chaotic auditions for a new sidekick, and threatens to make more movies (why do you think they call it dope?). Their true legacy is in all the stoner duos we've come to know and imitate. Without Cheech and Chong, there would be no Bill and Ted or Beavis and Butthead. (bruce)

Cheerleading I remember the day it happened. I was innocently eating lunch with my friends when someone came around with cheerleading try-out information. I ignored it, thinking all my friends would surely ignore it as well. I mean, we always made fun of cheerleader types. But some of the squirrelier girls were soon chatting about the tryouts, and then, to my dismay, even the tougher and brainier of the crowd were posing the concept to me, like, "Why not?" It was one of those days when my faith in my fellow fems went right out the window. Of course, most of them made the squad and soon after stopped playing on the AYSO (American Youth Soccer Organization) soccer team and instead squeaked and played dumb and became the prissy, catty snobs they were destined to become. Surely it was all for the best. (darby)

Chest Hair The symbol of manhood in the '70s. If you didn't have at least a few tufts sprouting from your half-open shirt, then you could forget about driving the chicks truly wild. In the swanky Vegas of that decade, rumor has it that the King took some style counsel from his pal Tom Jones, the King of Chest Hair, and adopted the shirt-unbuttoned-to-the-rhinestone-studded-belt-buckle look in order to better flaunt his pectoral pelt. Yet by the clean-shaven '80s, the chest carpet was as dead as Elvis, and buff studs too squeamish for the smooth operator–approach of shaving or waxing opted either for T-shirts or for buttoning their shirts all the way to the neck to hide their offending fur. But as all things Retro Hell refuse to truly die, we can definitely look forward to a hairier tomorrow. (nina/angela) (See also LAS VEGAS, MUSTACHES, and TOM JONES)

Chia Pets *Ch-ch-ch-chia!* What poor people would buy from Thrifty's as Christmas gifts for friends, though secretly desiring one for themselves. (ju-ji) ☘ There was recently this one of a terra-cotta woman with a chia hair pie called Barbara's Bush. (riley)

Chick-O-Sticks Really odd peanutty things which came cylindrically shaped in a clear plastic wrapper. (morgan and ferris) ☘ The wrapper had a chicken on it, which always led me to believe the candy was chicken flavored. (lisa aa) ☘ It wasn't?! (darby) ☘ They were *originally* shaped like chicken legs, hence the name. (bruce) (See also STICKS)

Chick Tracts California's Inland Empire–based Jack T. Chick has been providing us with flyer art and yuks aplenty for as far back as I remember, with his mini–comic books that demonstrate every possible way to relegate yourself to an afterlife in hell, including drugs, rock and roll, Ouija boards, and Dungeons and Dragons. Of course, as long as you accept Christ as your personal savior any time before you die, you'll be okay. There are even some full-size color books, but they're not free. (gwynne)

Chinese Jacks These were plastic rings in different colors with which you played a version of jacks (without a ball). They were as big as pogs with the girls during maybe '78 or '79. Much fun, and strangely enough most can't remember

them; though somehow they found their way to a minimal retro comeback (only because they are available again) in a cheaper format, with a lighter, uglier plastic that is less conducive not only to the game playing but to the jewelry you could make from the linking pieces. (darby)

Chinese Jump Rope It kinda looks like a thin circular bungee cord. You'd have to play with three people (or use chairs). Two people are on opposite ends with the rope around their ankles (it gets higher as the game goes on), and you have a routine of jumping in and out of the rope with a double dutch sort of feel, but you go at your own pace. (selina)

Chippendales Started in 1979, this was a very important liberating thing for mommies (on TV and in reality). They showed women can act just as wild and sexually crazed as men. (ju-ji)

Choose Life Someone explain to me what this was all about. Was this a Wham! thing, because they were wearing the T-shirts in their video? Or were they just following an already massively popular fashion fad? I always feared this was some kind of anti-abortion statement. (gwynne) ☘ Gwynne, you ignorant slut. The Choose Life shirts were merely a part of a huge British media campaign against mean old Mr. Heroin. The ad blitz targeted what was perceived (no doubt accurately) to be the most at-risk group: impressionable young music fans. Magazines like *The Face, Flexipop, NME,* and *Melody Maker* featured full-page photos of proto-waif teenagers, complete with sunken eyes, hideous purple needle marks, and, given the time frame, the most frightening consequence of all: bad hair and unfashionable clothes! (don)

The Chronicles of Narnia There were seven volumes, and the first one was *The Lion, the Witch, and the Wardrobe.* You had to read them in order, but sometimes the next one was checked out of the library so you were forced to skip. They were about four preteens, two boys and two girls, who discovered a magic, secret world in a kind of parallel universe. The cool thing about Narnia was that no matter how long the kids spent there, when they returned it was like no time had passed. The animals could talk. And when the older siblings became "cool" and started to care about clothes and hairstyles, they were banished! (mikki) ♣ But it was all a sinister, Christian, soul-snatching plot! (skylaire) ♣ Oliver North named his Virginia ranch Narnia, after these books. Scary. (bruce)

Cigarette Ads The televised cigarette commercials exist in the dim subconscious of all who were born before the first Nixon administration. Most memorable: Winston ads that featured the line "Winston tastes good like a cigarette should!" In one TV ad, a professor type is getting gas and remarks to the pump jockey that for the slogan to be grammatically correct, it should read, "Winston tastes good as a cigarette should." Whereupon the pump boy pulls him from the car and dunks his head under water, shouting: "What do you want? Good grammar or good taste?" (nick) ♣ Each brand had its own macho guy: Marlboro had the cowboy, Camel had the Turk (another schoolboy crush), Salem had the Salem Man (a basic outdoorsy white guy). Tareyton had a campaign whose line was "Tareyton smokers would rather fight than switch." The ads simply showed a satisfied smoker with a black eye. Lots of sexy black-eyed women stared down from billboards in those days. And note to all the tough guys out there: Prior to 1960, Marlboro was marketed primarily to women. (bruce) (See also NEWPORT ADS)

Cigars The sign that people are running out of retro items to make them unique. Inspires images of future cancer problems for all those action hero studs and super models to help kick off the new millennium. (jaz) 🐿

The Clapper "Clap on, clap off." An obvious entry but one that can't be ignored. A classic American product and commercial. (ju-ji)

Clockwork Orange Disturbing Stanley Kubrick movie ('71), mixing ballet-like sexual violence with classical music, representing a very conservative writer's (Anthony Burgess) view of a dangerous mutated youth gang culture. Of course, the movie became a favorite of just the sort of deviant youth culture Burgess predicted and feared. (brian)

Cloves Clove cigarettes were super big in the early '80s. They had that sweet flavor, so it wasn't a terrible leap from candy cigarettes. They were really harsh though, so when I think of that sweetness on my lips I immediately recall the dizziness I'd feel just moments after. There were rumors that some parent must have started that smoking these caused your lungs to bleed. (darby) 🐿

Coca-Cola, Sucking Through Straw Up Nose We all did this. Think Shakey's after a baseball game or during a birthday party. Burned and sizzled as it ran through your sinuses. You only did it a few times before you learned it hurts more than it is funny. (darby) ♣ And I thought shooting up vodka was stupid. (don)

Cocaine My first live rock show ever was the U.S. Festival 1983. I was a rather inexperienced fifteen-year-old, and my best friend's parents (the permissive, post-hippie type) were best friends with one of the people who put on this enormous three-day music festival in San Bernardino. My two pals and I had VIP backstage passes and were offered just about everything you can think of in exchange for them. I had a lot of firsts that weekend, but cocaine was not one of them. Far from being a punk rocker (not that I'm any closer now) my favorite person on Planet Earth was Stevie Nicks. And when my naïve eyes saw her go back to the top of her piano between songs time and time again to snort up a white powder, my adolescent adoration was irretrievably lost. As I grew older, I decided that drugs weren't just for evil people and I had better reasons to dislike Stevie Nicks. (jen d.) ♣ Freebase, razor blade, gold charms, special

C

mirrors, rolled-up gazillion-dollar bills, and cocaine T-shirts: *coke* in fake Hebrew script; "Enjoy Cocaine"; "If coke's a joke I can't wait for the next line." Cocaine was the thing to do, despite the fact that it was a horrible drug (at least to snort). This was the kind of drug guys bought and gave women in hopes of gettin' something in return. The only drawback being that once high on cocaine, the mirror was the main thing on one's mind, not sex. Not too long ago Duran Duran did a decent version of the infamous Grandmaster Flash song "White Lines" — the anti-cocaine song that *almost* makes you want to do some when you hear it. (ju-ji) ❀ I just have one tip if you're going to do this crap: Don't do it with acid. (jaz) (See also *BRIGHT LIGHTS, BIG CITY;* DRUGS; THE U.S. FESTIVAL; and watch the movies *Less Than Zero* and *Scarface,* to name but a few) 🐾

Nadia

Cold Showers A very very hilarious sitcom joke. Writers got a lot of creative points inventing those silly scenarios where the guy would have to go and take a cold shower when confronted by a sexual situation he couldn't deal with for one reason or another. Ha ha ha. Think Jack Tripper. (ju-ji)

Colorforms Vinyl cut-out images, usually of some cartoon or toy character, that you placed (and would magically stick) onto two-dimensional dress-up boards and dolls. They're still around, but not exciting enough for most. (ju-ji) ❀ Had Smurfs and Barbie. (jen g.) ❀ Spiderman all the way! (howard)

Colors Essential as the first film representation of the new wave of gangs which sorta portrayed Los Angeles's Bloods and Crips (i.e., red and blue). Directed by Dennis Hopper and starring Sean Penn, Robert Duvall, Maria Conchita Alonso, and an early peek at Damon Wayans. (ju-ji)

Coma This was a bestselling book and haunting movie starring Michael Douglas which dealt with the scarcity of body parts. But the mention of comas also brings to mind a real-life woman named Karen Ann Quinlan, whose family brought the whole right-to-die issue to public focus after Karen slipped into a coma, believed to be caused by a mix of alcohol and painkillers, and remained in a coma for a number of years. Her parents wanted to have her taken off life support and fought a long arduous court battle to do so. This was also made into a TV movie with Brian Keith starring as her father. (bruce/darby)

Nadia Comaneci Nadia was every girl's hero — maybe that's why every girl growing up in the '70s (at least in the Midwest) went a couple days a week after school to gymnastic lessons. We glided across the balance beam, hung from rings, and twisted our little selves around the uneven parallel bars. We jumped on trampolines and practiced floor routines, straddled horses and flipped, cartwheeled, and back-bended our way into pubescence. (jes) ❀ I loved the Romanian team's uniforms. (ju-ji) ❀ She had that weepy theme song, basically the onset of death rock. (noël) (See also "NADIA'S THEME")

Commercials

TV affected us growing up more than our parents did (unless your parents didn't allow you to watch TV). We learned how to spell relief, what to do to stains, what to like and dislike, and what we wanted to buy. We innocently sang and mimicked the tunes of Dr Pepper, Oscar Mayer, and *meow meow meow meow* Meow Mix. Even if you try to avoid mainstream culture, advertising always makes its evil way into the brain and replays itself anytime you need to use the product, or during just about any moments of possible silence, through the use of rhymes, reason, and bad show tunes. A few of these may seem as if they were only yesterday: Morris the Cat (9-Lives cat food); I love my calendar cat; Lauren Hutton and the Nestea Ice Tea plunge; "You've Got Ring Around the Collar" (Wisk); Herb Albert music; "He likes it! Hey, Mikey!" (Life cereal); "AIMs Home Loan to the rescue"; "And like a good neighbor, State Farm is there"; "Do you know me?" (American Express); "Baseball, hot dogs, apple pie, and Chevrolet"; "Beef, it's what's for dinner"; little Rodney Allen Rippy trying to take a bite out of the big burger (Jack in the Box); "You deserve a break today" / "Two all-beef patties, special sauce, lettuce, cheese, pickles, onions, on a sesame seed bun" (McD's); "Connect Four! Where?! Here, diagonally. Pretty sneaky, Sis!" (game); "When you play Perfection, you gotta move on fast, move on fast, before the pieces pop-up, before you put in the last, and that's Perfection!" (game); "You sank my battleship!" (game); "I'm the Sole Survivor" (game); battery on the shoulder of Robert Conrad, who dared you to knock it off; O.J. jumping turnstiles in the airport (Hertz rental car); "Sorry, Charlie!" (Star-kist tuna); margarine commercial where a crown suddenly appears on someone's head (Imperial margarine); "It's not nice to fool Mother Nature" (Parkay margarine — "Butter!"); "You think it's butter, but it's not, it's Chiffon"; "Pepto biiisssmmmoool"; "One spicy meatball" / "I can't believe I ate the whole thing"/"Plop plop, fizz fizz, oh what a relief it is fast fast *fast*" (Alka-Seltzer); "How do YOU spell relief? R.O.L.A.I.D.S."; "You get a big delight in every bite . . ." / Fruit Pie the Magician and Twinkie the Kid (Hostess); "How many licks does it take to get to the center of a Tootsie Pop?"; "If you believe in peanut butter, clap your hands" (Peter Pan); "Choosy mothers choose Jif"; "Leggo my Eggo" (Eggo waffles); "When it rains, it pours" (Morton salt); "4 out of 5 doctors recommend chewing Trident"; "pick a pack of Juicy Fruit — off the Juicy Fruit tree"; "Who wears short shorts?" (Nair hair removal cream); "I'm gonna wash that gray right outta my hair"; "Gee, Your Hair Smells Terrific!" (shampoo); Mom . . . do you ever get that . . . not-so-fresh feeling? (Massengil); pretty girls washing off a face full of cold cream (Noxema); "Calgon, take me away!" (bubble bath); scrubbing bubbles; Mr. Clean; Old Spice; Irish Spring; lots of Jay Ward; "Look left, right, and left again" (public service announcement); "Ancient Chinese secret, huh?"; "You're soaking in it" (Palmolive); "Adee-do" (plumbing and heating); "Hi, Emma! Hi yourselves, cuties! Whatcha doin' in my laundry basket?" / "Hey, it's the Fruit of the Loom guys!"; "Attention, shoppers, this is a stick-up . . . no, *this* is a Stick Up" (air freshener); Chiquita banana with dancing banana lady; stewardess offers "Coffee, tea . . . or a flick of my Bic"; Jane Russell with the eight-hour girdles; fast-talker John Moschitta (Federal Express); "It's Cal Worthington and his dog, Spot" (car dealerships); "You call that kid a Cracker Jack"; Uncle Sam offering the world a good car for only a buck (Matchbox); Frankenberry and Count Chocula argue about who is scarier and a cat scares them (cereal); the Quaker Oats guy; "I coulda had a V8"; "Hey, Kool-Aid!"; "A&W root beer's got that frosty mug taste"; "Doin' it Mountain Dew"; I'm picking up good vibrations (Sunkist); "I believe in Crystal Light, and I believe in me"; "I'd like to teach the world to sing" (Coca-Cola); Mean Joe Green "Tab for beautiful people"; "From the land of sky blue wa-ater" (Hamms beer); Spuds Mackenzie (Budweiser); "Thanks for your support" (Bartles & Jaymes); "Libbys Libbys Libbys on your label label label, you will like it like it like it on the table table table"; silver cleaners; Ginsu knives; Ronco; Donna Dixon on that Beautyrest bed; "When E. F. Hutton talks, people listen"; "Please don't squeeze the Charmin" (with Mr. Whipple); "You asked for it, you got it, Toyota" (with people jumping in the air); "If you want to be a model, or just look like one" (Barbizon); "Double A (honk, honk) M.C.O." (transmission shop); "Sorry now, so sorry now" and "Lipstick on your collar . . ." (before infomercials, one of the longest commercials of its day was for this stinkin' Connie Francis Collection); Chung King; "Muncha buncha Frito's go with lunch" (Frito's corn chips); "Here, kid, have a Life Saver" (dad tries to make it up to his son by offering this candy); "Take a bite outta crime" (McGruff, the creepy raincoated beagle); "Only you can prevent forest fires" (Smokey Bear); "Anytime is the right time for milk"; "Riunite on ice . . . so nice"; "Sugar in the evening! Sugar in your—vitamins?"; "Nothing comes between me and my Calvins"; "Heard it through the grapevine" (California Raisins); Wheat Thins with Sandy Duncan in fields of wheat; "I don't have a lot of time, I don't want to spend a lot of money" (Sizzler); "Kibbles and Bits! Kibbles and Bits! I'm gonna get me some Kibbles and Bits!"; "Healthy is the High Pro Glow" (dog food); Toss Across with the dog; "My Buddy, My Buddy, My Buddy and me!" (My Buddy doll); "Weebles wobble but they don't fall down"; commercials brought to you by the Church of Latter-Day Saints; "I got it from Sandy, who got it from Paul. Paul got it from Ernestine who could've got it anywhere at all. And with my love, I gave it to you. Now that we've got it, what're we gonna do? VD is for everybody" (public service announcement). (darby/lorraine/jessica g.) (See also CEREALS, FARRAH FAWCETT-MAJORS, GRAVY TRAIN, L'EGGS, LITTER, McDONALD'S, MR. MIKE, MASON REESE, SHAMPOOS, TY-D-BOL, WHERE'S THE BEEF?, and WOODSY OWL)

Combs More than just a grooming device, a fashion accessory! Came in more colors and styles than the hair they were meant to sculpt and looked extra-sexy peeking out of a designer back pocket. Those bulgy folding comb/brush combos were super handy for the long-haired ladies, but oh so uncomfortable to sit on in the classroom. (lisa a.) ❧ Goody unbreakable combs were *it*, especially the tortoise-shell kind. (noël) ❧ The small ones used in place of barrettes, most frequently for an asymmetric, holding-one-feathered-side-behind-your-ear look. (allison) (See also SITTING BACKWARD IN A CHAIR)

Comic Books *Howard the Duck; Conan the Barbarian; Tomb of Dracula; Quake; Fabulous Furry Freak Brothers; Love and Rockets; Zap; Weirdo; Fat Freddy's Cat; Young Lust; Zippy the Pinhead; Heavy Metal; Vampirella; Eerie; Creepy;* and numerous *Mad* rip-offs (*Cracked; Crazy; Parody;* and *Sick*). (martin) ❧ *Sgt. Rock; Nick Fury and His Howlin' Commandos; Red Sonja; The Avengers; The Defenders; Doctor Strange; The New Mutants; Alpha Flight* (with the first openly gay character!); *Fantastic Four;* and *Spiderman* (these two were still cool in the '80s). (paul h.) ❧ Plus a whole wave of new small-press comic artists including Julie Doucet (*Dirty Plotte*); Jim Woodring (*Cartoons Magazine, Jim, Frank*); Joe Matt (*Peep Show*); Seth (*Mr. X, Palookaville, It's a Good Life If You Don't Weaken*); Peter Bagge (*Comical Funnies, Neat Stuff, Hate*); Roberta Gregory (*Dynamite Damsels, Naughty Bits*); Aline Crumb (*Dirty Laundry*); Mary Fleener (*Slutburger*); and Dan Clowes (*Lloyd Llewellyn, Eightball*). (darby/eric) (See also CARTOONS and X-MEN)

Computers Remember the Timex-Sinclair with only 4K? The first home computer was the Altair, which you had to build from a kit! (steven) ❧ TRS-80, Commodore 64, Wang computers, Amiga (first with color), Atari, Tandy, Franklin, the enormousness of the one-meg drive. Computers used to be amazing things with whirling tape drives that were astounding because they were so huge. Then sudden-ly they got small, tiny, friendly. Next thing you know the things were turning up in the house as *personal* computers. You ran them off a cassette deck and hooked them up to your TV. They didn't do much of anything but everybody told you how important they were. By 1980 anybody that was hoping to surf the third wave had to have one of these lest they suffer that indignity of coming back sad-faced on the train from college. Frightened buyers started buying up anything with a keyboard and a screen, then finding out the thing had the calculating power of an abacus. The boom quickly turned to bust. The only survivor was Nintendo. It took another five years before Macs came out and people could finally do something with the damn things. I'm still waiting for them to get easy. (bruce)

The Coreys Corey Haim and Corey Feldman. Somehow both these child stars turned child bombs at around the same time and placated themselves by starring in some of their bomb vehicles together, which linked them forever in Retro Hell as "the Coreys." When people mention the Coreys it's usually with a little giggle under their breath. I ran into Corey Feldman a few times in my life: Once as a kid, at a middle-class hamburger resturant in the Valley, all innocent with his mommy and friends, and then about six years ago in an L.A. club, where he was decked out in a sorta '80s pimp-style suit with a hat, hangin' at the bar, all squinty-eyed cool with a smirk, hoping *someone* would notice. I did. He was way too baby-faced and dorky to pull it off, and it was more like a character in a movie 'cause no one would have done that in real life. Very recently, *Retro Hell* contributor Howard Hallis signed up to take his acting class, Corey Feldman's Act Naturally, but it was canceled. (darby)

Howard Cosell Howard Cosell was a great hustler. And he created a lot of the excitement for Cassius Clay, before he became Muhammad Ali. He was one of the few people that treated black fighters and sports figures as intelligent human beings — up until that time it was like they were all considered idiots. He would ask good questions, instead of a typical sports announcer who would say, just after you lost a game 17–0, "How do you feel?" Cosell would just go in there and say something like, "You guys really look bad, how can you get any better with the bozos you have on your team?" He was really fun, and he was good for sports. But like a lot of personalities he began to believe he was more important than the whole picture, so sometimes he got a little out of hand. But he was

Howard Cosell

no doubt the best announcer. To think that some jock could ever take his place! (dad) ❧ Annoying, slow-talking sportscaster, particularly for *ABC's Monday Night Football*, who got shit for referring to a black player on the Washington Redskins as a "little monkey." (noël)

Counseling Therapy techniques: screaming, rebirth, hitting your loved ones with sponge bats and pillows, yelling "I'm mad as hell" out the window. Seen in large doses on the sitcoms *Bob Newhart, The Jeffersons, Three's Company*, and many movies at the time. I think it was during this period that seeing a therapist came into vogue. (darby) ❧ I told my therapist that I didn't have any friends and she said, "I'm your friend" and I said "Yeah, I'll be your friend too if *you* pay *me* $50 an hour!" I didn't have to go back after that. (riley) (See also NEW AGE and SELF-HELP) 🐿

Cousin Oliver "Six weeks of work — six weeks! — and for twenty years I've been Cousin Oliver!" So says Robbie Rist, known to the unenlightened as "unlucky" Cousin Oliver on *The Brady Bunch*, the bespectacled blond John Denver look-alike who was brought on the show toward the end of its run, when the other kids had grown too old and gawky (or

buxom, in Jan's case) to be cute anymore. "If I get asked one more time if I had sex with Cindy, I swear I'm gonna punch someone." The truth is, Rist has been working nonstop since that infamous venture. In addition to featured guest spots throughout the '70s on *Lucas Tanner, The Mary Tyler Moore Show*, and *CHiPs* (to name but a few), he had the honor of being made into a Saturday morning animated character for mid-'80s New Wave rock-toon *Kidd Video*. Not much of a stretch, as the real Robbie has been playing in bands around town since puberty. He continues to do commercials and voice-over jobs, including Michelangelo in the Teenage Mutant Ninja Turtles movies. He is currently playing three instruments in twelve local bands and has almost single-handedly spearheaded L.A.'s Bubble Gum Crisis power pop scene. He's also really fucking cool and funny. So invite him to your next party. (gwynne)

Cowlnecks These were turtlenecks with an overly large and saggy neck. Gold chains usually dangled from the cowlneck, and vests were often worn over them. Think Joyce DeWitt on *Three's Company* (and think browns or russets, heathery lavender or pink). They were and still are very ugly and repressive and screaming for a retro comeback. (darby) ❧ Cowlnecks were also the foundation of the mid-'70s *Rhoda* look popularized by Valerie Harper in her *Mary Tyler Moore* spin-off show. While Mary's look was uptown classy, Rhoda's was downtown trashy. With the cowlneck sweater, Rhoda might opt for a hip-length crocheted vest, a belted cardigan, a pair of slightly flared double-knit polyester slacks or gauchos, a trench coat, loud socks, and a pair of wedgies. Rhoda was queen of the more-mixed-than-matched layered look, always appearing as if she hadn't been able to decide what to wear so she just threw on everything she owned, but *always* making sure to throw on a scarf and belt to "pull it all together." Somehow it worked beautifully, and being so easy to emulate, the look made a big impact on the fashion of the day and on the style of the '90s homeless population. (nina) (See also PLASTIC SURGERY and THE WEDGE) 🐾

Crazy Straws A drinking straw shaped into a convoluted pretzel of a design at its midsection. Pleasure was derived by watching fluid course through the ganglion of tubing before either swallowing the liquid or letting it drop back down into the glass for an encore performance. Such straws brought much in the way of entertainment to meals but did little to promote good table manners. (cliff) 🍀 Sure it was fun to watch the drink whirl and race through the straw, but alas, one's lungs almost collapsed before the precious fluid of choice could reach the mouth. When the glass emptied, the stream of juice would break up into little slow-moving bits, with the entire straw looking like the freeway at rush hour. (bruce) 🍀 They really lose their charm after you've spent any amount of time in a hospital room watching a loved one have his/her stomach pumped. (gwynne)

Creem Magazine For a time during the '70s, my mom worked at the local library in our neighborhood. My sister and I were about nine and six years old, respectively, and we spent a lot of time there, especially in the summer. Most of it was spent perusing the comic magazines like *National Lampoon* (which we had to sneak because they kept it tucked behind the counter due to its "adult subject matter"), *Mad* magazine, and *Dynamite!* But also in this part of the magazine section were the music periodicals, one of which would have more influence over my later life than I ever could've imagined at the time. Though I wasn't quite old enough to appreciate the articles in

Creem, many were undoubtedly written by my present heroes of rock journalism — like the late, great Lester Bangs, or Legs McNeil, even Greil Marcus. But this was the era of the glitter rock scene, and the flamboyant, gaudy colorfulness of people like Bowie, Marc Bolan, Gary Glitter, Iggy Pop, and Lou Reed impressed me in a way that still shines in my memory. My sister and I would wait eagerly for the next issue and run down to the local liquor store to check out the much-publicized first-ever photos of Kiss without their make-up — only to be foiled when they turned out to be photos of the backs of their heads! This really only added to their image. *Creem* provided me with my first exposure to an exciting-looking counterculture that had previously been unknown to me, growing up as I did in the northeast corner of the San Fernando Valley and being effectively removed from any smattering of hipness. (karrin) 🍀 It's still around, but it's really hard to find and it's not at all funny or interesting anymore. (gwynne) (See also KISS ARMY)

Crimping Iron Big in the New Wave/death rock period. For some good examples see Kim Richards (of *Nanny and the Professor*, *Escape to Witch Mountain*, and *Hello, Larry* fame) in *Tuff Turf*, Lea Thompson in *Howard the Duck*, or Siouxsie Sioux of Siouxsie and the Banshees. More innovative girls (i.e., girls whose parents wouldn't buy them things like crimping irons) made tight, small braids and slept on them for the same effect. (darby)

Crock-Pot A cooking utensil favored by working mothers who due to time constraints were unable to find the time to prepare an evening meal. The device allowed the working woman to simply throw table scraps and leftovers into the time-controlled pot in the hopes of passing it off as dinner. (cliff) (See also FEMINISM and KITCHEN APPLIANCES)

Cross Tops Way before crack cocaine, we met in the bathroom between classes to smoke cigarettes and buy cross tops for a buck a pop. That's before realizing they were $10 per 100 mail-order, and that No-Doz worked just as well. (darby) ❧ Also black beauties, pink hearts, et cetera, advertised in the back of magazines like *Creem, High Times, Hustler.* (laurel) ❧ Actually, the cross tops from the early '70s were sometimes decent-grade methamphetamines, not the early '80s–style caffeine crap. They were also referred to as whites, or, for the indecisive, white crosses, and were sold by the $1 unit called a rack in tightly foiled increments of four, five, or ten, depending on the quality of the drugs or the dealer. (don) (See also DRUGS)

Crystals Good for whatever ails ya. Sleep with them, exorcise with them, put them under your pyramid. (amy) (See also NEW AGE)

Curb Jobs When you went to mod clubs you could witness or hear gory stories of nasty skinheads giving these to people. The basic idea is you'd get the person, put his head sideways against the edge of the sidewalk with his jaw hanging over, then some skinhead with heavy steeltoes would stomp his boot into the person's jaw so it would break. Today they'd simply shoot 'em. (darby)

Curling Iron Most girls used it to curl, but I ran it through my hair to straighten the shit out. One out of five times we'd end up with some type of hickey or Adam Ant–looking burn on our face from the thing, which we'd goop lots of liquid make-up over to hide. (darby) (See also CRIMPING IRON)

Roald Dahl Most famous for the books *Charlie and the Chocolate Factory, Charlie and the Great Glass Elevator,* and *James and the Giant Peach.* Willy Wonka was a harsh man and actually most of the characters in Dahl's stories were despicable in their own special ways. Many don't know about his even darker side, which you can see in his adult novels like *Kiss Kiss* and *Switch Bitch.* When I was trapped in France for a few months I read every book at the library that they had in English, and for some reason these were there. There was this one short story about this lady finally being with the man of her dreams. He walks out on her because she is too dry down there because she is getting old. She goes into the bathroom and slashes her wrists because of it, which I enjoyed. I really wanted to interview Roald for this, but he's retro dead. (darby) (See also *WILLY WONKA AND THE CHOCOLATE FACTORY*)

Dallas Cowboys Cheerleaders The dazzling Dallas Cowgirls of the late '70s were famous for their all-American blond hair and blue-eyed charm. Distinctively marked by their teeny white shorts, huge lipsticked red smiles, and knotted royal blue blouses cradling their jubilant boobs, the Dallas Cowboys Cheerleaders were every little girl's dream and every heterosexual man's fantasy. Their skyrocketing popularity led to a made-for-TV movie. (noël) ❧ The Cowboys and the Steelers were two of the most perfect '70s teams. Dallas especially, with their shiny silver metallic and stars. In the tight-T-shirt,

silver-metallic-star, little-backpack '90s, Dallas is in again. 🐢 (winnie) (See the movie *Debbie Does Dallas*)

Dance Fever Mid-'70s Merv Griffin–produced dance show hosted by Deney Terrio, who choreographed John Travolta in *Saturday Night Fever.* Denny would appear with two female dancers (collectively named Motion) and then lead celebrity panelists (e.g., Dick Van Patten, Barry White, Joyce DeWitt) in judging contestants for originality, style, and talent. In the early '80s, Terrio's place was taken by similar-looking ex–*T.J. Hooker* co-star Adrian Zmed. (nick)

Danskin Outfits Mine was a bronze color with the leotard top and matching wrap-around skirt. Wore it to the sixth-grade disco that I went to with the boy next door. We won the dance contest (just before we left, my parents taught us how to dance '50s hop style to disco music and it was a big hit), and I got a real nifty disco gold charm as a prize, and we shared a gift certificate to the Warehouse, which we spent on Rod Stewart and Rick James 7"s, thinking we might keep practicing our hot dance moves and enter more contests, though we never did. (darby) ❧ I wore one of these ensembles to the formal opening of a musical when I was fourteen. I took off my coat in the lobby of the Kennedy Center and my skirt had somehow come untied, so of course the whole thing fell to my ankles in front of all these rich old famous people

d

Dallas Cowboys Cheerleaders

like Carol Channing. My parents got mad at me for being upset. "Shut up, no one noticed!" Now I do stuff like that on purpose. (gwynne) (See also DISCO CHIC)

Dark Shadows *Dark Shadows* was so far ahead of its time. An anomaly in the mid-'70s soap opera world, it quickly became ultrapopular, especially among kids and teenagers (not housewives) because of its content. It had all the usual soap opera infidelities, financial scandals, love triangles, murder, and mayhem, but it was set in Victorian times, at the fictional Collins House, and most of the action centered on some ultrasexy vampires — Quentin, Gerard Styles, Samantha, and the most famous of them all, Barnabas Collins (played by Jonathan Frid). The opening featured spooky, unearthly music (I think it had a theramin on it, or at least that's what it sounded like) and a grainy film of waves crashing on a desolate, rocky beach. There were all sorts of sexy, cleavage-heaving women fainting in tight-bodiced dresses, and lots of carnal love bites to the neck, flashing capes, people getting bricked up into walls, evil laughter, and always a cliff-hanger on Fridays. *Tiger Beat* and the other teen mags were full of the cast because they were all so damn good-looking (Quentin looked kind of like Adam Ant, if I recall correctly). The show came on from 4:00–4:30, so everyone would rush home from school, gather in the living room, pull down the shades so it was real dark, and get the shit scared out of them. I remember my sisters had to push their dollhouse to the wall because they thought it was Rose Cottage, the haunted dollhouse on *Dark Shadows*. Aaaah, those were the days. There was even a movie called *House of Dark Shadows*. If it was on now, it'd blow *Sunset Beach* right out of the water! (pleasant)

Davey and Goliath *"Daaaaaaveyyyy!"* Maybe I liked this show so much because I am Jewish. Claymation with a moral. (katy) ❧ I remember watching this and being absolutely *glued* to the TV on Sunday mornings. I loved the animation, but I was always bummed when the God/moral thing ended it. (e. c. cotterman) ❧ Produced for the Lutheran Church by Art Clokey of *Gumby* fame, they were made during the height of Art's extensive drug use, which may be why there is an underlying bizarre edge to them. I just know that Davey's sister's hair scared me. (bruce)

Dear Alex and Andy "I'm desperate!" "What should I do?" For all the kids who needed help getting past their typical life dilemmas, there were your friends Alex and Andy, on TV Saturday mornings. They'd always have a charming little folk ditty about a positive solution to your personal problem. (mike v.)

Death Rock In the Midwest, country-western showed up one day and never left; in L.A. it was death rock (today referred to as Goth) that arrived one dark and eerie night, has been with us ever since, and from the looks of things will not be going away anytime soon. It's as undead as the vampires its adherents emulate. The whole thing started around 1982 with the kids at London's Bat Cave (unless you want to count unwitting pioneers Dave Vanian, Siouxsie, Joy Division, and 45 Grave), but soon, as with all English fashion trends, Hollywood could boast its own version of the death rock scene, complete with its own clubs and plenty of young and frail ghoulings to support them. Fetish, probably the first Goth-friendly club, was the brainchild of Joseph Brooks and Henry Peck, of Vinyl Fetish record store, and played a danceable mix of Goth and its happier sister, Glam. Even punk dive Cathay De Grande had one night a week devoted to death rock called the Bone Club. Things went a bit further with the advent of Scream, Helter Skelter, Sanctuary, the Crypt, and Zombie Zoo. Some wonderful dances were developed by these nouveau creatures of the night, like the oh-so-interpretive Taffy Pull, and the dramatically swooping Penny Scoop. The monsters of Goth at first were Siouxsie, who is still a staple, Bauhaus (with their Bela Lugosi's Dead video playing nonstop), Virgin Prunes, Specimen, Joy Division, Alien Sex Fiend, and speed demons the Sisters of Mercy. Later there were Fields of the Nephilim, Christian Death, the Mission U.K., and KROQ-fueled groups like Soft Cell, Depeche Mode, and the Cure. There are many theories as to why Goth refuses to die; I guess (A) death is *muy* sexy (just take a gander at *Alarma* or any other Mexican Gore, Guts, and Cheesecake tabloid), and, more important (B) Who *wouldn't* look incredibly gorgeous with all that make-up? (don) (See also *THE HUNGER* and SIOUXSIE CLONES)

The Death of Ritchie This 1977 TV movie starred Robby Benson as a troubled teenager battling his way through severe drug abuse and a poor relationship with his family. Based on a true story, this movie affected *everyone* who saw it. Another depressing media exploitation of the failed post-hippie teen, complete with simulated psychedelic visuals and ghoulish, nightmarish traumas. Ritchie, a good-looking, suburban, middle-class kid, is the stereotype misfit who doesn't know how to fit in and learns how to freak out instead! All the girls liked Ritchie, but with his fucked-up mental condition, he inevitably scares them all away, making himself a bigger wreck. Ritchie had a secret room, accessible through his closet, where his friends and he would get high while bad '70s rock was ablarin', with cheap strobe lights and more accessories than a head shop! (Every kid I knew envied his interior decorating skills.) Invariably, his parents would break up the party and give Ritchie the third degree while he was still peaking, ultimately leading to traumatic conflict. In a dramatic ending, Ritchie drunkenly threatens his father's life, but Father takes *his* instead, saving him hundreds of dollars in therapy bills and stopping those loaded troublemakers from coming around again. (mike v.) (See also DEPRESSED-DRUGGIE-GIRL MOVIES)

The Decline of Western Civilization Those who didn't get to run wild and live in squalor in the big city (in this case Los Angeles) finally got a real peek into the lifestyles of the folks who did via Penelope Spheeris's crude, dare I say, rockumentary. Starring the Circle Jerks, X, Black Flag, Alice Bag, Catholic Discipline, and the Germs featuring the immortalized Darby Crash ("Give me a fucking beer!"). This "decline" occurred about the time most said punk was dead, and maybe it was true. Like the bad kids in old '50s flicks, the bad kids who were into the more outrageous music-oriented activities of the mid- to late '70s were all punks! But somewhere along the way divisions were made, and perhaps the real decline occurred as subdivisions were formed: death rock, new wave, hard-core, and so forth. Where once all groups fit together somehow, *Decline* seemed to expose one final flash of a moment long lost. And sure, punk is still dead, so don't let anybody tell you different. And let's not even bother wasting space on *Decline of Western Civilization Part II: The Metal Years*. (jaz) (Also worth a look: Penelope's second flick, the punk soap operaesque *Suburbia* — not to be confused with Richard Linklater's *SubUrbia* — which is listed as *The Wild Side* in later movie guidebooks.)

d

Tony Defranco and the Defranco Family

Similar concept as the Osmonds and the Jackson 5, but Italian, so my grandma approved! I played their hit single, "Heart Beat It's a Love Beat" so many times I'm surprised my mom didn't start beating me to her own love beat. The Defrancos were necessary in the early '70s when Italians constituted the Latin element of America; they were later replaced by Menudo. (nina)

Dep

(alias Dippity-Do) With the '50s comeback, my parents were finally sorta hip, for a moment. My mom gave me her old argyles she wore in high school (which I still have) and my dad told me how to get my fuzzy hair more slick. Most girls utilized Dep more in the early '80s though, when we had the sides either shaved or totally slicked back. (darby) (See also MOUSSE)

Depressed-Druggie-Girl Movies

My favorites include *Foxes, Christiane F.,* and *Out of the Blue.* All were filmed in '70s depresso-vision and are about girls who get caught up in sex, drugs, and rock 'n' roll at a frighteningly young age. (dave) ✿ *Times Square; Ladies and Gentlemen, the Fabulous Stains; Go Ask Alice;* made-for-TV *Sara T. — Portrait of a Teenage Alcoholic; The Late, Great Me;* all the teen prostitute movies, and that one about the bulimic. The little sister to the Depressed Housewife genre of books and movies: *Diary of a Mad Housewife, Haywire, A Doll's House, Bed/Time/Story.* (gwynne) (See also *GO ASK ALICE* and *SARA T.*)

Dexy's Midnight Runners

Haunting one-hit Irish or Canadian band (think overalls and armpits) with that evil song "Come on, Eileen." The way it slowed way down in the middle and then sped back up to the original cheerful tempo was particularly devastating.

(nina/darby) ✿ To be accurate, Kevin Rowland and Dexy's Midnight Runners were actually from Birmingham, England. Don't ask me why I know this — I think it's contained on the same neuron that has that "Eli Whitney/1793/cotton gin" factoid. Although their second album was faux-Celtic cheese (and their third album, *Don't Stand Me Down,* was a painfully bad attempt to approximate *Astral Weeks*), their first album should not be forgotten, being one of my very favorite major-label oddities. It's called *Looking for the Young Soul Rebels,* and it basically sounds like Stax/Volt soul — but really, really wrong. It's actually pretty great, in a Shaggs-y sort of way. If you see it in your local 99-cent bin, snap it up. (jesse geekcore)

Diamond Dave

Arguably the '80s' most flamboyant rock 'n' roll frontman, Diamond Dave embodied the excess of that decade. For those of you too young to remember, David Lee Roth handled the vocal chores for Van Halen before their acrimonious split (they said he was fired; Dave said he quit). Dave was cresting a big wave at the time with the success of his solo album and video, which featured him in

David Lee Roth and Friends

the role of talk show host on *Dave TV*. However, this transition to solo artist–multimedia explorer proved a bumpy one. The movie was shelved and subsequent albums rubbed their bellies on the floor of rock 'n' roll purgatory. Diamond Dave was renowned primarily for two endearing characteristics. First, he was rock's "great communicator," biggest mouth in show business. The author of such memorable quotes as "Critics love Elvis Costello because most of them actually look like him," and "I consider myself a family man, I've personally started three or four of my own in the last year." Second, he was known for his lack of discerning taste in clothing, regularly donning a pair of rodeo chaps with nothing underneath. A pair of spandex pants and cowboy boots were also a wardrobe staple. Mr. Roth surfaced a couple years back reincarnated as a Las Vegas showman, briefly taking up residence at Caesar's Palace and performing a greatest-hits show that confused diehard fans and vacationing geriatrics alike. Most recently, scandal reared its Hollywood head when the original V.H. lineup convened on stage at the *MTV Music Awards* to a standing ovation. While Dave orated about the big reunion, the other members kept quiet about this being nothing more than a publicity stunt for the release of their greatest hits package. (cliff) (See also OVERPLAYED VIDEOS)

King and queen of the teen movie scene

Diet for a New America Book written by the heir of the Baskin Robbins fortune, who gave it all up to document the true evils of the world through animal consumption and factory farming. A new very righteous and political vegetarian movement sprang up in the late '80s that went hand in hand with global warming, Hans Ruech's vivisection books, Peta, and the War Against Fur. (darby)

Digital Watches My first was Texas Instruments. Ugly silver metal for that fashionably futuristic edge. It had a light and a stopwatch and my parents actually had the piece of shit engraved — totally cool. (darby) ❧ The first models (circa 1972) were expensive and featured only a flat black screen. These were LED (light emitting diode) watches. One needed to press a small button to see the time light up inside; and you can imagine how impractical this soon became. Gillette introduced a LED with a gravity-activated light-up switch, but it ate batteries like crazy. Eventually, people opted for the far less cool gray-faced LCDs we know today. (bruce) ❧ The best watches had games on them like Pac-Man or Frogger. TV watches never quite caught on, but it's only a matter of time. (noël) (See also CALCULATORS and VIDEO GAMES)

Matt Dillon The most rad teen idol of our time (though Robby Benson was pretty *mmmm* in *Ode to Billie Joe* and *Ice Castles*). *Little Darlings*, *My Bodyguard*, *Tex*, *The Outsiders*, *Rumble Fish*, all the way to *Drugstore Cowboy*, Matt's best in a tight T-shirt, jeans, a cigarette dangling from his mouth, and wearing that cockeyed confused-puppy-dog face. Just steer clear of him speaking on late night talk shows today (or in that ridiculous movie with Sean Young a few years back). He's still not too bad, though I'm worried he's looking more and more like Henry Rollins. He more recently played duh in the movie *To Die For*, and the character really seemed to suit him. I don't know. (darby) (See also *THE OUTSIDERS*)

Director's Chairs Popular because they were cheap and you could put decals and lettering on the material. Colorful and easy to fold and store. Fat people and director's chairs do not go together. (darby/dad)

Disaster Movies When I was nine, *The Poseidon Adventure* ('72) was the only R-rated movie I was allowed to see. We went on vacation and it was showing on the hotel room's movie channel and we watched it again and again, always getting choked up when Shelley Winters has her heart attack and Stella Stevens falls off the catwalk, but never, for some reason, when Gene Hackman eats it. Irwin Allen gave new life to every has-been actor under the sun with such follow-ups as *The Towering Inferno* ('74) and *Earthquake* ('74). Subgenres include plane-crash movies (*Airport, Lost Flight*), submarine-crash movies (*Fer de Lance, The Abyss*), and rat movies (*Willard, Ben*). Like any other trend, the works got worse with each copycat production — but for some reason, these films churned out a lot of Academy Award–winning theme songs. (gwynne)

Disco Where blacks, whites, gays, and straights all danced together. The '70s brought the races together on the disco dance floor, learning about each other, accepting people who were different from you, hanging out and partying with them, doing illegal things with them. It was a quest for greater understanding between people. (cliff) ❧ In the earliest days of disco, there was a big glitter crossover. "Bohemian Rhapsody," "Bennie and the Jets," and "Aladdin Sane" were played alongside of Disco Tec and the Sexolettes doing "Shame, Shame, Shame." Glitter never died, it just re-emerged as punk rock three

years later. Believe it or not, before *Saturday Night Fever*, disco was pretty underground — big in both the gay and the black scenes. Lots of times the after-hours drug-drenched discos were filled with fags and drag queens, chic hairdressers and fashion plates, straight men, superfly black men, pimps and whores, drug dealers, and downtown denizens of all denominations of street life. Disco began to develop its own music and style, incorporating lots of funk and goofy lyrics such as "I'm your rubber-band man." Recently I had the pleasure of listening to several hours of old disco songs on a Walkman, and it dawned on me that every single song was about sex. (patty) ❧ It was around '78. I was still sorta into Kiss when I went to see *Saturday Night Fever* with my sister and got caught in a disco inferno. I burned baby burned, boogie oogie oogied, and shook my groove thang for a solid gold four months which in grade school time is close to five adult years. I was the disco dancing queen, convinced I was incredibly chic doing the Hustle and Le Freak. Thank God it was Friday, every day! Then I saw Blondie on TV singing that song "Denis" in French. It was over as fast as it started. The next day, I was listening to Elvis Costello and if you asked me, of course I would have told you disco sucked. It did then, but I was thrilled when it snuck back in as dance music a few years later. Once a queen, always a . . . (nina) (See also *STUDIO 54* and *DONNA SUMMER*) ❧

Disco Chic No more grass-stained jeans, puka shells, and tie-dyed hippie threads. Throw out your throw-ons, bid adieu to the late-'60s to mid-'70s hype of *au naturel*. The late-'70s disco craze ushered in a whole new eurotrash aesthetic that was all about trying hard to be chic. Dress codes at discos insisted you dress to impress, so "come as you are" was no longer an option. The easiest way to achieve this unnatural look was to take a clue from the disco ball spinning above the dance floor; that's right, shimmer and shine from head to toe! The sheen of unbuttoned satin shirts, gold chains, and sweaty chest hair; the glimmer of little sequined disco bags and spandex

Danskin dresses; the sparkle of opalescent eye shadow, metallic Lurex-threaded scarves, and gold-glittered high-heeled sandals transformed you into the shining star you were born to be — even without the cocaine. (nina) ❧ **Essential disco gear:** synthetic (satin, quiana, polyester, velour) anything; gold lamé anything; lots of designer shoes and clothes from Halston, Gucci, Diane Von Furstenberg, Yves St. Laurent, Charles Jourdan; designer "French-cut" jeans from Gloria Vanderbilt and Calvin Klein; gaudy Huck-A-Poo printed polyester shirts; high-waisted, superwide pantsuits with short bomber jackets worn with strappy high heels; spandex bodysuits; slinky wraparound skirts; halter tops, tube tops, or blouses with puffy sleeves and wide gathered waists; Foxy Lady belts; tiny stretchy gold belts; tuxedo-striped hotpants; scarf dresses with spaghetti straps; off-the-shoulder flowing flower-printed dresses; one-shoulder dresses; poppers, lighters, or zip-up coin purses hung from the necks; turbans; and strong perfume by Halston and Chloë. (patty/candi) (See also JEANS and POLYESTER) 🐾

Disco Parodies "Disco Lucy": The Wilton Place St. Band, 1977, got up to number 24 with this *I Love Lucy* theme with a disco beat and a woman singing, "Ya ya disco Lucy." This was that same summer *Star Wars* by Meco was cluttering the airwaves. ❧ **"Disco Duck":** "Try your luck, don't be a cluck." I think this was done by L.A. deejay Rick Dees. Also Disney's "Macho Duck" and the *Sesame Street* disco albums, *Sesame Street Fever* and *Sesame Disco.* (jaz) (See also TV SHOW SONGS ON RADIO)

The "Disco Sucks" Movement
"Disco's Dead, Crank the Led," "Disco's Dead, Crank the Ted [Nugent]." (jory) ❧ Today, we think of it as a nutty late-'70s fad, rather like disco itself. However, back in the Midwest, it became a holy cause, a mission to drive out the candy-assed invaders from the West Coast and return rock to its rightful place! The movement reached its crescendo on the steamy night of July 12, 1979, in Chicago's Comiskey Park. The White Sox were playing the Detroit Tigers in a twilight double-header. Between games, Chicago's famously fat morning zoo deejay, Steve Dahl, took to the field. The night's entertainment was to be an anti-disco rally, featuring the largest pyre of burning disco records the world had yet seen. After whipping several thousand drunken fans to a Nazi-like frenzy, Dahl set fire to a huge wooden crate containing several hundred copies of the *Saturday Night Fever* soundtrack as well as twenty pounds of TNT. The blast was far greater than expected, showering screaming bleacher bums with flaming flying vinyl. The second game was delayed by the ensuing riot (as well as the crater that now dominated the field). It was a seminal event for all young Rust Belt Reactionaries. A few years later they would be smashing Japanese cars, listening to Johnny Cougar, and voting for Reagan. (bruce)

Diseases Some of the most popular of our time included herpes, mono, toxic shock, Guillain-Barré syndrome (to prevent the predicted swine flu epidemic a massive vaccination program was started; the vaccine caused this particular syndrome with side effects much worse than the swine flu), Epstein-Barr, Hong Kong flu, rubella (formerly known as German measles), V.D., and the clap (the nickname for the popular retro STD gonorrhea — the friendliest of the diseases, to the point everyone joked about how many times he or she had had it). An often seen but little understood button of the day said: "Trap Clap, Wear Rubbers." So very long ago. (jaz/bruce) (See also AIDS)

Dittos Before nothing came between Brooke and her Calvins, before we ooh-la-la-ed over Sassons, all the foxy mamas zipped into saddle-back Dittos for the ultimate cameltoe — the '70s pant fashion essential. Chicks in Luv It pants just didn't know where it was at. (nina) ❧ Dittos and Luv Its were for elementary school, then you got to grow into Chemin de Fer! (darby) (See also JEANS and O.P. SHORTS)

Divorce Nowadays one in two American marriages ends in divorce, but before the early '70s it was rare and sort of dirty. At my Catholic prep school, divorce crept in, family by family, like some sort of disease we couldn't innoculate ourselves against. The divorced kids seemed bewildered at first then quickly readjusted themselves to spending weekends with their dad's new girlfriend and weekdays with a newly embittered mom. Those of us with families still intact felt vaguely unhip and behind the times. (mikki) ❧ Spawned the license plate holder "Divorcees Are Hot to Trot," which gravely offended my Catholic mom in Sunday traffic. (jeff) (Also check out the movie *Kramer vs. Kramer*)

Dixie Cups In every house (especially homes with kids). We went through a box a week. There were the Dixie Cup holders which were in every house as well. (darby) ❧ Originally, they were in these fiestaware colors and had musical notes walking like Egyptians around the edge of them. And then they just got plain with sunny happy colors, and *then* came the Dixie riddle cups, with horrible, horrible jokes on them. Even five-year-olds would throw their Kool-Aid down and walk away because these jokes were so bad. Example: "What do you call a sleeping bull? A bulldozer!" There was, however, one joke that I did actually kind of like because it was faintly clever and the visual image of it in my mind was so wonderful: "What does an ape sleep on? An ape-ri-cot!" Ha ha ha. (bruce)

Dolls Baby Tenderlove; Baby Thataway; talking Bozo doll; Love-Lee; Katie Kachoo (raise her arm and she sneezes); Angel Babies; Annie; Baby Crissy; Barbie and Ken (of course); the big life-sized bust of Barbie (you could do her makeup and even her hair); Superstar Barbie; Dawn (poor man's Barbie — sexier/hipper); Candi; Crissy; Dressie Bessie and Dapper Dan (the dolls with snaps, zippers, buckles, and laces so you could learn how to work these important objects); the Get-a-Long Gang; talking Grouch doll; Growing-up Skipper (you cranked her arm and her chest grew); Holly Hobbie; Little Red Riding Hood/Grandma Wolf puppet; "Love Is . . ." dolls; Muffie; Pippi Longstocking; Raggedy Ann and Andy; Rub-A-Dub Dolly (for the bath); Sailor Sue; Skipper; the Sunshine Family; Tiffany and Tuesday Taylor (with hair you could change from blonde to brunette and back again — also a black version); trolls; Wake-up Thumbelina (the doll that lifts her head and then turns over); also the scary three-faced doll (sleeping, crying, happy) with a knob on top; the red-haired doll with joints who rode a battery-operated bike; the wind-up baby with a butt that wiggled; and the dolls that your grandma kept in the bathroom which hid the extra roll of toilet paper. ❧ CARTOON DOLLS: Archie; Bugs Bunny and friends; Care Bears; Charlie Brown; Garfield; My Little Pony; Pebbles; Sippin' Bam Bam; Strawberry Shortcake. ❧ CEREAL DOLLS: Dig 'Em (Sugar Smacks); Tony the Tiger. ❧ COMMERCIAL DOLLS: Jolly Green Giant with Sprout; Ronald McDonald. ❧ CELEBRITY DOLLS: The Bionic Man and Woman (with real bionics!); Captain Marvel; Jimmy Carter; Andy Gibb; Dorothy Hamill; *Happy Days; Hardy Boys;* Kiss; Kristy McNichol; Mork and Mindy; the Osmonds; Dolly Parton; *Planet of the Apes;* Brooke Shields; *Star Wars;* Joey Stivik ("Archie Bunker's grandson is a physically correct boy doll, and we think that's terrific"); Sonny and Cher; *Star Trek;* Tiny Tim; John Travolta; *Waltons;* JJ Walker; *Welcome Back, Kotter.* (See also ACTION FIGURES, BABY ALIVE, CABBAGE PATCH KIDS, CARTOONS, G.I. JOE, STRETCH ARMSTRONG, and ROCK FLOWERS)

Dolphin Shorts At some point in elementary school these shorts were banned because they were *so* short your ass would stick out the back end. I would pull mine down a bit and get away with it, but the up-the-butt sluts couldn't. Dolphins were made of a thin, fake satin material and had different-colored panels (in front one side would be white and the other blue and then opposite on back). Other fancy selections were striped and solid colors. These can still be found in West Hollywood, but otherwise the massive Dolphin comeback just hasn't clicked yet, though the company has tried. (selina) 🐾

Don Kirshner's Rock Concert
Kirshner might have had a hand in creating the Monkees, I'm not sure. He was the guy who created the band Kansas. Premiering as *Don Kirshner's In Concert*, November 24, 1972, his syndicated TV show was aired opposite NBC's *Midnight Special* (staring Wolfman Jack) in many TV markets. The show is notable for padding out its menu of second-rate bands with music videos. Very innovative for its time. (bruce) ♣ I saw Patti Smith sing "Gloria" on this show around 1976. It permanently changed my life. "Humpin' on the parkin' meter." Fuck yes. (carla) ♣ The Ramones were on in '78 and my sister and I spent the whole day trying to figure out what they would do about Joey's little white, cakey drool problem. They actually greased the lens for his close-ups. (gwynne) (See also MALCOLM McLAREN)

Donny and Marie
I saw Marie once. I was working at this little boutique inside a Florida resort. We had really nice cigars and toiletries and stuff, and the only thing she bought was toothpaste. I started cracking up. You know, her and her teeth! (laurel) ♣ The Ice Angels — back-up dancers in Vegas showgirl outfits on ice skates? Brilliant. A little bit country *and* a little bit rock 'n' roll. (enrique marie) ♣ Don't forget the Paul Lynde drop-ins, Jimmy Osmond's brilliant trumpet playing, and the older dorkier Osmonds doing the occasional back-up vocals. (mike v.) (See also VARIETY SHOWS)

Double Dutch
A crazy superfangled jump rope game with two ropes spun into each other at opposite beats, played by coordinated sassy black chicks on *Sesame Street*. They still got double dutch teams touring and competing. Superbly retro. And don't forget that funky double dutch song. (ju-ji)

Down Vests
The winter look of the mid- to late '70s was all about down jackets. So what if they were big and violently colored. Sure they got lumpy after being wet and made you look like the Michelin man. Who cares, they were warm! They were *cool!* (bruce) 🐾

Dr. Demento
I listened to this every Sunday night on the radio at midnight, and, by placing a tape recorder upside down on top of the radio, made tapes of songs like "I Like Chinese," "They're Coming to Take Me Away," many Spike Jones and Weird Al classics (in this way I knew the words and tune to "Yoda" before I heard the original "Lola"), and the song that went "I think I had a wet dream cruisin' thru the Gulf Stream" and included many fish puns. Next day all this was fodder for a playground rehash with pals Steve "Bophelius" Poole and Ryan O'Neil. (pete) ♣ The song you are thinking of is called "Wet Dream" by comedian Kipp Addotta. He appeared in the film *Used Cars*, and now shows up as a sleazy lawyer on TV. Also, Weird Al's first song, "My Bologna" (a parody of the Knack's "My Sharona"), was on a

All-American big-toothed singing duo Donny and Marie

d

tape he sent to the good doctor. Barnes and Barnes of "fish heads, fish heads, roly-poly fish heads" fame features the singing of Billy Mumy, Will Robinson of *Lost in Space*. In Detroit, I'd hear him speaking of the Smogberry Tree in Sherman Oaks, and have no idea what he meant, but it was a lovely image to me, this crazy man in a funny hat lying under a tree thinking of strange songs to play. (bruce) ❦ I heard "Shoehorn with Teeth" by They Might Be Giants on his show a few years ago. It made me really happy. (gwynne) (See also WEIRD AL, and check out Dr. Demento's 25th anniversary collection double CD out on Rhino Records)

Dr. Martens Long before this type of footwear could be purchased in any mall, Dr. Martens combat boots were fuck as punk. If ever there were status symbols in the punk community, Docs rated up there with mohawks, safety pins, and black leather and flight jackets. They could pretty much be found only in independent stores that carried subculturaphanelia (studded dog collars, bondage pants, black lipstick, et cetera), which were not nearly as abundant as they are today. The three-holed Gibsons were okay (especially if they had a bulging steel-enforced toe), but let's face it, the higher up the boot, the more punk you were: you could mail-order twenty-holes direct from NaNa before their contract license with Dr. Martens (who hold the patent for the oil-, fat-, acid-, petrol-, alkali-resistant sole) expired. Other acceptable alterna-shoes you could own were: monkey boots, Converse high-tops (preferably with your favorite bands Sharpie-markered all over them), Creepers, and for those leaning toward death rock, Witchy shoes with ultrapointed toes often replete with skull buckles or stilettos. (lorraine) (See also SHOES)

Dr. Who This distinctivly low-tech sci-fi show first aired in Britain, November 23, 1963, and was first distributed in the U.S. in 1975. There were a number of actors who played the good doctor, but the best-known was Tom Baker, with a curly brown mop of hair and a really long scarf. He traveled around the universe with a lovely young assistant and a faithful mechanical dog, K-9, in a converted English telephone booth, the *Tardis*. (lisa aa.) (Also check out the recent book that features the *girls* of *Dr. Who*.)

Drugs There was a really jolly period in the '70s before everyone figured out how bad drugs were for you and got all 12-Steppy. Jargon like "One day at a time" and "Easy does it" was the province of alkies (aka your parents). **Soft Drugs:** Marijuana: The $10 lid was fading into the '60s, to be replaced by Bud and Thai stick. THC content was a consideration. I knew a guy who was invited and taken blindfolded to the Northern California Marijuana Growers Association *tasting*. By the '80s maybe even your parents had gotten high (scary thought). **Medium Drugs:** I knew a guy who took MDA and wandered nude into the surf on a beach for old folks in Miami. He said he "made love to the ocean." Yuck. **Hard Drugs:** Like I said, at first no one grokked (see EST) how hard they were. Thank Studio 54, Keith Richards, and Mick. Then you had John Belushi's speedball death at the Château Marmont and Richard Pryor torching-on with his crack pipe. Party over. (amy) (See also SCANDALS)

The Dry Look In the beginning there was Bryl Creme — a little dab will do you — that gave every guy that patent leather *My Three Sons* look about the head. Then in 1970, Vitalis, the makers of Bryl Creme, declared in many ads that "The Wet Head is Dead," to introduce their new hair-care product, the Dry Look. Just the perfect thing to use with your hot comb. (bruce) (See also HOT COMB)

Dubonnet Van Dyke Parks was drinking on this stuff during his 1991 concert at McCabe's, which was very hip and retro of him. (gwynne) ❦ Remember when Pia Zadora was the TV (and print) pitchwoman for this product, wearing a très sophisticated beret and crooning the jingle? (allison)

Dungeons and Dragons By the late '70s, D&D had become a favorite pastime of certain sorts of socially awkward, too-smart-for-their-own-good adolescents who preferred thinking of themselves as

d.

Chaotically Good Elves in a mystic realm rather than as the Chaotically Dressed Geeks they were in real life. If you played this back in the early '80s, you were likely to own a TRS-80, and by the time you got to college (and you probably did go), you were annoying your dormmates with your aggravating penchant for reciting entire Monty Python routines (*The Holy Grail* was probably your favorite). This king of all role-playing games subsumed the ideas of almost all extant fantasy literature from Moorcock to Leiber to Vance to Tolkien (the game originally used the term *hobbit* for a kind of character, until told to desist by the Tolkien estate, and used the lame disguise *halfling* from then on instead). It provided a framework so rich and elaborate that players need never, if they so desired, deal with the real world. The potentially all-consuming quality of the game, in which the players took on the identity of characters questing through mystic realms and coping with perilous and eldritch situations crafted by the game leader (called the dungeon master, or DM), helped create an elaborate mythos of its own. Many people became convinced D&D was Satan worship in disguise, or drove its devotees to insane mayhem, or at least bore a strong danger of completely disconnecting its players from reality. Mostly, all it did was waste a lot of your time (D&D could pretty much go on forever) and a lot of your money on things like dice with 4, 6, 8, 10, 12, 20, and 100 sides; molded lead figurines of wizards and trolls; and the interminable series of hardback guidebooks that told you things like the hit points and alignments of the various sorts of characters the players could pretend to be and beasties they might meet and have to fight. The game was constantly adding new detritus, rules, and situations (and thus new things to sell) to the whole mythos, with the last major rule revamping coming with the second edition of *Advanced Dungeons & Dragons*, which hit the world in 1989. (brian) ❧ "Magic — The Gathering" cards have

taken its place today, even though role-playing games still abound. (howard) (See also MONTY PYTHON and SATAN, and check out the movie *Mazes and Monsters*, and read also *The Dungeonmaster*.)

Duran Duran In '84, being a Duranie meant I was writing programs in BASIC to print the lyrics to every song from *Rio* on the screen in synch with the music warbling from the tape drive of my Atari 5200, or painstakingly embroidering the classic slanted *DD* in stitchery class. In '85 it meant writing comparative essays for eighth-grade English class on D2's superiority to Mötley Crüe and using their biography (a classic source of new romantic/Nagelesque visual stylings engineered by the masterminds of their look, Assorted iMaGes) to lure cool girls into friendships that would last decades. In '86 Duran Duran were already retro, but it was still necessary to dress Planet Earth on Simon's birthday and do the Nu-Ro dance in the school hallways with my best friend so everyone thought we were lesbians. And while we'd known for

years that their pastiche of Japan/Roxy Music/Classix Nouveaux/Bowie was at best a poor one, we still had to be there in '87 when they finally came to the Shoreline Amphitheater so that Simon could see us, fall in love, and sweep us onto the stage, whispering, "Let's yacht." (jessica g.) (See also OVERPLAYED VIDEOS)

Dynamite Scholastic kids' magazine — sort of a *People* with training wheels — that was available through schools (though I always read it in the doctor's office), where we first learned to worship stupid celebrities. It covered all the *Teen Beat*–type stuff, with a balance of cooler things thrown in. (jaz) ❧ Does anyone remember Marvel Comics's short-lived rip-off of the format, dubbed *Pizzazz*? (steven s.) (See also *BANANAS*)

Ear Cuffs Big around the bolo era. These pieces of curved metal, usually silver, clipped around the upper regions of your outer ear. Often had something like a chain or charm hanging from it. Judd Nelson wore one in *The Breakfast Club*. Piercing fanatics sometimes wear them today. Very geeky. (ju-ji)

Earth Shoes Earth Shoes ruled. They had a funny design that was supposed to be more healthful than regular shoes. The sole was shaped like a wedgie triangle, with the narrow end at your heel and the wide end where your toes were. Additionally, the shoes sloped upward instead of down, so your toes were slightly higher than your heel. They were mutated and backward, like Australian mammals, and they felt good. (mikki) ❧ My older sister once told me that since they were the opposite of high heels, Earth Shoes actually made you *shorter*. I think she was serious. (gwynne) ❧ The fad died down amid rumors that the shoes' orthopedic benefits were overstated. (ju-ji) (See also SHOES)

The East Bay The origins of the umpteenth wave of punk rock in the mid-'90s were born out of a zone called The East Bay (East of San Francisco's Bay) in the late '80s. Their brand of fun, sometimes political, punk rock would be regularly showcased at the local all-ages kid-run club Gilman Street (and featured in zines such as *Maximum Rock 'n' Roll*, *Flipside*, and even *Ben Is Dead*). Now famous for giving us Green Day, some of these bands from those good ol' days that should not be forgotten include Operation Ivy, Crimpshine, Sweet Babys, Isocracy, Kamala and the Karnivores, East Bay Mud, Sewer Trout, Stikky, Yeastie Girlz. (darby)

Clint Eastwood He was *the* biggest actor in the '70s. Dirty Harry was Mark Fuhrman without the racism. He was the only actor that always put some blacks in roles as good people and at the same time wasn't afraid to show blacks as the bad guy in the same movie. He was your basic "I hate bad guys and I'm gonna put them away" and a "What do you mean there's a Bill of Rights?" kind of guy. Americans loved him for it. When he would say things like "Make my day" or "Do you feel lucky, punk?" everybody in the entire theater would cheer. (dad) ❧ Growing up in Carmel, where Clint was elected mayor, I saw a lot of him. As mayor, the only piece of legislation he changed that I remember was a city ordinance that allowed you to eat ice cream on the street (this had previously been illegal, as the dripping action associated with such a crazy food caused unsightly sticky streets. *Quel* horror!). (morgan)

e

Easy Edges In 1974, up-and-coming architect Frank Geary came up with a brilliant idea — furniture made of corrugated cardboard. Taking advantage of the strength of the material, he shaped it into a series of art nouveau designs. The press ate it up and went crazy. It was proclaimed the Volkswagen of furniture. After six months on the market, Geary freaked. He didn't want to be stuck as a furniture designer and left to become a postmodernism architect. I saw one sell on Melrose for $2,700, and that was about five years ago. Today, his Easy Edges furniture made of disposable cardboard sells for $4,000, when it's found in decent condition. (bruce) (See also FURNITURE OF THE '70s)

The Edge of Night The only soap we could make it home in time to watch after school. A thirty-minute show that came on after *General Hospital* and which didn't survive the talk show generation. Spit out a few of today's stars, but the only names I can recall on demand are Lori Loughlin (*Full House*) and Grant Show (*Melrose Place*). (ju-ji)

8-Tracks Why it was cool: It was the first practical way to play recorded music in your car, and it was invented by Bill Lear of Learjet fame. Why it was uncool: The tracks were too short to hold the album-side-long rock compositions that were popular in the '70s progressive-rock era. Just as you were getting lost in the music, it would fade out, then chh*kunk!* the deck would change tracks before continuing the music. Strange fact: There were 4-track and 2-track tape players too. Best 8-track player: the early-'70s Panasonic Dynamite 8 plastic portable player, in red, yellow, or blue, shaped like a dynamite detonator (push down the plunger to change tracks). (candi) (See also 8-TRACKS AND UFOs)

The Electric Company *The Electric Company* was the kids' show that I actually learned the most from, despite the fact that it's mainly remembered for live-action *Spider-Man*. I always liked it better than *Sesame Street*, and in hindsight, I think it was the fact that *E.C.* actually was a step up, teaching kids to read and comprehend. Watching *Sesame Street* now (not that I'm a regular, but passing through), I notice that a lot of the learning appears to

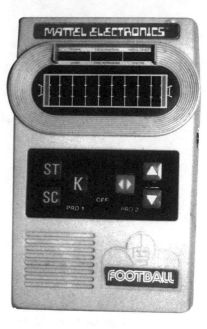

be memorization, which isn't all that good. *E.C.*, like *Zoom!* (which I remember less), taught older kids. Plus, it had Tom Lehrer songs and quite an opening ("Hey you guys!"). (sean) ❖ The part I remember most was the silhouette of the two faces, each saying one of the two syllables of a word, which would visually fly out of their mouth as they spoke, thus creating the word: "C" "AT" "CAT," and then a little jingle played after it. (jaz) (See also *SESAME STREET* and *ZOOM!*)

Electronic Hand-Held Games When I almost died from food poisoning after eating a bad BLT after a big soccer game and was asleep in the hospital for over a week, the first present I was given when I awoke was a Mattel hand-held electronic soccer game. You can imagine how glad I was to be alive. This was technology at its finest. *Bleep bleep bleep.* (darby) ❖ My favorite was the baseball game. Players were represented by tiny red LEDs. I can't figure out how you were supposed to master such low-techness. (noël) ❖ Dataman; Little Professor; Li'l Genius; Spelling B; Mr. Challenger; Merlin; Head to Head; Tiger Raceway; Time Out's Fireman; the Exterminator; Toss-up; Kingpin II Electronic Pinball; Zap; Missile Invader; Super Galaxy Invader; Melody Madness; 2XL; Chess Challenger; I Took a Lickin' from Chicken; Electronic Battleship; Stop Thief;

Maniac; Milton; Melody Madness; Simon (and a million copycats, including one from Tiger actually called Copycat); Einstein; Electronic Quarterback . . . (See also SIMON, SPEAK & SPELL, and VIDEO GAMES)

Elvira Sassy death rock–like temptress with a pumpkinful of witticisms who's also known for her oh-so-fabulous cleavage, usually seen hosting some kind of B-movie flick or Halloween show. (noël) ♣

Elvis Dies August 16, 1977. Long past his prime, a bloated joke of a legend, the King had retired into his own magical world of Graceland. Here he supposedly slept all day, feasted on fatty foods, and shot at his TVs. When Hollywood beckoned his return, the El went on a strict regimen, resorting to enemas and a liquid protein diet, all bolstered by a fabulous array of prescription drugs. On August 16, 1977, as Americans everywhere flocked to see *Star Wars* for the twelfth time, Elvis Aaron Presley took care of business by placing his hunk of burning love atop one of Graceland's many toilets. As the drugs and enemas took effect, our hero pondered the pages of *The Search for the Historic Face of Jesus*, and Elvis the Pelvis gyrated one last time as he strained a fateful stool. The pressure of the chemical-packed poop proved too much for Presley. His pulse got all shook up, and rock 'n' roll's greatest legend fell to the floor, bound about the ankles by his enormous underpants. There he was found, and thus saw the face of Jesus for himself. He's been "sighted" by fans ever since. Such is the stuff of modern American legends. (bruce) (See also CHEST HAIR)

Emergency Breakthrough Precursor to call-waiting, this is what you had to do to reach your friends who talked on the phone for too long — can you imagine! I think it cost a dollar, but that meant nothing to a teen whose parents still pay their phone bill. (ju-ji)

Emergency Cigarettes These were cigs in thin glass tubes, which you'd have to break open in order to get to the cigarette. It was a great concept really, since so many would probably break down and actually tweak enough to smoke these, adding another couple of bucks to the cost of the cig. They'd probably repurchase the emergency cigarette too, out of guilt for having no self-control. Great gimmick. I think it's funny. (darby)

Emergency Plus Four Jack Webb productions briefly branched out into Saturday morning cartoons with this spin-off from *Emergency*. Our two favorite firemen tooled around with a van full of ethnically balanced kids who couldn't stay out of trouble. (bruce) (See also CARTOONS)

Energy Crisis The energy crisis of 1974, combined with a series of severe winters in the mid-'70s, produced a profound sense of doom. Rumors abounded that it was all the fault of the Soviets, who had used theories of Nikola Tesla to screw up our climate. Others pointed to the fact that Lake Michigan had frozen over for the first time in twenty years as a sign that the Ice Age had returned. This all made sense in a darkened house set at a patriotic 68°. (bruce) (See also PHENOMENA)

Epilady Scary means for hair removal that pulls the hair right out of your skin. That's dedication. (ju-ji) 🐾

ERA Wasn't this a bumper sticker? (jaz)

Erasable Pens Essential school supply in the early '80s. When they first came out they were the most important invention. They did what no pen did before — and they worked too, sorta. At least, better than the pen before it, which had an eraser for no reason because all you'd do is rip the paper apart trying to get it to erase the ink. So who the fuck uses these erasable pens today? That's what we want to know. (darby/mike v.) ♣ Probably the same people who still use those thick multicolored pens, which you could click for green, red, black, or blue. (jaz) ♣ The special thick ink came out of the pen like jam onto toast, and it stained hands and clothes just as well. I'm sure the inventor was expecting to make a fortune. (bruce)

8-Tracks and UFOs

Saucer Stories and the Lear Family

In the early '60s the Air Force worked overtime to promote the notion that UFOs were merely illusions or misinterpretations of natural phenomena and not extraterrestrial craft. But on April 24, 1964, New Mexico highway patrolman Lonnie Zamora watched a bright, shiny, humming disc touch down just a few feet away from him on the dusty desert floor. When the UFO shot off into the cosmos, it left behind a big, ugly burn in the brush that couldn't easily be explained away by the Air Force or anybody else. Reports of UFO sightings followed all that summer, jamming the lines at Project Blue Book and anywhere else there was someone to listen. But then the strangest thing of all happened. In the fall of 1964, late at night in a dark laboratory in Southern California, William Powell Lear gave birth to the 8-track tape. Bill Lear, glamour boy and eccentric scientific genius, a man who was on the verge of unleashing the amazing and mighty Learjet on the world, created the endless-loop tape cartridge. Right away, Bill Lear got on the phone to RCA, who agreed to provide music from their vast library, and Ford would later offer the Lear Stereo Eight in its Lincolns, Galaxie LTDs, and Thunderbirds.

One does not have to be a disciple of the fringe to begin to suspect that, indeed, something was, and is, up. And the deeper one looks, the weirder it gets. For starters, Lear's son, Bill Jr., a well-respected pilot, reports on his very own close encounter and a whole lot more in Timothy Good's recent book *Alien Contact: Top Secret UFO Files Revealed*. Bill Lear's younger son, John, also highly honored and regarded in the aviation world, is now a noted UFOlogist and publicly states that on April 30, 1964, the aliens agreed to provide technology and we agreed to overlook the abductions, crop circles, the messing-up of our cattle, and whatever other sinister stuff they wanted to do.

What About Bill?

Was Bill Lear in cahoots with the government all along? Was he being fed the goods on alien technology and passing off all those inventions as his own? It's no secret that Bill Lear's government connections go a long way back. According to Richard Raske in his Lear biography, *Stormy Genius,* Bill made so much dough from government war contracts that, as a result of the 1944 War Profits Control Act, he had to give back $1.4 million. Imagine, in 1944, Pepsi was probably only a nickel.

While in the heat of the research and writing of this article, I received a strange message from someone who identified himself only as Ghost Rite. It came to me on August 8, 1994, at 13:15:09 EDT, via America Online. Ghost Rite's note read, "I recently spoke to an engineer who did considerable consulting work with the government. This man, now in his 80s, worked on the Manhattan Project in Chicago. He knew Lear well, flew with him many times, and was also involved with some of the plane's design. He didn't go into a whole lot of detail, but did mention that Lear had told him about seeing UFOs." Is it possible that Learjet technology was over Bill's own head? When quizzed about his inventions and how he alone had made these quantum leaps of science, Bill Lear would often respond with evasive, mysterious answers like, "Could five hundred men have painted the Sistine Chapel?" or "You never have to repair or replace what you leave out of the design" or "I have a mission." Bill's own engineers, a group of very bright guys, were reportedly "shocked" by the technology of the Learjet. How had he gotten from A to Z? Even thirty years later, Bill's own biographer can explain it no better than to state, "Lear was driven by a vision of beauty and simplicity in which every part sang harmony." Huh?

But our concern here is not so much whether or not the aliens handed Bill the blueprint for the Learjet or the Electrical Resistance De-Icing Means for Aircraft Windshields or the Torsionally Deformable Support for a Gyroscopal Gimbal. What about the 8-track tape?

An 8-Track/UFO Testimonial

In 1969, an anonymous girl we'll call Lisa turned fifteen and she and her mother—we'll call her Louise—took off for Roswell, New Mexico, in a '58 Chevy low rider. Driving across the desert they listened to Marty Robbins and Merle Haggard and watched for tornadoes. But it wasn't a funnel of wind that Lisa saw that night just outside of Roswell. It was about sunset, and Louise had just slipped Johnny Paycheck into the deck, when Lisa grabbed her mother's arm and screamed bloody murder. Then Louise saw it, too. "Holy shit," they said in unison as they stared up at the big silver cigar hovering over the car. "Floor it, Mom," cried Lisa, and Louise did just that. But the UFO stayed right with them. It wasn't until they passed the Roswell city limits sign that the big cigar finally vanished, as quickly as it had appeared.

When they arrived at Louise's sister's house, they rushed inside and told her sister—who we'll call Goldie—of their hair-raising experience. But to their shock and amazement, Goldie just giggled. "Oh, hell," she said, "them damn UFOs are always buggin' everybody around here. Bobby Joe has a hell of a time with 'em." As it turned out, Lisa's cousin Bobby Joe drove a tow truck and was out most every night making his pickups and dodging UFOs. He swore that all he had to do was put Uriah Heep in his rig's deck, especially *Demons and Wizards*, and wham, the UFOs would come around like a swarm of giant, metallic horseflies. Goldie claimed that she'd once been taken aboard a UFO. The aliens had shown her a short film about spores, and not much else had happened. Goldie hadn't noticed any particular aftereffects with the exception that, from that day forward, she could get ten hamburger patties out of a pound of ground beef.

Strange Day Indeed

John Lennon stood naked on the terrace of his New York City penthouse and watched a dome-shaped UFO flashing a circle of red and white lights hover past the United Nations Building. He asked himself, "What the Nixon is that?" On *Milk and Honey,* Lennon sings in "Nobody Told Me," one of the last songs he wrote before his murder, "There's UFOs over New York and I ain't too surprised."

Many other legendary musicians have had close encounters. The band Hot Chocolate describes their UFO encounter in the number-one hit single "No Doubt About It." On *Passage,* the Carpenters recorded "Calling Occupants of Interplanetary Craft," an anthem for an International Contact Day. But some may be less forward about the sharing of their UFO experiences, and perhaps more cryptic. Consider: Electric Light Orchestra's "Out of the Blue," Led Zeppelin's "Houses of the Holy," Elton John's "Captain Fantastic and the Brown Dirt Cowboy," Jefferson Starship's "Freedom at Point Zero," anything by Earth, Wind & Fire, and K-Tel's *Starflight,* which gave us the hits "Heaven Must Have Sent You" and "Ain't No Stoppin' Us Now." It's just too ugly to consider the notion that the 8-track was passed to Bill Lear as part of some alien mind-control plan. I prefer to think that maybe the 8-track slipped through a cosmic crack. That a good-spirited band of alien trackers somehow managed to sneak the 8-track to us, knowing that at some point down the line there would be others here on Earth who would come to know that they know we know. And this knowledge alone may be enough to sustain us. (jean erhardt)

Eraser Burn A bored fifth-grader who either had finished his homework or just wouldn't do it would rub his eraser against the top of his hand until it bled, resulting in a scab that inevitably became a big, ugly, useless scar that made kids feel fraternal with their equally stupid friends who would do the same. Now they say these scars are from working on their car. (mike v.)

Eraserhead The *Citizen Kane* of midnight movies. (thomas c.) (See also *BLUE VELVET*)

Erasers First and foremost are those good-smelling Sanrio erasers that I just wanted to chew on for eternity. But then came those erasers that were shaped like spaceships or Barney Rubble. Perhaps best explained as a natural extension of the pencil-fighting phenomenon of the early '80s, erasers became a big fucking deal, so much so that the elders at my grade school installed a gumball machine just to sell those things to us stupid kids. Milk sales went down that year. (noël) ✿ When I was eight I gave my pink car eraser to Ronny Stockton as a symbol of my love. I was so nervous and thought it would ensure his true deep feelings for me, but he never returned my love and kept my eraser too. (selina) ✿ In the first grade, I stole Melinda Smolin's Frito Bandito eraser. It was the only thing I'd ever stolen and the only time I lied until long after puberty. I finally gave it back to her in the fifth grade. (gwynne) (See also HELLO KITTY)

ESP (Extra Sensory Perception)

General rubric for all things telepathic. Tiresome ESP debunker The Amazing Randi is still to be seen on *Good Morning Wisconsin*, et al., stoking the fires of rationalism, but he is as boring as the ESP-ites. Honorable mention goes to Uri Geller for ruining countless sets of silverware. Get a life. (amy)

Esprit You could not officially be a trendy bitch without a closet full of tear-dropped-zipper-wear encrusted with that disconnected *E*. It always made me think of Laverne and her scripty *L*. You could be poor and still have Esprit-wear, like those big square cotton bags they made in all the shades and hues of primary colors. You could read the white letters from one end of the Galleria to the other. (morgan and ferris) (See also NEW AGE)

Esso Jumpsuits Workers, unite! Fashion for the people! (gwynne)

EST (Erhard Seminar Training)

Masterminded by former door-to-door encyclopedia salesman Werner Erhard, famous for conducting long, expensive seminars in which you weren't allowed to get up and pee. (amy) (See also NEW AGE)

Esthole Person who practiced est techniques. Term originated from enlightening program sessions where the leader would challenge an initiate by referring to him or her as an asshole. (krista)

E.T. The mania over that cuddly beer-swilling alien produced paraphernalia like those sick leathery dolls and rubber E.T. fingers that lit up when you pushed on them. (wendy) ✿ I remember seeing *E.T.* at a drive-in and it changed my life. Maybe someday *I* would meet an alien and have the opportunity not only to befriend it, but to return home with it! *E.T.* provided my escapist fun when other children were dreaming of Cabbage Patch Kids or John Schneider. E.T. was the only consumer frenzy phenomenon that I have ever gone for: I had the plush E.T., the midsize leather E.T. doll, the molded plastic E.T. with the string that when pulled would make him say the most endearing things. I had glass-blown E.T.s, E.T. TV trays, E.T. birthday plates, E.T. buttons, soap, and even a now-tattered E.T. marionette that was purchased in Tijuana. My fascination with the UFO phenomenon was no doubt begun by this fellow; although when I read *Communion* a few years later, my opinion of the benign, enlightened, otherworldly space visitor was smashed somewhat to bits. On occasion I still stare wistfully at the heavens. (skylaire) ✿ Neil Diamond fell so hard for E.T. he made the song "Turn on Your Heartlight" just for him. Can you imagine?! (ju-ji)

e

Linda Evans Remember during the *Dynasty* peak when she was supposed to be the most beautiful woman alive? (ju-ji) ❖ John Derek has this thing for blondes who look like each other: Ursula Andress, Linda Evans, and Bo Derek. Now Linda's getting spiritual with New Age freak Yanni, who bears a striking resemblance to Oakland A's former relief pitcher Dennis Eckersley. (noël) (See also *MIAMI VICE* and SCANDALS)

Executive Toys Few could handle the minimalistic empty-white-office look, and most began to seek out things to complement their Spartan offices, expensive things that were passively fascinating. The most famous of these were the Newton Balls (invented by Sir Isaac), five silver balls in a row that were supposed to illustrate energy. After that came the Wave, a slow-motion blue wave in a flat bottle, a sort of traumatic aquarium. Eventually offices and fashionable homes filled with magic windows of dripping sand, Plexiglas puzzles, and a pile of diamond-shaped magnetic flakes called Creddle. Like most minimalist things, these got boring fast. Eventually, all these executive playthings could be found at the local head shop for sale to stoners tired of Lava Lamps. (bruce) (See also GAMES/TOYS)

Extended Food At the same time that gasoline prices were skyrocketing, around 1974, prices for meat, sugar, and coffee shot up too. Manufacturers responded with "extended" food products, like coffee thinned with wheat, burgers extended with textured soy protein that stretched one pound of meat into two, and bread made low-calorie by the addition of wood cellulose. (candi)

Linda Evans

f

"Face" It was awful to get faced. It meant you looked stupid in front of your friends. Example: "You look nice today in that acid-washed jacket and those neon jelly shoes." "Thanks." "Face!!" If you were quick, however, you could fend off this peccadillo with the "block" rejoinder. You held up your arm in front of your face and ostensibly halted getting faced, all the while exclaiming "Block!" Then you would fight over whether or not you blocked the face in time or not. (morgan and ferris) ❀ Also there was that trick where you'd claim, "Did you know your hand is as big as your face?" and when the fool tried it, you pushed his own hand in his face. (noël) ❀ Being "faced" used to mean being too stoned, short for "shit-faced." (paul)

Famous Amos Black man who started his own self-titled cookie business. My dad said he was a nice guy 'cause he met him when he opened his first Famous Amos cookie shop. We'd always go to his store in Tarzana, especially after seeing a movie down the street. His cookies were yummy, nice and fresh, but the bagged stuff didn't compare. He is not involved with The Famous Amos cookie company anymore and has since started up another cookie company under a new unknown, less popular name. (darby)

Fanny Packs Invented by some clever folks as an identification badge for geeks. (jaz)

Fantasy Island In the original pilot, a number of spoiled wealthy people came to the island, and they all died! Naturally, this wasn't going to work as a series, so they softened the edge. The producers had first approached Orson Welles to play Mr. Roark. However, Citizen Welles wasn't interested in playing a wheelchair-bound sage, even with a hot blond sidekick. (bruce) ❀ Dennis Cole (father of murdered best friend of Henry Rollins, Joe Cole) was an actor, a real popular actor, totally '70s: *Love Boat, Fantasy Island* . . . I remember seeing him in most of those episodes. He was that blond guy with the fuckin' hair — blond, feathered, with the part on the side, that's just tapered to his head — big smile, big teeth, real square-looking jaw, your perfect Ken doll face, and he was always with this blond feathered chick. He'd be walking down that plank to *Fantasy Island*. You know who I mean? I mean that was *him*, he was like *the guy*. (laurel) ❀ "Da plane! Da plane!" Oh Tattoo, you really pulled at our heartstrings. We heard you were a bitter little man after the series ended, but even after your suicide you're always #1 in Retro Hell with us. And I'll honor your memory by *not* seeing your porno. (ju-ji)

Farrah's Feathered Hair My dippy follower of a sister tried this one (though she now thinks she's the original dreadlocker). Over the shag and the bob, (blond) feathered hair reigned as the trendy 'do. Match that with some powder blue eye shadow, succulent, translucent cherry red lip gloss, and squeeze it into a pair of designer lace-up jeans and a lace-up bodice and the Farrah-be was good to go! (karrin) ❧ Girls would carry those big plastic combs in the back pockets of their cut-offs so they could brush their Farrah 'dos upside-down with their heads hanging between their legs and then flip the whole thing back, sometimes whipping passersby with their newly fluffed manes. I think I used to see this in a lot of 7-Eleven parking lots. (gwynne) ❧ A couple of teenage girls in Texas, jealous of a classmate's new Farrah 'do, waited by her locker and tossed acid at her face and hair, resulting in serious burns and hair loss. (allison)

Fat Albert and the Cosby Kids

Based on Cosby's records from the early '60s, *Fat Albert* was an animated show set in a slum in North Philadelphia. Colorful characters such as the epony-mous Fat Albert, Russell, Mushmouth, and Rudy. It always ended with a moralistic musical number in which the Kids played instruments fashioned out of junk. (nick) ❧ Hey hey hey. I always thought it was

Mr. Roarke and his favorite little man

weird, this black guy pretending to be hanging out with these black cartoon characters. Bill was a good guy though. And I always wished Fat Albert was *my* friend. But the character we'd imitate the most was the Mushmouth guy who talked *eyebadeyba* with big flubbering lips. They were a jammin' junk rock band (later influencing Einstürzende Neubauten, Pussy Galore, Artis the Spoonman, and Doo Rag) and always went to their hideout to watch the cartoon *The Brown Hornet*. We can only assume this influenced Matt Groening's *Simpsons* to have their own *Itchy and Scratchy* cartoon. (darby/noël)

Farrah Fawcett-Majors I don't know how worthwhile a memory this is, since I guess it's really the first time I realized my looks weren't up to society's snuff. My friends and I would gather excitedly to watch *Charlie's Angels* every week, minutely discussing Kelly, Sabrina, and Jill's every move, garment, facial expression, and oh-so-slightly-vary-ing coiffure. Of course, we all really want-ed to be Farrah, but it was tacitly under-stood that those of us with dark hair and ghostly skin were supposed to settle and pretend we would be happy to be one of the others. I refused and insisted I be Jill, much to everyone's disgust. (mikki) ❧ When we played *Charlie's Angels* at recess, I was always Jill. We snuck around build-ings aiming guns while bracing our arms for the backfire. I drove a pretend white Cobra and flipped my imaginary long blond tresses. Farrah was only on the show for one season, but it was enough to reel us all in. Remember those Fabergé (with milk and honey) commercials (🦋) with those immortal lines, "You tell two friends and they'll tell two friends and so on and so on . . ." while Farrah's face multiplied on the screen? Oh, sweet Jesus, that was heaven. I

Farrah by Jory C

had her poster on the wall in my room, all of the *Charlie's Angels* trading cards, and even the dolls. She was my idol. (jes) ❧ I thought she was kind of ugly, with a mannish, square jaw, weird nose, a smile that looked more like a "Who farted?" grimace, and small, droopy boobs. Cheryl Tiegs, Cheryl Ladd, and especially Britt Ekland I understood, but this *meeskite?* Years later, a lover tried to convince me I didn't need to lose any weight because he hated that "gross, skinny, Farrah Fawcett type." Still, *Vendetta* is a really rad movie. (gwynne) ❧ Note: Farrah's youthful *Playboy* spread showed her with smoother skin than she ever had twenty years ago — weird, huh? And what's up with those power nipples? (See also *CHARLIE'S ANGELS*, SHAMPOO, *SIX MILLION DOLLAR MAN*, and T-SHIRT TRANSFERS) ❧

"Feed the World" / "We Are the World" The Brits, led by supersensitivos Bob Geldof of the Boomtown Rats and Midge Ure of Ultravox, pulled together a bunch of their pop star pals (this is back in the days when Americans — beyond trendy L.A. KROQers — knew or cared about British pop stars) to sing a Christmas tune about starving victims of vicious government policies in Ethiopia, though the government part didn't get mentioned. Americans, flexing that mighty imperial muscle and showing that we were no one's colony anymore, responded with the star-studded "We Are the World" — Richie! Jackson! Springsteen! Lauper! Perry! Dylan! Turner! That song was terrible too. The whole process led to Live Aid, which I stayed up all night after my McDonald's shift ended to watch for some reason. I don't think either song has been heard by anyone since the end of 1985, and we're not missing anything. (brian) ❧ Live Aid, boasting two huge concerts with a dazzling array of artists on two separate continents, televised across the entire Milky Way. It was at that time that the then-chubby Madonna graced the stage with her new look for the world: floral-print pants. (noël) ❧ Michael Jackson changed a line in the song because it seemed to advocate suicide. The line was originally "There's a choice we're making; we're taking our own lives," but it ended up, "We're saving our own lives." (don) ❧ The Ramones did a kind of lame parody called "Hands Across Your Face," with all the Rodney Bingenheimer quasi-celebrities as extras. (gwynne)

Feminism Despite the fact that the early feminists seem to have mutated into shrill, menopausal, porn-hating, anti-sex victims, you have to admit they were pretty cool when they started out. Gloria Steinem was a fox and they had a message that you could be whatever you wanted to be — revolutionary indeed. (mikki) (See also CROCK-POT, ERA, and WITCH MOVIES)

Fad Diets

The '70s were the heyday of the fad diet, as well as more "reasonable" diet regimens like Weight Watchers. But who the hell wants to hear boring advice like "Eat less food, but be sure to eat a wider variety of relatively low-fat and low-calorie foods"? It's a lot more interesting to hear, say, that I should eat only one thing, or none of certain things, or some elaborate philosophical justification for eating only food overcooked to the point of mushiness. Fortunately for me and millions of diet-obsessed '70s denizens, diet fads — from the Atkins diet to the grapefruit diet to macrobiotics to raw foods diets — provided all that in spades.

Dr. Atkins's Diet Revolution, a bonafide six-million-copy sensation begun in the early '70s (with initial appearances in *Woman's Day* and *Cosmo*, to clue you in on Atkins's main targets), declared that you could lose weight and feel great while eating tons of bacon and eggs, steak and veal, and all the mayo you could hold — as long as you didn't put it on a sandwich, because you were supposed to eat *no carbohydrates*, to begin with, and then a bare maintenance minimum from then on. Y'see, as long as you keep stuffing your body with carbos, it'll never begin consuming itself from the inside. Oh. One slight drawback — the process of your body eating itself from the inside, known as ketosis, produces an abundance of ketones in your breath that smell pretty rank. A small price to pay for prime-rib-induced slimming. And if you miss bread in all its many uses — like for making sandwiches or as pie crusts — Atkins helpfully points out that fried pork rinds work just as well anywhere you might want to use bread.

Carbophobia, if not outright prohibition of the feisty food molecules, was central to some of the '70s more hippie-dippie diet crazes, like macrobiotics. The best introduction to macrobiotics is Sakurazawa Nyoiti's *You Are All Sanpaku*. Sanpaku, he asserts, is a condition — diagnosable by whether or not you can see whites underneath the pupils of your eyes — of desperate ill health. Almost all westerners are doomed to sanpaku because our diet consists of more than brown rice chewed 150 times per mouthful and the occasional tablespoonful of highly overcooked vegetables. To avoid sanpaku, avoid sugar, of course. Also avoid fruit, most liquids and spices, and remember, rotted food is best — it has been partially predigested, so less work for you! The whole macrobiotic system is based on classification of all foods into "yin" and "yang." You're supposed to stick to a rigid 5:1 ratio — but of which to which? Buy the book!

There was an opposing impossible-to-follow, make-you-feel-very-guilty hippie regimen based on raw foods, for which see 1971's *Are You Confused?*, by Paavo Airola. Airola's basic rule: Cooked food is dead food and should be avoided at all costs. The interesting thing about *both* these diets is that they essentially say the diet of most Americans is not only kinda bad but essentially nothing but endless rounds of deadly poisons. How life expectancy has continued to rise for those of us in the West remains a mystery. A special subset of this fad, guaranteed to make the easily suggestible feel queasy, is William Dufty's 1975 *Sugar Blues*. It was Gloria Swanson who first warned him about how bad sugar is, and you wouldn't believe *how* bad — this book blames almost every social and personal evil, from slavery to depression, on sugar. Note that Dufty also translated *You Are All Sanpaku*.

High-fiber diets were also big in the '70s. Yogurt and wheat germ came into their prime as miracle foods. The notion of making your diet consist mostly of a single item, like grapefruit or bananas, swept the credulous. Even the humble hawthorn berry got its own diet book singing its praises.

The most famous '70s diet fad, the Scarsdale diet, wasn't very entertainingly zany — your basic low-carbo, high-protein, no-sweets routine — except for its quasi-totalitarian hints that if you didn't follow *every* instruction to the letter you were wasting your time. Immortality descended upon it when its inventor, Herman Tarnower, was murdered by his assistant/lover Jean Harris. He's been losing weight steadily ever since.

What possesses people to obsess so much about their weight and toss so much lucre at more-or-less obvious monomaniacs, cranks, and quacks? Sociologists can and will debate this in learned tracts for decades, but I think an abundance of wealth, leisure, and general opulence are to blame. Diet crazes are just one more way of God's telling us we have too much time and money on our hands. Neither medical science nor popular fads of the past 2,000 years have added much to the ancient Greek advice about moderation — eat small amounts of a wide variety of things. Exercise more to lose weight. And for God's sake, eat at least six grapefruits a day. (by brian, a very healthy guy)

'50ʌ Revivalʌ like *Grease, Happy Days, Laverne and Shirley, The Outsiders,* Johnny Rockets (and other '50s knock-off diners), *Sha Na Na, American Graffiti, American Hot Wax.* We had a " '50s day," to be followed by an afterschool "sock hop," in the seventh grade. I wore my mom's old clothes and for the first time felt like I looked kind of good. Then some kid threw chocolate milk on me at lunch, and we got into a fistfight. He gave me a black eye, and we both got suspended. (gwynne) (See also *GREASE* and SHA NA NA)

Fiʌh Abe Vigoda from *Barney Miller* has been an underground scenester icon for many years now. You didn't know this? Yeah, he had a lot to do with the onslaught of grunge. (jaz)

Fiʌhnet Purʌeʌ The bigger the purse the better. These were colored plastic net you'd buy at Long's or Clark's Drugs and they worked really well during the New Wave period. They're always in with the grannies, along with the floral plastic variety. (ju-ji)

f

Fizzies They were these tablets that were supposed to be dropped into a glass of water and then sugar added. The flavor I remember was the bright red cherry. They looked like brightly colored Alka-Seltzers and fizzed and actually tasted like them too. (riley)

Flashdance Though *Fame, A Chorus Line,* and *All That Jazz* came first (recognizing of course the other level on which *All That Jazz* exists), it wasn't until *Flashdance,* the TV version of *Fame,* and later *Stayin' Alive* and *Perfect* that the whole dancewear phenomenon occurred full-force. If Jennifer Beals didn't look so good in those cut sweatshirts and legwarmers I doubt women would have gone for it in such a *big* way. This movie really made guys appreciate the ability most fems possess to change clothes in front of someone without letting them see anything. (darby) (See also AEROBICS and BIG)

Fonzie I never did understand Fonzie. Here's this short little Jewish guy and all these girls screaming their heads off over him. But I didn't give a shit, because I was selling a lot of Fonzie T-shirts at my store. (dad) ✿ This is a story I heard secondhand and never verified: Supposedly Henry Winkler's kids didn't think their dad was very cool — I guess they grew up when *Happy Days* was already off the air and just didn't relate to the Fonz. So when the Weezer video came out with all that *Happy Days* imagery, his kids were able to relate something that is cool today (Weezer) to something that was cool then (their dad). Rumor has it that Henry Winkler ran into Weezer, probably at some Planet Hollywood soirée, and he thanked them for making his kids think he was cool. Hey, Fonzie! (darby) (See also T-SHIRT TRANSFERS) ✿

The Fonzie Record I had an 8-track tape called *Fonzie Favorites* with cheesy novelty songs from the '50s like "You Talk Too Much" and "Charlie Brown." Drove my mother crazy by playing it all the time. It had nothing to do with Fonzie other than the picture of him on the tape. (howard) ✿ This *is* a weird fucking record. Besides Fonzie's '50s favorites there are "The Fonzarelli Slide" and "The Fonz Song," and then the "Impressionist Track" which is this Vinnie Barbarino impersonator doing Fonzie saying "Aaaay," "Cool," "Nerd," and "Sit on It!" Obviously made by a completely disturbed individual who is probably an alien. (darby) (See also 8-TRACKS AND UFOs)

Foosball It's lame in comparison to air hockey, but check out that scene in *Il Postino,* which is about as hot as foosball can get. (darby)

Free to Be You and Me It was this '70s liberal variety special TV show (based on the scary liberal kids' book of the same title), hosted by Marlo Thomas, that taught you about being yourself and live and let live through song and dance. The music was eventually released on vinyl. (riley)

Friendship Bracelets Bracelets woven from embroidery floss that you'd knot on your wrist (or ankle for the more adventurous) and wear until they got so scummy that the string disintegrated and it fell off. When summer vacation boredom set in,

The Fonz at his coolest

45 Spiders

Few ever knew them by this name, fewer today even remember them. But once upon a time, these little bits of plastic were so common, they didn't need a name. Their three swirling arms around a central hole allowed you to play a 45-rpm single on a quality hi-fi. Gone the way of spittoons now, look for them as Melrose Avenue jewelry objects. (bruce)

you could make them for all of your friends. If you were too lazy for that, they could be purchased at any hippie craft fair, head shop, or Grateful Dead concert parking lot. (lorraine) (See also ARTS AND CRAFTS)

Funky Phantom A Bicentennial-inspired cartoon about a dead Revolutionary War hero who helped three modern-day teens solve Scooby-Doo-esque mysteries. Funky's catchphrase: "Heavens to Hessians!" (nick) (See also CARTOONS)

Furniture of the '70s Anything made of groovy natural material qualifies: wood, wicker, bamboo, rope, cork, muslin, burlap, leather, suede, or earthenware pottery. In retrospect, this mottled, textured, stippled, sprinkled look kinda makes me feel itchy. Other trends: supergraphics; hippie or post-hippie posters; shag carpeting (in earth tones, full of munchie crumbs and flakes of marijuana dropped while rolling joints); peel-and-stick tiles; do-it-yourself cheapo furniture: board-and-brick bookcases, crate end tables, telephone-cable-spool dining tables (well, some things never change); cotton Indian print bedspreads in muddy curry colors; lots and lots of living plants (hanging in macramé plant slings!) and dried flowers or weeds; octagonal wooden end tables; director's chairs; spineless or unstructured furniture: waterbeds, beanbag chairs, giant floor pillows, inflatable chairs, foam-rubber cube furniture; modular conversation-pit sofas; woodstoves and ceiling fans. (candi) ❧ And we mustn't forget bubble chairs. (howard) ❧ And the primary-colored, pod-shaped chairs with a built-in radio, and the giant hand like the one in which Bobby Sherman sits on the inside flap of *With Love, Bobby* . . . (gwynne)

Furniture of the '80s Hi-tech: Bright colors on a backdrop of black or white, with lots of chrome; occurred often in sushi bars and clubs with neon lighting (as seen in movie *Less Than Zero*). Loft spaces with skylights (as in *Year of the Dragon*); Noguchi paper lamps; white furniture; bleached wood floors; stainless steel kitchen appliances; hi-tech TVs. **Southwestern:** Like living inside of a Georgia O'Keeffe painting. **Memphis Style** (or Pee-Wee eclectic): Budding bohemian postmodernism from Italy (as seen in movie *Ruthless People*). Black hi-tech with dabs of color and a little weirdness. This stuff went from high end to the copycat bargain stores within five years. Eventually all three styles ended up being reduced to a variety of "semi-disposable Scandinavian furniture." **Punk rock:** Can't forget the essential (and cheap) milk crates! (bruce/darby) (See also ART/POSTERS and *MIAMI VICE*)

Futons What was supposed to be a clever Japanese space-saving couch-bed was actually a big saggy ton of dead weight that turned ugly within the first year. People pretended they liked to sleep on hard surfaces because it was the thing to do. Those who hated sushi insightfully steered clear of these contraptions. (jaz)

Fuzzy Steering Wheel Covers These remind me of the fuzzy covers you use for toilet seats. It's a very daring statement today. Back then it was fashionably smart. (darby) (See also CARS)

G-Rated Live Action Brought to us foremostly by those G-rated specialists at Disney. Included such classics as: *Freaky Friday, Benji, Escape to Witch Mountain,* and *Herbie the Love Bug*. You gotta admit, there ain't too many G-rated flicks aside from those of the cartoon variety these days. (jaz)

Games / Toys This section is hard to fill since most of the standard American packaged kid games are still around, but one thing to note is that in the past few years a lot of them have been altered in various ways and reintroduced to the adolescent-conscious consumer. Some just have new packaging, like Don't Break the Ice and Cootie, which is real modern icky. While some have gone back to using their original, old-style packaging, enticing consumers with the better, older version (the one you remember playing as a kid!), there are others, like the board game Candyland, which are completely different games going by the familiar old name. I think there should be a law against that kind of blatant disrespect for our retro! A few other games include Fuzzy Pumper Barber Shop (Playdoh); Mr. Potato Head; Super Strong Plastic Blocks; Tinker Toys; Lincoln Logs (invented by Frank Lloyd Wright's son John Lloyd Wright); Lite-Brite; Spiderwriters; Pen-dul-art; Weebles; dominos; Parcheesi; Perfection; Sorry; Life; Mastermind; Mystery Date; Careers; Clue; Body Language (with Lucille Ball on the box); the Skywriter; the Ungame; Stay Alive; Gunfight at the O.K. Corral; Skyro; Zoom-It; track ball (kids' version of Jai-lai); rock tumblers; Merlin; Skittle Bowling (with the ball on a string you'd swing to knock down the pins); Magic Rocks (that would "grow" in a glass bowl); CB McHaul (a toy truck with a microphone and speaker in it, so you could pretend you were talking on the CB while driving a truck); water games like water ring toss and basketball; Scruples; Trivial Pursuit; Headache; Trouble. Speaking of which, I think the Pop-O-Matic ("Pops the dice, double moves twice") was one of the most important inventions of our time. Also think: charades; blinking contests; breath-holding contests; making yourself dizzy; et cetera. (darby) (See also CHINESE JUMP ROPE, COLORFORMS, EXECUTIVE TOYS, ELECTRONIC HAND-HELD GAMES, HACKEY SACK, MOUSE-TRAP, MR. MIKE, OPERATION, POGO STICKS, RUBIK'S CUBE, SEA MONKEYS, SIMON, SIT 'N' SPIN, SPINNING/HYPERVENTILATING, SPIRO-GRAPH, SUPER ELASTIC BUBBLE PLASTIC, TIN-KER TOYS, TOMY POCKET GAMES, VIBRATING FOOTBALL GAME, VIDEO GAMES, WHAM-O!, and *YES AND KNOW* BOOKS)

Garanimals A brilliant marketing strategy in kids' clothes. All the tops and bottoms had animal labels on them, so all that a kid had to do to look coordinated was to match an ELEPHANT top with ELE-PHANT pants, or whatever. Of course, half the adults in the world could use the assistance of Garanimals in getting themselves dressed and presentable. (candi) ❤ My sister always joked, "Garanimals are for Gardummies." (nina)

Garbage Pail Kids My personal favorite was Haunted Hollis. Stickers with gross-out graphics that took cute little Cabbage Patch Kids and turned them into derelicts. Kind of like what would happen when all those young mothers who adopted Cabbage Patch dolls get hooked on smack and abandon them in a city dump. There were two versions of each sticker in each set, with the only difference being a name change. What a clever way to make more money! These things were cool because they really pissed off your parents and you could stick them on the desk of your enemies when you found one with a matching name! (howard) ♣ Someone told me that Art "Maus" Spiegelman, who created Wacky Packages, came up with the idea for this after some pro-lifer shoved into his hands a pamphlet with a photo of an aborted fetus in a medical pail. If this is so, I wouldn't be the least bit surprised. (steven) (We wholeheartedly recommend you check out the movie of the same name!)

Leif Garrett The Filmography: *The Whispering* ('96); *Dominion* ('95); *The Spirit of '76* ('90); *The Banker* ('89); *Party Line* ('88); *Cheerleader Camp* ('87); *The Longshot* ('86); *Shaker Run* ('85); *Delta Fever* ('87); *Thunder Alley* ('85); *The Outsiders* ('83); *Final Chapter — Walking Tall* ('77); *Kid Vengeance* ('77); *Peter Lundy and the Medicine Hat Stallion* ('77, TV); *Skateboard* ('77);

Family ('76, TV guest appearance); *Flood!* ('76, TV); *God's Gun* ('76); *Three for the Road* ('75, TV series); *The Last Survivors* ('75, TV); *Part 2, Walking Tall* ('75); *Devil Times Five* ('74); *Macon County Line* ('74); *Strange Homecoming* ('74, TV); *Walking Tall* ('73). (katy) ♣ It's hard to imagine Leif not looking so hot, but it's true. And so what happened to this kid heartthrob? Today he appears randomly on retro-celebrating shows but mostly he makes handmade candles that he sells at small kitschy shops in Los Angeles. (ju-ji)

Gass Shoes Back when Bass shoes were the last word in high school style, Kinney's Shoes produced their own version, called Gass shoes. The folks at Kinney's insisted that they were not copies, and that GASS stood for Great American Shoe Store. They weren't that bad, but these Great American Shoes contained one fatal flaw. Like the Bass originals, their name was etched into the sole, in large stylized letters. If you wore them on a snowy day, your footprints betrayed your cheapness and made you the target of put-downs and snowballs. The unlucky became true fashion victims. (bruce) (See also SHOES)

Gas Stations, Full-Service The disappearance of these in the '80s went hand in hand with the mini-mart phenomenon (though Beverly Hills still manages a larger ratio of full-serve to self-serve pumps). With the addition of bulletproof glass and gas station attendants who never leave their cages, today's stations complement our fearful, unsupportive, and disconnected society. (darby)

Game Shows

Most game shows exhibited a profound disgust for humanity. They were, in effect, Mark Goodson/Bill Todman/Josef Mengele productions. Gimmicks, gimmicks, gimmicks. The "winner" on the *The Magnificent Marble Machine,* for instance, got a shot to play a thirty-foot (or so it seemed) oversized pinball machine that took two people to work the flippers. *Beat the Clock* made contestant and celebrity fools grimace grotesquely as they passed water balloons along cheek to jowl in pursuit of Rice-A-Roni, Rolltex Roll-On Paints, Turtle Wax, and other stuff. *Diamond Head* featured a Don Ho theme and a money tube in which the winner tried (alas, vainly) to grab money out of the air as it was blown by at hurricane velocity. *Almost Anything Goes* (a prime-time show) pitted whole towns against each other, competing in such Olympian contests as sliding huge mugs of "beer" down a seventy-foot bar. *High Rollers*, with a pre-*Jeopardy!* Alex Trebek, featured a craps table and oversized dice. Contestants would rattle those dinosaur bones and then a grocery-store checkout conveyor belt would slide 'em back up, easy as can be. Competition deluxe: *$100,000 Name That Tune,* featuring faceless game show host Tom Kennedy, squaring off against *Face the Music* in the same time slot, hosted by TV *Tarzan* Ron Ely. Both shows featured singers who would belt out tunes but insert "la-las" for the words. To wit: "La, La, my belle, these are words that go together well . . ." Name . . . that . . . tune! Who can forget ex-*21* host Jack Barry calling out the values on *Joker's Wild?*: "Jokah, Jokah, . . . no." *Celebrity Sweepstakes* included overweight stars in extremely narrow booths that simulated starting posts in a horse race. Somebody calculated the odds that a star would get a question right and then contestants would bet. Man-tanned ex–*Laugh-in* host Dan Rowan was the perennial favorite, usually at even money or 2:1. The long shot was almost always ditzy platinum-blond starlet Carol Wayne, who rarely came in at less than 150:1. *The Money Maze* was a '70s game show in which one spouse directed another through a lifesize rat maze filled with valuable prizes, thereby increasing already soaring divorce rates by about 100%. Hosted by George Clooney's father, Nick (the brother of singer Rosemary Clooney), who also sang the theme ("Life's just a chance . . ."). This show was just a nightmare to watch. Although they had the option, most couples let the husband descend into the maze while the wife stood next to the host on a dais overlooking the scene. Just beyond the husband's reach were all the riches that his wife, and all the viewers, could see. Nick would smile jocularly as furied insults issued up from the pit below. *Treasure Hunt,* hosted by Geoff Edwards — who had more game shows than McLean Stevenson had sitcoms — always ended the same way. Geoff would introduce Mr. Emile Aurturi III, resident of England, clad in derby and British suit, and ask him: "Emile Aurturi III, did you hide a check for $10,000?" And Mr. Whoopee would reply curtly: "Yes, I did, Geoff," and then wander about the set and pick it up. Bad prizes were called clunkers: a bowl of applesauce, a wheelbarrow of cantaloupes, a chimpanzee wearing a dress. Did it happen or did we dream it? An urban legend holds that a female *Newlywed Game* contestant was asked "Where was the strangest place you ever made whoopee?" The answer came back: "I'm gonna say he's gonna say in the butt." I have met at least four people who claimed to witness this historic TV discussion, but Bob Eubanks, emcee of the *Newlywed Game,* hotly denies it ever took place. Like the theory that Paul McCartney actually died in a 1966 car crash ("I was alone, I took a ride . . ."), this sounds so real it must be true. (nick) ♣ Other important games include: *Love Connection; Dating Game; $10,000 Pyramid; Black Jack; Hollywood Squares* (Paul Lynde, Joan Rivers, Phyllis Diller, Rose Marie, Rich Little among the regulars); *Family Feud* (with Richard Dawson); *Match Game* (one of my faves, with regular Charles Nelson Reilly); *Press Your Luck; Child's Play; Body Language; Card Sharks* . . . Very popular with the celebrities (like talk shows or *Love Boat*–style shows) for lulls or in-between-gig work. (darby) ♣ An FCC ruling in 1969 took the 7 to 8 P.M. time slot away from the networks and gave it to the local stations. The idea was that they would devote the time to local programming. Instead they bought syndicated programs and ran them for rating points. The most popular of these programs were nighttime versions of daytime network game shows. Who can forget those great game show celebrities, who never seemed to do anything else: Kitty Carlisle, Peggy Cass, Richard Dawson, Brett Somers, Arlene Francis, Anita Gillette, Jaye P. Morgan, et cetera. (bruce) ♣ (See also NIPSEY RUSSELL, and check out the Game Show Network, which has more than 50,000 episodes of hundreds of series from 1950 to today, including shows of the '80s like *Super Password; Card Sharks; Blockbusters; Body Language; Tattletales; Child's Play; Tic Tac Dough;* and *The Joker's Wild.)*

Phyllis Diller

Gauchos Ugly corduroy-pant-like things that were horrendously tacky and unflattering (like that ever stopped me). They were like big huge shorts that went to about midcalf, the predecessor to the big clothes thing that all the gang/scenesters are into now. Not to be confused with culottes, which were little skirts with legs. No fashion-conscious girl in the '70s was without this essential clothing item. (jes)

General Hospital Recording

Artists Guitar-wielding soap stars. **Rick Springfield** (Dr. Noah Drake) started off the bunch, becoming a singer on the soap opera and at the same time a singing star in the real world. Next up, kid punk Blackie, played by a young John Stamos ('82), went that route, though no one remembers any songs he did. And finally there was Jack Wagner (alias Frisco Jones — now *Melrose Place*) with his mushy "All I Need" ("is just a little more time, to be sure, what I feel . . ." It's just so damn catchy). The people in charge of that soap still try to make (bad) music an integral part of the show. Today Luke and Sonny own a "House of Blues"–type club in which miscellaneous famous guest stars whom I can't recall sometimes appear. There's also Wallace Kurth's version of rock god Eddie Maine (really an alias for businessman Ned Ashton), and recently that ex-Menudo guy playing Miguel, with thousands of screaming fans during his TV performances and that pukey song "Don't Stop Now." These may sound horrible, but compared to *The Young and the Restless's* Michael Damian (Danny Romalotti) and his *Amazing Technicolor Dreamcoat* nonsense, *G.H.* fuckin' rocks. ABC soaps rule. (darby) ✤ Totally. (selina) ✤ Fuck you both. (noël) (See also LUKE AND LAURA and RICK SPRINGFIELD)

Andy Gibb As a little girl I used to listen to Kasey Kasem every Saturday when he did the top-twenty countdown, and one summer (around '76) Andy Gibb had the #1 song in the nation almost every week ("Love Is Thicker Than Water," "You Are My Everything," and others). ✤ Andy's soothing, whiney preteen angst tunes were the best to make up dances to, besides Olivia's "Totally Hot" and Michael Jackson's "Off the Wall." Andy, I still miss you, and your shadow dancing. (ju-ji)

G.I. Joe By the time G.I. Joe got life-like hair and a kung fu grip he couldn't fight Germans and Japanese anymore. In the '70s the military was so discredited, G.I. Joe wasn't even a soldier; instead he became a part of the Adventure Team. Eventually he shrank in size to 3½" tall and fought terrorists. By 1980 he fought aliens. He regained his potency, and his full ten inches, after the Persian Gulf War. But it's not how big they are, it's how you play with them. (bruce/noël) (See also TOYS)

Girl Scouts Selling Thin Mints in front of Gemco in cool uniforms with sashes — not those lame vests they wear for merit badges now. I was kicked out of one Girl Scout troop because my mom got into some sort of tiff with the troop leader. To this day I'm a little unclear on the specifics, but it had something to do with the Girl Scout slumber party, which was at our house. From then on the troop leader would always yell at me and wouldn't let her daughter come over to play anymore. My next Girl Scout troop was where I met the girl who was to be my best friend ever since. We always had to sit in the punishment chair and were usually ostracized by the rest of the girls on all of the Scout outings and camping trips. We didn't care because we hated them, too, and went through their tents when they were off singing or whatever. (lorraine)

Girls Just Wanna Have Fun No, not the super hit by Ms. Lauper, but the movie. It starred various unknowns at the time but spawned three gargantuan starlets: Shannen Doherty, Helen Hunt, and Sarah Jessica Parker. It was sort of a *Flashdance* meets *Dance Party USA* and my sister watched it over and over on Betamax. (morgan)

Girly Posters Samantha Fox, Lynda as Wonder Woman, all of the Angels, Jacqueline Bissett, Bo Derek, Stevie Nicks, Linda Ronstadt. (bobby) (See also FARRAH FAWCETT-MAJORS)

Glitter/Glam Rock Certainly, the only worthwhile musical movement of the '70s, except punk. I suppose it began with Bowie, The Sweet, T. Rex, Gary Glitter, and, stateside, the New York Dolls, and maybe Alice Cooper. How the hell can Stone Temple Pilots sell a billion records when it would be much smarter for someone to find that first Dolls LP? It was all *so* much more interesting and exciting. How does the youth of today survive? Where *is* the justice? Glam kinda mutated into a joke, merging with bad metal guitar sometime in the mid-'80s. But when it was good . . . I mean, David Johansen *knew* how to wear high heels! The New York Dolls *knew* how to pull off thigh-high vinyl platforms! Who the hell are *you*? (skylaire)

G.L.O.W. (Gorgeous Ladies of Wrestling) A dim memory, frighteningly made-up hellcats clawing each other's eyes out and then singing and dancing to the show's theme song at the end in front of the giant neon G.L.O.W. sign. Reform school rejects or role models? I could never quite decide. (skylaire)

Go Ask Alice In the made-for-TV-movie landscape of the '70s, *Go Ask Alice* was *IT.* Jamie Smith-Jackson became my blueprint for teen girl-hood after the ABC movie, one of the first and still the best of the kids-getting-into-drugs-at-the-high-school genre, was broadcast in 1973. The movie is perfect — Alice gets mixed up with the stoner kids after they dose her with acid-laced soda ("Button, button, who's got the button?") at a party, while a bad cover of Traffic's "Dear Mr. Fantasy" oozes on the soundtrack. Soon she's slimmed down thanks to speed, replaced her cheerful plaids and carefully curled locks with superfine flares and floppy hats, run away from home, gotten really strung out, and encountered Andy Griffith as the weary "priest who knows about kids." Home again, trapped between her perkily naïve parents (her mom blithely overhears this exchange: "Hey, Alice, why don't you get off your high horse?" "Or your horse high!") and the ruthless kids who just won't let her get straight, Alice struggles to save herself. After being dosed while baby-sitting and hospitalized as a result, she's reunited with her whiny, pre-drugs best friend and ultrasquare boyfriend — the semiotics of this movie definitely run counter to its anti-drugs message. The movie ends with a freeze-frame of Alice poised to start a new school year as her mom's voice informs us that Alice died of "an overdose of drugs" shortly after her sixteenth birthday. To quote an ABC press release, "How 'mellow' is a down? How 'soft' are the drugs? Go ask Alice. I think she'll know." Perfection. And Jamie Smith-Jackson's performance as Alice, complete with diary-entry narration, remains a definitive image of teen angst. Currently Jackson makes art ("altar-like box constructions") and, in a sublime '70s union, is married to Michael Ontkean (*The Rookies, Making Love, Twin Peaks*). (allison) (See also DEPRESSED-DRUGGIE-GIRL MOVIES)

The Godfather No one wants to tackle this entry, it's just too epic, what can we say? Perhaps it's in my blood (my dad says my great-grandfather worked for Bugsy Siegel), but personally this movie ignited in me an out-of-control lust for the decadent and fascinating world of the Hollywood version of the gangsters. Italian, dark, sexy, rich, scheming, vindictive, submission, aggression, violence, and, what's most important, of course, "the family"! Well, I also learned to love the Asian and black and Hispanic gangsters as well. But no matter how many times I watch it, the second Al Pacino appears on that screen I nearly cream my panties. (darby) (See also *BLUE VELVET*)

The Gong Show Chuck Barris introduced the Unknown Comic, the flounder dance, and greatly influenced modern-day performance art with this cool talent show. Spin-offs: *The $1.98 Beauty Contest* and *The Gong Show Movie.* (howard) ♣ We all know someone who made it on the show, even if it was just Rerun from *What's Happening!* executing his far-out breakin' moves. Started in 1976, this was an amateur talent contest in which celebs would judge contestants and, after pretending to control themselves, give a really bad act the "gong," which was sorta their version of the cane. They'd always throw in one or two people who were actually talented to win the prize — though I can't recall what it was, surely something silly. Lotsa camps and schools would hold their own similar *Gong*-style talent shows for a while during its peak. It was the epitome of bad TV and a good example of what could pass for entertainment at the time. It seems they're always trying to bring this baby back — and who would mind exchanging one talk show for it? (darby) 🐾

Gravy Train This was dog food that claimed that when you added water, it would make its own gravy. I think they just discovered that a bag of dog food made a bunch of dog food dust from all the kibbles rubbing against each other, and that this stuff sort of coagulated into a paste when you got it wet. American creative marketing at its best. (jon) ♣ Made famous by their commercial with the dog chasing the Gravy Train covered wagon; something akin to chasing the dragon. (ju-ji)

Grease Besides *Rocky Horror,* no movie encouraged so many revisits by preteen girls. It was quite common for many of them to have seen this flick more than twenty times, know the complete dialogue and dance movements, and actually get into trading cards. (darby) ♣ The scene was third grade. Last day of school. I was wearing my John Travolta tight black T-shirt and pretending I was Danny Zucko. I had seen *Grease* twenty times in the movie theater and was about to pounce on my Sandy — a young girl by the name of Beth — 'cause, hey, I had three whole months to live it down. Jump forward to ninth grade. Drama. Doing the play *Grease.* I was

Johnny Casino. Sang "Born to Hand Jive." Got all the little girls dancing. I'm such a fucking moron. What the fuck was I thinking? (howard) ♣ *Grease II* was *way* better than *Grease,* no matter what anyone says. When Michelle Pfeiffer sang about her "Cool Rider," I connected. It creeped me out when I found out Maxwell Caulfield was married to Nanny from *Nanny and the Professor,* especially since she was like one hundred years older than him, but I got over it. (katy) (See also '50s REVIVALS, OLIVIA NEWTON-JOHN, and URBAN COWBOY) 🐾

Great Space Coaster "It's the Great Space Coaster, get on board! On the Great Space Coaster, we'll explore! Come and ride a fantasy, to a place where dreams fly fast and free!" Gary Gnu rocked, and the prissy pink bird looked like a toilet brush. (morgan) ♣ The only thing really worthwhile about this puffy-character-littered kids show was "No Gnews is Good Gnews," where a foam rubber gnu puppet gave a newscast of absolute irrelevancies, successfully prophesying the current status of the news media. (jon)

Groupies Once upon a time, there were girls — and occasionally guys — who took pride in the mere act of bedding rock superstars. They became celebrities in their own right and honed this ability to an art. Some even turned their experiences into art, like the legendary penis-sculpting Plaster Casters, and the groupie's answer to Uncle Remus, the infamous Cherry Vanilla, and Miss Pamela Des Barres. Now everyone has to hide behind some kind of bogus career motive — their own band, booking/promoting a venue, writing for *Ben Is Dead* ... And the clothes aren't as good. (gwynne) ♣ Of all the various shatterlings of the candy-assed world of glam rock, perhaps none is still as interesting as groupies. Just porking the gi-tar man wasn't enough. Like vestal virgins of some cult, many of these folks not only chased the bands across the planet, but perfected a certain scary style. (sky-laire) (See also the best retro groupie book, *I'm with the Band*)

The G-Spot Yet another thing men couldn't find. You can still buy this 1981 bestseller, the book that sent everyone scurrying into their own and other people's vaginas on a vision quest for the secret button. The clitoris became passé. Rumor was if you stumbled upon it, things got very gushy. (amy)

Gummi Bears Rising from the ashes of other childhood delicacies like Swedish Fish and Cola Bottles, Gummi Bears stormed the candy market in the early '80s in assorted flavors and colors. There are a number of different manufacturers of this chewy stuff, and depending on which brand, it was either rock hard or supersoft. (noël) (🏃) Also found in the newer renditions such as Gummi Life Savers and Gummi Worms.

Gunne Sax This is another one of those blocked-out memories. *Little House* was big on TV and natural colors were in. All the temple and church girls were wearing them, including me. Frilly, prissy, often high-collar, long-sleeved, cream-colored, lace-trimmed blouses with faux pearl buttons and classic-style flowery long skirts. Parents must have been so happy that we allowed ourselves to look that conservative. Trends can be so demeaning. (darby) Similar brands: Sweet Baby Jane, Organically Grown, Biba. Similar fabric: Indian cotton gauze.

h

Hackey Sack A way-too-hippie type of foot juggling game that was big early to mid-'80s, mainly among the Deadhead set. I have nothing but scorn for hackey sacks. (ju-ji)

Hairbrushes Just a few that were superpopular at the time: those round curling brushes that were big with the blow-dryer scene — think Jaclyn Smith; those now-standard plastic bristle Goody brushes; those thick '70s full hairbrushes that dad used with Bryl Creme; and those brushes with the pink rubber bottom and the white plastic brush bristles — the whole brush portion slid off the handle, though I'm still not sure why. Maybe it was so you could just replace the brush part when it was worn out and not have to throw the handle away? Or perhaps it was thought to be easier to clean. Well, number one, they'd sometimes slide off while I did my hair. Second, these things seemed to want to store hair grime in them to the point that a favorite nervous habit of mine used to be scraping the once-white now-brown cruddy bristles with my fingernails to get them clean. (ju-ji) (See also COMBS)

Halley's Comet Everyone looked for it on camping trips when it was passing through in 1986, but it wasn't really anything more than a fuzzy blob unless you had a telescope. More of an excuse to get drunk in the outdoors with a date and for producing comet-themed baseball hats. (wendy)

Hallmark Stores Tootsie Roll banks, Life Saver books, Ziggy boxes, the heart section, stuffed pillows, satin . . . (lisa r.) ❖ Also Coachhouse Gifts, the #1 shop for girls — especially for gift buying. Pins, unicorns, mugs, posters, everything *General Hospital* . . . I think they're gone now — at least from the major metropolitan areas. (ju-ji) ❖ Paper Moon Stationery — '80s supergraphics. Envelopes, cards, stationery, memo books, address books. Very pricey, encouraged me to shoplift. (laurel) ❖ Before these came along, cards were either dorky things you sent Grandma or poorly drawn things on recycled paper that looked like outtakes from the comic strip *Cathy*. Paper Moon's greatest contribution to culture was the blank card. (bruce)

Halloween Candies Razor blades in apples, cyanide in yer chocolate bar, and PCP-flavored candy. (wendy) ❖ Since it wasn't safe anymore to get unwrapped candy, M&M Mars came out with "fun-size" candies in 1971. Easier for Mom (until she had to check them for needle holes), but more of a gyp for kids. (bruce)

Halloween Costumes Prepackaged all-plastic supermarket costumes started in the mid-'60s. Many people wanted costumes in bright colors and very reflective. The big company to do this, Ben Cooper, had the all-important marketing contract with Walt Disney and Hanna-Barbera. Of course, aside from the mask, the costumes barely resembled the characters. Popular with wimpy kids who used character lunch boxes. (bruce)

Marvin Hamlisch Show tune–making *uber*-nerd. Penned a number of memorable '70s showbiz jingles, including "The Entertainer" (theme from *The Sting*), "The Way We Were," "Nobody Does It Better," "What I Did for Love" (showstopper from *A Chorus Line*), "They're Playing Our Song," and so forth. Took himself very seriously on TV talk show interviews. (thomas c.) ✿ Loved by Gilda Radner's Lisa Loopner. (darby)

Hands Across America I think this was some communist plot to take over the world, but I might have been too young. (ju-ji) ✿ Oh sure, We Are the World was a good cause, but what about all the needy here at home? USA for Africa answered with Hands Across America. This supercause sequel was to be an immense, sponsored chain of hand-holding that would stretch from coast to coast that summer and join the whole country in a single touchy-feel of hope and caring. A stirring new theme song was written for the event, and millions were spent buying up three solid minutes of ad time to premiere it during the Super Bowl. But then Michael Jackson's song "We Are the World" was chosen to be the theme song of all USA for Africa events, including the upcoming Hands Across America. The Moonwalker had a lot of clout in those days, and the Super Bowl ad was redubbed with Michael's divine song, as was the entire promotional campaign for the event. The nation at large first learned of Hands Across America during the halftime show at Super Bowl XIX and collectively groaned as it heard "We Are the World" played for the fifty thousandth time. The Hands Across America song was finally released a mere month before the event (does anyone out there have a copy?), but few took notice. Fewer still actually joined hands, so their line was pathetically strengthened in many spots with hundreds of miles of red ribbon. Maybe it *was* a communist plot after all. (bruce)

Handwriting Analysis This was very big in the '70s. I met this lady on Olvera Street in Los Angeles who was a handwriting analyst to the stars in the '70s. She has lots of great stories and her whole entire little booth is lined with pictures of Erik Estrada. Handwriting analysis was so *sacred!* I remember trying so hard to write perfectly when I first had it done. (laurel) ✿ I remember this huge Univac-looking thing at various trade shows. It was often manned by a sad-looking old man who promised you a scientific analysis of your scribble via his Space Age wonder. The thing was comically old then, and we just laughed at his pathetic punch cards. (bruce)

Happy Days Out of all the TV shows I watched as a youth, this one had the biggest impact. I can remember now how we'd discuss the show in detail each day in elementary school, during lunch, as we waited in line, through notes and whispers. I didn't really remember until now how much we bonded with it. I sometimes wish I was smarter than all that, but alas, it was many many years until I had larger concepts of existence. (darby) (See also CHACHI and FONZIE)

Sunday, Monday . . .

Hand Games

One thing that never changes about kids is that they're easily bored. If not constantly occupied with something, they start climbing the walls. The only thing more dangerous than a bored fifth-grader is a bored fifth-grader after eating one of those huge Pixie Stix that came in the three-foot plastic straws. In a simpler era, before Mortal Kombat II, we had to come up with cheap ways to fill the time between feedings, especially when our parents wouldn't let us watch TV. This often meant resorting to playing games with our hands. We played different ones depending on what state we lived in, what city, what school (or McMartin school) we went to, and the crowd we hung out with, but for the most part these games were universal. Actually, not all of them were really games; they could also be creative expressions, functional tools, and a children's sign language of sorts. The face and hands are often the best tools for expressing oneself — when one can't find the right words, or just hasn't learned them yet. Here's a few of our favorites: (jessy/darby/wendy)

The Arm Chair

Make a chair of arms by holding your wrist with one hand and grabbing on to the other person's wrist with your other hand, while your partner's doing the same thing. Can be useful in emergencies. More fun to ride in than to make.

Arm-Chair Dreadlocks

Make funky, nappy mini-dreads out of someone's hairy arm by rubbing circles with a spit-wet palm into the top region of the arm near his or her bent elbow.

Bloody Knuckles

Make fists and put them palms-down in front of you. Your opponent does the same, so your fists are nearly touching. Then whoever's turn it is tries to smash the other person's fists, while the opponent tries to pull away in time to avoid having his hands bashed into bloody stumps. When you missed, though, it was your turn for punishment. Like "hot hands" for kids in parochial school.

Cheek Pop

Make a popping noise by putting your finger in your mouth and then popping it out. Hard to master, but, just like riding a bike, you never forget it.

Chinese Pee-Pee Joke

You put your hands together and pretend it's a refrigerator and then you open the door, take out a Coke, sip it, then return it to the imaginary Frigidaire. Here's the hysterical part: you speak with a heavy Oriental accent and say, "Me Chinese, me play joke, me put pee-pee in your Coke." Ha ha, you sure fooled them.

Crack Your Nose

Tell someone you can crack your nose bone. Put your hands together and cover your nose, and secretly put your thumbnail under your front teeth. Then while you move your hands as if you were actually cracking your nose you snap your thumbnail and make a *crack* sound. A totally convincing gross-out when done correctly.

Flicking People in the Nose

When you trick someone into looking at his shirt by saying, "Ooo! What's that on your shirt?" or by saying, "Smell my hand," and when he looks down, you flick his nose with your finger. *Ahaaa!*

Flipping Off

Raise middle finger with all other fingers held down with the thumb. ✣ The next stage is having your ring and index fingers partly raised. Really hard-core when accompanied by phrases like "Sit 'n' spin!" ✣ Do the same gesture but have the inside of your hand face out. ✣ The Judd (as in Nelson): Face your hand in flipping-off position toward the ground and say, "Can you hear this? Do you want me to turn it up?" Also rubbing your eye or scratching your ear with your middle finger is a good way to flip off an authority figure without getting caught. ✣ Snapping your thumbnail under your front teeth. There's the Italian one where you put one hand in the elbow crease of the other and bend it up. Extraharsh if you complete it with the basic bird or finger/tooth combination like the older sister did in *Poltergeist.* ✣ Brush the back of your fingers under your chin. ✣ Hold up three fingers and say "Read between the lines." ✣ The first time someone showed me how to flip someone off they told me to keep all my fingers up except the middle one — a sort of opposite fuck-you. When I (darby) was forced to stay in my room I remember sitting on my bed looking out the window, down at all the big kids playing in the parking area, and feeling mighty superior flipping them off this way.

Gimme Five

Gimme five, on the side, in the hole, you got soul! ❖ Gimme five, up high, down low, too slow! ❖ Gimme five, way up high, gimme a nickle, tickle, tickle! (That scary one Jes came up with.) ❖ Gimme five (hold out both hands, they give you ten), here's your change (slap 'em in the face). ❖ Walk toward your friend and pretend you're gonna give him a high five. Miss his hand up high, then slap his hand as it comes back down to his side. (Note: There's an infinite number of these.)

Handshakes

Put arm out to shake someone's hand, then pull it away just as he or she is gonna grab it and slick back your hair with it instead. ❖ Tickle someone with your middle finger while you shake that person's hand to let him know just how interested you are. ❖ Variations are really up to you, but some super combination shakes to mix 'n' match might be the wrist shake (hold on to the other person's wrist), the homeboy shake (grab the heel of the other person's hand, your fingers just above his wrist, with thumbs crossed on top), and the finger shake (hook the end of your curled fingers with his). Add in a finger gun or snap and you can start your own exclusive club. The person with the most smooth moves per shake wins. Has semisexual connotations — a needed outlet for male-to-male contact.

Hand/Underarm Farts

Get the suction going, maybe add a little spit or sweat for good measure, and liven up your math class with disgusting boy noises. I tried and tried but was never agile enough to execute these classic stunts.

Indian Wrist Burn

Grab hold of a friend's arm with both hands and twist *hard* — like wringing out a towel. Then quickly reverse the motion. Repeat rapidly. It'll burn like a mother, and he or she will want to punch your face in.

Mumblety-Peg

Spread your fingers out on a flat surface. Get a sharp knife (or perhaps a twig or something for starters) and stab the space between your thumb and index finger, then stab the space between your index finger and your middle finger, then between your middle and ring finger, then between your ring finger and pinky. Then do it in the other direction. Eventually you gotta go really fast. Then, with practice, try it with your eyes closed. Scare the girlie girls with this amazing feat. We find that boys who perform this trick these days are incredibly agile with their hands and fingers, and have a sense of confidence. Practice, practice, practice!

Patty-Cake Games

More than any other game, patty-cake games had the most possible variations. Deviations depend on your geographic location, ethnic and economic upbringing, and the year you were born. Our most memorable are Eli Eli Chicali Chicali, Miss Mary Mack, Down by the Banks of the Hanky Panky, Say, Say Oh Playmate, and Miss Susie.

Pinky Pressure

Bite the tips of your pinky fingers until they hurt. As soon as you take them out of your mouth, hook the tips together and pull — *hard!* If you do it right, it will hurt like nothing else.

Pinching

The monkey bite — the most painful pinch in the history of the time. Make a regular fist, but instead of having your thumb resting on top of your index finger, you stick it under your index finger, so that it is pointing out between your index and middle. When you get some skin between your thumb and middle finger and squeeze with your thumb, it should hurt like hell.

Punching

"Let's see who can punch the softest. You go first." Someone punches you really soft. Then it's your turn and you hit really hard and say, "I lose."

Quarter Elbow Catch

Made famous by Fonzie's klutz cousin on *Happy Days,* who was trying to get into the *Guinness Book* (which, for the record, didn't exist at that time in real-world history). When the episode appeared on TV for the first time, my entire elementary school was engrossed with the game. What you do is bend your arm and point your elbow out in front of you with your palm facing up, and place some quarters at your arm's bend. Then you quickly move your hand down in a swift motion to catch the quarters. You keep adding more quarters as your skill improves. Mucho fun.

Some Girls Sit Like This

Some girls sit like this (make two little legs crossed together with your middle and index fingers), and some girls sit like *that* (make two legs spread wide apart). The girls that sit like that (make the wide legs) get *that* (flip 'em the standard middle finger) like *that* (snap your finger).

Spider Pushups

Put the fingertips of both hands together with palms apart and put your palms together, then repeat. Then ask somebody, "Do you know what this is? It's a spider doing pushups on a mirror. Hahahha!"

String Games

Cat's cradle, kitty's whiskers, canoe, ladder, rabbit, glasses, butterfly, witch's broom. (Too hard to explain on paper — ask a girl.)

Talking With Someone Else's Hands

Hold your arms behind your back while a friend slips his arms through yours. The friend makes your gestures and usually talks and says really stupid things that you lip-synch to.

Willies

Stick a moistened finger into some hapless person's ear and swish it all around. Icky!

Other Miscellaneous

Includes Rock, Paper, Scissors; snapping (to do it while you're dancing is the ultimate Retro Hell); making the Vulcan sign; church and steeple; This Little Piggy; mercy; hand shadows; thumb wrestling; Johnny Whoops.

The Happy Hooker Also known as Xaviera Hollander. When I was in the sixth grade this boy brought some *Happy Hooker* paperbacks to school, and he and this other guy and I would read them in the library (hidden inside other books, of course). They got me really horny, and I wished either of them would try to have sex with me. I tried to hint around a lot, but they acted like it would never have occurred to them. (gwynne) ♣ There was a nice picture, a couple years back, of Xaviera in the *National Enquirer* wearing a bikini on the beach and looking a few hundred pounds scary. (ju-ji)

Hard and Soft '70s people loved to divide things into "hard" and "soft" categories, which usually meant "bad" and "not so bad." For instance, there were addictive hard drugs, like heroin or speed, and recreational soft drugs, like marijuana or Valium. People spoke of hard pornography, as opposed to soft porn, the kind of stuff printed in *Playboy*. Rock and roll split into hard rock and soft rock, and TV newscasters were accused of covering fewer hard news stories and giving more time to soft news. (candi)

Hardware Wars That great *Star Wars* parody short film with a Princess Leia with real buns on the side of her head and flying toasters. I recall they even showed this to us in my English class — why, I'm not sure. (darby) ♣ It was the creation of a small-time filmmaker who became the Weird Al of film with this 1977 short. Alas, he tried to parlay its success with two awful shorts, *Pork Lips Now* and a

Close Encounters rip-off. Where is he now? (bruce) ✿
The distributor of the short was Pyramid Films, out of Southern California, and their primary market was and remains grade and high schools. So, it's very possible they pushed this picture to local 16mm film bookers at schools and/or offered it as a package deal. As for the filmmaker, his name is Ernie Fosselius, Jr., and he comes from the Bay Area. He made a go of it in Hollywood after his short film parodies were noticed, but his career as a director never really took off. However, you can still occasionally spot his credit as a sound recordist/editor on cable flicks from time to time, so I assume he's a working pro. (d.h. coleman)

FYI: In our massive retro research we discovered Michael Weise's Web page recently (he was the producer and cameraman for *Hardware Wars*), and he was selling copies of the mini-flick for $19.95 plus shipping! The tag line read: "Hardware Wars: a saga of romance, rebellion, and household appliances!" The rest of his site was pushin' some business seminar shit he's doing today. There was actually a remastered release of this flick, to coincide with the re-release of the Star Wars trilogy, which got minor retro attention. ✿

Hardy Boys/Nancy Drew Once-foxy Parker Stevenson and Shaun Cassidy are now bow-wows. The end. (ju-ji) ✿ Ellery Queen for the playground set. They were series of books about crime-solving kids (predating *Scooby-Doo* and *Encyclopedia Brown*) that we all read because our parents had read them when they were children. The Hardy boys were two brothers (for young adult males to read — these were written in the '30s — what wholesome, all-American boy would be caught dead reading *Nancy Drew*?), and Nancy was the detectin' apple of her father's eye. Sometimes she had a different color hair and was always aided by her gal pals and her trusty boyfriend, Ned Nickerson, who endured all of his romantic plans being preempted by Nancy's nose for a mystery. Not once did Ned ever try anything more daring than a congratulatory peck after a tough mystery had been solved by our heroine; that is, until someone had the bright idea to come out with The New Nancy Drew/Hardy Boys Collection some time in the '80s — then Ned and Nancy had fights all the time, as well as passionate interludes in attempts to relate to the more modern, less innocent young adult readers of today. (lorraine) (See also BESTSELLING BOOKS and BOOKS [KIDS/YOUNG ADULT]) ✿

Harlem Globetrotters All-black basketball team from Chicago actually founded in 1927 but made famous via TV in the '70s. Gimmick was that they were the ultimate pranksters and super ballplayers. There were actually two teams, with Meadowlark Lemon and Curly Neal leading one and Geese Ausbie and Marques "The Magician" Haynes leading the other. They only got together as the stars of their TV show *The Harlem Globetrotters Popcorn Machine* and as guest stars on *Sesame Street* and *Scooby-Doo*. (darby) ✿ They always played the same team, the Washington Generals, who were mostly white and always lost. (noël)

Harvey's Bristol Cream The nicest-sounding and -looking resident of my parents' liquor cabinet. Bottoms up, Harv! (pete)

Tom Hatton Popeye was another one of those cartoons I hated, but because I was addicted to TV, I inevitably watched hours of it a week. Tom Hatton was the sweatered Popeye expert who, every Sunday, would speak to us between these cartoons on *The Tom Hatton Popeye Show*. After that he'd play some old movie on the *Family Film Festival* and sometimes have a guest from the movie visit and they'd talk after commercial breaks. Today you can hear him in L.A. doing celebrity gossip on KNX 1070 news radio — the AM station where the guy who was the voice for Cecil in the superpsychedelic cartoon *Beany and Cecil* gives the news. (darby) ✿ The King of the Squiggles appeared briefly in the Dan Aykroyd/Chevy Chase piece of shit *Spies Like Us*. (howard)

h

Hawaiian Shirts From '79 to '81 these were worn by all types in my school. It was a pitiable mix of these, sailor shirts, Izods, Hang Ten, and those shirts with the rainbows across the chest. (darby) (See also SURF CLOTHING and TUBE TOPS)

Headbands Rolled à la Pat Benatar and Loverboy. The hot-aerobics-instructor look was in! Also in this category were stretch terry-cloth headbands and wristbands, for that tennis-pro look. (pleasant) ❧ Not only of the sweatband variety, but thin ribbons of various colors banded together with gold elastic and tied around the head as a fashion statement. Unbelievable but true — I wore them a couple of times and thought it very daring. (darby) (See also AEROBICS; OLIVIA NEWTON-JOHN; RIBBONS; and watch the movies *Perfect*, *Fame*, and *Xanadu*)

Head Shop Accessories Black-light posters Scotch-taped to the walls, incense burners, Lava Lamps, bongs and pipes, Odors Away drops on the light bulbs to camouflage pot smells, velvet paintings, rock posters, et cetera. (pleasant) ❧ Is it because pot smokers are so damn slow that these shops never seem to change? (darby)

Heathers The only movie I've seen more times than *The Breakfast Club* — I would come home from school every day and watch this until it was time for *Request Video* to come on and wish that I could kill off the popular crowd one by one, just like Winona Ryder and Christian Slater did in the movie. One of the many great things about this flick was how the dialogue coined its own slang ("How very" and "What's your damage?" to spout a couple). I usually didn't watch the last fifteen minutes though, because Winona chickens out and saves the school from Christian's boiler room bomb and watches as he blows himself up instead — what a waste! (lorraine)

Heavy Metallers These folks consistently ruled the '80s, which is *why* there was alternative music then. They took the rock posturing of Kiss and left the sense of humor behind. Heavy metallers were so clueless it was difficult to like anything about them, regardless of their occasional hook. They inspired headbangers, suicides, and, of course, Tipper Gore. I went out with one who had that long shag and talked about Randy Rhoads a lot. Actually I did kinda bang my head on Sabbath and Mötley Crüe. (ju-ji) ❧ We called 'em boogie idiots. (gwynne) ❧ A noteworthy motivator for the creation of *Ben Is Dead*. (darby) (See also SATAN)

Hell H-E-double toothpicks! (jes) ❧ ... double hockey sticks! (jaz) ❧ Where we're all headed, with AC/DC playing in the background. (noël) ❧ 7734 on the calculator. (bridget)

Motivation for Spïnal Tap and *Ben Is Dead*

Hello Kitty Sanrio (1979) is the Japanese manufacturer of Hello Kitty and all her pals: the Little Twin Stars, Tuxedo Sam, My Unico, My Melody, Robbie Rabbit, plus numerous ever-arriving new characters (the second wave starting with KeroKeroKeropi) that I no longer have the endurance to keep up with. These cartoony characters appear on every exorbitantly priced school item (pencils, smelly erasers, stationery, stickers, tape dispensers, you name it) that any young girl could ever dream of. Entire stores (and even a theme park in Japan where Sanrio is equivalent to Disney) are still dedicated to the jewelry, stuffed animals, and purses/bags/ boxes/containers to store all of these precious treasures in. The desire for Hello Kitty and Co. (and we *did* jones for these items — the mere scent of the Sanrio store was enough to bring tears of ecstasy to fourth-grade eyes) bridged the consumer gap between when a little girl wants toys and when she starts obsessing over clothes. However, there are many who can never bear to part with the serene childhood security/rapture that comes from owning said accessories and harbor/nurture this fixation for the rest of their days (which Sanrio is only too happy to provide for, with many items geared toward a more "adult" audience). I'd continue extolling the virtues, but I'm on my way out the door to go buy a new battery for my Little Twin Stars ring watch. (lorraine) (See also PATTI AND JIMMY)

Hesher (also Heshen or Hesh) A term used to define that guy with the long scraggly hair who lived at the end of the block, always seen in flannel or rocker T-shirts; who lived with a divorced mom who often worked; who would likely ditch school and have stoner blacklight parties in his room with the scraggly hesher chicks. Lotsa Doors and Zeppelin, marijuana and 'ludes, and definitely an old muscle car if at all possible. (See also HEAVY METALLERS, THE MULLET, SHARK TOOTH NECKLACES, and the Dead Milkmen Song "Bitchen Camaro")

Jon-Erik Hexum A studmo type introduced to audiences via the 1983 made-for-TV movie *Making of a Male Model*, starring Joan Collins as the owner of a modeling agency. He became a hot young star while co-starring with Jennifer O'Neill in a weekly series called *Cover Up* ('84–'85) in which they played dashing detectives. (allison)

Hickeys They were fun to give but a curse to receive. I wore turtlenecks to cover them up, even in the summer. And if my parents asked what the hell *that* was, the answer was always that the faithful curling iron burned me (again). (jes) What *was* the concept of using a frozen spoon? Other excuses: wrestling with an octopus, hit by stray golfballs. (jaz)

The Hillside Strangler Every kid in L.A. County had nightmares about this guy. I can't count how many times I double and triple checked to make sure the house was all locked up. (darby) I wasn't in Los Angeles when this was going down, but it seems that almost every kid anywhere had some local mass murderer to fear in the post-Manson '70s. (bruce) (See also *THE NIGHT STALKER* and SON OF SAM)

The Hip Hypnotist The Hip Hypnotist was a big fat lady named Pat Collins who'd dress in '70s sequined muu-muu-ish dresses, wear lotsa makeup, and cash in on the vacationing middle class in Vegas and Reno. My mom and I went when my mom was visiting me in my scary boarding school near the Nevada border. She actually went under the spell of the Hip Hypnotist and probably barked like a dog, but I was so embarrassed I guess I blocked it out. After the show she did that trendy thing of getting hypnotized by Pat to never *ever* smoke again — which lasted about a week. (darby)

John Hughes

h

One of the most prolific contributors to the once-funny, subversive, and perverse periodical *National Lampoon,* John Hughes was, at some point in the Reagan '80s, captured by guerrilla conservative forces, killed, and replaced by an *Invasion of the Body Snatchers*–type pod whose primary purpose was to extol, via his films, the virtues of midwestern conformity and Reagan-Bushesque family values.

1985's nerd wish-fulfillment epic *Sixteen Candles* demonstrated the same anarchistic aplomb of his *Lampoon* work, established the reputations of otherwise one-dimensional young actors known as the Brat Pack (particularly Molly Ringwald and Anthony Michael Hall), and earned him the reputation of Teen Angst Guru. But follow-up *Weird Science,* another triumph of the nerd fantasy involving two boys' initiation into studhood through a computer-generated beautiful woman, foreshadowed things to come with its wussy ending. Once the said woman's initial purpose is fulfilled, she tearfully bids adieu to the two teens, as they are now popular enough to get girlfriends their own age.

The Breakfast Club is a wolf in sheep's clothing, packaged as a film advocating tolerance for "different" people, but sneakily turning into a convincing argument for conformity. It is therefore even more offensive than if it had been blatant in its intent from the get-go. Five teens from opposing cliques are forced to share an eight-hour detention, and though they learn how to get along, it is still the macho guys, the Jock and the Greaser, who wind up getting chick action, while it is the Nerd's fate to write the paper for everyone. Worse yet, though they've spent the whole day learning that she's really very nice, the Weird Girl only becomes appealing to the boys after she lets the Popular Girl give her a nauseating mall-rat makeover. Though it seems almost impossible, *Pretty in Pink* went even further in equating conformity with success and happiness. Not only does the Nerd Guy lose Girl to the Popular Asshole, but Annie Potts, as Girl's Older Best Friend, demonstrates her romantic fulfillment by changing from a way-cool Cyndi Lauper–type to a yuppie.

The title character in *Ferris Bueller's Day Off* (played by Matthew Broderick) is the most goody-goody rebel since Greg Brady was caught smoking. He pulls off an elaborate school-ditching ploy just so he can go to a ball game, a museum, and a parade. Thank you, John, for creating a truant Pat Boone could love.

When he ran out of steam with the teens, Hughes went on to pro-breeder turf. He dabbled in Yuppie Baby movies like *She's Having a Baby,* wherein the sophisticated urban couple learns to live in pea-brained, white suburbia and like it. And his Cute Little Kid romps put him over the top, both in box-office cash and artistic hideousness. *Curly Sue,* in addition to being a G-rated rip-off of *Paper Moon,* appealed to the audience on the same basic level as a Formula 409 commercial, by throwing dirt all over two attractive actors and giving the audience the satisfaction of seeing them hosed down and dressed for dinner. And *Home Alone* deserves kudos only for the dubious achievement of making a live-action film version of Tex Avery's classic cartoon "One Ham's Family." But hey, at least he's creating wank fodder for the pedophiles. (gwynne)

h

Hippie Food Goes Mainstream By the end of the decade, many weird hippie health foods had crossed over from natural-food stores into the mainstream supermarket. As they were assimilated, many products lost the very qualities that had given them nutritional appeal. Strange sour yogurt was disguised by lashings of sugar, or made into frozen yogurt, or that meal-in-a-bowl granola bar (Frógurt). Megacorporations marketed their own prepackaged granolas, and even the most synthetic foods bore names that suggested Grandma's farm kitchen: Country Time (lemonade powder), Home Pride Butter-Top white bread, Hidden Valley Ranch salad dressing, Autumn 100% natural margarine (which could just as accurately be called Autumn 100% artificial butter). Other products, like herbal teas and pita bread, moved unchanged from health-food stores to conventional supermarkets as American tastes broadened. Grocery stores even copied health-food stores' scoop-it-yourself bins and barrels, but filled them with jelly beans and chocolate-covered raisins instead of prunes and millet. (candi) (See also BROWN VS. WHITE)

Hitchhikers Today I seem to pick up only young girls or old ladies, but when I first started driving I even picked up those scary guys at the freeway on-ramp. Sometimes hitchhiking was the only way to get around, but now I only hitchhike when my car breaks down or I'm stranded and have no other choice (besides truckers, people rarely stop). A sign of the times? Perhaps I just read one teen girl horror book and saw one hitchhiking movie too many. (darby) (Check out movie *The Hitcher*)

Holly Hobbie My favorite female stuffed dolls that I slept with were Holly Hobbie and her best friend Heather. They both wore their hair in braids and dressed like *Little House on the Prairie* people — but Heather was a bit more upper-class-looking. They were cartoons, Colorforms, and Shrinky Dinks too. (selina) (See also DOLLS and GUNNE SAX)

Homo Hankie Code Brought to mainstream consciousness by the 1979 homocop film *Cruisin'*. There was (and still is) a pamphlet available at the Pleasure Chest (the only place in L.A. you could purchase spiked leather wristbands before the advent of "New Wave/punk" boutiques like Poseur) with the entire list of colors and their meanings according to which back pocket of your jeans it was worn in. For example, "Dark blue, right = blowjob, dominant; dark blue, left = blowjob, submissive." It got really out of hand toward the bottom, like "Fur, right = bestiality, dominant." The guys at the store all laughed at me when I asked what *scat* was: "Well, what color is the hankie?" "Brown . . . Oh!" (gwynne)

h

Hot Combs During the early '70s, hair dryers evolved from conical dinosaurs to phallic blowhards. Along the way, a few startling mutants were born, and quickly died. The earliest one was the hot comb, the first hair dryer for men. It was needed to help the "new man" keep his new Mark Spitz coif looking "natural." Hot combs were decidedly butch; they were large, clunky, and powerful, and were available in nice manly colors like black or dark brown. Like any power tool for men, these came with lots of attachments, which could give you that look liberated ladies dug. Alas, hair-drying technology was then in its infancy, with the early models being far more powerful than practical. Many a man looking for that feathered look had to adopt a Mike Brady–style perm after a fiery encounter with his hot comb. (bruce)

Hot Tubbin' Wrapped up in this one object are all the feelings and obsessions of the '70s: hedonism, sexual liberation, Californianess, communal activity, do-it-yourself 'tude, and wood splinters in your butt. Hippies invented them, cutting big old oaken wine barrels in half to create Japanese-style hot soak tubs. Manufacturers stripped away the funky elements, designed premade indoor fiberglass tubs with pulsating heater jets, and mass-marketed them to wild-and-crazy suburbanites. (candi) ✥ I don't know what the swingin' couples did with their Jacuzzis, but most teen parties ended with everyone crammed into them. Especially big at the time were those portable, above-ground types, which poorer families like mine splurged on. They were so small that if two slightly dirty people went in, the water would turn brown like a dirty bathtub. Totally bunk. (darby) ✥ For some reason, when I think back to the '70s, my impression of hot tubs had something to do with swingers, the Playboy Mansion, and some kind of hetero-male sex fantasy. In fact, whenever I'm in California and I end up having sex in a hot tub, I feel pretty ridiculous. It seems so stereotypical and retro that I bust up laughing, much to my partner's horror. (patty) (See also PARTY FLICKS and *PINK LADY*)

Rock Hudson Dies of AIDS No one even knew he was gay, let alone HIV positive, especially Linda Evans, whom he had wetly kissed on *Dynasty* a few months before his death, in 1985.

The Hunger Peter Murphy singing in a bar, lesbian sex between Susan Sarandon and Catherine Deneuve, a sexy svelte Bowie vampire . . . I didn't think much of this film, but it made my girlfriend — who didn't like having sex with me — *really* want to have sex with me. Darby calls the movie the equivalent of ecstasy for women. (brian)

Hysterical-Women Roles Just like the witch movies that were big in the '70s, these seemed a direct response to the role women were playing in the world. The message was to beware of these wild and free women: Evelyn Draper (*Play Misty for Me*), Barbara Jean (*Nashville*), Nurse Ratched (*One Flew Over the Cuckoo's Nest*), Carrie (*Carrie*). . . . (jaz) ✥ In the American cinema, a strong woman is more often than not an evil woman. This genre really got under way with *What Ever Happened to Baby Jane?*, as many survivors of Hollywood's golden age kept on acting as disturbed moms and grandmas. My favorite gem is *What's the Matter with Helen?*, with Shelley Winters and Debbie Reynolds. (mike s.) ✥ Perhaps Glenn Close in *Fatal Attraction* ('87) marks the apotheosis of the genre. (adam s.) (See also DEPRESSED-DRUGGIE-GIRL MOVIES)

"I Love You This Much" Statuettes
These sentimental figurines were about five inches tall (usually with disproportionally large heads) and stood on a base proclaiming "World's Greatest Grandma," "Congratulations, Graduate," one's undying love, or any other sentiment celebrating any occasion you would possibly need to buy someone a tacky knickknack for. Al Hoff from the popular zine *Thriftscore* has the largest collection of these in the free world. (lorraine)

"I'm a Pepper . . ." There is no drink more retro than Dr Pepper. (jes) ❀ And the jingle was written and sung by soft-core god Barry Manilow for added '70s flavor. (darby) ❀ And the "I'm a Pepper" guy was the star of *An American Werewolf in London*. (howard) ❀ In the Free-to-Be-You-and-Me '70s, advertisers found themselves trying to get millions of self-proclaimed individualists to all buy the same thing. The folks at Dr Pepper came up with a rather creative solution to this problem. Cultivating an image as an alternative soft drink, they got you to feel you could drink Dr Pepper *and* be an original, along with the hundreds of other people dancing in the street with you. (bruce) (See also 7-UP)

Incredible Edibles Like the now-reissued Creepy Crawlers, but the machine to cook the goop looked like this big sphere-shaped head that opened in half like a giant mouth, with eyes on the top half. The rubbery snakes and bugs you made out of a special goop you could eat! (riley)

Indian Earth This was that powder blush in a small terra-cotta container with the cork lid. To use it you'd tilt the bottle over and then dab your blush brush on the lid and do all your blush zones: the puckered cheeks, the sides of your eyes, and maybe your chest to give the illusion of cleavage (pre–push-up bra days). The container led one to believe this was some natural product that the Indians actually used; at least *I* fell for it. So instead of looking natural we looked like slutty little girls playing in Mom's make-up. (darby)

"In 'n' Out Burger" Bumper Stickers
Who could resist transforming these freebies into the phrase "In 'n' Out Urge." Whoa! Righteous! (jory)

Invisible Dogs Plain good clean fun. The toy was simply a leash made out of a stiff metal that everybody in the world had. You saw them every day but still they were very very funny. Can you imagine the kids in your neighborhood today being entertained by something that doesn't make noise, isn't run by a computer, doesn't emulate a violent act or cost a hundred bucks? (jes) ❀ An empty dog harness, a long leash, and a stiff wire, and you had the stuff of *Candid Camera*. These were sold under the name No-Dogs. I had one when I was twelve and used to freak out folks at the mall by taking mine out for a walk. Later models had a tacky little tube inside which would squirt water out the rear end upon command. (bruce)

Isis The premise of this show was that a young lady archaeologist finds an Egyptian amulet on a dig and is compelled to put it on. The next thing you know — *blammo!* — she's become the living embodiment of Isis, the Egyptian goddess of fertility! Along with this fancy new outfit, she gets all these funky superpowers and flies around (with her arms outstretched behind her in a very un-Superman–like style) doing good deeds and righting wrongs — you know, all that superheroine stuff that you would expect, with the requisite moral to be learned at the end of the episode. I definitely had a crush on the classy chick who played Isis. (creepy mike) (See also *SHAZAM!*)

Joe Isuzu Skinny shmuck whose specialty was selling Isuzu Troopers, which were essentially motorcycles with boxes on them. I don't know where he came from, but he later became a regular character on *Empty Nest,* with Richard Mulligan and Kristy McNichol. (jon)

Itty-Bitty-Titty Committee Inspired three buxom women in the '70s to form a group, called the Itty-bitty-titty Pity Committee, supposedly for busty gals in need of over-the-shoulder boulder holders. (bruce)

Invisible dog, with visible arm

J. Geils Band Where do ex–rock stars go to die? The J. Geils Band had only a few hits, but "Centerfold" was so big, it hurt. Today the singer, Peter Wolf, has been having shows for his art in New York City. His new band, Peter and the Houseparty 5, exists somewhere too . . . beware. I read that Faye Dunaway married Peter Wolf on August 7, 1974. If that doesn't top the charts in retro-weird! (ju-ji) ❧ They were a Boston band that no one took seriously in their hometown, and for good reason. Eventually they found a place in the world that would have them — Detroit. They were the Oingo Boingo of postindustrial Detroit. They would sell out an arena *five* nights in a row. You couldn't have a party without one of their records, and no Friday night was complete without hearing "Ain't Nothin' but a House Party." Of course, all their songs sounded the same, the driving piano, the "Moobie Doo!" and *wamma-jamma* with the harmonica. "Centerfold" was their only national breakout hit, but by the time that came out their fans were like "Bullshit, man, they sold out, it's bullshit disco motherfucker crap, man." (bruce) (See also OVERPLAYED VIDEOS)

Janet Jackson Michael's baby sister started off her public life as the young neighbor of J. J.'s family on the sitcom *Good Times*. She was cute, lovable, and a natural as the sharp little kid. We didn't hear too much from her until she appeared on, and survived, the career-wreckin' *Diff'rent Strokes*, as Willis's girlfriend (basically playing the same character but older

and more toned down). When she made the weirdest move and appeared as a chubby, sorta talentless underdog in the TV version of *Fame*, you had to appreciate her gusto. As her bro was *beating it* all the way to the top, Janet was planning her own version of Jackson fame. After a make-over that would have made any talk show host proud, a few tips from Paula Abdul, and some help from mega-producers Jimmy Jam and Terry Lewis, Janet took *Control* ('86). She asked, "What have you done for me lately?" and the world replied, "Bought your albums, Miss Jackson." By the release of *Rhythm Nation 1814* ('89) her fame momentarily eclipsed Michael's without her even meaning to be *nasty*. And suddenly that rhythm nation was all eyes on foxy Janet. I remember shopping in Fedco for some electronics the night of her big live concert. Every TV in the store had her on it. When she started singing about those Nasty Boys I swear the whole store stood watching in awe. (darby/nina)

Michael Jackson's Nose The last time we saw little "A-B-C as easy as 1-2-3" Michael with an afro, ebony of skin and nose, was on the cover of *Off the Wall* ('79). When he whittled away a little of the nose for *Thriller* ('82), some of us may have even thought he looked better. No doubt he thought so, because as his skin got progressively whiter, his nose kept getting smaller and smaller until his *Leave Me Alone* ('89) video, when it totally disappeared — just a scar contoured on either side with make-up. On *Oprah*, he explained away the ever whitening skin by saying he had some rare pigmentation disease. Perhaps we buy that, Jacko, but the nose? Maybe it was an aftereffect of his hair catching on fire in that Pepsi commercial? Maybe he spent too long in an oxygen tank? Maybe Bubbles bit it off? Who knows, and furthermore, who cares? Being a moon-walking, child-friendly freak without a nose gives him that added edge all pop icons need. (nina) (See also HANDS ACROSS AMERICA)

The Gloved One

James at 15 Seminal TV movie, starred Lance Kerwin as a sensitive boy whose best friends were a shrill, army-jacketed feminist girl (in a likable way, though) and a low-key African American boy. Nothing like it before or since. (allison) ❀ I just remember the scene in the TV movie where James was finally going to do it with that girl and they were sorta camping out and getting naked and it was thoroughly romantic and I masturbated over it for months. (darby) ❀ Incidentally, James didn't lose it in the icy cold Oregon woods with his girlfriend; the implication was that he couldn't get it up because of the temperature. The real cherry-popping took place a year later in Boston with the hot Scandinavian exchange student. It was quite a controversy at the time, a teen having sex, although it would be an even *bigger* deal today. Additional screaming revolved around James's request for condoms from a pal, something that did not appear in the episode as aired. Just as well; it would have deprived us of seeing the aforementioned student saying, in her inimitable accent, "Vat if I am pregnant?" the morning after. (john m) (See also BED-WETTING)

Jaws This has to be listed separately. Because it, above all other scary movies, seemed to go way beyond, touching on deep dark fears in each and every one of us — ones we never even knew we had — to this day, making us scared to death of the deep blue sea. And scared to death of sharks. After this movie most of us had problems swimming in the deep end of the pool (especially alone) or even going to the toilet (because of the slight possible chance that Jaws might go up the pipes and break through and eat you, butt first). When my dad took me to see the movie he told my mom we were going to *Bambi* — which made it even more exciting. I remember the whole thing, when the barrels were under water for a while and all was quiet and suddenly one popped up and my dad was so scared that he dug his nails into my arm and jumped out of his seat. Whadda wimp! (darby) (Refer to the book *The Seventies* for more enjoyable data and check out the zine *Shark Fear*.)

Jean Naté The commercial was of a lady jockey horse-racing as if that splash of Jean Naté stimulated her to win, smelling good and femme while she did it. I remember whenever I used the stuff, I tried to splash it on just like the lady on TV did, and I'd pretend that I was getting just as stimulated while the nice bouncy theme song played in my head: "Jean Naté Jean Naté du dudu, dudu dudu du . . ." (darby) (See also SMELLS)

Jeans Denim was *the* '70s fabric of choice, turning up on everything from shoes to caps to cars (AMC came out with a special edition of the 1973 Gremlin with Levi's upholstery!). There were more brands and more types of jeans fashion than we care to remember: Kelly Girl, Chemin de Fer, Gloria Vanderbilt, Jordache, Sasson, Lee, Wrangler, Charlie's Angels, Chic, Sergio Valente, Cham de Baron (with those fabulous low-budget commercials of a guy at customs in an airport being asked if he had anything to declare and answering, "Chams . . . Cham de Baron"), and Code Bleu (totally overpriced trendywear whose jean jackets had a big fag tag on the upper back to let the world know you were the shit); unisex jeans (fitting neither man nor woman) like Faded Glory and Britannia; the Canadian favorite, Fancy Ass!; Oshkosh B'Gosh overalls; elephant bell bottoms that dragged on the ground; tie-dyed jeans; metal-studded jeans; patchwork jeans; embroidery-pocketed jeans; skirts made from splitting jeans at the inseam and sewing in a piece of triangular fabric; jeans purses; and jeans tucked into boots! The early '80s brought us Guess, Bongo, Calvins; the *über*-dark indigo San Francisco Riding Gear jeans; Normandie Rose; stonewashed jeans, and, as a backlash against '70s styling, we had cuffed jeans, tapered jeans, ripped jeans, ankle zip jeans, and finally Levi's 501s. (nina/wendy/howard/riley/morgan and ferris) (See also DISCO CHIC; DITTOS; PAINTER'S PANTS; PATCHES; and SASSON)

Jelly Bellys Had John Hinckley, Jr., finished off Ronald Reagan like he should have, these gourmet jelly beans might never have been so big. I remember sampling the good stuff, like bubble gum, coconut, and lemon-lime flavors, at the local ice cream shop, but I could never afford to buy them. They were for rich people. (noël) "In 1976 the first eight Jelly Belly flavors were born: Very Cherry, Lemon, Cream Soda, Orange, Green Apple, Root Beer, Grape, and Licorice. [Soon after] I was named America's Best Jelly Bean in C. Paul Luongo's book *America's Best 100!*, and became the favorite candy of celebs like Larry King and Jeanne Dixon. And then, of course, there was President Ronald Reagan, who made me a staple in the Oval Office and on *Air Force One*. And guess what? I was also the first jelly bean in outer space. I was served on the space shuttle — on the same mission that boasted another first — the first American woman astronaut, Sally Ride" (Quote from Mr. Jelly Belly himself via the official Jelly Belly site, which you can connect to at http://www.jellybelly.com/.)

Jelly Glasses I think it was Welch's that used to have *The Archies* (I have Betty and Veronica's Fashion Show with a bas-relief of Hot Dog on the cup's bottom), *Josie and the Pussycats*, and *Scooby-Doo* imprinted on them. Now they're so dull I wouldn't even buy that sugary jelly just to get the free glass it turns into once you've cleaned it out. (darby)

Jem The rock star, the doll, the cartoon, the role model. "Jem is her name, no one else is the same!" (skylaire) Truly outrageous! By igniting her earrings she was transformed — "Synergy power, on!" But beware of the Misfits! The anti-Jem band who sang in the opening credits, "We are the Misfits, our songs are better, and we're gonna get her!" (morgan)

1976 (4TH GRADE): **MY FAVORITE PANTS.**
i had two pairs of these, because i loved them so much--- one in yellow, one in peachy-orange.

RAINBOW STITCHING UP THE LEGS...

(FAKE POCKET)

...AND OVER THE BUTT.

VERY SNAZZY.

(i was also pretty attached to my soccer t-shirt. actually i really sucked at soccer-- my mom swore i joined the team just for the shirt.)

J.J. Everyone called me J.J. when I was little and therefore I really felt connected to J.J. on *Good Times*. I even requested that people pronounce the initials with an accent on the second *J* for authenticity. If there was anybody I wanted to be, besides the president or Nadia Comaneci, it was J.J. Walker. I wanted to be tall and lanky and funny with a big ol' afro. I loved his hat and his cool ghetto clothes. But I was forced to wear Garanimals instead of the fashionable stuff J.J. had. And why couldn't my sister be as understanding as Thelma? J.J. also had the smoothest way of jive-talkin' Mama and the horny chick who lived downstairs. I wasn't allowed to call *my* mom *Mama;* I had to call her *Mother*. I begged her to take me to get an afro. Finally the years of pleading paid off. Ol' Mother cautioned me that an afro might not be very flattering on my little head, but I guess she was fed up with my whining and begging. Off I went to the local midwestern beauty salon and after sitting through hours of chemical torture, I got me an afro. And I cried because it stung like all hell. And fuck, did I look bad. That's when I started my campaign for a Dorothy Hamill 'do . . . or was it the Farrah Fawcett flip? (jes) (See also BLAXPLOITATION and GARANIMALS)

Jogging Today people just plain *run* for exercise, but in the early '70s when the modern obsession with fitness began, folks talked about "jogging." Soon, whether one actually exercised or not, it was cool to appear in public wearing jogging suits: matching sweatpants and jackets with stripes down the side, plus jogging shoes (three-stripe Adidas were the first major brand) and a sweatband. (candi) (See also POWER WALKING and SWEATSUITS)

Ray Jay Johnson Unfunny comedian whose tired routine (Youse can call me Ray or youse can call me Jay, but ya doesn't haveta call me Johnson) disgraced any number of mid- to late '70s commercials, sitcoms, and variety shows. (nick)

Johnson and Smith Catalogue Gift and novelty catalogue heavily advertised in comic books, it offered such memorable items as chest-hair toupees, garlic gum, dog doo, exploding cigars, whoopee cushions, elevator shoes . . . (nick)

Jokes, Dirty Kid Do you wanna hear a dirty joke? The white horse fell in the mud. Isn't that funny!? There were so many stupid dirty kid jokes, like "deeper, Danny, deeper," or "Whaddya eating under there? Under where?," but the most ultimately famous one, actually one of the only jokes I remember telling in my whole life (tho' Jes is the one who remembered the details), was the Snake in the Grass. Oh man, it's really great . . . Okay, so there's this little boy who asked his dad if he could take a shower with him. "Please, daddy." "No, no." "Pleeaase, I'll hold my breath until I die." "Oh, okay." So they take a shower and the little boy asks, "Daddy, what's that?" "That's my snake, son." "Oh." So the next day the little boy asks his mom, "Mom, can I take a shower with you?" "No." "Pleeaase." "No." "I'll hold my breath until I die." "Oh, okay." So they take a shower and the little boy asks, "Mommy, what's that?" "Those are my headlights, and that's my grass." So, the next night the little boy walks into his parents' bedroom unannounced while both his parents are having sex in bed and screams, "Mommy, mommy, turn on your headlights, there's a snake in your grass."

Okay, maybe I don't remember it too well. I was always bad with punchlines. But it's really funny, don't you think? (Other versions include the Gorilla and the Banana, the Fire Truck, and the Garage.) (darby)

Jonathan Livingston Seagull The '70s equivalent of the *Bridges of Madison County*, this '72 *and* '73 bestselling Richard Bach tome investigated the possibility that seagulls do more than eat garbage and crap on you at the beach. Later spawned a movie featuring a Neil Diamond soundtrack. (nick)

❧ What the hell was going on in the '70s? I was assigned this waste of pulp for a book report in sixth grade and was flabbergasted by its vacuous platitudes! Imagine my shock when I discovered it had been written for *adults*! Millions of them read it, and worse yet, *believed* in it. It swelled into a *Garp*-sized phenomenon. There were posters, pendants, and even a parade float with the *Jonathan* theme. This was all from the goddamn book! I guess the age was afflicted with a critical mass of soulless adults wondering why their marriage failed and dreaming of moving to Big Sur. Faith *is* an eternal human weakness. To this day, I'm still not sure which was more pathetic, the follow-up movie or its soundtrack album. (bruce) (See also BESTSELLING BOOKS)

Ed "Too Tall" Jones

In the late '70s, the all-star Dallas Cowboys had it all: patriotic charm, Dallas Cowboy Cheerleaders, Super Bowl rings, and Ed "Too Tall" Jones (although rival Pittsburgh Steelers did have "Mean" Joe Green, who will always be remembered for his pivotal role in an old Coca-Cola commercial). Even with the household-name talents of Roger Staubach, Tony Dorsett, and Thomas "Hollywood" Henderson, Too Tall was not just another shining star in the Cowboys' lineup. He had surely arrived when his tallness was thrown into a cameo role for *Diff'rent Strokes*, which featured His Shortness, Gary Coleman. The twenty-foot height difference alone was nonstop American-made comedy for the masses and, boy, did we have fun or what! (noël) (See also DALLAS COWBOYS CHEERLEADERS)

Jonny Quest

Or, Jonny has two daddies. First animated series to showcase a positive portrayal of a gay couple, *J.Q.* followed the adventures of young Jonny; his father, Dr. Quest; his father's muscular companion, Race Bannon; Indian orphan Hadji; and lovable pooch, Bandit. A Hanna-Barbera production, *J.Q.* took place in a world without women that was populated exclusively by thawed-out cavemen, ex-Nazi commanders, and Third World industrialists with pet Komodo dragons. (nick) ❧ I still desperately want to live the Jonny Quest lifestyle and careen through an all-male realm of exotic adventure. I still want to travel the world in a supersonic jet with my bearded scientist dad, who can deflect a laser beam with his watch. I still want Race Bannon to swing down, rescue me, and keep me safe in his big buff arms. But more than anything else, I want to hear twangy spy-guitar music playing everywhere I go. (bruce) (See also CARTOONS) 🐾

Josie and the Pussycats

Saturday morning cartoon, 1970 to 1974. A fondly recalled gem from the days when every cartoon had to have its own rock group. In this ditty, an all-girl group toured the globe and just couldn't seem to stay out of trouble. Kasey Kasem did the voice of Alexander, the hippie manager, and future *Charlie's Angels* star Cheryl Ladd was the voice of Sheri, the dumb blonde. During the second season, the Pussycats found themselves launched into space, where they found even more trouble and adventures. Each episode would feature the gals doing a horrid song. Capitol Records eventually put out an album of them and sent a band of studio hacks on tour with it. Rumor has it that Kim Carnes, of "Bette Davis Eyes" fame, was one of the singers. They also did tie-ins with Kellogg's, who put Pussycat records on the backs of "specially marked boxes." One obscure note: CBS used this as the flagship of its 1970 Saturday morning season and went so far as to create a series of informational vignettes featuring various Pussycats explaining facts about the world. The vignettes ran between other cartoons, under the title "In the Know," with the gals doing the theme song. After *Josie and the Pussycats* was canceled, CBS revamped the vignettes and retitled them "In the News," which they ran under this title until 1992. (bruce) (See also *CHARLIE'S ANGELS*)

Junk Dressing

Madonna and Cyndi Lauper rule in this category, though we *all* dressed this way in the early '80s; it was street fashion. Cat collars, white lace shirts with different-color bras underneath, big bows in way-moussed and teased hair, leopard-print scarves, and about five hundred necklaces, bracelets, and ear-piercings with endless hoops and wiggly goldfish and leaf earrings. Lots of eyeliner, pink eyeshadow, red lips. Petticoats and fishnets, lace-up boots or retro pumps with bobby sox. (pleasant) ❧ Whaddya mean, "early '80s"? I still dress like this! (gwynne) (See also MADONNA WANNABES and MOUSSE)

Junk Food Though junk food isn't particularly retro — considering it never went away — we did participate in its overwhelming upsurge, and each culture seems to focus on certain ones more that others. Some of those in which we regularly partook: Beef Jerky (fatty tube–style or shredded); raw cookie dough; Cheetos (and other styracorn products); Wonder bread; Laughing Cow Cheese cubes; string cheese; the rise of drive-thru fast food; Otter Pops; all the variety of Ding Dongs, Ho-Hos, Chocodiles, Twinkies, Devil Dogs, Suzie Q's; Eggo's; toaster oven pizzas (and most toaster foods); macaroni and cheese; pot pies; Tater Tots and other Ore-Ida fried mush. (darby) ❧ I believe the term *junk food* was popularized by Euell Gibbons — a big natural-food writer of the '60s. From '72 to '75 Grape Nuts hired him to do a series of commercials. His big phrase was "You ever eat a pine tree? You know, some parts are edible." During the whole brown versus white age Euell became a sort of Yoda. Junk food by definition means food in which the amount of fat and calories exceeds the amount of nutrients. It quickly came to mean munchies (or almost anything that was sold in a wrapper). (bruce) (See also CANDY, CEREALS, THE MUNCHIES, PILLSBURY COOKIE DOUGH, SPACE FOOD STICKS, and TOASTER FOODS)

j

K

Kareem Abdul-Jabbar Original name: Lew Alcindor. Besides *Airplane,* he was in that Bruce Lee movie *Game of Death*. A Los Angeles Lakers favorite for many, many, many years. (bruce)

Kazoo Harvey Korman was the voice of the Great Kazoo, a Martian on *The Flintstones* that had been exiled from the twenty-sixth century. He had that big head and he zapped the Flintstones into the future and they actually met the Jetsons in a traffic jam. He was just this sort of bored guy with this big hat. You could tell they were really running out of ideas for *The Flintstones* when he showed up. (bruce)

Kennington Shirts Fuzzy shirts made of either terry cloth or velour. Came in a variety of designs and kooky nature-color combos (think brown). Kennington has reintroduced their terry-cloth and velour shirts thanks to their retro popularity. (noël) 🐿️

Killer Pussy With all the retro comebacks, you could only hope this saucy band would find their way back. Killer Pussy taught me about important things like enemas ("Teenage enema nurses in bondage") and pocket pool ("Mama's little baby plays pocket pool pocket pool, Mama's little angel is a pocket pool man"). (darby) ♣ There's a lame CD *More Music from the Soundtrack Valley Girl,* on which you can find "Pocket Pool." Highly recommended, as anything that begins "More Music from . . ." is obviously queer. *Especially* since that song is not even *in* the movie (although it does have "Eaten by the Monster of Love" — the only song I wanted to be on the original LP). (liza) ♣ Most of my best friends (and some members of bands I was in) in Phoenix were in this group. Gary Russell, the leader/guitarist, was a total genius, not to mention a great guitarist. He was a deejay on legendary Arizona pirate station KDIL, made some of the best prank phone calls, wrote the weirdest, funniest shit you'll ever read, helped fellow Phoenician Freddy Snakeskin (ex-KROQ deejays) create amazing Xerox collage-art zines a decade before punk rock made it fashionable, and was just about the only guy who could pull off what I've come to call Improv Pop. An all-around surrealistic wunderkind, who was seen driving a cab in Phoenix. At least he's alive, unlike the drummer, who was the guitarist/singer in most of my Phoenix bands, including the Yvonnes, Kray-zee Homicide, and the Consumers. One of the first in my seemingly never-ending series of dead friends/bandmates. (don) ♣ FYI, Killer Pussy is available on the CD comp *The Obscurity File Vol. 1* from Oglio Records (aka the New Wave Connection) and *New Wave Theatre Vol. 1.* (vince) (See also JACK LA LANNE)

King Tut In the 1920s, despite legends of a curse and the wrath of the pharaohs, archaeologists dug deep into the tomb of the ancient Egyptian King Tut. Disturbing the grave proved to be lucrative, as hundreds of priceless artifacts were discovered and examined. Fifty years later, select pieces from this collection appeared in museums around the world, giving thousands of curious historians a glimpse of ancient history at one of its finest moments. But, like most events of this magnitude, capitalism is not far away and it reared its ugly head everywhere Tut appeared. Jewelry, posters, books, key chains, postage stamps, novelty songs, TV specials, coke spoons, you name it. King Tut was re-throned and the world bowed down to him. Everybody was an overnight intellectual/historian, and you were square if you weren't hip to the triangles. This kickstarted the mega-fad pyramid power, ripping people off with "pyramid-purified bottled water," new age philosophy, and numerous other get-rich-quick scams. (mike v.) 🍀 Despite evidence to the contrary (most people directly involved in violating his tomb lived to a ripe old age), it's still widely believed that a curse is attached to him. But then again, Steve Martin hasn't had a hit in years. . . . (brian) (See also PHENOMENA and STEVE MARTIN)

Kirlian Photography

Russian thing where they photograph your aura. Pictures of live leaves with colorful, glowing outlines, and plucked leaves looking forlorn. Kinda cool. (amy)

Kiss Army

Fan clubs were for pussies who liked the Bay City Rollers; Kiss fans had an army and, fuck yes, I was enlisted. I joined after my dad and sister and I saw them and Cheap Trick at the Forum in '77, and accepted Ace Frehley as my own personal savior. At ten, all I wanted was to go on a "rocket ride" to "Detroit Rock City" and "pull the trigger of your love gun" — even if I didn't know what it meant, it sounded, and more important, looked, F-U-N. Kiss infused all my prepubescent fantasies with the mystery of the dark and unknown. They had their own comic book, and even starred in their very own movie, *Kiss Meets the Phantom of the Park*. They were more than rock gods, they were superheroes. (nina) 🐾

Kitchen Appliances

In the years after pop-up toasters and before the arrival of microwaves, America's kitchens brimmed with all sorts of electronic gadgets that helped usher in the era of junk food. First there was the toaster oven, which allowed any stoner to enjoy the special thrill of watching cheese melt all over the place under a groovy red light. The folks at a company called Presto soon gave the world a device called Hotdiggity. It was a little plastic hut with electrified prongs that cooked your impaled hot dogs by induction. They followed this triumph with something imaginatively called the Burgermaker. It was a hinged pair of hot plates that squeezed and fried an idly torn hunk of ground beef into something not unlike a hamburger patty. When you were done you had a crispy black meat shell with pink beefy goodness inside. It was just like fast food! The task of french fries went to Presto's next invention, the Frybaby. It's horrific name proved perfect for what it was, a stout metal cauldron of boiling oil that sat, and often spewed, right on your kitchen counter. Many discovered the fun of plunging anything into its waiting maw and hearing it pop and sizzle into an unrecognizable puff of "food." For convenience' sake, the Frybaby came with a plastic lid that allowed any indifferent chef to keep the same fetid fat for later use. There were many other appliances of this ilk, such as the Woks-a-lot or the vividly named Salad Shooter; also ice cream makers, fondue makers, food dehydrators, food processors (La Machine). Eventually we all learned that one cheap microwave could replace a shelf of costly gadgets. (bruce) (See also CROCK-POT and MICROWAVE OVENS)

Klick-Klacks The Pinto of toys: two marbles about the size of Ping-Pong balls attached to a string. You were supposed to hold the middle of the string and "click" them together. If you got really good at it, you could do fancy tricks with them, not unlike those done with yo-yos. But, alas, they allegedly had a nasty habit of breaking and exploding in a shrapnel-like shower of glass. The teachers at school told us some kid was blinded by a flying shard, and they banned and confiscated our Klick-Klacks. (gwynne) ❧ We all knew it was a conspiracy because the wimpy grown-ups hated the sound they made. (carla) ❧ The horror stories of shattering glass were often attributed to a cheap Klick-Klack knock-off called "Klikies." But even before this, the ill-conceived toy had earned a lethal reputation. The similarity between a pair of Klick-Klacks and the South American hunter's weapon called a bolo was soon evident to every boy who watched adventure shows on TV. I must say that in this capacity they proved surprisingly effective. This same toy has recently returned in a very tame form. The new model is made entirely out of stiff plastic and holds no potential for creativity or mayhem. (bruce) (See also EXECUTIVE TOYS)

Kmart Girl china dolls, karate shoes, "Mia" knock-offs, Icees, the Kmart cafeteria (popcorn, slushies — I once had Thanksgiving dinner there), sweat clothes, underwear, stealing make-up . . . (lisa r.) ❧ The deglamorization of Jaclyn Smith, and now Kathy Ireland. (ju-ji)

Knickers You were cool if you wore these half-pants that buttoned at the knee. An ugly classic look for men that was adopted by women for this brief unfeminine period. They were the fad along with vests, argyle socks, and topsiders and pennyloafers. (selina)

Knuckle Writing Where you'd write *Ozzy* or *Fuck* on your knuckles and it was still shocking. Mainly part of the stoner/metal culture at first, and then very punk rock. (jaz)

Koala Bear Clip-Ons There were koalas, pandas, unicorns, and bears, and they were basically a small stuffed animal built around a metal clip, so when you pinched its back its arms would open and you could clip it on to things like your pencil. (darby) ❧ I had my seventh grade school photo taken with one clipped to my uniform collar and a superdorky I-hate-you look on my face. (riley)

Koogle This existed for a short time only, for about two years (my guess is '73–'74, but I could be wrong). It was a line of flavored peanut butter–type spreads with a wacky Kool-Aid guy mascot who resembled Rat Fink and sang the virtues of peanut butters that tasted like cinnamon, chocolate, banana, and vanilla. The Koogle Monster often hung out in odd locales (one was in a locker room after the big game) shouting "Fooot-foootio-fow!" and hassling the kids with the hard sell. Needless to say, the folks who devised this product thought it was so great they rushed its release without first perfecting its flavor. The chocolate tasted like a mud slab. The cinnamon was very chemical-gritty; and I was too afraid to try the other two flavors (that, and my brother and I couldn't con our very food-conservative mother into forking over the cash for such a frivolity). It has been stated that every kid in America had a jar lying around with just one big spoonmark indenting the surface. (kevin c./mike g.)

H

Kork-Ease Platforms Worn with tight Chemin de Fer or Britannia jeans and a pastel-colored french-cut T-shirt, Kork-Ease were these great platform sandals. They usually only came in "natural," and the straps were leather while the platform was suede. They came in three different heights, and of course, the sluttiest chicks wore only the highest, which was like the Frankenstein-platform size. I had a pair with baby-pink metallic leather straps that I got from Fred Slatten Shoes in West Hollywood, and also a bootleg Kork-Ease in silver glitter — in addition to my countless other pairs. They were really comfortable (must've been the cork in the soles) and really sexy-looking. The way we wore 'em was to get the tipedge hem of your bell bottoms about $1/2$ inch above the sole, so that just a hint of the shoe was visible and your legs in their tight jeans looked ultralong. Also, they looked real tough with straight Levi's, which we wore cuffed up and custom-sewn with a seam up the front of the legs to look like old-fashioned ski pants. You'd wear the Kork-Ease, jeans, and a striped T-shirt with a beret and big hoop earrings — it was a style we stole from New York Puerto Rican girls that Johnny Thunders also used to wear, only he wore lace-up platform boots. (pleasant) (See also JEANS and SHOES)

Krofft Superstars If the name *Lidsville* doesn't key you off to where these two kiddie-show lunatics are coming from, you've already had too much to smoke. They're responsible for the generational brain damage resulting from bizarro Saturday morning fare such as *The Bugaloos, Dr. Shrinker, Wonderbug, The Great Space Coaster, Sigmund and the Sea Monsters,* and *Jurassic Park* precursor *Land of the Lost.* One of the Spumco (*Ren and Stimpy*) animators told me he'd once scored 'shrooms for a Krofft; in return, he'd been informed that H. R. PufnStuf's initials stood for *hand-rolled.* But I still have my own theory about that show's homosexual/castration anxiety subtext. An evil witch plots to steal

a pretty young British boy's magic flute, until he is saved by a chickenhawk-like father figure who calls himself "Puf" (as in "pouf"?). (gwynne) ♣ Sid and Marty started out doing puppet shows at the '64 World's Fair and eventually produced *Donny and Marie.* Along the way, they left a freaked-out swath in the minds of a generation. After *Donny and Marie,* these folks went on to open an indoor theme park in downtown Atlanta. It featured an enormous pinball machine you could ride in. (bruce) ♣ Recently there was a Sid and Marty tribute-type event at the Hollywood Directors' Guild. My sister and I went, forced our way into Sid and Marty's face, and — despite the rest of the crowd waiting for some of their attention — made them take pictures with us, sign our souvenirs (I hate that!), and handed them a copy of *Ben Is Dead* while professing our gratitude for their inspiration. When inside they spoke of the

new upcoming movie versions of some of their Saturday morning shows, and I uncontrollably blurted out, "Can my sister and I be Electra-Woman and Dynagirl?" Gulp. Silence. And then, I can't believe it, they completely ignored me! What*ever!* At least I learned the correct lyrics to the very important song "Oranges Poranges," sung by Witchiepoo's punk rock band: "Oranges poranges, who said. . . there ain't no rhyme for oranges." (darby) ✿ At the end of every H. R. PufnStuf episode, Puf exclaimed, "Keep those cards and letters coming!" I took this to heart and wrote Jimmy (Jack Wilde), who set my five-year-old heart aflame. A love letter in an envelope crayoned full of X's and O's. When I received a type-written letter in return I felt like Marcia Brady after meeting Desi Arnaz, Jr. It wasn't until more than a decade later that my mother admitted to the interception of my letter and forgery, with the lame excuse that the show was already in reruns. (lorraine)

K-Tel Famous for their commercials pitching their mass-market compilation tapes/LPs in the '70s and '80s, which would combine the oddest groups. My friend has one called *Pure Power* with Alice Cooper, the Doobie Brothers, Paul Anka, K.C. and the Sunshine Band, and Hall and Oates. I've got one called *Rock 80* with Gary Numan, Sniff 'N' the Tears, Pat Benatar, Joe Jackson, the Ramones, and M (the ones who do that song "Pop Muzik"). Blondie seemed to appear on about 90% of their releases — and all their records said "As advertised on TV," as if it were a big selling point. P.S.: They were also later responsible for the despicable "Hooked On" series. (darby)

Kung-Fu Theater It was either Saturday or Sunday mornings, but I remember watching *Master of the Flying Guillotine* over and over. I think that was the favorite out of the three or so they played. I would watch them (sometimes they would have them back to back), then my friends and I would go out to the wooded field behind our tract and recreate the whole movie, complete with jumping out of trees and throwing chains, and we even learned to make nunchaku from the master, Bruce Lee. Later I found they have a Hong Kong film festival every year so the tradition lives on, sort of. (e.c. cotterman) ✿ "Everybody was Kung-Fu fightin'. Hya! . . . Those kicks were fast as lightnin'. Hya!" (nina) (See also JACKIE CHAN)

H

Jack La Lanne One of the guys in Killer Pussy married the daughter of the person who owns Jack La Lanne's name, and because of this I've seen videotape of a party at his house featuring Jack La Lanne singing a god-awful version of "My Way." (don) (See also KILLER PUSSY)

Lancelot Link, Secret Chimp The greatest live-action children's show ever, this all-primate (as in, *no humans*) rock 'n' roll spy spoof ran for two precious seasons only starting in 1970, though it has since been rerun on Nickelodeon and The Comedy Channel. Cast, in addition to simian 007 Lance, included Mata Hairi; Inspector Darwin; (negative German stereotype) Baron von Butcher; (negative Spanish stereotype) Creto; (negative Asian stereotypes) Dragon Woman and Wang Fu; (negative Arab stereotype) Ali Assassin; and (Brit stereotype who looked eerily like Queen Elizabeth) the Duchess. ABC/Dunhill released an album of Lance's groovy group the Evolution Revolution, easily one of the most brilliant rock albums of the era. (gwynne) 🌼 After its two-season run on ABC, the producers realized this entirely dubbed show could be redubbed and shown in almost any TV market in the world. Alas, the secret-agent formula didn't translate well in most markets. However, the show did very well when it ran in Central Africa, and in 1987 it became the number-one show in Zaire. (bruce)

Lanyards Key chains made from colorful polyvinyl-plastic-flat-stringlike compound called gimp (was it named for those who could not master the art?) by use of a technique called the box stitch. If you wanted to pass summer camp, you had to weave several of these, often by hooking the key-chain end on to the bark of a tree. (lorraine) (See also ARTS AND CRAFTS)

Las Vegas Retro capital of the world! No matter what is or is not (usually not) in style, Las Vegas isn't scared to keep it proudly displayed. In this, the decade of the comebacks, Las Vegas is truly the proud forefather. Where old tried-and-true has-beens can *always* find a home when the rest of the trendy world thinks them a bit *too* Retro Hell. (darby) (See also ELVIS DIES) 🐘

Cyndi Lauper Why is this goddess of song relegated to has-been status while mushy wussy pop groups rule the airwaves? The music business sure sucks. (gwynne) 🌼 Briefly made professional wrestling hip in the mid-'80s by casting Captain Lou Albano in her music videos and promoting WWF matches with her husband/manager. (howard) (See also JUNK DRESSING) 🐘

L'Eggs Popular pantyhose that came in those *Mork and Mindy*–type plastic eggs. They were all wrinkly and sick when you took them out. (wendy) 🌼 The egg-shaped containers made people feel like they were getting some kind of great bonus along with

Jack La Lanne

Lamps That Lit Up When You Touched the Leaves of a Plant

Who knows what these were actually called, but this was hi-tech sci-fi right there in the house of your parents' richer, neater friends. The plant would be sprouting out of a lamp base and one, two, three, the light would grow brighter with each touch, until it finally shut off and you could start again. Hours of orgasmic kid play. (darby)

each pair of pantyhose. Supposedly you could use (no, recycle!) the eggs for Christmas ornaments and other crafts projects. I have a whole book of these projects, put out by the pantyhose company. Pretty lame in retrospect. (candi) ❧ Retired quarterback Joe Namath did the oddest thing by wearing L'Eggs pantyhose in one of their commercials. "If these can make my legs look good, imagine what they could do for yours." The zenith of '70s androgyny chic. (jes/bruce) ❧ Namath needed money. It's embarrassing. (dad) ❧ R.I.P. Juliet Prowse. (darby)

Le Bag / Le Sport-Sac Very French, no? Le Bag was the oversized, great-for-shopliftin' tote. Le Sport-Sac was made out of parachute material that came in an array of sizes and styles and which if you close your eyes you may still be able to picture in some ugly rust color, with lots of make-up stains on it, that you kept for one too many years. (darby) 🐾

Legwarmers With tight jeans and legwarmers for the Pat Benatar aesthetic, or on top of your Frye boots (I think those may have been a special item called boot toppers, though). (allison) ❧ Kate Bush had the *best* legwarmer collection. (gwynne) ❧ *Xanadu*, the movie Olivia Newton-John starred in, was my great inspiration to wear these knitted, footless stockings with everything I owned. (laurel) (See also AEROBICS and FLASHDANCE) 🐾

Lipgloss The kind with the syrup in a glass tube and a plastic ball on top that you would roll on your lips. The popular flavor was, of course, bubble gum. You put this stuff on your lips until they were practically dripping with this sugary slime. It was good for school too, 'cause when you got bored in class you could spend the whole time putting it on and licking it off. Lisa AA. says they were called Kissing Sticks, others say Max Factor Kissing Gloss, but there's also the one with the sponge-tipped applicator, which was Kissing *Potion* — unless I've got them all mixed up, which seems probable. (darby) ❧ There was another popular type in a small tin with a sliding top and an antiquey-looking fruit drawing on the lid. (lisa aa.) ❧ Stagelight's Blue Roses ruled. (gwynne) 🐾

Lips I think the whole lips thing started with that Rolling Stones logo, and it progressed to lip-shaped pillows, lip-shaped couches, lip-shaped phones, etcetera. (riley) (See also PATCHES)

Lipsmackers Strawberry, grape, orange, bubble gum, root beer, 7-Up, Dr Pepper . . . The smart folks at Bonne Bell (besides this and Ten-O-Six, what else do they make?) caught on to the retro phenom and brought these tasty lip stuffs back, but I've only seen them in the smaller sizes. They used to be extra large and people would wear them around their necks on strings. Personally I never liked the way they tasted much. (darby) ❧ My friend Dru used to eat the watermelon one. (riley) 🐾

Lipstick I always wore bright orange or fuschia with frost over it. (ju-ji) *The* only two colors to have were Frosted Brownie and Zinc Pink, and if you didn't put it on every five minutes (so that it looked like caked-on frosting), what was the point of wearing it in the first place? Example: My stepmother once snapped at me, "Enough with the lipstick, Lisa! This is summer camp, *not* a fashion show!" (lisa r.) The mini white Avon lipstick samples that Grandma always had. There'd be that little cap you'd pull off and the lipstick would be there, and you wouldn't have to twist it up. They were called Fire and things like that. (laurel) (See also AVON)

Liquid Silver Necklaces Usually accented with turquoise teardrops, mother-of-pearl doves, or coral clumps. Replaced by gold S-chains. (gwynne)

Lite Beer Today you can choose from light, dark, ice, draft, and nonalcohol beers, as well as nutty combinations of these qualities, but not so very long ago beer was beer, period. The first successful light beers were promoted in the '70s, including an early success, Anheuser-Busch's Natural Lite. I'm not sure how much more natural it was than any of its competitors, but the word sure sounded good to '70s consumers. (candi) At my school the jocks on one side of the gym would scream "Tastes great!" while the jocks on the other side would yell "Less filling!" They never seemed to tire of this. (lorraine) (See also BUSCH GARDENS)

Lite-Brite "Lite-Brite, makin' things with light. What a sight, making things with Lite-Brite!" Another of my fave toys, though owing to electrical currents, an adult had to be present during use. Bummer. (katy) The glowing grid, an early trainer for the generation destined to work at glowing screens. Real chunky graphics, cool colors, and those tiny pegs you'd always lose. Few toys of its era are as fondly recalled. (bruce) (See also TOYS)

Litter The most noteworthy retro litter memory, beyond Woodsy Owl, is the commercial featuring Iron Eyes Cody, the Indian who shed that deep tragic tear which kept us kids guilt-ridden for years to come. (jaz) "Seemingly the Indian doesn't mind the highway that cuts through his land or the cars that pollute his pristine sky. No, it's those bottles and wrappers on the side of the road that have prompted his silent crying. . . . After politically charged American history classes in elementary school, I was already painfully aware of my passive role in stealing land from Native Americans [and] the ad cleverly capitalized on this guilt, but at the same time it implied that we could right our wrongs toward Native Americans simply by refraining from pitching Coke bottles out our car windows" (Pagan Kennedy, from the book *Platforms*). A friend of mine would throw his Jack-in-the-Box trash out the car window in the parking lot before we left, saying, "I'm not littering, I'm creating minimum-wage jobs for America." (jeff) I always thought there were three places it was okay to litter at: school, McDonald's, and Disneyland. (darby)

Little Kiddles Miniature Mattel-made cutie poseable dolls with tons of accessories. They eventually spawned a more advanced form, the Skiddles, which moved in a lifelike fashion once you shoved a spooky Vespa-looking device into their tiny little backs. Kinda scary. (bruce/allison) (See also DOLLS)

The Littlest Angel This terrifying Christmas television special featured Johnny Whitaker as a little shepherd boy who falls off a cliff to an undoubtedly gruesome death while chasing a dove. Thousands of youngsters freaked out during the scene where he returns as a spirit to his mother, gives her a hug, then realizes she has absolutely no knowledge of his presence. The plot concerned the earning of his wings in heaven but was probably lost on children, who had never faced the consequences of death quite so literally. Remembered by all with shudders and existential horror. (lisa m)

Logan's Run A good example of what passed for sci-fi before *Star Wars* came out. A real '70s vision of the future. A century after the apocalypse, a bunch of happy white people live inside the ultimate singles complex, a huge domed city that looks suspiciously like the Texas shopping mall it was filmed in. Here they lounge around in skimpy disco clothes, do drugs, beam up sex partners on demand, and wait to turn thirty, which is when they get to float around in this real cool zero-gravity area and blow up in front of a cheering crowd. I think the producers spent too much time in Orange County. This flick is so '70s that it featured Farrah Fawcett in a small role. I used to think this was pretty cool until my hand crystal started blinking red. Later, it became a really dumb TV series starring Gregory Harrison, who later was on *Trapper John, M.D.* (bruce) ❧ Even more than my thing for Lance Kerwin (*James at 15*), I have the worst fetish for guys who look like Michael York. (gwynne) ❧ I so very much loved this movie. (darby) ❧ I think you subconsciously loved it for the abundance of kitty cats at the end. (noël)

Lookyloos The type of people who are looking but never buy. Made famous by a series of commercials for Twentieth Century real estate. Today a term used by traffic reporters to describe the annoying types who stall traffic by checking out the accident on the side of the road. (darby)

The Loud Family The PBS show, à la *Real World*, entitled *An American Family*, peeked into the life of "the Loud family." Famous for the scenario in which one of the kids, Lance Loud, comes out. Today Lance is a successful writer for *The Advocate* and other publications. (darby) ❧ Also the name of the band Scott Miller (Let's Active) is in. They're not bad. (jesse g.) ❧ And a sketch on *Saturday Night Live* about a family who talked really, really loud! (jaz)

Love, American Style There is no other decade this show could have inhabited. Actually it first aired in September 1969, but it was ultimately '70s and lasted until January 1974. "Love seen from all sides: young and old, rich and poor, unmarried, just married, long married, and multimarried." Each program consisted of a bunch of cute one-act plays with *love* in the title: "Love and the Practical Joker," "Love and the Legal Agreement," "Love and the Hot Pants," "Love and the Hippie Girl," "Love and the Pill." It was a wonderful vehicle for ABC sitcom stars to stretch their abilities, and also soon became a haven for washed-up old actors of the Rudy Vallee and Caesar Romero variety. The one running theme is that every house in every episode had the same brass bed. In between there would be these terrible blackout skits featuring the loveless loser Lamar, played by the actor who later became Angel of the *Rockford Files* (Stuart Margolin). Every episode ended with an iris-out in the shape of a heart. Other Miscellaneous Info: Guest stars included Phyllis Diller, Sonny and Cher, Paul Lynde, Milton Berle, Ozzie and Harriet, Tiny Tim, Jacqueline Susann, Martha Ray, and Burt Reynolds; *Love, American Style* never made it to the top twenty-five shows during any year; the intro song "Love, American style, truer than the red, white, and blue, love, American style, that's me and you" was sung by the Cowsills. It was released as a single but failed to make the charts. The pilot of *Happy Days* first appeared as a segment of *Love, American Style*. It was called "Love and the Happy Day" and featured Ron Howard and Anson Williams as Richie and Potsie. (bruce/darby)

George Lucas Like any good film geek of the late '70s, I hated him while secretly envying him. The man who gave the world *Star Wars* had led a checkered past. From teenage hot-rodder to Hollywood god, his story inspired many equally wimpy boys with a taste for fantasy. He earned my respect by realizing his limitations as director and letting others direct his productions. George retreated to his own movie ranch, complete with fake farmhouses that housed million-dollar studios. Eventually, the solitude got to him. He tried to turn the Force into a religion, sat at Joseph Campbell's feet and called him Yoda. Today, he still talks about the importance of myth in our lives and is working on the *Star Wars* prequel movies. Now I can hate him honestly. (bruce) ❧ Interesting Side Facts: George Lucas originally wanted to change Anthony Daniels's British-sounding voice for C-3PO and hired veteran voice-over artist and comedian Stan Freeburg to redub all his dialogue. However, he changed his mind when he saw how difficult it would be. Princess Leia was to be Amy Irving, not Carrie Fisher. Han Solo was originally to be Nick Nolte, not Harrison Ford. Harrison Ford practically begged Lucas to have Han Solo's character killed in *Return of the Jedi,* feeling this would "complete" the character. The idea of forest-dwelling primitives defeating a hi-tech empire was a big part of *Star Wars'* post-Vietnam origins, but it was scrapped when Lucas felt that the Wookies were not primitive enough. So they were made smaller and the name was shrunk and reversed to become Ewoks. George Lucas on the success of *Star Wars:* "It just had to do with people liking dumb movies." (bobby) (See also STAR WARS)

The infamous nuptials of Luke and Laura

Luke and Laura I remember when the president got shot. I remember the earthquake. And I remember Luke and Laura's wedding. They're fuckin' retarded now. (selina) ❧ The most famous soap opera couple ever — despite the fact that Luke was a total dog! (I thought he was hot. I can't believe you didn't like him. The Bradys all had curly hair and I loved them too. — selina) In Hallmark-type stores during their heyday you could find everything Luke and Laura: stationery, posters, pins, mugs. I know they made their comeback already (a few times), but they *never* talk about the rape that originally brought

them together. As a youth I found it quite shocking. *And poor Scotty!* (darby) ❧ For a period of time around '77, *General Hospital* was in danger of cancellation for its poor ratings. Desperate, they made some drastic changes, and with a few new writers, characters, and acting teachers, the ratings soared up to third-place within two years. *The Soap Opera Encyclopedia* said that *G. H.* entered a highly controversial but phenomenally popular period. And after a controversial writer from *Days of Our Lives* joined, the pace picked up even more as they made one of the most notorious moves in the history of daytime drama. On October 5, 1979, Luke, who was convinced he would be killed in mob activity, forced Laura to dance with him to the throbbing music of Herb Alpert's "Rise" in his deserted disco. He then pushed Laura to the floor and raped her. Crying in fear and humiliation, Laura screamed "No!" repeatedly before the fade-out. The married Laura had expressed interest in Luke, but from Francis's gut-wrenching, painful performance as a rape victim afterward, it was clear that the incident had been more than a seduction. Laura was hospitalized and attended group therapy sessions for rape victims for a while, but as the months passed it became clear that there was powerful chemistry between Genie Francis and Anthony Geary, who had created a fascinating antihero in Luke Spencer. *General Hospital* had become enormously popular and the stories were moving with such momentum that the show was not about to slow down by sending its new male lead to therapy or jail. Instead, the show ignored the rape issue, thus appearing to condone the incident, and later got around to calling it a "seduction." Meanwhile, at the actors' personal appearances to promote the show, teenage fans screamed at Tony Geary, "Rape me, Luke! Rape me!," much to the dismay of both actors. (jaz)

Lunch Boxes They stopped making metal lunch boxes in 1986 because kids kept bashing each other over the head with them. The last one ever made was Rambo. Lunch boxes became a hot retro collectible item shortly thereafter. I remember waiting for the schoolbus in the fourth grade and teasing my friend's brother so badly he swung his lunch box and it caught the corner of my eye. I guess that was also about the age that I started to get self-conscious about my appearance because I remember feeling like the whole class was watching my black eye grow bigger and bigger during the day. The first lunch box I ever bought as a collector was a Campus Queen lunch box at a church rummage sale. Me and the other punk rockers from school had gone rummaging for the

cool garb. There were huge piles of lunch boxes, and Campus Queen was on top. Since I was completely *not* the Campus Queen, I found great joy in the irony of carrying this wonderful '50s-esque pink box to school every day. If only I would have had the foresight to buy the whole bunch of them, but I didn't know how lunch boxes would grow on me. I now have about sixty of them. They are perfect pop art. They're colorful, portable, 3-D, have all those cool panels, and they each represented something that kids were obsessed with: TV shows, movies, cute rock stars, or cartoons. It's that obsession that fascinates me about pop culture and therefore about lunch boxes. They're getting harder and harder to find, and each time I go to some out-of-the-way-town's Salvation Army, I desperately search for a huge box of lunch boxes that cost only a dime each, just like the one in which I found my Campus Queen. (jennifer)

m

Bob Mackie Bob Mackie gowns: extravagant, decadent, extreme, sexy. What Cher and Carol Burnett would always wear to get attention. What every desperate queen dreamed of owning. Before his recent comeback with lovely Barbie gowns, there was a really harsh article about his has-been status in *Vanity Fair* (the magazine devoted to building them up when they're already on their way up, and bringing them down when they're already down). Guess with the lack of variety shows, Mr. Mackie just wasn't *the man*. The business can be so cruel. (darby) ✿ He once did a gown for Carol Burnett that was made entirely of dishrags. He also did all of Judy Garland's outfits for her nightmare TV specials in the early '60s. Girlfriend can't get herself more fabulous than that! (bruce) ✿ One year when Cher was a presenter at the Academy Awards she wore a Mackie gown that was made of beads placed over her breasts and around her pelvis. She looked nude. It was scandalous back then. The only reason anyone watched *The Sonny and Cher Comedy Hour* was to see what she was wearing — especially during her big number at the end of the show. (patty) 🐘

Macramé Was never cool. Even back then, it was only for hippies or bored convicts. These days it's back in a small way. It's regained some dignity and has been renamed "knotting." (lisa aa.) ✿ I lived for macramé. (carla) ✿ *It was cool!* You could make belts, plant hangers, clothing, wall hangings . . . fuck you, it was cool. (jes) (See also ARTS AND CRAFTS)

Mad Libs Even though they were only fun if you used a lot of words like "toilet," "belly button," and "gross," at least they taught us the parts of speech. (gwynne)

Madonna Wannabes The look we had to have in '84 was straight out of Madonna's video "Borderline" mixed in with a little "Lucky Star": neon, fishnet, rubber bracelets, belly shirts, exposed navel, the net shirt, overlined lips, white lace, green lace, black lace, torn lace, random hair ties, having a mole, underwear as outerwear, the bustier with visible cleavage, rat's-nest hair, ripped nylons, ripped denim, fingerless gloves, crinolines, leopard print, '50s shades. She did Cyndi Lauper's clowny look one better — she made it sexy! We thought she had more sensuality in her ear than most women have in their whole bodies. Unfortunately her look changed so much that it got hard to keep up, and most teenage girls stopped trying once she gave us the "Papa Don't Preach" pixie haircut minimal idea. (jessica g./nina) ✿ Madonnamania pushed the push-up bra, as well as virtually every other punk apparel staple, into the ultramainstream. This meant that good, strong, pretty multicolored bras (as well as garter belts, lace stockings, whips, and muzzles) were available at most major department stores, sometimes even in my size, 34D. Madonna offered me salvation from the mid- to late '70s' skin-tight and braless look when the only bras made were those whisper-thin, totally sheer, little-more-than-nude nylons-for-your-knockers variety. My boobs are forever grateful. (gwynne) (See also JUNK DRESSING and SIOUXSIE CLONES)

Mad Magazine God, I loved *Mad* magazine when I was a kid. The fold-ins, Spy vs. Spy, Al Jaffee, Don Martin, Sergio Aragonnes's teeny little gag drawings in the margins. *Furshlugginer! Portzebie! Eccch! Mad* used to put out these big fat Super Specials all the time, collections of old material (mostly jokes about Spiro Agnew, as it turned out) with a few new pages and some stickers and posters and stuff like that thrown in. I bought 'em all, but the ones I liked best had these little pull-out booklets that reprinted stuff from the '50s, back when *Mad* was still a scuzzy little color comic book instead of a big black-and-white magazine. Those old comics scared the hell out of me; they were so sweaty and stubbly and horny and evil-looking, and every corner of every page was crammed with psychotic, cross-hatched detail. They were so nasty, I was a little scared about my mom finding out that I had them. (stymie) ❧ The *Mad* board game was rad. (darby) ❧ Once upon a time, it was read by pseudoslacker college-drop-out guys, but this was in the early '60s. By the late '70s, its adolescent core readership had discovered the *National Lampoon* and its naked babes. Many would argue as to the exact period of this magazine's halcyon days. It all depends on when you were a lonely, introverted adolescent who was too sarcastic to have friends. I caught a recent issue, and it was *grim*. (bruce) (See also NATIONAL LAMPOON)

Mad Max For as much as some original fans can't stand Mel Gibson today, the first *Mad Max* (1979) was a great flick. Postapocalyptic sci-fi with vicious cyclists, over-the-top punk rock clothing, and rude weaponry that spurred more than a few good nightmares (especially the part where Mel's wife and son were killed). Though this Australian film was originally dumped by its U.S. distributor, who dubbed it with American voices, it eventually became a big cult hit, which we all rented for late-night after-party viewing. *Mad Max 2* (retitled *The Road Warrior*) was an even bigger success, with amazing stunts; and the one that rightfully finished off the trilogy, *Mad Max Beyond Thunderdome*, co-starred Ms. Tina Turner during the peak of her comeback (with a bunch of annoying children) and had her singing the wretched Thunderdome song. (ju-ji)

The Magic 8-Ball When I was nine I got one for my birthday. I was so happy. After building up a lovely relationship I dropped it and cried so much because I thought I'd killed it. My parents said they'd get me another one, but I wanted that one, because I thought of it as a friend and I didn't want it to be with anyone else. My family consoled me by taking pictures of me and it together and saying it would go to a doctor and get fixed and then go to a needy girl. So I accepted that and got a new one. When I was ten I used it to make money. I made my friend dress up in my sister's Halloween gypsy outfit and I dressed up in mine and we took a table out on the front lawn and made a sign announcing, "Fortunes told by Exelda the Great for 25¢." Lemonade was too passé. (selina)

m

Magnets Refrigerator variety starting with the alphabet in many colors to the scary detail-oriented cutesy kinds that moms would collect and get mad at you for breaking when you slammed the fridge door. (darby)

Mahogany Shoot me, but this 1975 cinematic camp classic of a female fashion designer's fierce climb to the top never fails to brings tears to my eyes. Diva Diana Ross is amazing as she manipulates a multitude of men including psycho-photog Anthony Perkins and dreamy Billy Dee Williams for fame and fortune until she realizes the shallowness of her pursuits. By the time the credits roll with Miss Ross crooning the lyrics of its hit title song, "Do you know where you're going to? Do you like the things that life is showing you?," no doubt millions of filmgoers *almost* kicked their coke habits. But the real stars of the show are the fashion-forward clothes actually designed by the talented mind of Miss Ross herself: Afro-Japonesque chic that was years, decades, perhaps even centuries before its time. Sheer brilliance. (nina) (See also *THE WIZ*)

Chris Makepeace Star of such retro hits as *Meatballs* (Wudy the Wabbit) and *My Bodyguard* (Cliff Peach). It sucks that Chris never made a poster for those young girls who like the sensitive type in piped jogging shorts and striped tube socks pulled up to the bony knees. (winnie)

The Mall Huge, yet welcoming. Cold, yet comforting. The source of all pleasure, the point of all purpose. A vast, timeless void at the navel of soulless Suburbia. It sheltered us, provided for us, and eventually employed us. At the center of the adolescent world stood that sacred ground, the mall. No mere village green or marketplace, the mall was an all-encompassing environment where everything you could want to want was found. Bigger than cathedrals, and more revered, they were the temples of the money changers! Even without money, we still came to pay homage, to stroll, to see and be seen, and perhaps even to fall in love. Alas, when money came to matter more than mischief, the scales fell from our eyes and we saw the malls for the empty shells they were. One's faith in commerce cannot survive such a rapture. (bruce) (See also VALLEY GIRL/DUDE)

Mall Walking A scary form of exercise in which mommies would go to the mall at opening time and do laps around the thing in the air-conditioned (or heated) inside. They'd know how many laps equaled a mile and everything. With what other sport could you actually shop and exercise at the same time? (ju-ji)

"Man" to "Dude" In the '70s, the interjection/familiar pronoun/adverb/can't-think-of-another-word word of choice was "man." "Hey, man," "No way, man," "Maaan!" — no self-respecting liberal could form a whole sentence without at least one "man." But sometime in the '80s when no one was paying attention and all the hippies went corporate (which left only underemployed surfers, skateboarders, and high school kids in charge of street slang), the "man" became a "dude." While "man" was older and wiser, "dude" was younger and, well, dumber. Aided by the success of such megahits as *Bill and Ted's Excellent Adventure* ('89), the concept of "dude," its meanings and implications, grew so expansive, it somehow became appropriate in any context on its own. With the nuances of its pronunciation, dudes who said "dude" had no problem communicating. Pronounced "Duuhuhude," it meant "Right on, I'm into it if you are," or "Check out that Harley," or just a simple "Awesome." Pronounced "Duuuude," it might mean "No, thanks," or "I think that girl he's hanging with is way harsh," or "See ya later," while "Dude!" expressed surprise — "No way, I can't believe it" — or a greeting: "Hey, what's up?" "Dude" also became an ambisexual appellation and was used to address either a guy or a girl, so there was the possibility in daily conversation for the double-dude sentence. For instance, "Dude, duuhuhude" could mean "Hey, dude, I heard you scored with that chick from chem class, way to go." But the triple-dude sentence was usually reserved for the close intimacy of the "dude" couple. To this day, if I hear "Dude, duuude, duuhuhude" I interpret it to mean "Hey, love, I hate to put you out, but if you could pick me up a pack of Camels on your way home, I'd be so psyched." (nina) (See also SAYINGS/SLANG)

Steve Martin leads the hoedown

Twisted Sister. Tish and Snooky were the den mothers of the punk scene, and killer dressers. They'd show up at Cramps' shows done up from head to toe in fishnets, spider webs with rubber spiders sewn on, and beehive hairdos with bat-wing barrettes. Or go out looking like perfect '60s airline stewardesses, or mod chicks with round glasses and orange paisley miniskirts. You've gotta remember that in those days, the general public was flabbergasted when they saw stuff like that. They were two of the most fun and crazy, creative, intelligent, pioneering people I ever came across, and they were sisters. Man, what a gene pool! (pleasant)

Marathon Bars A braided candy bar. What a concept. A caramel braid, covered in waxy chocolate. Marathon referred to either how long they were (one foot, with a ruler printed on the back of the wrapper to prove it) or how far you could stretch the gooey caramel. (winnie) (See also CANDY)

Manic Panic Tish and Snooky, sisters from the Bronx, who were part of the Lower East Side punk scene in Manhattan circa '76–'82, were far more than familiar faces in the crowd at CBGB's. They owned and operated Manic Panic, a little hole-in-the-wall on St. Mark's Place in the East Village, which along with Trash and Vaudeville and Screaming Mimi's became *the* place for punks and wannabes to shop. The whole area was cool, but Manic Panic was cooler, due to their introduction of the superbright colorful hair dye (of the same name) and to how amazingly cool Tish and Snooky were. They knew absolutely everybody who was anybody — hung out nightly at the Mudd Club, Max's, the Four Roses, Mercer St. Arts Center, the Palladium, and CBGB's. They had completely diabolical senses of humor, made great clothes, found the best crap in thrift shops, and sang in their own band called the Sick F*cks (the band the Plasmatics modeled themselves after) — besides singing backup for Blondie (before they were eventually replaced by a keyboard player), and a variety of others like the Dictators, the Del-Lords, Squeeze, RuPaul, even

Steve Martin Who else could get away with such obviously stupid skits like wearing a fake arrow through his head and telling suave stories about "Happy Feet," Grandpa buying a rubber, bad pot jokes, or "Cat Juggling," all the while ending every joke with "*Well, excuuuuuuuse me!!*" (mike v.) L.A. local boy Steve Martin excelled at magic and playing the banjo. This was enough to land him several years' work at Disneyland's magic shop. Eventually, he became one of the writer/performers on *The Smothers Brothers Show.* Emerging from the dust and rubble of their cancellation, he grabbed his banjo and some jokes and headed for the stage. He rode out the end of the Aquarian age in a white suit, a conservative haircut, and a big fake grin. The look was normal, but the act was not. He'd come out and read the phone book, introduce a Boston fern as his

m

partner, or play inaudible tunes on the dog whistle. By 1975, there were enough people on drugs to get his act. They filled theaters and arenas to see him do his "wild and crazy thing." By the time *Saturday Night Live* premiered, he'd already worked with much of the cast and crew. He became their frequent guest and the decade's king of stand-up. His first few comedy albums were best-sellers, and his first feature film soared, despite predictions to the contrary. He dated Bernadette Peters (star of many Mel Brooks comedies) for a while, before losing her to Broadway. As his stand-up got limp, he moved further into films. Today he has settled into playing slightly unfunny middle-aged men, with a conservative haircut and big fake grin intact. It has served him well. No excuses needed. (bruce) ♣ Like a few other comedians — such as Robin Williams and Tom Hanks — Steve Martin has transcended his stereotypical goofball roles to become a well-respected figure in the acting community. Who would've thought that some silver-haired freak who penned and recorded the song "King Tut" ('78) with the Toot Uncommons and starred in the movie *The Jerk* ('79) would go on to such greatness? There's hope for us after all. (noël) (See also KING TUT and *SATURDAY NIGHT LIVE*)

Mary Hartman, Mary Hartman

Norman Lear, at the height of his programming prowess, created the brilliant *Mary Hartman, Mary Hartman* as an intentional spoof of the vacuity of televisual melodrama and soap opera plot-twist inanity, but he went so over the top with this that none of the three networks would touch it. Essentially, the show revolved around the edge-of-sanity acting style of Louise Lasser, who played the title role of a pigtailed, apron-and-platform-shoe-wearing distressed housewife, and the relative normalcy of the remaining cast. Plot twists depicted the kitschy, lower-middle-class small-town world of Fernwood, Ohio, a town composed of geriatric flashers, child preachers, C&W lounge singers, kidnappings, freak accidents, slutty teens, lecherous but cute cops, smarmy politicians, and concerned citizens' councils. Being not fully able to cope with all of this, Mary would typically crawl down into the kitchen sink cabinet or launch into non sequiturs about her favorite household cleansers. *Mary Hartman, Mary Hartman* was shown in syndication and was a huge late-night hit, but lasted only for one magic year. Louise Lasser got embroiled in a cocaine controversy and quit. (thomas c.)

M*A*S*H

M*A*S*H may have been depicting Korea in the '50s, but it was clearly a '70s commentary on the Vietnam War of the '60s. Talk about Retro Hell. (bruce) ♣ The surreal episodes were certainly impressive for typical television. I still get depressed about Colonel Blake dying (though it didn't faze me much when the actor McLean Stevenson recently died). This version of the Korean War, on which the show was based, went on longer ('72–'83) than the actual war did. "True" fans of the *M*A*S*H* movie, which inspired the television spin-off, found the TV version weak and blamed it all on Alan Alda. (darby) ♣ Alan Alda is your typical wimpy liberal. He was *sensitive, caring*, and turned a fairly funny Korean War movie into an egotistical piece of shit. They were always right, never wrong. They turned what was originally an anti-military movie into an anti-*war* TV show. Not exactly one of my favorites. (dad) ♣ It might not have been one of Dad's favorite shows, but we were all forced to watch it every week! (selina) ♣ Alan Alda personified the '70s American male. (mike s.) ♣ Alan Alda even to this day is my perfect dream man. He had the quickest wit, passion, and biggest yummy smile of anyone ever. (jes) ♣ I still watch late-night reruns of this to see if I can get a glimpse of Radar's left hand with the missing fingers. (e. c. cotterman) ♣ All the middlebrow people would say, "I don't watch TV . . . well, except for *M*A*S*H* and PBS." (jeff) (See also PBS)

Masters and Johnson The George and Martha Washington of the Sexual Revolution. Picking up Dr. Kinsey's banner, this pair of St. Louis shrinks begat the entire field of sex therapy. From sex surrogates to AIDS panic, this multidivorced duo blazed the trail for others. Along the way, they became household names, and man and wife. Next time you're horny, thank these good doctors that you are able to think of sex as something natural and fun. (bruce)

Max Headroom A really innovative science fiction television series that began as some quick Coke commercials of a computer-generated celebrity named Max Headroom, a blond-haired head in a box with the personality of a game show host, played by Matt Frewer. When they made this digitized spokesman into a TV series, they set up a postapocalyptic future where television studios rule the world. It was kind of cool actually. Really unique for prime time. That is exactly why no one watched it besides a few cult followers who still obsess over it to this day on the Internet. I really liked Amanda Pays, who played the main love interest on the show (she's now married to *L.A. Law*'s Corbin Bernsen). She was really hot because she looked like supermodel Paulina Porizkova. Frewer didn't work much after the critically acclaimed show was canned, but he has turned up in a few bad movies recently. He was exceptionally good as the principal in that piece of shit National Lampoon movie *Senior Trip*. (howard) (See also MODELS)

Bob McAllister Pervert or genius? Host of marathon kiddie shows like *Wonderama* and *Kids Are People Too*, and a helluva songwriter! I wonder if he ever found that aardvark? (gwynne) ❧ Last sighting was in a summer '93 advertisement on the score sheets at Bowlmor Lanes on University Place, N.Y.C. He was advertising his services as a private entertainer for parties. The ad read: "Do you remember this man?" with a bad drawing of him, telling you to flip it over for the answer. And then on the back it said, "It's Bob McAllister! The *Wonderama* Man!" (steve m.) (See also WONDERAMA)

McDonald's The magical land Ronald inhabits was a much trippier place in the early '70s. It wasn't so built up. There were still Fillet-o-Fish in the pond, and patches of french fries for the picking. Whatever became of those shaggy creatures with their googly eyes that grazed there? What became of Grimace's extra arms? Why is the Hamburglar still on the loose after twenty-five years, and where is Chief Big Mac during all his sprees? The Chief is gone now, along with Mayor McCheese. Ronald must have arranged a coup d'état. He had himself installed as omnipotent ruler of McDonaldland, using his black magic to transform the place until it all became a single reflection of his own caloric soul! These days McDonaldland looks more like upper-class suburbia: kids in safety helmets, and a McDonald's on every corner. It's all so nice, so tidy, and so controlled. All magic in the land now flows from Ronald, whom all children MUST adore. Ronald's rule is benevolent, but absolute. Man, I gotta stop eating here when I'm depressed. (bruce) ❧ What lurks behind that sinister grin of scary clown mascot Ronald? McDonald's has the most recognizable brand name on the planet, in seventy-nine countries, eager to share its homegrown happiness and comforting convenience. (skylaire) ❧ I worked there. I'd leave school at lunch just in time for the rush. My favorite thing to do was give out free food in the drive-thru. To any cute, skinny, snobby popular girl that came through I'd give extra Big Macs, shakes, and apple pies. They'd like me for it and never know I was just trying to fatten them up. My favorite Mickey D's story (though no one called it that pre-'80s) was when I was testing out being ultrafem like my friends who all had fancy long fingernails. Mine wouldn't grow so I got the Lee Press-On variety. I remember it was impossible to even button my shirt to get dressed in the morning, but I vowed to try them for a full day and went to work with them on. As I was putting together a drive-thru order, I removed my hand from a bag to find that three of the fingernails were gone! I guess it was the greasy steam. It was so busy, though, I gave them the bag anyway. It must have been disturbing finding fingernails in their food, but I figured most people who eat there probably don't look at what they're eating anyway. (darby) ❧

Meat Crisis

Though largely forgotten today, the 1973 meat crisis became a seminal event in American gastronomic history. Of the era's many crises, this is the one that has had the longest-lasting impact on our daily lives. Dinner, in those simple times, meant meat — not chicken, not pasta, but formerly four-legged flesh. A steak and baked potato were considered eating light, salads were called "rabbit food," and vegetarians were spooky waifs with flowers in their hair. Into this mindset came a series of economic calamities known as the Nixon administration. Numerous government policies intruded into the marketplace like never before. Inflation was the culprit then, but remained just a buzzword to many. However, its point drove into everyone's home when the price of ground hamburger rose to an unbelievable 99¢ a pound! Middle America had gradually and grudgingly forgone steaks and chops, but this was different. This was hamburger, a staple, the essential building block of the American diet! How could this have happened to the ruler of the Free World, the country that won World War II? How could any red-blooded American be expected to survive on fewer than two daily servings of red-blooded meat?

Throughout the harsh winter, some tried to get by with newly introduced "meat extenders" like Hamburger Helper and Manwich — and soy beans were touted to be our savior. Others dug up survival strategies from the Depression and the rationed 1940s. Sales of Crock-Pots soared, while some enterprising souls began selling horsemeat to major supermarkets. The curious tried this chewy crimson flesh, and it enjoyed a brief novelty (one entire episode of *All in the Family* involved Edith trying to sneak horsemeat past Archie). After a few months, it wasn't funny anymore. There was talk of shortages and retirees reduced to eating pet food. Meat began vanishing from supermarket shelves, leaving only chicken in its wake. Sales of deep freezers jumped, and the government warned against hoarding. Stories in the press told of large-scale cattle rustling and a growing mafia for black-market meat. The government, grim-faced and distrusted, even began printing tickets for possible meat rationing. In March, consumer activists called for a nationwide one-week boycott of meat by every man, woman, and child.

It was perhaps the most successful act of consumer defiance ever seen. What began as a last thrash of counterculture ire received the backing of the USDA, who now said Americans were eating too much meat. Even hardhat types joined this bandwagon. Housewives everywhere swapped recipes for the upcoming week without meat. During the first week of April, school lunches went patriotically meatless, and families picketed their local Burger King. When the week was up, the boycott continued on Tuesdays and Thursdays. By May, there had been a 60% drop in meat sales nationwide, and packing plants had begun laying off workers. Supermarkets began cutting prices, as did wholesalers.

Gradually, meat prices began to come down, but they would never return to their pre-crisis levels.

There was an unexpected benefit from this crisis and the boycott. What began as a panic soon turned practical and then became a principle. Millions discovered life after eating death, finding they got along just fine on less meat. The swapped recipes stayed with us, and dinner became more adventurous. Many people felt better, not just about themselves, but actually better. We now eat far more chicken than beef, and many of us go meatless for health instead of money. Gardenburgers and pasta dishes appear on more restaurant menus. True, we are fatter than ever, and junk food is now an entire food group, but our diet has grown more diverse and varied as our waistlines have grown larger. We have gone through a subtle and substantial cultural change, one that began in this half-forgotten crisis.

Epilogue: New York City's main garbage dump is a place charmingly known as Fish Kills. Here stands a pile of garbage that is arguably the most massive thing ever made by man. Its total volume surpasses that of the Pyramids and the Great Wall of China. In the early '90s, a local professor of archaeology hit upon the amusing idea of using this humongous heap as a convenient training site for his students. Here they could study and date successive layers of the civilization that made it and draw conclusions about its people. As his students began their methodical excavations, they found they could date their findings from old newspapers. When they reached a level corresponding to 1973, they found an unusually rich deposit of rotted meat. The students were puzzled by the findings and brought them to the professor. It appeared that consumers of the time had bought far more meat than they could ever use, only to wind up throwing it away. The professor solved the puzzle by telling them of the meat crisis they were too young to recall. He then congratulated them on being the first to turn up solid archaeological evidence of its existence. (bruce)

McDonald's Happy Meal Conveniently packaged fast food (cheeseburger, small fries, small beverage) wrapped in a candy-colored activity fun box with a surprise toy for added orgasms. These were geared toward getting kids to pester their parents for McDonald's wholesome greasiness and who in turn would buy themselves some fatty foods, proof of the power of impulse shopping. Unfortunately, the toy aspect of the Happy Meal has since been bought out by movie companies and others of their ilk who want to advertise their products through the guise of fun. In the year 2000, Happy Meals will have been around for twenty-one years if you can believe it! (noël)

Malcolm McLaren Brilliant conceptual artist or the Don Kirshner of punk? The only consensus people have reached about this guy is that he's very, very shrewd. He first appeared on the music scene in the early '70s when he became the manager for the New York Dolls. He gave the band a makeover to look like commies, a gambit guaranteed to piss off Americans in a big way. Everything about the band became red: they wore red, they used the word *red* in every song, they even waved around Chairman Mao's *Little Red Book* onstage. Eventually the band broke up, and Malcolm headed back to England to open Sex, a bondage boutique on London's sleazy side. It wasn't long before he was auditioning local kids for a new band he was putting together, a band he'd decided to call the Sex Pistols. He picked four of the meanest, mangiest pups ever to walk the streets of London, and within a few months they were a sensation. At first the Pistols were content just to make noise and let Malcolm do the thinking ("Submission," for instance, grew out of one of Malcolm's directives to write a song about bondage), but the band was just too scrappy to take orders for long. The Pistols eventually had a nasty breakup, but Malcolm never quite made it out of the spotlight. In the '80s he created a bunch of upbeat dance bands like Bow Wow Wow and the Supreme Team, and he even started putting out his own records featuring weird, irritatingly catchy songs like the scratchy "Buffalo Gals" ("Four buffalo boys goin' round the outside, round the outside . . .") These days he makes his bread and butter writing commercial jingles (the Virgin Airlines theme is his), but he still puts out an occasional solo album. He was last seen devising a publicity campaign for Warsaw, perhaps the weirdest twist yet in a very weird career. Don't be surprised if Poland becomes the in place to be in a few years. (stymie) (See also NEW ROMANTIC)

MDA No doubt your future kids will thank you if you were clueless to this infinitely stronger and deeply more satisfying mid-'80s hallucinogenic precursor to ecstasy. Otherwise, try to imagine, if you can, the difference between acid in the '60s and what passes for a hit today, then apply this to the MDA and ecstasy equation to figure out the total possible sum of your remaining brain cells — take your time if you need to. (nina) ❧ It cost $5 a hit and looked like this grayish-whitish powder, which you wrapped in a corner of paper and ate — though to get the best high from it you were supposed to put it in a capsule and shove it up your butt. (riley) (See also ACID)

Members Only Expensive early '80s jackets with those snaps on the shoulders. This was among the few things in life I was happy not to be able to afford. (darby) ❧ Actually a whole line of clothing, but they are best remembered for their distinctive jackets. Although aimed at active youthful guys, they were priced way beyond their range. Instead, they became far too popular among aging men who responded to their quasimilitary styling. Trying to recapture a little of their WWII youth, these guys were soon trying to zip over guts they'd never hide. The jackets made one's dad look stylin' for about five minutes. Later, they could be seen on less successful drug dealers. (bruce) (See also *MIAMI VICE*)

Metric System This was the wave of the future. In the '80s we were all going to use it. What happened? It's still 3,000 miles to N.Y.C., I'm still 5 foot 7 inches tall, and I'm still buying gallons of gas. Was it because they taught it in math class and alienated everyone? Are we afraid of size 90 jeans? Doesn't a 30-degree summer day sound good about now? We've moved no closer to the rest of the world than a 2-liter Pepsi. (bruce) ❧ I was Miss Metric in the 1976 Independence Day bike parade. I wore a 2-liter Tupperware hat and measuring-tape hair ribbons. I represented excitement and promise for the dawning of a new way to measure. The metric system was such a joy for third-graders and teachers. Everything divisible by 10! No more silly fractions, just use a millimeter or two instead. Unfortunately, big business, grown-ups, or someone wasn't as thoroughly taken as I was with all these centimeters and kilos. By the time I graduated from grammar school, rulers were back to inches and *Zoom*'s recipes were again broadcast in cups and tablespoons. (lisa aa.) ❧ People still work through the math metrics unit in the L.A. unified school district (no budget for books in the last twenty years). (jeff) (See also *ZOOM*)

Mexican Jumping Beans Is it magic? High technology? Nope! Just nature, pure and simple, *but amazing!* Little worms in the beans made them actually jump! (Or at least turn over.) These beauties were mesmerizing! However, once I learned the secret I became disconcerted, caring less about my pleasure and more about the well-being of my little worm friends. (jory) ✿ When you thought they were dead, you'd just throw them in a skillet and they'd wake up! (laurel)

Russ Meyer The Wizard of Bras hasn't released a new film since the 1981 pec-tacular *Beneath the Valley of the Ultra-Vixens.* He claims to have been putting the final touches on his fifteen-hour orb-obsessed autobiography *Berlin Alexandertits.* If there weren't such an ample market for his old melondramas on home video, he'd probably be flat busted by now. But he's still tops with me, and his body of work will forever be branded in my mammary. (gwynne) ✿ He is effectively retired for all practical purposes, à la Orson Welles in the '80s — and like Welles, a genius of the American cinema who will be remembered forever. *Beyond the Valley of the Dolls,* more than *Woodstock,* epitomizes the hippie era. (mike s.)

Miami Vice Based on a glamorous yet crime-laden '80s Miami, this prime-time TV action series ('84–'89) about two cool undercover cops, starring Don Johnson as Detective Sonny Crockett and Philip Michael Thomas as Detective Ricardo Tubbs, had all the trappings essential to the gilded decade of indulgence: flashy sports cars (Crockett had a Ferrari Spider), yachts (Crockett lived on a boat), gratuitous girls with big boobs in tiny bikinis, too much money, too much cocaine, bad-guy drug dealers in Members Only jackets, Italian designer linen suits in pastel colors, skinny ties, neon-lit bedrooms, music-video-style

Cocaine busters Crockett and Tubbs

quick-cut editing, nonstop crankin' tunes in stereo (a TV first), and a postmodern pastiche of pop-culture references (Crockett had a pet alligator named Elvis). The only other TV show that comes close to rivaling its '80s appeal is glitzy *Dynasty* with the never-under-dressed-always-ready-for-a-catfight duo of Joan Collins and Linda Evans — but then again, *Miami Vice* did have Sheena Easton on it for a while. (nina) (See also BLAZERS and COCAINE)

Micronauts These were cool space-age toys from Mego that included such galactic characters as Space Glider, Biotron, Microtron, Baron Karza, and Time Traveller. They all had removable small parts that kept getting lost, forcing Mom and Dad to return to the toy shop to buy your sorry ass a replacement. Some of them moved by themselves with batteries and they had cities and submarines and space ships made out of die-cast metal! Inspired a comic book by Marvel you could get at Pic 'n' Save. They were briefly revived under another name in the mid-'80s. (howard) ✿ The above neglects to mention that Micronauts are the coolest toys on planet Earth. Imagine combining Legos and K-Nex with *Star Wars* and the *Superfriends* (not the human ones but the messed-up ones from the Bizarro world) and you have Micronauts. Sparkly, shiny, interconnecting clear plastic metal toys from the microverse. (brandon spoons, editor of the zine *My Friend the Micronaut*)

Microwave Ovens It is perhaps impossible to convey the wonder and awe these things inspired upon their introduction. Cooking food on paper plates and five-minute cookies were the stuff of sci-fi. Yet here was the proof, right in your mouth! In an age when nuclear power and DDT were held as modern miracles, a small glass-lined box could not possibly pose a danger. I first saw one in action during a mall demonstration that was titled "A Taste of Tomorrow." Batter placed in ice cream cones rose and bubbled to pale perfection before my widened eyes. It was like seeing those Pillsbury rolls on TV, but in real time! The rest of the crowd shared my rapture. They gasped in unison at the sight and pushed us dumbstruck children to the front so that we could all have our own taste of tomorrow. No carnival snack was ever as marvelous to me as that unadorned "micro-muffin." Their arrival was to be our last slow dance with big science before an equally unadorned future filled with bubbling burritos spinning away at the all-night mini-mart. (bruce) (See also KITCHEN APPLIANCES and TOASTER FOODS)

Midnight Movies *Rocky Horror Picture Show; The Wall; Heavy Metal; This Is Spiñal Tap; Thank God It's Friday; The Groove Tube; The Phantom of Paradise; Fritz the Cat; The Nine Lives of Fritz the Cat; Dynamite Chicken; Kentucky Fried Movie.* What else could you do late at night when you were totally stoned in suburbia? (ju-ji) ❧ Plus the rock 'n' roll variety: *Rainbow Bridge* (Jimi Hendrix); *Rust Never Sleeps* (Neil Young); *Pink Floyd Live in Pompeii; The Magical Mystery Tour* (Beatles); *Ladies and Gentlemen, the Rolling Stones; Tommy; Quadrophenia* (The Who); *Lisztomania* (Roger Daltrey); *The Song Remains the Same* (Zeppelin). ❧ Before MTV, before Blockbuster, before Betamax, the only way most of us could ever hope to see those legendary alternative films, or rock 'n' roll concert films, was the midnight movie. Either you went to a legitimate movie house that did this on the side, or better yet, you went to a head theater. This was usually a dilapidated old movie palace that survived by the owners' showing whatever they could get their hands on. Since they were just getting by, the management never complained if you smoked dope in the front row or shot up in the bathroom. A solid rule was that you didn't just sit down and watch the flick. You hung out, wandered around, visited friends, or got a blowjob in the balcony. No wonder they didn't last. (bruce) (See also *SPIÑAL TAP* and *ROCKY HORROR PICTURE SHOW*)

Minibikes Not to be confused with dirt bikes, these were nasty little bits of steel, usually driven by nasty little brats. They were cheap, *loud,* and dangerous. No wonder they were so big for a while. Not even the bikers liked minibikes. Soon they became the mode of choice for feral young boys with too many dogs and stepdads. (bruce)

Mister Rogers One man whose contribution to kiddie culture is so extreme as to be nearly immeasurable is Fred Rogers. A lot of people like to think that Mister Rogers is some sort of pedophiliac weirdo, like the popular *Saturday Night Live* caricature portrays him ("Can you say *nambla?*"), but in reality Fred Rogers is a pretty normal if slightly overachieving guy who really does care about kids and does his darnedest to entertain and edu-

Mister Rogers and friends

cate them without talking down to them or relying on a bunch of technical tomfoolery to bedazzle 'em. His show, *Mister Rogers' Neighborhood,* is still shown every day on PBS and features some great puppet surrealism in the "Land of Make-Believe" segments. He does all the voices for the pantheon of puppets, including King Friday the Thirteenth, Daniel Striped Tiger, Lady Elaine Fairchild, Ex the Owl, and my personal totem, familiar, and role model, Henrietta Kitty. Besides being the hardworking puppetmeister in the secular world (now that Uncle Sam doesn't have Jim Henson to kick around anymore), Mister Rogers is really into music, and it shows. An accomplished jazz musician in his own right, he scores all the music on the show, and his LPs and a lot of his stuff is actually pretty listenable. The man is an awesome lyricist to boot. Check out "Meow Meow Meow Meow Beautiful" which is sung, predictably enough, by Henrietta Kitty, and has some of the best lyrics that have ever been spewed (or is that "mewed"?) by man or puppet: "Meow meow meow meow beautiful; oh, Mister Rogers, meow." Meow, it's enough to make one weep, meow. (don)

Models Cheryl Tiegs, Christie Brinkley, Patti Hansen, Rosie Vela . . . blond and basic was a big thing in the early '80s — quite depressing if one was looking for a feminine image with dimension. That Kim Alexis is now doing hemorrhoid and Monistat™ vaginal yeast preventive cream commercials is quite amusing. (ju-ji) ❧ Early '80s model-turned-drug-addict Gia, who is most famous for dying of AIDS, opened the door for younger, healthier Cindy Crawford, who looked so much like Gia she was called Baby Gia. (jaz) ❧ Gia also opened the door for the whole controversial heroin-chic, strung-out-models look which pushed healthy Cindy Crawford and her buxom supermodel friends like Claudia Schiffer and Elle MacPherson off the runway. Other models with Retro Hell appeal: Paulina Porizkova (for being in The

Cars' video and then marrying Ric Ocasek); Lauren Hutton (for still hanging in there); Iman (for marrying David Bowie); Jerry Hall (for being on Roxy Music's *Siren* album cover and finally getting Mick Jagger to marry her); Yasmin LeBon (for the Duran Duran connection); and Isabella Rossellini (for doing *Blue Velvet*). (nina) (See also *BLUE VELVET* and PHOEBE CATES'S BOOB SCENE)

Monchhichi "Monchhichi, Monchhichi, oh so soft and cuddly, with his thumb in his mouth he's really neat . . ." blah, blah, blah. Some ugly trollish monkey-doll thing that looked like the uglier kids in school, who you'd soon call Monchhichi. (And perfectly described my first boyfriend.) (darby) ❧ This scary primate had a plastic thumb that fit snugly in its mouth, and you could interlock them together like a chain. Its face was really hard plastic and would hurt the person you hurled it at. (morgan and ferris)

Cheryl Tiegs with her fabulous self

Mod

Mod, short for Modern Jazz, came about in England in the late '50s through early '60s. A bunch of straight white kids started hanging out in jazz clubs with the black kids and gay artists. They would dress like the musicians and the artsy crowd, in Italian three-button suits with thin lapels and five-inch side vents, button-down shirts, inch-wide ties, tie clips, Italian pointed-toe shoes called "winkel pickers," or Clarks' desert boots. To support such an expensive clothes habit meant getting a full-time job. To get to work and nightclubs, they needed transportation that was affordable, cool, could be customized to their idiosyncratic, detail-obsessed taste, and was, of course, from Italy: a Vespa or Lambretta scooter. England's weather dictated clothing protection; the scooter's leg shield would keep their pants legs and shoes clean while their parkas protected the rest. To stay alert at their jobs, be able to dance all night (some clubs actually started as early as the afternoon, and some stayed open till dawn), and somehow find time to shop for clothes, records, and scooter accessories, they took speed: purple hearts, cross tops, et cetera. By the early '60s, in addition to modern jazz, some "black music" acquired lyrics and was called soul. Since black music was so popular in the clubs in England, a man named Chris Blackwell helped bring ska over from Jamaica (and founded Island Records), and kids started skanking.

What about girls? To fit in the boys' world, girls had to dress and act somewhat boyish in ski pants or pencil skirts, button-down shirts, pointed flats or loafers for shoes, and wear their hair in a short bob. This way they were ready to jump on the back of a scooter and go-go-go without getting in the way of the boys' narcissism. Local bands like the High Numbers (who became The Who), The Yardbirds, and the Small Faces started imitating the black artists they loved, playing blues, R&B, and soul, and wound up with their own sound later to be called Power Pop. The scene grew and soon the mods were getting noticed by the post-teddy-boys-turned-long-haired-rockers who listened to American "white music" (which was actually also imitating black music).

The gay-looking clean-cut mods got picked on and the fights eventually became rumbles and riots. From the British papers came stories about the rumbles, and soon the American press discovered the word *mod*. Eager to label things and warp definitions, the American press succeeded in completely changing the definition of mod for their own capitalistic gains, and the term *mod* was taken and used to mean "modern" to sell clothes and many other things. As the scene waned, the mods in the southern part of England got more into psychedelic hippie music and music later called Garage Punk.

The mods in the northern part of England kept listening to soul, and by around 1969, some mods who had really gotten into ska shaved their heads and were called skinheads (nothing to do with the racists the tabloid media has told you about), while the British Invasion had taken America. Flower power, acid rock, glam, M.O.R. (Middle of the Road), bubble gum, funk, then disco, which sucked, in case you didn't know. In 1977, The Jam started releasing Power Pop revival music, and by 1979 the movie *Quadrophenia*, starring music by The Who, ensured a huge mod revival with a bunch of Power Pop bands (the Merton Parkas, the Chords, the Purple Hearts, and the Secret Affair) and (later to be called Second Wave) ska bands (the Specials [who started the Two-Tone record label], Madness, and the Selecter).

The mod revival was worldwide and finally making its way to America. In Los Angeles, a group of friends returned from a trip to Europe where they had seen mods for the first time. They realized record stores had an Import section carrying the British Two-Tone ska records they'd heard. Clubs that played punk rock would throw in a ska and Power Pop show. A guy from England started deejaying at the Oriental Nights Klub (the O.N. Klub) in Silver Lake, and it became the first mod club in L.A. Bands that played mod music started forming, like the Boxboys, the Untouchables, the Crosstops, the Bangs (who became the Bangles), the Rebel Rockers, the Question, and the J-Walkers. Scooter clubs were forming and having scooter rallies. Mods came out of the woodwork, showing up at the rallies and shows; scooter clubs from Orange County, the Valley, and Pasadena areas formed and would rally to wherever the cool clubs were. After the O.N. Klub came the Bullet, which took place at the Lhasa club in Hollywood. Mods had been researching their roots and started listening to '60s soul and old ska and Power Pop.

At the 1982 Who concert, mods came from everywhere, and the mod scene in L.A. was huge through about 1985, by which time there were new kids just getting into it and looking to start fights with anyone interested. All the cool vintage James Bond suits had been bought from all the thrift stores, and the good vintage clothing stores on Melrose had closed due to the insane rent increases since the media had "discovered" (read: *ruined*) the street. There are continual attempts at reviving the scene with northern soul (remember those mods in the northern part of England? The northern soul scene was really big in England in the mid- to late '80s but it never really took off here) with ex-mods deejaying, playing obscure soul records. And there are always ska shows with a bunch of skinhead ska boys, some on scooters, skanking to the rude ska beat. Today mods have been seen about, finally, with partial thanks to the neo-anglophilic Brit Pop kids, and mod dance clubs have been popping up again! (riley)

Monster Trucks One of the more curious offshoots of '70s trucker culture. There were two basic schools of monster trucks. The first was a humble semi-cab hot-rodded and loaded with anything that would make smoke and noise. When that got boring you could always see how much stuff you could haul with the fucker. With that very American combination of style and excess, shade-tree mechanics gave birth to the monster pickup. Outfitted with aircraft engines, tree-topping exhaust rails, and tires the size of asteroids, these butt-ugly things just reeked of macho. Some cracker figured he could con folks outta beer money by charging admission to watch these things trash arenas. By the '80s, this fine bit of diesel folk art had degenerated into ersatz demolition derbys. The chief attraction was watching some gaudy truck roll over and crush a bunch a helpless cars, sort of Evel Knieval in reverse. Just before leaving Michigan, I attended one of these charming social events. Eighty thousand fools packed the Silverdome on a snowy night to see the show. Never in my life have I witnessed a crowd so in need of dental hygiene. It was the only time I've seen shots of whiskey sold at concessions stands. The halftime event featured Walt Lazar, a local Chevy dealer. He was a small Lebanese man whose TV spots featured him dressed like General Patton, waving Old Glory, and riding a WWII–era tank over a Toyota. Tonight's show would feature General Walt and his tank running over twenty new Corollas. The very appearance of Walt's tank merited thunderous applause. As he approached the first "Jap car," a chant slowly rose from the crowd. It was Walt's own ad slogan, "Tanks but no tanks to imports." The chant began to build — it was a low but loud moan progressing to a mantra. Once the first windshield cracked, the crowd exploded, with "Tanks but no tanks. Tanks but no tanks . . ." Toothless grandmas, tear-stained daddies, sugarhopped sons, were all adrift in the swelling chant. Walt continued his mission. Now the scene was mayhem. There was no sound of the crushed metal, only the chant, now punctuated with Indian calls and rebel yells. The balcony folks were pounding on the rails. A shirtless teenager waved the Stars and Stripes. With the last car crushed, Walt began a slow victory lap as he was showered with cheers. As tow trucks pulled away the carcasses, an equally deep and profound *boo* went up from the masses. I wasn't laughing anymore. Instead I felt like I was at Nuremberg, a witch-burning, and a public lynching, all at the same time. (bruce)

Monty Python "I am *not* a witch. *They* dressed me up like this." The most brilliant comedy team since the Marx Brothers, Monty Python was the brainchild of Spike Milligan, who with Peter Sellers revolutionized British radio comedy in the mid '50s on BBC's *The Goon Show*. In 1968 he did the same for British television comedy, when he combined two college comedy groups with BBC comedy veterans John Cleese and Graham Chapman and secured a BBC series commitment for this new comedy troop. An American underground comic book artist named Terry Gilliam was brought in to do linking animation, and the series went into production. What the series didn't have was an air date, a time slot, or even a name. With episodes already being filmed, the troop found themselves under pressure from the BBC to name their show. The troop informed the network that the new comedy series would simply be titled *Its*. The network was not amused. The series was given a Siberian time slot, at 10:30 on Sunday nights, and told to come up with a better, more memorable name. Eventually they came up with the moniker of *Monty Python's Flying Circus*, and took to the air. The series limped through the first season, barely surviving its time slot, critical confusion, and indifferent ratings. Slowly, a cult following was built up for the show. A few years later, the series was aired in Canada, and was soon canceled. A devoted bunch of new *Python* fans braved sub-zero weather to picket outside the CBC headquarters, and the series was restored. Such fan devotion was industry news, and helped *Monty Python* eventually to come to the U.S. Ironically, its 1975 debut on America's PBS occurred just as the Pythons had stopped production of the show after four hectic seasons on the BBC. The series and two feature films (*And Now for Something Completely Different* and *Monty Python and the Holy Grail*) all exploded in America's face during the fall of 1975. High-class madness entered college dorms and the lives of geeky people everywhere. The Pythons eventually reunited, made more episodes, more movies, and even toured the USA. For me, this tour made for their coolest moment; their big-screen religious spoof *Monty Python's Life of Brian* was then in theaters and was raising the ire of many. Among the irate was the much younger wife of U.S. senator and Big Bang survivor Strom Thurmond. Mrs. Thurmond was leading a campaign against the film, which prompted the Pythons to open each show by lowering an enormous picture of her ancient husband. In between observations on the senator's odd name, they revealed interesting "facts" about him, such as his prehensile tail and his ability to shed his skin twice a year. They informed a baffled U.S. press that each show would be a benefit for Senator Strom Thurmond, whether he liked it or not. Strange and subtle was a Python trademark, then and always. (bruce)

Mood Rings Black meant anger, red meant kinda mad, green was okay, blue meant feeling good. Did any escape being boiled in water or frozen in refrigerators? (nick) ❧ They were useless outside in winter, they just turned gray and stayed that way. There were many incarnations of the personal mood detector. There was the big flat butch ring, a watch that changed color (the Moodwatcher), pendants, and even nail polish. A high school pal of mine broke up with his girlfriend when he saw hers change colors four times in fifteen minutes. Martin Landau and Barbara Bain showed up on *Mike Douglas* wearing matching gold ones, showing them to the cameras, and the audience applauded. They later divorced. (bruce)

Moog Rhymes with vogue, by the way. The keyboard-controlled Moog synthesizer was a breakthrough in electronic musical instruments. It let musicians mimic existing instruments or create sounds no human ear had ever heard. Most people first heard the Moog when Walter (Wendy) Carlos's album *Switched-on Bach* became a big hit in 1968, giving a futuristic sound to centuries-old classical music. Soon, Moogs were required equipment for every self-respecting progressive rock band. (candi) ❧ First released in 1967, the first batch wound up going to Pete Townsend, George Harrison, Paul Beaver, Roger McGuinn, and, oddly enough, Mickey Dolenz. Moog was the sound of the future. (mike s.) (See also PROG and SCANDALS) ⟡

Moon Boots There was a period when people thought that if you went into the snow you had to be wearing these cushy, warm, hyper–space age, platformesque Kiss-wannabe boots. Practically everyone in Southern California had a pair that they'd break out at any sign of winter weather — like they'd wear them twice before they grew out of them. They were probably called Moon Boots because they looked like the boots the astronauts wore up there, or they used some newfangled NASA material to make them, or maybe because they sorta moon-bounced when you walked . . . but really these weren't a utilitarian type of shoe; you mostly used them to get from the car to the ski lodge when you took that yearly trip to the snow. (jes/darby) ❧ I'd wear these halfway to school, duck into a Holiday Inn parking structure, ditch the boots, and switch into sneakers, reversing the process on the way back. This simultaneously kept my mother happy and kept me from getting pummeled in junior high. (jeff h.)

Mooning Still done by frat boys and five-year-olds. (winnie) ❧ The presumably insulting act of bearing your butt at someone was a forgotten relic of a simpler time. Until it was shown in the film *American Graffiti* ('73), and it all began again. (bruce) (See also STREAKING)

Mousetrap A game in which players take turns building a Rube Goldberg machine that eventually traps a mouse. I have yet to meet anyone who actually followed the rules. (nick) ❧ I did *once*, and then the goddamn trap didn't work! (bruce)

Mousse This fizzy, foamy '80s hair product that squirted out of its bottle like whipped cream was marketed to men *and* women and everyone fell for it. Its pluses were that it supposedly made thin hair "thicker," added control without stiffness, gave you the "wet" look, and you were hip and stylin' if you used it. Guess these pluses aren't very '90s, as most now opt for newer, more technologically advanced hair products. (darby)

Mr. Bill *Saturday Night Live* had their own cartoonish short way before Tracey Ullman had the *Simpsons*. Mr. Bill was the supreme tragic character. It was the story of a naïve Play-Doh man with a high-pitched whine and a cute dog Spot, trying to make it in this hard cruel world and being the ultimate victim and continuously suffering at the hands of Mr. Hand — a godlike father figure who *pretended* to be Mr. Bill's friend (he wasn't!). Chopped, baked, blended, boiled, smashed, and destroyed — Mr. Bill and poor Spot had it worse than Wile E. Coyote. Strange to think a man of clay being destroyed endlessly was adult humor at the time. Or maybe not. (darby) ❧

Oh No! Mr. Bill!

Walter Williams and Vince DeGeneres (older brother of comedienne Ellen DeGeneres) made the first Mr. Bill vignette on Super 8 and mailed it into *SNL*. Their little film was an immediate hit, and the show wanted more. Walter claimed to be Mr. Bill's inventor and signed a deal with producer Lorne Michaels, without Vince. Vince later sued Walter, and lost. In the early '80s, Walter tried to market Mr. Bill merchandise, but lost out to a refurbished Gumby. Recently, Mr. Bill was himself parodied in a series of Pizza Hut commercials. (bruce)

Mr. Coffee Scary commercials with Joe DiMaggio. The most popular and worst coffeemaker of the time. The coffee addicts loved the whole automatic turn coffeemaking was taking. The good variation was the Braun brand, especially if it came in rust. (darby) (See also MUGS)

Mr. Mike "This party is really dull, I think I'll liven it up with Mr. Microphone." The idea of a home wireless microphone had been a big hit in Japan, where karaoke and other acts of group humiliation are enjoyed. Americans showed little interest in singing through their own radios, so it ended up here as a cheap children's toy. (bruce) Note: Donny and Marie had their own version of this wonderful gift idea. 🦫

Mr. T Besides his character in *Rocky III,* Mr. T's most notorious role was on *The A-Team.* This character really challenged Mr. T's acting skills: B.A. was big and tough and wore lots of gold rings and necklaces. His dialogue consisted of soliloquies like "You foo" and yet he was sensitive enough to expose his fear of flying and to have a love scene. His acting prowess in such classics as *D.C. Cab* forged the way for fine and multifaceted actors such as Urkel, Alf, and Arnold Schwarzenegger. (jes) ❧ Mr. T Myth — Mr. T used to live in this posh neighborhood called the Land of the Trees and the entire community was pissed off at him for lowering the property value of the area because he liked to get really drunk and take out a chainsaw and chop down trees in his front yard in the middle of the night. (wendy) ❧ Mr. T Reality — Mr. T had a short-lived cereal that . . . like its *Gremlins* counterpart . . . tasted like a low-grade version of Cap'n Crunch. He also had a comic book a few years ago that ran for about twelve issues. (noël) ❧ More Mr. T Reality — His real name is Laurence Tureaud; he wore chains to remind him of slavery. (bruce) (See also *THE A-TEAM*)

MTV How new and bold was it? It was the first cable channel to broadcast in stereo (the first stereo television in North America, even before there were stereo-ready televisions!). To get the full sound, you had to get an adapter from the cable company that plugged into your rack stereo system. If this sounds like a million years ago, it was. (bruce) ❧ Before he became the star, Beck used to call MTV "the Beast." MTV came into my home as part of the package when we first got cable and I can still remember with what excitement I watched the Buggles sing "Video Killed the Radio Star" (the first video they ever aired). It seemed so innocuous, hard to imagine with what aggression it would grow into its present stake of media territory. (karrin) ❧ Launched sometime in 1981, Music Television seemed like a very good idea. The then-fledgling video channel reached only the few million people who were lucky enough to be in the right county. Original veejays included among others Alan Hunter, Martha Quinn, JJ Jackson, Mark Goodman, and Nina Blackwood, who hosted the show twenty-four hours a day and played a slew of New Wave videos from Duran Duran, Thompson Twins, Adam Ant, Devo, Toni Basil, etcetera. "I Want My MTV" was a big catch phrase for a while. Fifteen years later, the channel is viewed by millions worldwide on a daily basis. At this point, MTV commands way too much influence on public opinion. The PBS documentary *The History of Rock 'n' Roll* reported that MTV initially did not promote many black artists; that is, until CBS convinced them to play a Michael Jackson video. (noël) ❧ Before MTV, it actually was possible for your little incestuous club scene to stay

Mr. T as Mr. T

virtually unspoiled by poseur geeks imitating you, but now anything you do gets shown all over the world instantly, as some complete moron tells the pimply-faced teenagers that they are "the Next Big Thing." (riley) (See also OVERPLAYED VIDEOS)

Mugs Every kitchen had at least one hippie craftsperson–made giant crude pottery mug for making a big cup of Celestial Seasons Red Zinger herbal tea while thinking heavy thoughts. Squarer folks, like your mom and dad, had matched sets of normal-looking coffee mugs (maybe avocado green, with a mushroom or strawberry design on them, or later with hearts, rainbows, Ziggy, or personalized with their names) that hung from the pegs of a wooden or wrought-iron curlicue *mug tree* that sat on the kitchen countertop. So absolutely commonplace that you'd think they were required by law. (candi) ❧ I think they were! What amazes me is that the whole mug thing happened in an era when most people still drank instant coffee and couldn't pronounce espresso. The mug trees were as impractical as they were dumb. They fell from favor when people finally realized how ugly dangling coffee-stained cups could be. (bruce)

m

The Mullet Hesher/rocker-style 'do. Short (often spikey) on top and at ears, long in back. (darby) ❧ Think Journey. (nina) ❧ I always called it "the Fresno," because when I went to Fresno all the guys still had it. Besides that, nowadays I only see it on very butch lesbians. (gwynne) (See also THE SHAG)

The Munchies Sponsored by Doritos and Crunch 'n' Munch. (darby) ❧ One of the funniest side effects of marijuana smoking was that irresistible, bottomless snacky hunger called the Munchies. Any kind of junk food would do, but there was one manufactured snack that specifically targeted the doper market: Screaming Yellow Zonkers, a fancy caramel corn in a Peter Max-ish box. Trippy. (candi) ❧ In the '80s, a cartoon corn-kernel man came on between Saturday morning cartoon shows and sang "When you're feeling bored or blue, watch out for the munchies, they find ways of making you munch when you're not hun-gry," and he then introduced healthier snack items because "soon you're not just bored, you're fat!" (ju-ji) (See also JUNK FOOD, SUNFLOWER SEEDS, and TIME FOR TIMER)

Muppets Okay, who else thought they were real when they were little kids? *Sesame Street* was cool until you outgrew it and moved on to *The Electric Company,* then it was *3-2-1 Contact,* and then you were ready for the big time — *The Muppet Show* (begun in 1976). Featuring guests like the *Star Wars* characters, Debbie Harry, Liberace, and GG Allin (What? You don't remember that one?), the Muppets revived the variety show for the next generation too young to remember *The Smothers Brothers* or *Donny and Marie.* There were hints at animal crossbreeding between pigs and frogs, the Mad Bomber, the Swedish Chef, Pigs in Space, Beaker, and a host of other cool characters. Remember how fucking awesome Animal was? I had an Animal puppet I used to carry with me everywhere and got this girl to go out on a date with me in second grade by convincing her it was the pup-

Jim Henson, Miss Piggy, Kermit

pet's birthday! Pretty smooth, huh? I still think one of my best opening lines has to be when I walked up to a beautiful Hollywood sex goddess and said, "So . . . who's *your* favorite Muppet?" (howard) ❧ Miss Piggy was sooo big at one point, she reached the closest state to being human a nonhuman creature can reach. I think she even went to one of those gala affairs with Michael Jackson or something. She was sexy, and tough, and I bet she got a lot of marriage proposals. (ju-ji) ❧ Jim Henson (R.I.P.) created these in the early '50s, specifically for TV. He coined their name by combining the words *marionette* and *puppet.* Kermit has been around since the beginning, and Miss Piggy was originally called Piggy Lee. The muppets were a fixture on the old Ed Sullivan show. Even before *Sesame Street,* I had a stuffed ventriloquist-style doll of Rolf (the gravel-voiced dog who played piano). Almost forgotten today are the grotesque reptilian muppets who appeared on *Saturday Night Live*'s first season. They lived in a steamy primordial world, where they all worshipped a stone idol that spoke with a Brooklyn accent. The humor of these bits was decidedly adult. When Lily

Tomlin hosted the show, she sang a duet of "I Got You, Babe" with one of these muppets named Scrag. Side note: Deep in the bowels of the NBC building at Rockefeller Center, there is a notoriously crappy dressing room. It is tiny, and has a "closet" that is actually a simple pipe access. Jim Henson and Frank Oz got stuck with this room in 1956 when they were doing *The Steve Allen Show*. Pissed off at the crummy quarters, they painted all sorts of trippy muppetlike faces onto the pipes. Now legendary, the faces are still there! (bruce) (See also *SESAME STREET*) 🐾

Muscle Cars They're huge, but there's barely any room inside! The trunk won't hold an amp, but they get worse mileage than a van! That these reached the pinnacle of popularity at the height of the gas shortage made about as much sense as jeans that you had to lie on the floor to zip up but were still loose, baggy, and unsexy. (gwynne) 🐾 Back in the postwar days of jalopies, young toughs like John DeLorean were burning up the streets of Detroit in retro-fitted junkers from the '30s. Others, like Lee Iacocca, were in school finding ways to increase engine power. By 1963, both of them were climbing the legs of the U.S. auto industry with knives in their teeth. That model year saw the introduction of the first factory-issue muscle cars. For the next decade, Detroit kept turning out a series of "lower, wider, faster" models. Too expensive for teenagers, too wild for adults, these behemoths found a niche among the dead-end types who built them. They kept the engineers horny and could pass anything on the road, except a gas station. Today, the few middle-aged men who can still afford to maintain these heaps like to speak wistfully of the muscle car era. According to them, this era ended either with the federal safety laws of 1972, the oil crisis of 1974, or their first marriage around the same time. (bruce) 🐾

"Music Box Dancer" Like "Chariots of Fire," or that Chuck Mangione hit, this song was a rare instance of an instrumental getting in the Top 10. Played by dweeby girls at piano recitals for the next five years. It's hard to believe that people could get so hyped on a song inspired by a little, plastic, spinning woman on the end of a spring. I wanna do this song at karaoke. (winnie)

Mustaches Those big, furry, ugly ones sported by such dubious hunks of the era as Tom Selleck, Kenny Rogers, Richard Pryor, Cheech Marin, Burt Reynolds, Mark Spitz, and so on. Hell, even Santa had one! No wonder he was so scary. (karrin) 🐾 Mustaches are back. Push from Palace Brothers sports a bushy one while the singer from Six Finger Satellite has a pathetically chintzy one, though he does bear a remarkable resemblance to Schneider from *One Day at a Time*. (noël) (See also CHEST HAIR, QUEEN, and BURT REYNOLDS) 🐾

MV3 I really found punk rock and New Wave through my old best friend Paula, whose sister, Rina, was older and hipper and danced on *MV3*. We'd run home from school, turn it on, and watch all the New Wave and the new music video trends. Hosted by none other than KROQ's Richard Blade and some val-girl chick, they featured music videos from small bands like Gary Numan, Talking Heads, and Devo. This was about the same time some new music television phenomenon was emerging — I wonder whatever happened with that? (darby) 🐾 This show was a revelation to me when I was living in postindustrial Detroit. I'd keep hearing about all this New Wave music, but it all seemed very far from my gray world, where people still thought "Smoke on the Water" was pretty cool. You couldn't find this music on the radio, no club played it, and it wasn't sold in stores. My only window on this brave new world was *MV3*. It aired every afternoon on a UHF station that showed black religious programs the rest of the time. On my screen I saw wondrous images of Boy George and Thomas Dolby. Imagine, rock stars who made little movies! What really captured my imagination was the show itself, a neon-lit studio full of happy tanned folks in cool clothes, doing cool dances to way-out tunes, all of it hosted by a genuine English deejay and a real live valley girl! As quickly as it came, the show was gone. I knew I'd have to move to California if I wanted more of it, and so I did. (bruce)

Ralph Nader The godfather of consumer activism spent much of the '70s as a certified celebrity. He first gained fame with a book titled *Unsafe at Any Speed*, which exposed design flaws in GM's sporty and popular Corvaire and was instrumental in the car's demise. In the '70s, there were still plenty of people wanting to get back at "the Man" but who were now equally interested in "changing the system from within." To these sunshine rebels, Ralph and his struggles were the next logical step. Soon the term *consumerism* was coined, and Ralph became the leader of a movement. Ralph Nader was gifted with gangly looks and an unimpressive speaking voice; his star could only have risen in the same era Woody Allen's did. The most media-impressive aspects of Ralph's celebrity were his Gandhi-like acts of self-denial. He'd drive to Congress in a beat-up five-year-old car, and show up for interviews in a rumpled suit ten years out of date. Whatever he had to say was always far less impressive than how he said it. His books and lectures galvanized consumers, giving them an empowerment they'd never missed. Almost any action of Big Business brought on the wrath of consumer activists, who became known as Nader's Raiders. Like Don Quixote, he turned his attention to the boundless ineptitude of Big Government. He became the last hero of the crumbling counterculture, but also met his match. Whatever fire he had left was eventually lost to Reagan-era greed and cheap imitators like David Horowitz. (bruce)

Nadia's Theme After Nadia Comaneci kicked Olga Korbett's butt and showed herself to be the prettiest little sprite to ever mount a balance beam, Nadia-mania swept the country. Tiny girls everywhere sought fame and happiness in gymnastics. When *ABC Sports* showed the umpteenth ultra-slow replay of Nadia's poetry in motion, some producer decided to set it all to music. The music chosen was the main title theme to a forgotten '70s film called *Bless the Beasts and the Children*. Naturally, someone in Nadia-mad America thought of putting this out as a single. The tune was quickly rereleased as "Nadia's Theme," the name many people still remember it by. I do recall that some moron band actually covered it, adding their own inane lyrics. To further cloud the issue, the same piece of music was also put to use as the theme music to the CBS soap *The Young and the Restless*. (bruce) (See also NADIA COMANECI)

Name-Plate Necklaces All the coolest chicks in my junior high had them — they made fantastic bat mitzvah gifts from the folks or your grandparents from Florida. (katy) ✿ My tenth-grade photo is living proof that I was the geekiest of dweebs — my name-plate necklace is easily readable and blends nicely with the lovely sleeveless knit sweater in swanky pink and gray. Mmm, stylish! (bridget) (See also PERSONALIZED SHIT)

National Lampoon It used to be funny. I swear, it used to be funny! Fine, don't believe me. (gwynne) ❧ Didn't survive Reagan. (mike s.) ❧ Some will argue as to when its heyday was. A few say it's the stoned hippie-esque days of 1969–1974. Others will claim it was the cocaine days of 1975–1980, when its smug and sassy words were fortified with lots of naked babes. One thing both camps agree on: by 1980, middle age had destroyed whatever talent cocaine hadn't. A few loyal readers later went on to *Spy,* but most got a life. (bruce)

Naugas Circa 1967, this was Uniroyal's promotional giveaway for their new wonder fabric Naugahyde ("Every year, the Nauga sheds his beautiful hide"). These lovable owl-like creatures are much sought after by geeky knickknack collectors like myself. (gwynne) ❧ In 1968, I was a seven-year-old monster freak. One day I saw a Nauga in a print ad and went nuts! The creature was shiny, scary, and lovable. Soon the Nauga was turning up on small tags attached to luggage and furniture made of Naugahyde. I started collecting these, as well as print

ads, promotional flyers, and anything else with the Nauga's image. Eventually, Uniroyal, who made Naugahyde, sent a guy in a Nauga suit on a national promotional tour. He turned up on *Laugh-In* and the local Bozo show. Bozo announced that the Nauga would be appearing at the local mall. I begged Mom to take me. For some reason, the six-foot-blue creature with fangs frightened most of the children there, except me. For my birthday that year, Mom made me a Nauga of my very own, and my big sister made a baby one as well. For Christmas, the lady next door, who worked at Uniroyal, gave me a present of a genuine promotional Nauga. My Nauga family was now complete. I slept with them every night, reasoning that they were scary enough to keep the other monsters away. In time, my homemade Naugas wore out, but the authentic one endured. I took it everywhere with me, and yes, it was as tough and stain-resistant as the ads proclaimed. It is with me still, a quarter century later. We've slept together longer than most married couples, my Nauga and I; maybe that's why I'm so into leather. (bruce)

Needlepoint For a great book on the subject try *Celebrity Needlepoint,* by Joan Scobey and Lee Parr McGrath (1972), with lovely needlepoint work by Janet Leigh, Princess Grace, Cathy Crosby, Mary Tyler Moore, Amy Vanderbilt, and miscellaneous U.S. Cabinet wives to name a few. Quite exciting! Needlepoint made the leap from a purely female hobby to a unisex art form when I was growing up, and Rosey Grier was its poster boy. (darby)

Our own Bruce Elliot and his beloved Nauga

Neighborhood Dealer Always some heavy metal guy whose parents are never home. You timidly knock on the door and he answers it saying, "Who told you to come here?" Rush is playing in the background and some girls with heavy black eyeliner are hanging around near the stairwell, eyeing you. He acts like he hates your guts as he doles out the marijuana/pills/shrooms and you hand him the money. You race down the driveway into your chickenshit friend's VW Bug and roar away, knowing you can stave off another day of tedious nothingness. (lisa m.)

Nerf Football The Nerf Ball dates back to about 1972. In purple, orange, or green, these turned ugly after a few days because there was no coating on the ball and everything would stick to it (cat hair, grime, et cetera). The Nerf Football with a harder coating came later and it took off like wildfire — everyone seemed to have one. They made a whole lot of Nerf things after that. They were actually meant to be indoor balls but they were always played with outside so they'd get waterlogged and heavy and dogs would chew them up. These were cuddly athletic toys. (bruce/darby) ❧ If I remember correctly, the first Nerf was the basketball with the hoop you'd attach to the back of the door. We'd throw the ball at our cat and she'd try to bat it with her paw but the thing would just stick on her claws. (dad)

New Age Shirley MacLaine — will she be remembered for her legs or her channel? Shirley disgraced the Rat Pack and all her fans by going megahard-core New Age. She starred in a long, narcissistic miniseries devoted to the story of her life and spiritual awakening. The main thing I remember is her sitting in a hot tub, grooving on her change of life and displaying her already-retro multiply pierced ears. Yuk! Seth Speaks: Seth was the entity channeled by anorexic-looking Jane Roberts. Jane died of cancer from chain-smoking. "What's your sign?" accompanied by "Rising?" and "Moon?": I once had a blind date ask for my birth information before we met. As I entered the café he jumped up, declared us soulmates, and frantically waved papers at me showing our matching trines. ESP Tests: Your best friend held a playing card facedown while you tried to guess which suit it was. It felt very bad to fail. Space-Invading: Psychic intrusion. Crossing the boundaries of someone else's aura or electromagnetic field. Trolling around in their mind or being: considered very bad form. Raising Your Kundalini: A kind of yoga that movie stars did, where you meditated and energy rose up your spine to the back of your skull, giving you a buzz. It had something to do with sex. Primal Scream Therapy: Arthur Janov's invention, made famous by rock stars and other celebrities. Basic program was to go into a room and get *way* down: kick out the jams, yell like there's no tomorrow at Mommy, Daddy, whoever fucked you up first when you were a sprite. I once lived next door to "a primal scream therapy household." Bummer. Zero-Gravity Things: There was a hanging-upside-down-by-your-ankles fad (in 1980, Richard Gere did this very sexily in *American Gigolo*) and there were the ubiquitous immersion tanks (think *Altered States*, also 1980). Possibly had something to do with John Lily and dolphins. Esalen, Group Therapy, Sensitivity Training, Encounter Groups, Feelings: Go figure. Astral Projection: Robert Monroe wrote a book about how to fly around outside your body while it's still in bed. Vegetarians: Vegetarians fall under the general rubric of New Age because their driving force is arrogant superiority — the same I-know-better snottiness that characterized pyramid power, *I'm OK, You're OK*, and open marriages. Michael Jackson was a vegetarian, and that was *rad;* it was also tried by John Lennon and other hipsters (although during one period he and Yoko lived on an exclusive diet of sushi, heroin, Gauloises, and Hershey Bars). Favorite cookbooks were *Laurel's Kitchen* and *Diet for a Small Planet*. Also don't forget fruitarians, airtarians, high colonics, and Leonard Orr, the bathtub guru. Which brings us to rebirthing, which might have something to do with Alice Miller, Arthur Janov, and others. As the saying goes: What goes around, comes around. (amy) (See also *DIET FOR A NEW AMERICA*)

The New Coke Fiasco I remember this being a big event in my formative years. Mom drove me to the 7-Eleven the day they released New Coke and with baited anticipation I took a sip. Another. And another. "This is Pepsi!" For the next two weeks we bought all the regular/original Coke we could find and stored it in the garage. It was carefully rationed until the New Coke scare was over. (morgan and ferris)

Newport Ads The idea that some ad agency is still making money off the creation of Newport cigarette ads is a Retro Hell phenomenon with no logical explanation. Take a '70s Newport ad and hold it side by side with a '90s version, and only the partially yellowed paper might give away its true place in time. They're all green, with men and women in posed situations, where something cute and goofy is taking place, usually sporty with lots of smiles and teeth. I often wonder if they just shot an unlimited number of these back then and have just continued recycling them ever since. (darby)

New Romantic (Nu-Ro) This was a really distinctive music/fashion genre in the early '80s that sprang up as a reaction to hard-core punk. Anyone could go out and wear a Ramones-style T-shirt and jeans, or cut some holes in a trash bag and put it on, but to look like a New Romantic, you had to really try hard. The look was overblown and the only rigid standards it had were lots of make-up and wild hairdos for girls and boys — think early Duran Duran, Adam Ant, Toyah Wilcox, Annabella Lwin's braided mohawk, Haysi Fantayzee's crazy-colored dreads all tied up with yarn and rags. Even Madonna was influenced by the fashion — her gigantic hair-bows and lacy gloves are direct appropriations. Fantasy dressing was in: ruffles, embroidery, Jimi Hendrix military-style jackets, jodhpurs, pirate clothes, clown clothes, Caribbean sarongs in wild jungle prints with leggings worn underneath and little ska hats on top of a pile of braids, dog collars, rhinestone broaches, chains, fingerless gloves. Spandau Ballet even wore kilts! The look is now so classically '80s and dated that it wouldn't be a surprise to see it all resurface on the runways any day. And the Nu-Ro sound was distinctive — driving, tribal drums, lots of pop harmonies, bits of ethnic music. It was pure ear candy. (pleasant) (See also MADONNA WANNABES and SIOUXSIE CLONES)

Olivia Newton-John Before there was Men at Work, Paul Hogan, or Yahoo, Australia had sweet (bland) Olivia Newton-John to boast about. Although she was a well-known pop singer who crafted '70s-style sensitive songs, she won the world over with her classically clichéd transformation from a virginal, goody-two-shoes cheerleader to black-leather-clad roadster betty in the film *Grease*. She went on to superstardom with her seminal hit song "(Let's Get) Physical" and sparked a fashion craze that encouraged women everywhere to wear multicolored leg-warmers for no reason. When her fame died down and babymaking became her forte, she invested her well-deserved royalties into a number of shopping mall stores that went by the name of Koala Blue. Word has it that her stores have since gone bankrupt. (noël) ❀ Liv was everyone's peaches-and-cream wet dream. Whether you wanted her during her sweet "Have You Ever Been Mellow?" days, the naughty-but-nice incarnation of her "Totally Hot" and "Physical" period, or when she was the hot Helmut Newton dominatrix of "Soul Kiss" and "Deeper Than the Night," she always seemed capable of pushing more than a few buttons. (enrique marie) ❀ Her best role ever — the rollerskating mystery muse in *Xanadu!* (bridget) (See also AEROBICS)

New Zoo Revue This one was for the truly devoted TV watcher. Most of the other kids with more discerning tastes, or whose parents kept an eye on them and the TV, didn't know what this disturbing show was. It was similar to another whacked-out kids' show at that time, *The Magic Garden,* and had a slew of people in big puffy costumes: Henrietta the Hippo (flamboyant like Miss Piggy), Freddie the Frog (goofy like Gilligan), Charlie the Owl (owls are always the conservative intellectuals), and the two humans who were their friends (Doug and Emily Jo). All I remember thinking about it when I was a kid is that these people were so stupid to think we were this stupid. This and *Three's Company* were the archetype of TV shows that tried to *lower* your IQ level — and who knows, they may have succeeded! Their theme song went something like "It's the *New Zoo Revue*, coming right at you!" (darby) ❧ I used to look at Henrietta Hippo's nostrils, thinking they were her eyes. (noël)

The Night Stalker Now doomed to be forever known as "the '70s *X-Files*," this was the coolest shit I'd ever seen on network TV circa 1974, and it still is as far as I'm concerned. Sad-sack Chicago reporter Carl Kolchak, who toiled for the truth, pounded the pavement, used up shoe leather, and otherwise worked for the Independent News Service, fell into an eerie series of completely coincidental supernatural mysteries and monsters. No overarching conspiracy was posited, nor even any explanation as to why this one guy was unlucky enough to run into all this crazy supernatural shit. Kolchak's foes ranged from the obvious vampires and werewolves to aliens sucking bone marrow out of zoo animals to voodoo zombies to Indian bear spirits to flesh-eating Hindu demons to succubi to runaway androids. Kolchak, an easily ruffled fella in a trench coat and slouch hat, made a much better audience surrogate than those antifreeze-blooded FBI agents so popular today. Darren McGavin starred; the Sci-Fi Channel shows reruns today. (brian) ❧ The Night Stalker is also the name given to notorious L.A. serial killer Richard Ramirez, who pillaged Southern California in the summer of '85, slaughtering at least fourteen people and sexually assaulting more than twenty. Young and old, male and female, no one was spared. He was a self-proclaimed Satanist obsessed with the rock group AC/DC (which the media claimed stood for "anti-christ devil's child") and apparently used to play their song "Night Prowler" over and over

before he went out for the kill. After he was finally caught, he didn't even bother faking any remorse, waving and yelling, "Hail, Satan!" to reporters. The reason he gave to a fellow inmate for committing the murders: "I love all that blood." (See also SATAN)

Night Tracks The pre-MTV video show. It aired on late weekend TV and was very Rick Dees. There wasn't a lot to choose from because no one was making videos back then. (morgan and ferris)

Nixon When I became a sentient being, aware that I was a human, in a country, with a government, Nixon was president. He, Julie, and Pat all seemed so happy and stable in the White House, which, I was sure, never housed the kinds of violence and hypocrisy that went down in mine. I loved Nixon, and even cried when he had to resign. It wasn't until a year or two after that, when I figured out a little more about politics, that I realized what he had done, and denounced him. But I still have a soft spot reserved for Tricky Dick — I like bitter. (mikki) ❧ I spent long, hard hours on the playground jumping rope singing pro-McGovern songs prior to the '72 election. My uncle was in Vietnam and my mom told me that if McGovern defeated Nixon he could come home. I cried my first-grade eyes out when Nixon won. That election finally confirmed my suspicions that our

Nixon gives the "whatever" sign

1984

George Orwell smeared postwar Britain by inverting the year 1948 into 1984 and gave the world a case of the jitters that lasted thirty-six years. For decades, one could allude to 1984 as a shorthand for any worst-case scenario, especially where civil liberties were concerned. As the year itself approached, pundits went into future shock and spoke at length about the place of liberty in our lives. Finally 1984 came and went, with freedom as big a myth as ever. Mention 1984 today and people will be more likely to think of pink neon and purple hair. Living in the postmodern age means that the nightmare future is now the good old days; ya gotta love it! (bruce)

world was indeed irrational. (nina) ❧ Watergate ushered America into the real world, politically speaking. While nations such as Spain, France, and Italy always held their politicians in the utmost contempt, Americans idealized their leaders to unrealistic heights. It's remarkable how pre-Vietnam America regarded itself as superior to and different from the rest of the world. (mike s.) ❧ I remember the day Nixon resigned; my sister, my mom, and I were at the Alberts' house at the end of the cul-de-sac on our block. The TV was on and us kids were just hanging out and playing. When he said the "I resign" part, all of our parents jumped up and cheered! (riley) ❧ 1979. I was staying at a house in San Clemente. On the beach, I could see a bluff at the far end. It was flat and ringed with tall palm trees. "That's it," a cousin told me. "That's Nixon's place." As luck would have it, the ex-president was moving out that week. Around sunset, a large helicopter emerged from the ring of palms and flew low over the beach. A loud chorus of "Boo" rose up from the crowd. Even the folks out in the surf gave it the finger, while little kids tossed clods of wet sand heavenward. I even joined in, as I saw the helicopter head toward the falling sun. A true California curio. (bruce)

Noodles When did they turn into "pasta"? (riley) ❧ It was circa 1980, Riley. Spaghettios, Raviolios, Roller Coasters, and so on. The '70s marked an explosion in canned noodle products aimed straight at kids. Where there had once been only lame imitation Italian things, there was now a universe of pasta extruded into "fun shapes," all deluged in the same ultrasweet tomato sauce. Fatty, Salty, Sweet, and Starchy — these happy four became the constant dinner companions of a generation of latchkey kids. (bruce)

Noogies On *Saturday Night Live*, Todd (Bill Murray) gave these knuckle rubs to the head to Lisa Loopner (Gilda Radner) as an expression of love and affection. Warning: Most girls don't like it, and they can cause dreads in curly-haired individuals. (darby)

Novelty Telephones Until the '70s, Americans used bland, functional, boring telephones; even the Princess phone (Barbie had one!) was pretty clunky. Then AT&T started loosening up and making telephones in fashion colors and shapes, even coming out with reproductions of '30s two-piece candlestick phones — sturdy but too tasteful to be anything but dull. Then in a flash of genius, they introduced the Mickey Mouse phone — a jaunty full-figure of Mickey helpfully holding the receiver. Time

1984 Olympics

Joan Benoit, Mary Decker (who tripped on Zola Budd), Mitch Gaylord, Greg Louganis, Carl Lewis, Mary Lou Retton . . . it's when everything in L.A. became a "collector's item." I remember going to the Olympic baseball games and convincing my dad to buy those stupid 15¢ pins for $20. By the way, does anyone want to buy a few lovely 1984 Olympics pins cheap? (darby) ♣ The city decided that all these people were gonna flock to L.A. in the summer of '84 to see the Summer Games here, so they started preparing things in '83 for an influx of billions of tourists.

O.J. Simpson and friends

They tried to "clean up the city" and did this huge hooker roundup in Hollywood and for almost ten years after that you rarely saw hookers working it on Sunset or Hollywood Boulevards (), which was really weird. The city got these temporary new accent colors in an attempt to decorate: these weird sort of pastel blue, peach, mint, and pink triangles, circles, and squares were seen around. They built all these new ways to come and go from LAX, preparing for the masses of people. All the locals got really scared because we were all told that traffic was gonna be horrific, so everyone left for the summer. In the end, not many tourists came here after all, so the traffic actually *improved* until the paranoid Angelenos who had fled finally returned. (riley)

traveler Malcolm McDowell is confused by one of these in the 1979 movie *Time After Time*. Soon the market was flooded with nutty, tasteless, goofy novelty phones — more cartoon characters such as Snoopy, neon phones, pianos (which played notes), lips, mallard ducks, footballs, hot dogs on buns, high-heeled shoes, et cetera. (candi) ♣ FYI: All of this was made possible through a federal ruling. Prior to this, people did not own the phones in their home; they were the property of Ma Bell. You couldn't take them with you when you moved, nor plug them in where you wanted. They were big, plain, dependable things with bells inside. After the ruling, people were finally allowed to own phones, and the rest is marketing history. (bobby)

Nucleus Group that existed to create the epitome of early '80s robotic New Wave dance club music with the song "Jam on It," with the unforgettable "wicky wicky wicky wicky." (jaz)

N.Y. Versus L.A. I remember this like the generations before me remember the threat of nuclear war with the nasty Reds. Being that I was a native New Yorker living in L.A., I didn't think the New Yorkers were *too* nasty. If there was anyone who documented the feud best, though a *bit* prejudiced, it'd have to be Woody Allen. For example, when his character in *Annie Hall* was asked to move from N.Y. to L.A. his response was: "I don't want to live in a city where the only cultural advantage is to make a right turn on a red light." Many New Yorkers still talk this way — makes them feel better. (darby) ❧ Don't forget the punk rock rivalries — N.Y. versus L.A. versus S.F. versus the U.K. versus the Midwest. . . . (don) ❧

1989; I'm visiting Manhattan. I stroll through Midtown and notice an area sealed off with police tape and a lot of people standing around doing nothing. Being an Angeleno in training, I assumed this was a movie shoot. I asked one of the bystanders if they were shooting something. His response, "No, they ain't shot nobody yet," illustrates the essential difference between N.Y. and L.A. (bruce) ❧ This rivalry really got played out in the Dodgers versus Yankees 1981 World Series! (lorraine)

#1

Who you "looked out for" during the Me Generation of the '70s. Just in case someone forgot who exactly #1 was, #1 gold charms were often worn on gold S-chain necklaces to avoid confusion. It's kinda interesting that the TM (transcendental meditation) craze aiming to get beyond the self had its biggest boom when everyone thought he or she was #1. There could be a lesson here for Generation X to learn from this blatant indulgence in one's own hypocrisy. Though what exactly that lesson might be is open for interpretation. (nina)

П

The Occult An integral part of many an adolescent's life. Whether it was fooling with a Ouija board, dabbling in Dungeons and Dragons, or sleeping in cemeteries, some interest in the occult served for many as the first step for those beginning to question the carved-in-stone explanations for everything they received from their parents, school, church, and society. (skylaire) (See also SATAN and SLUMBER PARTIES)

Billy Ocean A Lionel Richie without the ego and Jeri curls. Carried into the mainstream by his hit single "Caribbean Queen" ('84), Billy Ocean flew past us before we realized he was a rare specimen from the near-extinct breed of suave male black singers who make no excursions into rap or hip-hop. (nina)

Officer Bird The safety-conscious parrot is right up there with "Say Nope to Dope and Ugh to Drugs" puppet Lester as being an accepted means for the pigs to influence our young impressionable minds by using a cute spokesperson to teach us those little lessons we so desperately needed to hear. I met Officer Bird and his partner Officer Dan at my local library when I was a kid and remember wondering how he drove that fucking car around. (howard)

Oil and Gas Crisis OPEC (Organization of Petroleum Exporting Countries) was not really the problem. What made it a big deal was that there was a price freeze on oil, which created a shortage. If you just let prices rise — like in the case when Iraq invaded Kuwait and Bush let the price of gas go up and everybody and their brother started selling us oil — there will never be a shortage. This is called Economics 101, supply and demand, and price theory. The only thing that I personally remember about the gas crisis was having to get gasoline on alternate days, even or odd depending on your license plate, and waiting a half-hour for gas. Since I was a salesman, I got a sticker saying I could get gas any time I wanted to, but I still had to wait in line. (dad) ❀ Many memories of stewing in the back of the station wagon as we waited hours in line at the gas station for a half fill-up. Special thanks to the warring OPEC nations for inducing my entrepreneurial side and teaching me how to siphon gas out of the tanks of cars in the Cabin John Mall parking lot and selling it in plastic bottles around the corner. (pete) ❀ The definitive tale of this period remains to be written. So too is the study of its legacy in our souls. Suffice to say, those of us who lived through it as children gained an insight into how vulnerable our civilization really is. (bruce) (See also ENERGY CRISIS)

Old Movies on TV Long, long ago, before cable, before videos, and even before colorization, TV was filled with old movies. Not classic movies, just old movies. They were cheap, dark, and full of dead people. Such films cluttered up the forgotten parts of the TV schedule. Despite their faults, it was like having a wealth of Hollywood history at your fingertips. Today, no part of the twenty-four-hour TV schedule is available for such dusty concepts. Why air some black and white war movie when you can have *A-Team* reruns in color? Why show some scratchy old movie when you could be selling the Flow-Bee in that timeslot? (bruce)

On-TV Pioneer in pay-per-view programming. I think it cost like $25 to order a movie. (winnie) ♣ While the masses waited for cable to come their way, clever entrepreneurs thought up a way to beam programs over microwaves, charge for the service, and sell the special antennas needed. Those who took the bait found out quickly how dull cable could be. The rest of us would have to wait years for this insight. (bruce)

Operation A complex electronic board game involving a labeled anatomical representation of the male form complete with a red nose that buzzes and lights up. The object is to successfully remove the man's organs with tweezers without touching any part of him except the organ being removed. "It takes a very steady hand." (jen g.) ♣ It was a good way to learn medical slang: Charlie Horse, Tennis Elbow, Broken Heart, Adam's Apple, Water on the Knee, Funny Bone, et cetera. (lisa aa.)

O.P. Shorts It's 1980. I'm envious of my twelve-year-old boyfriend. Not because he's bitchin' or cool or foxy, 'cause he's kind of a loser, but because he gets to wear O.P.s every day and I'm stuck with Jordache and Sasson. Just a few years ago, they finally got rid of Luv Its and Dittos and now they've come up with this nasty Italian shit. Well,

it's not Italian, but it reminds me of hairy men with gold chains and little dicks. I suppose I could buy myself some O.P.s, but I'm not sure I've achieved the level of self-confidence I would need to be cross-dressing in the seventh grade. Fortunately the 501 epidemic hits in a few years and saves me. (nancy) ♣ "O.P." stood for "Ocean Pacific," but mothers thought it was funny to claim it was for "Over Priced." These and the Lightning Bolt variety were ultimate '80s surfer/suburbia wear. Today they are all about geek "normal" guys with skinny legs. (darby) (See also SURF CLOTHING)

Orange Important color when we grew up. It was a color that always looked dirty. BART (Bay Area Rapid Transit) Station/Tomorrowland Orange. As a matter of fact, it was one of the main factors that made Disneyland's Tomorrowland so absurdly dated. A few years ago they finally changed what they could of it to a more safe, always in, blue. (darby)

Orange Julius Where high school girls work in cute outfits in the middle of the mall. The julius was considered a healthy drink. I always liked strawberry. (jaz) ♣ Ahh, the foamy synthetic yumminess — the froth that never seemed to dissipate . . . (bridget)

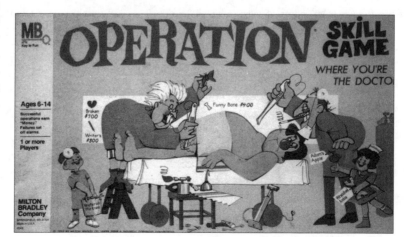

$1.98 Beauty Contest

TV show hosted by campy flamer walrus Rip Taylor, who made these "beauty" contestants do ridiculous, embarrassing things in order to win $1.98 and the opportunity to hang out at the end of the show, when Rip sang the theme song at them while prancing all over the set. All I remember of this fantastic tune is the very last line, where Rip Taylor says, "And you win the $1.98!!" One of the great ones, for sure. (don)

Organizers "Let's do lunch" was only possible after you checked your thick-with-papers-and-notes vinyl personal organizer with the Velcro closure. I know the idea was to organize people and their new superbusy schedules, but the unorganized people were just as unorganized with the thing, and on top of it they were weighed down by having to carry it around everywhere they went. They're the ones who still use the same organizer from 1985 'cause they didn't finish filling out the day-to-day scheduler yet. (darby)

The Outsiders They would occasionally show this movie in English class because the screenplay was adapted from S. E. Hinton's award-winning book. It was the age-old story of greaser versus soc (pronounced "sosh," as in short for *socialite*), narrated from the greasers' point of view (who all had cool names like Pony-boy and Soda-pop). This movie was made pre–Brat Pack, but was crammed with teen heartthrobs-to-be: Tommy Howell, Matt Dillon, Ralph Macchio, Emilio Estevez, Rob Lowe; even Tom Cruise and Patrick Swayze were young and hunky. (lorraine) (See also BRAT PACK)

Overplayed Videos We may bemoan the fact that MTV no longer even plays videos, but back in the early '80s that's all they played — over and over. A few we may never forget: Pat Benatar/"Love Is a Battlefield" ('83) — Pat and her street-trash New Wave dancing-troupe buddies shake their boobs in syncopated rage over the plight of the teenage runaway-turned-hooker. Eurythmics/"Sweet Dreams (Are Made of This)" ('83) — How many people thought Annie Lennox was a man when this video clip first aired has yet to be calculated. And what was with the cows? A-ha/"Take on Me" ('85) — Real girl gets sucked into comic book but is saved by the cute Norwegian band guys from this terrible animation takeover. I still have no clue what "take on me" means. Howard Jones/"What Is Love?" — Nebbish contemplates the meaning of love as he wanders through a park looking to get laid. ZZ Top/"Legs" ('84) — Three trailer-park bimbos use their legs to get a car big enough to drive the hell away from three bearded perverted hillbillies with a fetish for the letter Z. Billy Idol/"Dancing with Myself" ('84) — Billy sneered and sang about masturbation on a giant building in the postapocalyptic world of the future. In "Eyes Without a Face," he sneered, sang, and pouted! Ratt/"Round and Round" ('84) — Edie Sedgwick–esque girl jumps out of an attic onto a table of a dinner party at which Milton Berle plays both host and hostess. Michael Jackson/"Thriller" ('84) — More a miniseries than a music video, in which Vincent Price narrated Michael's make-up-enhanced transformation into a werewolf/zombie; it foreshadowed his real life body-manipulation horrors.   Men Without Hats/"The Safety Dance" ('83) — Disco at the Renaissance Pleasure Faire. Thomas Dolby/"She Blinded Me with Science" ('83) — Science! Prince/"When Doves Cry" ('84) — Even the bathtub in the video was on platforms. Wet and steamy! Madonna /"Papa Don't Preach" ('86) — Very Catholic undertones as Madonna plays a teenage girl who tells her father she's pregnant and, the shocker, going to "keep my baby." Plus, gave us a whole new minimal look at Madonna — sleek and svelte. J. Geils Band/"Centerfold" ('81) — Started and ended the whole milk-in-snare-drum craze. Duran Duran /"Hungry Like the Wolf" ('83) and "Rio" ('83) — See Simon and the boys in exotic locations you've never been in with exotic girls you'll never have. All Van Halen videos with David Lee Roth — When "Jump" and "Panama" came on the tube, you knew you had time to reload that bong. These were lengthy performance videos by Van Halen with Diamond Dave strutting his stuff or flying through the air on a bungee cord to the radical licks of the brothers. Also unforgettable, "Hot for Teacher" ('84), in which Van Halen, portrayed as fourth-graders, turn their classroom into a strip club and hoot as their babe teacher gets naked! Man, put that band on detention! Talking Heads/"Burning Down the House" ('83) — That big ol' face of David Byrne projected on that house still haunts me. Twisted Sister/"We're Not Gonna Take It" ('84) — "What are you gonna do with your life?" "I'm gonna rock!" Twang. Robert Palmer/"Addicted to Love" ('86) — Comatose women dressed/made up to look like sex-bomb mannequins sway out of rhythm with instruments hanging on them, backing up a white-man-in-suit singer. It scandalized people for its blatant objectification of women. Whatever. (nina/howard) (See also MADONNA WANNABES, MTV, and *MV3*)

P

Pac-Man Fever All of us old enough to have lived through the '80s are familiar with an era of greed and excess ushered in by Reaganomics, where our models of fame and fortune were highlighted by TV shows like *Dynasty, Silver Spoons,* and *Diff'rent Strokes.* I wasted a big part of my youth watching little Arnold Drummond cavorting about in a number of ill-fated adventures, redeemed only by the hogwash moralizing of his authoritative but gentle, rich, white dad ("Mr. D."). One episode I remember well started out simply enough with a typical breakfast scene. Arnold was voraciously shoveling cereal into his big mouth, and an observant Mr. Drummond commented, "Arnold . . . you're eating so fast, you look like Pac-Man!" As far as Mr. Drummond was concerned, it was only appropriate that a little goofy yellow gobbler like Pac-Man — whose appetite was never quite satiated — should be a topic for conversation. As bad as the joke was, the crowd just about died. You see, in 1981, Pac-Man was *it,* revolutionizing the game industry in one fell swoop. Not only was it the first successful departure from outer-space-oriented games, it was responsible for converting hard-core pinballers into full-time Pac-Maniacs. Originally deemed "too cute to be successful" by press and trade alike, Pac-Man proved all naysayers wrong. Soon the whole world had Pac-Man Fever. As with other pop-culture crazes, Pac-Mania was accompanied by bloodthirsty opportunists who flooded the market with colorful, tacky goods bearing the image of the little yellow muncher. But even more amazing was his intense popularity that propelled him beyond super-stardom. No longer was Pac-Man just a video game character, he was a celebrity. It even got to the point where prominent mayors across the nation gave him keys to their city, not to mention the twenty-seven cities that officially declared April 3 Pac-Man Day in 1982. I wonder if it's still observed. (noël) ☘ Also part of the mania, the hit song "Pac-Man Fever" ('82) by Buckner and Garcia, and of course Ms. Pac-Man, who many contend makes for even better video game play. (jaz)

Painter's Pants Those pantaloons with the gazillion pockets on the side (one of which perfectly housed your unbreakable comb, one in front to hang your sassy thumb, and one in back for the thumb of your true love). (darby) ☘ Were very hip among the gay disco scene long before it hit the straight college scene. Always worn with a sweater tied around the shoulders. Very chic. (patty) ☘ And what about those silly painter's hats? (lisa aa.) (See also DISCO CHIC) 🐾

Palm Tree Ponytail worn on the side of the head and puffed up, usually crimped and occasionally streaked with a temporary spray-in blue, green, or pink hair paint, for very trendy disco girls or wimpy New Wavers too timid to do anything really radical to their long, blond surfer locks. (gwynne) (See also STICKSHIFT)

Paper Dolls A 1982 TV movie which starred Joan Hackett, Jennifer Warren, Joan Collins, Daryl Hannah, Alexandra Paul, Marc Singer, Barry Primus, Craig T. Nelson, Antonio Fargas, and Eric Stoltz. All about young fashion model girls who deal with their new life of suffering from their beauty and fame and the horrible adults around them. The spin-off TV series lasted about as long as the TV show *Models Inc.*, which no doubt currently resides in its own pre-retro purgatory. (ju-ji)

Paranoia Pot paranoia: Cheech and Chong needlessly flushing their stash down the toilet; being convinced that oblivious strangers are staring at you; having a teacher or parent ask you the reason for your bloodshot eyes and coming up with the snappy answer, "I got pinkeye!" while trying hard not to bust up. Coke paranoia: Peering out the window to check for cops and helicopters with infrared detectors; suspecting that your girlfriend is going to run off with your dealer who you *know* is stepping on your coke; wiping your nose obsessively; relating too well to Rockwell's "Somebody's Watching Me" ('84). Acid paranoia: Being convinced that your neighbors are aliens from another dimension; hearing the voice of Satan tell you to kill your neighbors while listening to Pink Floyd; worrying that you may never be the same again (okay, maybe you were right on that one). (nina/lisa m.)

Paraquat I remember a pot rally in Greenwich Village sometime in the late '70s and the following crowd participation chant: "We like pot/And we like it a lot/Stop spraying it/With paraquat!" (thomas c.)

Parcourse A strange incorporation of the morning jog with this series of plaques set up usually in public parks some distance from each other. You jogged from plaque to plaque, and at each stop were instructed to do some simple, quick exercise: so many jumping jacks, sit-ups, chin-ups, etc. Then you jogged on to the next. It was supposed to be a scientifically designed, perfect time-motion-study way to exercise. As my friend Nick points out, mostly it just interrupts calisthenics with pointless jogging or a good jog with pointless calisthenics. A great relic of the days when we thought we could combine everything into one experience — the TV dinner of exercise regimens. Though these things still exist, strangely no one I mention them to seems to have any idea what they are anymore. I haven't a clue as to why they're called "parcourses." (brian)

Party Flicks Once a giant of the movie theater scene, the '80s party movie has gone the way of the horror flick — relegated mostly to video. Attempting yet failing to imitate the classic *National Lampoon's Animal House* ('78), which was itself trying to capture the essence of the early '60s fraternity scene, the plot of the vapid party flicks revolved solely around scoring chicks and booze. No togas in sight, but lots of falling in the pool, girls' bikini tops coming off in the Jacuzzi, pizza on the turntable, sex in the folks' bed, and inane pranks pulled on stuffy authority figures and passed-out friends. A few we remember: *Porky's* (with Kim Cattrall), *The Wild Life* (with Eric Stoltz, Randy Quaid, and Sherilyn Fenn), *Easy Money* (Rodney Dangerfield, Joe Pesci, and Jennifer Jason Leigh — actually anything with Rodney Dangerfield seems to apply), *Where the Boys Are '84* (with Lisa Hartman), *Joysticks, Spring Break, Hardbodies, Bachelor Party* (with Tom Hanks), *Summer School* (with Mark Harmon, Kirstie Alley, *Little House on the Prairie*'s Patrick Laborteaux and *Melrose Place*'s Courtney Thorne-Smith), *Revenge of the Nerds* (with John Goodman and *Married with Children*'s Ted McGinley), *Party Party* . . . (brian/jaz) (See also CAMP MOVIES, HOT TUBS, *PORKY'S* and TEEN IDOL FREAKOUT)

P

Paper Games

Paper Football: Where you finger-flick the football and try to get it close to the edge of your opponent's side of the desk, without its falling off. Battleship: Where you take turns trying to sink each other's battleships. To fire you make a mark with pen on your side of the paper, then fold the paper over and in the same place you marked (but on the opposite side of the paper) you go over the mark. This causes the ink to rub off on your opponents' side of the page so when you unfold the paper you can see if your mark hit one of their battleships. Tank War Game: Where again you use a piece of notebook paper, fold it in half, and then you each make a fortress on the bottom edge of the page with mines in the middle. (You can also play it like space ships and space stations.) Then you move your tank by taking a pen, holding it vertical to the paper, and letting it slide out from under your finger. You then move your tank's position to where the ink stops. Other miscellaneous paper games include spit wads; paper towels that you get wet and throw up to the ceiling so they stick; sticking "kick me"–type notes on goobers; paper helicopters and airplanes (sticking pins into the front so they'll stick into whatever they hit, e.g., the teacher's ass); straws (great as a weapon for spit balls and also to take off the wrapper by pulling it down the straw and condensing it, then adding a few drops of water and watch it grow like a worm); even school notes could fit in this section. (darby) ✿

Mash: Another favorite retro paper game used to humiliate your friends. You start off by writing *mash* really big at the top of a piece of notebook paper. Then you ask your friend to name four guys/girls — they can be famous or real, but most important of all one of the guys/girls has to be the grossest mate your friend can think of. Next they have to pick four numbers, and at least one of the numbers has to be really high, like 200. Then they have to name four cars, and at least one has to be something he hates (Pintos and Gremlins were popular for the gross choice). In the space in the center you draw a spiral and ask them to tell you when to stop. When they tell you to stop, you count the lines of the spiral, and you use that number to start the process of elimination, hoping, of course, that they will end up with the worst combination possible. If there are seven lines of the spiral you start off with the *m* of *mash* and cross off every seventh word, until you have one left in every category. *M* = mansion, *A* = apartment, *S* = shack, and *H* = house. The names of girls/guys = your friend's mate. Numbers = the number of kids he will have, and the cars become the car he will drive. Example: You live in a shack with Getty Lee, you have forty kids, and you drive a Grand Torino. Probably the most unforgettable paper game involved the Cootie Catcher Fortune Teller: This involves minor origami but is well worth it. The outside flaps of the cootie catcher should have four different colors, the inside ones should have eight different numbers (half even, half odd), and under the numbered flaps are housed eight different fortunes. Poise the CCFT on your fingers and tell a friend to pick a color. If she chooses, for example, green, open and close the CCFT five times (G-R-E-E-N), and stop on the inner flaps that will reveal four numbers. Tell her to pick a number and open and close accordingly. Repeat this process over and over. When your friend is nearly exasperated and ready to walk away, lift up the flap of the last number called and read her fortune. She will wrongly believe that the fortune is extratrue because of the time involved in waiting for it. Naturally, it will be a horrifyingly dismal fortune. Snicker as your friend turns away and the next friend eagerly steps forward for his turn. Variation for further unfair and immature humiliation of your friends: Write one extrafancy, beautiful, special, lucky fortune and memorize what number it lies under. When your favorite friend chooses that number, lift up the flap and read aloud. Your favorite friend will beam with delight as the others truly crumble under the weight of their misfortune. Sample fortunes: You will die in a fiery auto accident; You are so ugly; Your BO smells like swiss cheese; You will have to eat your own boogers for the rest of your life and will never have any good food; Why are you so fat?; Glen Danzig is your mate for life; Everyone talks about you behind your back; You suck. (amra/d'arcy) (See also SLAM BOOKS)

Party Line I'm not sure why, but when you called Time (853-1212) you used to be able to talk to other people who were calling it at the same time. You'd yell out where your party was or find out about others or try to set up dates that you would never keep. Around the time they made it impossible to talk to others was the period when 976 numbers started up. (darby) ❧ Also known as "pipelines." Some bored crank caller had stumbled upon a curious fact of analogue phone exchanges. When you called *any* number with a recording, you could also hear distant voices of other callers. What was more, you could actually *talk* to them. Not just one on one, but you could talk with several people at once. I took to this like mad. Not that it was easy; you could only talk and listen during the ten seconds it took the recording to recycle. The voices would be faint and distant and confusing because everyone would talk at once. Different recordings would also have different crowds hanging out on them. The weather number had little sixth-grade kids, "No Longer in Service" was mostly girls, and so forth. All the kids at school who were into this called themselves "pipeliners." We'd often talk and swap notes about the different lines and the different people on them. One night, I reached nirvana when I accidentally clicked my receiver multiple times and got a brief recording about line trouble, the recording then took a full *five minutes* to recycle! There seemed to be dozens of people on this line, many of them were high school age and were pros at this. I'd "call" this number all the time. The crowd would change during the day, yet there were certain regulars who would talk about anything to anyone. (I recall one guy who never said anything except, "Any of you chicks ball?") I actually managed an afterschool date with two high school girls via this line. I told the other pipeliners at my school about this incredible click number, and they freaked. Unfortunately, they also freaked the night they called it and heard two guys planning to buy some dope. I persevered for several more weeks, until one day when I clicked in while the area phone lines were being serviced, and our phone went dead for three days. I still fondly recall the pipeline, and how an underground adolescent culture briefly flowered in a forgotten technological crevice. Today's digital technology has now filled in those crevices, and we have 900 party lines and the Internet. It's similar, but not the same. (bruce)

P

Pass de Duchie on the Left-Hand Side In 1983 a song with this odd title became a minor hit. It was by a U.K. reggae-style band called Musical Youth, whose members were all under eighteen. Inevitably, there was much confusion over what the title referred to. *Duchie* is Jamaican slang for a dutch-oven cooking pot. The song was a remake of an old standard by reggae legends the Mighty Diamonds. Their original version was titled "Pass the Coochie on the Left-Hand Side." The "coochie" of the title is a Rasta concoction of cooked marijuana, which one cooks in a duchie. In partaking of the coochie, one samples from the duchie and then passes it to the left. Musical Youth altered the song slightly, so as to clean it up and make it more commercial. Incidentally, passing to your left is also considered proper etiquette when sharing a joint with friends. (bruce)

Patches Sewing patches all over your jeans was one of those chicken-or-egg '70s fashion trends, like crotch snaps on leotards. Did the patched look arise from a need to cover actual holes caused by wear and tear or did the endless patching and repatching to a quilted perfection cause all the holes and thus the need to decorate over them? Whatever the reason, hardly a leg of bare denim could be spotted without at least one patch. Some of the favorites: happy faces, band logos, Rolling Stone lips, mushrooms, unicorns, butterflies, rainbows, peace signs, Zig Zag man smoking a joint, Keep on Truckin' guy, Black Power fists, and other patches of fabric, even patches from other pieces of patched jeans! In the '80s, patches became obsolete when visible holes in your jeans were stylin', and the decorating urge moved up to the jeans jacket, which was mercilessly stuck with pins. (nina) (See also JEANS and RAINBOWS)

Patti and Jimmy Much cooler than that satanic Hello Kitty, P&J were discontinued years ago without warning. From the Sanrio family, Patti and Jimmy were often seen practicing very chic pursuits such as tennis, polo, and golf. (katy) (See also HELLO KITTY)

PBS Any living American of discerning taste owes Public Broadcasting a profound debt. In 1969, the federal government created the Public Broadcasting Service out of the old National Educational Television. Where NET had been mostly educational, PBS was substantial, showing opera, science, and children's programming. Nixon hated it, and tried to end it all, so you know it was cool! It didn't gain much mass-market recognition until Carl Sagan's *Cosmos*, in 1980. (bruce) ✿ Largely subsidized by oil companies, *Masterpiece Theatre* is now officially called the *Mobil Masterpiece Theatre*. (darby) (See also *THE ELECTRIC COMPANY*, SLIM GOODBODY, *SESAME STREET*, and *ZOOM*)

PCP Also known as "angel dust," "sherm," and "superkools," this rhinoceros tranquilizer was the most high-risk high of all times. Just think: a drug that affects everyone who does it completely differently! Some got mellow, some got a speedy effect, some had hallucinations, others went completely

Musical Youth

bonkers, and some just died (among them *Pink Flamingos* star David Lochary). Since replaced in demographic popularity by the comparatively tame crack, ice, and St. Ides malt liquor. (gwynne) ❂ In my high school speech class, two angel dust enthusiasts described their personal experiences as research in the Drugs: Pro and Con debate. (jeff) (See also DRUGS) 🐌

Peace Sign   The ubiquitous icon of the Aquarian age. It was designed in 1964 by Britain's Controlled Nuclear Development antiwar lobby. Within the eternal circle, it combined a stylized version of the semaphore letters *C, N,* and *D.* A masterpiece of design, it looked equally good on a letterhead and in spray paint. Anyone could draw it, and by 1970, *everyone* knew what it stood for. Even thirty years later it is still a potent symbol, though more for partyin' than peace. A famous right-wing bumper sticker of the early '70s compared its shape to that of a bird's foot and read "Footprint of the great American chicken." (bruce) ❂ Some said it was the sign of the broken cross and if you drew it upside down it meant Satan. I never could remember which way was up, so it frightened me. (lisa m.)

Pearl Drops   Sold in a distinctive but strange upside-down bottle, Pearl Drops was not a tooth*paste* but a tooth *polish.* So exclaimed the ad model as she seductively licked her teeth on TV. Was she inviting others to do so? (bruce) (See also 7-UP)

Pee-wee   *Mecholecha-hi mecka-heiny-ho!* Paul Reubens was a veteran of comedy clubs and several Cheech and Chong movies when he hit upon the persona of Pee-wee Herman. Crossing Pinky Lee with Harry Langdon and adding bits of Jacques Tati and Jerry Lewis, he came up with a frantically bizarre man-child. Paul took this character on stage and hit big. Eventually he created an entire stage review, modeled after a '50s kiddie show, that was like the real thing on acid. He developed a cult following and became a frequent guest on talk shows, always as Pee-wee, never as Paul Reubens. His first film was an inexplicable hit, and CBS began looking at him to head a show to compete with *Saturday Night Live.* Something got lost in the translation, and by the time the smoke cleared, CBS had given this parody of a kiddie show host his own kiddie show, right smack dab in the middle of Saturday morning! *Pee-wee's Playhouse* was the wackiest thing to hit kid-vid in years. It became an immediate hit. The newly revamped Nielsen ratings indicated that it was the most videotaped show on television; they also showed that most of the people taping would watch the show around 11 PM Saturday nights. CBS was making plans to rerun each week's show at 11:30 Saturday nights, but then the ratings began to slip. After the novelty of Pee-wee wore off, one was left with a pretty strange half-hour of TV. Paul's crew thought they were doing a children's show; Paul had other ideas. Though when the show returned, CBS made it much more sane, it soon went out of production (but not off the air). Pee-wee's next movie bombed, and he started showing up on talk shows with a different look, more haggard than harried. Pee-wee Herman was consuming Paul Reubens. He left Hollywood and moved to Florida, near his parents. One night Paul Reubens was arrested for masturbating in a sleazy Florida porno theater. He showed up at the MTV awards a few weeks later, asking, "Heard any good jokes lately?" But the joke was on Paul. (bruce)

Pelé   The Conqueror! Brazil's soccer superstar came to play for the fledgling New York Cosmos and did his part to convert the football heathens of America. He was fantastic, fabulous, and friendly; even the man's name was fun to say! Here was a big, bronzed, beautiful sports star who didn't have to use his hands. Fortunately, he didn't have to speak much either. Pelé's English might have been as limited as a New York cabbie's, but he was still able to do plenty of endorsements and even a film with Sylvester Stallone. The Cosmos and their league never really worked out like everyone hoped. Today we have junior soccer teams, even soccer moms, but twenty years on, Pelé is still the best-known soccer player in American history. (bruce)

Pelé, the Conqueror

Pencils There was a whole pencil craze, like the 3/4" diameter Husky brand coated in metallic paints and the "bendable" pencils that came in psychedelic swirl paint jobs. (noël) ❧ Also stupid pencils with lead cartridges, high class clicking pencils, "mood" pencils with heat-sensitive coatings that changed color when you held them. Pencil Accessories: Frustration pencils, those things that were just a wad of furry material affixed to the top of a pencil with two wiggly eyes attached. Such fun it was to straighten the hair and then spin it between your palms, creating a wild Don King 'do for your pencil pal. (morgan and ferris) ❧ I liked to give mine dreadlocks, but it was a girlie thing and I got beat up so I ditched it after P.E. (e. c. cotterman) ❧ Also there was that triangular rubber piece you slid the pencils into to get a better grip. Made writing impossible. (jaz) Pencil Fighting: Pre-pog obsession: a pencil-breaking game where you chop each other's pencils until the loser's pencil breaks. My Pal pencils worked best. (jory) (See also ERASERS and MOOD RINGS)

Pens Scented (I used to hoard the black licorice ones and snort away during art class); T-shirt markers; metallic gold and silver paint pens; Erasermate 2 (hell for lefties); the two-color clickable; the four-color clickable; the insanely useless and fat ten-color clickable, the naughty disappearing-swimsuit pen. Hats off to pens! (jeff h.) (See also BANANAS and ERASABLE PENS)

The People's Court Tuning in to Judge Wapner was a last resort in afterschool-TV viewing. Two mini-trials in thirty minutes with an aging judge, a tall hunky court clerk who reminded me of Bull from *Night Court*, and a cheeseball announcer, Doug Llewelyn, who would hype the show at the beginning and during any break so you'd stay tuned. The best was when he'd confront the bitter losers after the trial and sorta egg them on in his detatched, smarmy, TV-guy way. These were real trials. I know 'cause when our own photographer was sued, they called and asked if we wanted the case settled in their forum, *The People's Court*. So we had Dougy calling *Ben Is Dead* a pornographic magazine while we sat in the audience in our *Ben* T-shirts. Our photographer won, but even if he'd lost, the deal was *The People's Court* paid your expenses in trade for appearing on their show. More fun than being an extra on any other TV show. (darby)

Pepsi Light When Pepsi Light came out it was aimed straight at the youth market. With its lemon-twist, calorie-free aura and pretty blue packaging, we had no defenses. I used to drink it after school and before parties with a slug of Jack Daniel's. Yum. (mikki) ❧ It was a part artificial sweetner, part sugar combo with a twist of lemon. It was the only kind of Pepsi that actually tasted good to me. (riley)

P

Perfection "When you're into Perfection, stay on your toes, you gotta be quick, cause here's how it goes: Set the timer, put the pieces in place, don't be late. With perfection, you gotta move on fast, move on fast . . . before the pieces pop up before you put in the last. And that's Perfection." You might think I only played with toys that had cool theme songs and you might be right. (katy)

Perfume and Cologne Love's Baby Soft was a girl's fragrance in a pink bottle with white polka dots. I don't really know exactly what it smells like, but I remember its being something like sweet baby powder, and boy-oh-boy did I feel sexy. It was essential for entrapping boys at the roller rink. Jean Naté was another fave and it came in assorted forms like bath beads, a mist spray, sachets. Incredibly potent stuff. "I can bring home the bacon, fry it up in a pan, and never, never, never let you forget you're a man! 'Cause I'm a woman, Enjoli!" Charlie was another magnetic scent from the '70s because of the supermodel/actress Shelley Hack sporting a suit and tie getting whatever she wanted from any man on the planet. Very ERA. (jes) ❧ Before Love's Baby Soft, there was Love's Lemon. After Baby Soft everything went musk, which lasted for years — until patchouli oil. In the disco era everyone wore Halston and Chloë. Very strong, repulsive scents, but *very* chic. (patty) ❧ Don't forget Babe by Fabergé, with its glamorous spokeswoman Margaux Hemingway (of *Lipstick* fame). (allison) ❧ Or Zany!, for the girls that just wanted to have fun! (nina) ❧ I liked Tinkerbell perfume. It smelled just like those expensive perfumes my mom would get — gross. (ju-ji) ❧ I had the whole line of Tinkerbell scents and powders, which quickly smelled like alcohol. There were also the ever-popular men's scents — they campaigned these to appeal to swashbuckling pirates. (bobby) ❧ The liberated New Man of sensitive '70s was not shy about scents. A whole new arm of the perfume industry opened up to pamper him. Where his father's options had been Old Spice or Aqua Velva, he had Brut, Chaz, Gambler, High Karate, or Canoe (haughtily pronounced "Can-know"). There were many others, but the ultimate was musk. This was not a brand but a type. Squeezed from the glands of an unfortunate muskrat, this ingredient was supposed to exude a pheromone-like power from the New Man's chain-laden neck. However, I thought he wound up smelling like an old couch in the rain. Muskrat Luv indeed! (bruce) (See also JEAN NATÉ, POLO, and SMELLS) 🐇

Refrigerator Perry If memory serves, Mr. Perry played for the Chicago Bears in the mid- to late '80s. He was a big fat defensive lineman most famous for switching sides and playing fullback when the Bears were down close to the opposing team's goal line. They'd hand him the ball and the other team would get out of the way, fearing for their lives. That maneuver got a lot of attention in that Super Bowl they were in. He milked his girth for all it was worth, achieving notoriety far beyond the average blue-collar defensive-line grunt. (jessica g.)

Personalized Shit There was a period when everything had to be embroidered or ironed-on or embossed with your own personal name. The more common your name the better chance you had in finding your item prepersonalized. (darby) ❧ This stuff contributed to my immense feelings of alienation as a youngster. (skylaire) ❧ I totally know what you mean. The only time I ever saw my name on anything was during Christmas. (noël) (See also MUGS and NAME-PLATE NECKLACES)

The Pet Rock The biggest toy fluke (and pet fluke) of my generation. Can you imagine it happening today: people buying a rock decorated with animal features, tying a string around it like a leash, and actually taking it for walks? (Then again, there are those computerized pets. Hmm.) All I remember is that if you weren't rich or stupid enough to buy one of these you could make your own — which I did. Them were simpler times. (darby) ❧ Created by an advertising executive, Gary Dahl of Los Gatos, California. He brought the small smooth rocks from a Mexican beach and packaged them in a tiny box complete with air holes. The true genius was inside: the rock rested on straw and came with a tiny book that explained how to train, play with, and even housebreak your rock. They became the hot gift of Christmas 1975, at $5 a pop. (bruce)

P

Pez After saving numerous wrappers from this tiny brick-shaped candy, I was finally able to send away for the ultimate PEZ dispenser, which was available only by mail. It was the only dispenser made without a character head and sported a simple utilitarian top with a smartly notched grip. It was covered in metallic gold paint and looked like an expensive cigarette lighter. But the coolest thing was that it came with its own pentagonal display stand, with room in its base for five other dispensers. I arranged all my other goofy-looking PEZ dispensers so that they faced inward, to worship their golden PEZ god. (bruce) ❧ Note: European PEZ tastes a thousand times better than American PEZ. (tom)

Phenomena God was dead, the Moon was conquered, big science was discredited, the revolution was over, and the government couldn't be trusted. Despite all of this, people still wanted to believe in something bigger than Crystal Lite. Those who thought themselves too smart to find Jesus turned to the Unknown. The mysterious was safely beyond explanation, allowing one to believe whatever one liked about whatever one liked. The blend of Aquarian spirituality and Watergate paranoia proved a potent combo. You could cast a horoscope, talk to your plants, or sleep in a pyramid and still be taken seriously. The search for Bigfoot, Nessie, or Atlantis now looked like legitimate science. Belief in UFOs and government conspiracies was now only a jump to the left (with your hands on your hips). A jump to the right, and you had Arab oil intrigue and CIA mind control. Many never grew out of this phase, and many more have grown into it. By the '80s most Americans had rediscovered the one true faith that has always sustained and comforted us: money! (bruce) ❧ '70s Phenomena: Bigfoot, Loch Ness Monster, the energy crisis, pyramid power, UFO cover-ups, hot tubs; '80s Phenomena: Mt. St. Helens, Minimalls, yuppies. (See also BERMUDA TRIANGLE, KING TUT, NEW AGE, and PYRAMID MONEY SCHEMES)

Phoebe Cates's Boob Scene *Fast Times at Ridgemont High* was an amazingly great film, with enough raunch and laughs to keep our developing gonads reeling. The infamous Phoebe Cates boob scene was one of the fondest memories of my youth, way better than anything from *Animal House* or Bo Derek's *10*. Of course, I didn't realize that the Judge Reinhold character was beating off in the bathroom during that fantasy scenario nor did I realize what that carrot-sucking instruction in the cafeteria was all about. I was just a kid. (noël) (See also MODELS, VALLEY GIRL/DUDE, and VANS)

Photosensitive Glasses Outside, these magical lenses will change from clear to dark in just seconds! No need ever again for sunglasses, one pair goes anywhere! It was the dawn of multifunction products, when the conscientious consumer liked to cut down on excess manufacturing by making one product do as much as possible. Like "it's a candy — it's a gum" Razzles, some photosensitive eyewear did neither function well. Glasses were brownish indoors, making me look like a total geek in my eyewear. It was already bad enough just wearing aviators at age eight. (lisa aa.) (See also BUMMERS)

Picking Your Nose The fake bent-finger trick so you look like you're really going for it! "You can pick your friends, you can pick your nose, but you can't pick your friend's nose!" (bridget) ❧ Remember twisting up tissues and shoving them in your nose to clean it — how did that work? (ju-ji)

Pig Latin Uckfay ouyay! (howard) ❧ I never did get this one. We spoke what I call "I the Guy." It's a half-assed version but if you say it fast enough it works. I am now going to disclose the secret to speaking this very rare and mysterious language. It may be the first and last time you will ever see this in print! The best way to do it is by example, so if I wanted to say "You always act so stupid, you always talk so dumb," it would be spoken: "Youthegoo allthegall waysthegays actthegack sothego stupthegoop idthegid, youthegoo allthegall waysthegays talkthegalk sothego dumbthegum!" That's it. Pretty easy, huh? Well then, now go practice so we can have a decent conversation for once. (darby) ❧ Also, don't forget "ubby-dubby"! "Hu-bi, frub-ends!" My sister ordered the brochure on how to speak this irritating language just so she could tease me. She also used to write mean notes to me in her diary — knowing I was reading it. We had a heartwarming coming-together when we learned to put "ub" in the middle of words and talk in front of my brother about his nasty booger-eating habit. (winnie) ✿ The case of Mushmouth in *Fat Albert* mustn't be discounted. (adam s.) (See also *FAT ALBERT AND THE COSBY KIDS* and SIGN LANGUAGE)

The Pill Some women left theirs out on the bedside table, just so you'd know they were getting some. I used to hide my pill pack in the way back of the sock drawer where my mom would never find it. Every time I got stoned and felt a pain in my leg I thought I was experiencing a blood clot. (lisa m.) (See also BIRTH CONTROL and PARANOIA)

Pillsbury Cookie Dough The Pillsbury Dough Boy god came down to planet Earth and blessed us with raw prepackaged cookie dough that all the girls would pig out on after school and then purposely throw up. Was, and probably still is, an essential part of the bulimic's diet. (darby) ✿ Poppin' Fresh: The Pillsbury Dough Boy. For a while in the mid-'70s he did ads with his wife, Poppy Fresh. My little sister had an entire play set of Poppin's whole family, including Grandpopper, Grandmopper, and the dog, Cupcake. What ever became of Poppy Fresh? A nasty divorce? An illicit affair with the Hamburger Helper Hand? I heard she got a really bad yeast infection and just got *huge*. That's her as the Stay-Puf Marshmallow in *Ghostbusters*, honest, it is! (bruce) ✿ I had it bad for the Dough Boy. There was just something inexplicably sexy about him — his tantalizing texture, his pliable yet solid shape. I still don't understand it, but Casper the Ghost worked me over in a similar way. (nina) (See also JUNK FOOD and the comic book *Johnny the Homicidal Maniac*)

Pinball Arcades used to be filled with pinball machines and menacing sixteen-year-old stoners who chain-smoked and would beat you up for spare change. In other words, the greatest place to hang out in a suburb. When the greedy bastards changed it to three balls for a quarter instead of five, they killed the whole damned scene. Ms. Pac-Man? Give me a break! (jeff)

Pink Lady and Jeff Future students of television history may ask, "Who killed the variety show?" and discover the culprit is *Pink Lady*. In 1980, NBC executives, for reasons known only to themselves, produced a one-hour variety show whose stars could barely speak English. They were a Japanese rock duo known as Pink Lady, and its members, Mie Nemoto and Kei Masuda, had scored a minor U.S. hit the year before with "Kiss in the Dark." The show cast them as Me and Kay, two sexy Japanese gals who happened to host a variety show. They tried to learn about American customs through their friend and inter-

Pink Ladies and Jeff

preter Jeff (comic Jeff Altman). Altman was already a veteran of another equally infamous variety show, *Cos*, and of *The Starland Vocal Band Show*. He could not speak Japanese, so when he was interpreting for the two he simply faked it, yammering in oriental gibberish. Poor Me and Kay looked as confused as everyone else who bothered to watch. Every show ended with the stars in a hot tub and the ratings in the toilet. The network pulled the plug on the tub and the show on April 7, barely a month after its publicized premiere. Mie and Kei returned to Japan, and Jeff went on to appear on the final few seasons of *Solid Gold*. (bruce)

Daniel Pinkwater   The existentialist, surrealist, and just-plain-silly works of Daniel Pinkwater made the biggest literary impression on my twelve-year-old world. Pinkwater has been writing for twenty years now, populating his stories with calorically imbalanced spacemen, wise old blacks, mystic lizards, parallel universes with roadstop root-beer stands, and genetically enhanced monster chickens. What's not to love? *Fat Men from Space, Lizard Music, The Worms of Kukumlina*, are all filed in my permanent library alongside Nietzsche and the collected works of Charles Fort. (skylaire)

Pippi Longstocking   She was one of my idols. I had seen all her movies. She lives alone in Villa Villekulla with her horse General and her monkey Mr. Nilsson. Her dad visits sometimes but can't stay long 'cause he's a captain of a pirate ship. She inherited his strength and is the strongest girl in the world — even stronger than her father. She has two friends, Annika and Tommy. And Annika whines annoyingly about getting in trouble when Pippi takes them on her wild adventures. They do everything, even fly a car with gas made of Spunk, which is their made-up name for whatever they want. Pippi's infamous look: a supershort punk Holly Hobbie dress, with thigh-high tights (not matching), and cool witchiepoo shoes. She has freckles and red hair that's braided and sticking out on both sides. When I was younger I would dress in old clothes and pretend to be her, even dressing up as her for Halloween, putting on raggedy, ripped clothes, spray-on red hair, wires in my braids, and painted-on freckles. (selina) ❧ Great role model for budding tomboys. It seemed like Tommy and Annika were always getting naked to help out with Pippi's schemes. Pippi would build sails out of their shirts and pants, or they'd have to pretend to be orphans with no clothes. When we'd play, I always got to be Pippi despite my bossy best friend who I think preferred to be prettier li'l Annika. Could also be considered a major contributor to the large number of poorly dubbed foreign movies on TV in the '70s. (wendy)

Planet of the Apes   The other night I went to see a friend's band and I swear their bass player looked *exactly* like Cornelius from all those *Planet of the Apes* movies ('68–'73). Creepy, to say the least. Even more creepy is that apparently Oliver Stone was developing yet another *Apes* movie to star Arnold Schwarzenegger, *not* as one of the apes but as the marooned-in-monkeyland astronaut played originally by Charlton Heston. (nina) 🐒

Plastic Bead Jewelry   Ugly round plastic beads in gaudy bright colors that worked well for vals and New Wave chicks. Found cheap at Thrifty or any large drugstore. (darby) ❧ Good for the '60s go-go girl look, with matching Day-Glo-striped minidresses, fishnets, huge plastic Edie Sedgwick earrings, *That Girl* bouffant, and of course the white pointy-toed boots. (gwynne) ❧ All the rage in the early '80s, pop beads fit together to form jewelry. Came in clear plastic tubes. Were usually hot pink or turquoise. Mostly made unimaginative necklaces and bracelets. Was very uncool to mix colors at my school. Solid was the only way to go. (jen g.) (See also JUNK DRESSING)

Plastic Bottles Glass seemed so nice and natural and recyclable, but that didn't matter, because plastic didn't break. Soon everything came in a plastic bottle — and tasted more like plastic too. (ju-ji)

Plastic Surgery So many have horrified us over the past few years with their new expensive faces. Seeing Joan Rivers in person gave me a better idea of how these post-op results really end up looking, and how TV can hide the reality. Perhaps these people don't care about how they look in the real world. There's a good bit about Liberace in the recommended book *The Encyclopedia of Bad Taste*: "Liberace's plastic surgeon removed so much wrinkled skin from the aging pianist's face that when Liberace took off the bandages, he realized with horror that he was unable to keep his eyes closed. Unless squeezed tightly, they wanted to spring open, even when he slept, requiring him to use drops throughout the night to keep his eyeballs from drying out." Brutal! (darby) ❧ Back in the '70s, a nose job or face lift was major surgery; these days, no one blinks a collagen-injected eye at such commonplace procedures. Can you think of one woman in the limelight who doesn't have a little extra bounce? (nina) (See also BRAT PACK, COWLNECKS, and MICHAEL JACKSON'S NOSE)

Platform Shoes It was all about platforms in 1975. I lived for them. I had ones made of wood-grain soles with bunches of plastic fruit or satin flowers on top, or snakeskin (lots of snakeskin shoes back then). I had fabric wedgies covered with old floral-print drapery fabric, and my favorites were a gorgeous pair of red, white, and gold twelve-inch platform shoes I now use as book ends. These had ankle straps and little bows on them. They wedged from twelve inches at the heel down to nine inches in front and were less than an inch wide. Since our whole house was covered in shag carpets I used to carry them to the back door before putting them on. I remember one night, when I first bought them, I was just starting to get off on the acid I had taken when my dad came running upstairs with an ax in his hand screaming at me to give him my shoes so he could chop off a few inches. "Patty, they're going to wreck your feet. No daughter of mine is going to walk down the street in shoes like these." I started crying and screaming about how all the kids (I should have said "drag queens") were wearing them and that if he ruined my shoes I was moving out. I ran out the door a foot taller and stumbled to freedom. It's twenty years later (yikes!) and I am working out a scam on the Canadian health plan so I can get my bunion removed. I tried on these shoes the other day and, sure enough, every twist and bump on my misshapen feet fit perfectly between the bows and straps of those twenty-pound shoes. Of course, I won't ever tell him he was right. (patty) ❧ I remember getting bar mitzvahed, and I was really small and had five-inch platform shoes that made me as tall as Tammy — the hottest girl at the time. And by virtue of the fact that I was 5'5" in my shoes, instead of 5', my bar mitzvah was a little bit more of a special event than it would have been. Let's just say that I feel sorry for the short guys today who don't benefit from this fashion. (cliff c.) 🐚

Sylvia Plath Probably the most astute and expressive writer of the century. Her poetry is remorseless and incisive, and her one novel, *The Bell Jar,* was like a *Catcher in the Rye* for loner intellectual women. Acting like *The Bell Jar*'s heroine, Plath killed herself by putting her head in the oven when her poet husband Ted Hughes cheated on her. Since then, Hughes and Plath's conservative mother have been responsible for releasing her journals, taking care to first delete passages that they don't approve of. I often feel that if Plath could have hung on for a few more years, she would have escaped the stifling conformity of the late '50s and felt at home with the cultural renaissance of the '60s. We'll never know. Perhaps because of her exacting, brutal, nonclichéd writing (and perhaps just because of her glamorous Kurt-like death), rock musicians like me have been fascinated by her. Among the groups that have sung about Sylvia Plath: Peter Laughner, the Johnsons, Johnny Panic, Death of Samantha, and my band, the Leaving Trains. Later on, writer Anne Sexton, who was friends with Plath, would end up offing herself too. (falling james)

Playboy The magazine and the company were rich during most of the 1970s. *Playboy*'s circulation peaked with the November 1972 issue, which sold 7,161,561 copies. Almost all of the monthly circulation was distributed through newsstands. This would change during the early '80s when Jerry Falwell and Ed Meese and others targeted "smut," which curtailed sales in places like convenience stores. If you look back at issues from the early '70s, you'll find that the centerfolds are a bit more explicit than those before and those that followed. This was largely due to the "pubic wars" — the pictorials in other magazines left little to the imagination, and there was pressure on *Playboy* to follow suit. The first appearance of pubic hair in *Playboy* occurred in an August 1969 pictorial featuring an actress. The first Playmate followed suit, in January 1971. It was a big deal at the time. There were other firsts: the first Playmate to sign her centerfold (October 1975), the first Playmate datasheet (July 1977), and the last Playmate to have a staple over her navel (September 1985). *Playboy* was rich rich rich — it even had a black DC-9 called the "Big Bunny" that Hef and Barbi Benton used to jet around the world and back and forth between his Los Angeles and Chicago mansions. The plane had a galley, a living room, a disco, movie and video equipment, a wet bar, and sleeping quarters for sixteen people. In the mid-'70s, the company sold the plane and the Chicago mansion and moved to Los Angeles full-time. *Playboy* was profitable in large part because of its huge circulation and its casinos in London, which were bringing in tens of millions of dollars in annual profits. But after its casino licenses were challenged and *Playboy* sold its gaming operations (it's a long story), the company hit tough times. That's when Christie Hefner, Hef's daughter by his first marriage, became CEO. She dumped unprofitable businesses like the sentimental favorite Playboy Clubs (the last U.S. club, in Lansing, Michigan, closed in 1988) and other financial black holes such as the Playboy book publishing division. (She also discontinued those Rabbit Head air fresheners, if you're looking for one.) Today *Playboy* has a circulation of 3.2 million, is building an online pay site, and owns part of a new casino in Greece. Little-known fact: Hef hosted *Saturday Night Live* on October 15, 1977. Trivia: No playmates have been born in Alaska, Connecticut, Delaware, Iowa, Maine, South Dakota, or Vermont. (Chip Rowe, *Playboy* Advisor) (see also BARBI BENTON)

Play-Doh I can't recall ever *making* anything with this stuff, just sniffing it while watching cartoons. There's a game out now, similar to Pictionary, in which you're supposed to model things with Play-Doh and other people guess what it's supposed to be. Poor. (jeff h.) ♣ There are sure-bet scents that are guaranteed to hit you hard with Retro Hell memories. Get yourself a plastic container of this shit and sniff away. (jaz)

Pogo Sticks, Stilts, and Lemon Twists

Inventions which made it possible to have a whole afternoon of fun without leaving the garage and driveway. (jen d.) ♣ My dad built me some stilts when I was about ten. Towering over everyone was cool, but learning to walk on those suckers was superdangerous — especially if evil neighborhood enemies were around to facilitate your descent. (bridget) ♣ Lemon Twists were those plastic lemons on the end of a plastic rope that you'd attach to your ankle and then swing around in a circle under you and jump over as it passed. Incidentally, they had a previous incarnation around 1967 when they were called Ding-a-Lings, and had small bells on them. The sound of those things on driveway concrete can still give me riot flashbacks. Another hot jumping toy of the early '70s was called the Hoppity Hop. A one-piece sack of ultrathick rubber, it had a ring handle molded into the top. When it was fully inflated, one could squat on this thing and really hop around; I'm talking spastic jumps for joy. It came in a violent blue or a fire-engine red that made you look like a victim of scrotal elephantiasis. (bruce) (See also STICKS)

Polack Jokes Very '70s. Being Polish, I always enjoyed these a lot more than I should have. (winnie) ♣ '70s Polack: (Q) How does a Polack disco dance? (A) Dis go here, dis go there [as shuffling feet following dance instructions]. '80s Polack: (Q) How do you tell when a Polack's been using your P.C.? (A) There's white-out on the screen. A lot of the Polish jokes have been recycled as blonde jokes. (bruce)

Politically Correct (or P.C.) From the mid-'80s we started re-inventing our language in order to attempt not to offend people unintentionally with racially, sexually, or otherwise derogatorily slanted terms. Of course, this hypersensitivity to semantics made for even more unintentional insults. Some P.C. revampings: girls = women; postman = postal worker; handicapped = physically challenged; retarded = special; Mexican = Chicano/Hispanic; Spanish = Latin; Oriental = Asian; black = African American; Iranian = Persian; minorities = people of color; secretary = administrative assistant; Indians = Native Americans; ghetto = inner city; old people = seniors; hookers = sex workers. (thomas c.) ♣ Don't forget, stewardess = flight attendant! (lorraine) ♣ And Merry Christmas! = Happy Holidays! (jaz)

Polo Popular male fragrance that cashed in on the preppie appeal of the '80s. One of my favorite scents. (krista) ♣ Brother to Ralph Lauren's then-popular girl fragrance Lauren. Lauren's clean, refreshing scent never fails to remind me of Marlboro Lights, Tab, and coke drip. (nina) (See also PERFUME AND COLOGNE, PREPPIE, and TAB)

Polyester Just as I'm sure the '90s will go down in the history books as the age of rayon, so the '70s will have to be remembered as the polyester era. Polyester was created in the '70s, so is it any wonder that everything worn under the sun was made of it? Everything from leisure suits (open-collared, wide-lapeled, bad plaid) to spaghetti-strapped, elasticized disco gowns, and it reeked. The thing is that polyester is made out of petroleum products and doesn't absorb moisture the way cotton and other natural fibers do, so skin can't really breathe. Can't you just imagine the stench of your partner after a long night of doing the Hustle on the dance floor? How could they stand it? What were

they thinking? (karrin) ♣ Let's not forget to mention how highly flammable some of these clothes are. Premodern primitive burn victims ended up with pictures embedded in their skin. (noël) ♣ When it first came out my mom would always be having fires in the dryer. (patty) (See also DISCO CHIC) ♣

Pom Poms Those fuzzy little things were everywhere, on everything: bathroom curtains, girly bedroom items, ski hats, the back of tennis socks, larger ones on rollerskates, and some even had "weepuls," googly eyes and feet pasted on, which you'd get as a prize for selling chocolate bars for the school and your parents would stick to their car dashboard. (darby)

Pooper Scooper In the '60s they passed a law that said you had to clean up after your dog's mess in N.Y. — in L.A. it happened in the '70s. Common courtesy, but for your average self-obsessed dog owner it was a major uproar. To make it easier on them a pooper scooper was invented, which was like a smaller version of the "lobby pans" they clean up with at amusement parks. (darby) ♣ They started in cities like N.Y. where you had a hundred thousand dogs for every blade of grass so everybody was constantly stepping on shit — kinda like the buffalo on the Great Plains. So some guy came up with this design: a little scoop with a little shovel with a little plastic bag that was attached to it. It was absolutely a wonderful thing. So now in N.Y. you don't have shit in the streets, you just have piss from winos. (dad)

Pop Rocks A *huge* kiddie candy fad around 1979, these sugar rocks fizzed and crackled in your mouth. Then a rumor spread that they were dangerous, that "little Mikey" — the small boy who had starred in Life cereal commercials earlier in the decade — had eaten too many Pop Rocks washed down with soda and *exploded*. Another urban legend in action. (candi) (See also SCANDALS) ♣

P

Population Explosion   People used to think this was a bad thing. People also used to at least pay lip service to concern about this very real and ever-increasing problem, if only out of a sort of primitive political correctness. Now all you hear about are biological clocks and the race race. ("But, like, if we don't breed, white people will become the minority!) Am I the only one who finds this strange? (gwynne) ♣ A buzz word of the late '60s, when there were about half as many people as there are now. It ceased to be a concern to most Americans once they realized it mainly affected foreigners. (bruce) Even *Schoolhouse Rock* addressed the issue — "Elbow Room! Elbow Room! Gotta Gotta Get Us Some Elbow Room!" (See also BABIES and BIRTH CONTROL)

Porky's   In the heat of my trials with puberty, there were only a few outlets for my increasing rush of sexual frustration. For a pimple-faced wuss, all there was as far as naked women was R-rated movies on TV and pleading with some sympathetic adult to buy you and your equally horny friends tickets to the mecca of all T&A movies — *Porky's*. I remember the shower scene as if it were still playing on an endless tape-loop in my mind. I remember the sequels: *Porky's II: The Next Day* (where the guy goes on a date with a condom *already on!*) and *Porky's Revenge* . . . Ah, yes. (howard) (See also PARTY FLICKS)

Post-It Notes   In the early '70s, 3M's Spencer Silver attempted to develop a new adhesive but couldn't quite get it right. Several years later, another 3M guy was singing in his church choir and became frustrated because his hymnal markers kept falling out. He remembered Silver's loser sticky and used it to coat his markers. Praise the Lord! Another modern innovation for the always busy and disorganized denizens of the present. (skylaire) (See also the movie *Romy and Michelle's High School Reunion*)

P.O.W. Bracelets   P.O.W. bracelets were silver, M.I.A. bracelets were bronze. Wide metal bracelets with the name, rank, and capture date of a particular American prisoner of war in Indochina. Big clunky things that you were not supposed to take off until your particular prisoner came home. Very big with nerdy compassionate types. One girl in my fourth-grade class got hers after a three-month wait only to have her prisoner released by the North Vietnamese four days later — she was pissed. She loudly banged it against every hard surface to get the band off. (bruce)

Power Walking   It's gross and makes people look retarded. Chest out, butt tucked in, power walkers look like they're holding in their poo and are trying to make it to their house before it's too late. Dan Aykroyd did the power walk in the opening segment of *Doctor Detroit*. They even had power walk races. The point of power walking was that you wouldn't destroy your knees — and it was also great for fat people who couldn't run. (darby/noël) ♣ Also known as wogging (jogging plus walking). (winnie) (See also MALL WALKING)

Preppie, Save an Alligator Shoot A   (Also *The Preppie Handbook*) Oh gawd, it was so bad. The Buffy and Muffy and Biff and Skip infiltration of the early '80s. The punks/New Wavers on one side and the preppies on the other. War! Think bright-colored Lacoste alligator and Polo shirts (collars up, please!), Ray-Ban sunglasses, Bass penny loafers, Sperry topsiders (no socks!), waterproof duck shoes, hair bands, argyle vests, tucked-in oxford cloth button-down shirts, canvas webbed thin belts, blazers, monogrammed sweaters, L. L. Bean, J. Crew, bermuda shorts, country clubs/tennis/field hockey . . . oh, and President Reagan! A well-documented conservative uprising. (ju-ji) ♣ I have to admit, I made the ultimate preppie, even more so than Michael J. Fox on *Family Ties*. I spent at least an hour on my hair (I had to have the *perfect* bear claw). I used Aqua Net, though, so I had that Jimmy Johnson "My hair can't move/hair helmet" thing. Then I heard "Pretty Vacant" and related a little too much. (e. c. cotterman) (See also YUPPIES and the movie *Trading Places*)

Prince and People Associated with Prince

He trickled up as an underground rumor in the late '70s, a titillating mix of disco, New Wave, and New Romantic. Heavy rock, sexy and transgressive, naughty but nice, was he black or white, was he straight or gay? Lots of young freakazoids on the dance floor loved pondering the questions, until the irresistible one-two of his 1983 double album *1999*'s pop-single breakthroughs, and then his double threat hit film/superhit soundtrack *Purple Rain*, made 1984 the year of Prince. At least in my high school, the slightly mentally unbalanced, sensitive but tough loner types began adopting a look of frock coats, frills, and teased curls, abandoning the James Dean archetype for a while at least. As much as I loved Prince, I learned to avoid people who loved him so much they began wearing lace gloves as they rode their motorcycles. Unlike most other early '80s superstar peers (Madonna, Springsteen, Michael Jackson, and even — believe it or not, if you weren't there or don't remember, Cyndi Lauper), he refused to slow down and refused to kiss ass, releasing a new burst of peculiar genius every ten months or so to this day, until no one but the really serious fan cared about anything other than publicity stunts like changing his name to a symbol. But even at the height of his market power, he failed at building a Paisley Park empire out of such comparatively weak (sometimes downright pathetic) protégés as Sheila E., the Family, the Time, Jill Jones, Madhouse, Vanity 6, Apollonia 6, and Carmen Elektra (now Jenny McCarthy's replacement on MTV's *Singled Out*). He did manage to write huge hits for already established artists like the Bangles ("Manic Monday") and Sinead O'Connor ("Nothing Compares 2 U"). His 1988 album, *Lovesexy* — when everyone but the fanatics started to jump off the boat in droves — is the nearest equivalent to powerful and joyous psychedelic on wax, one of the best albums ever made by a major-league pop artist, which no one seems to have heard. I feel bad embalming him in the almost-sneering nostalgia that many will undoubtedly take this book for. (brian) ✿ I recently saw *Under the Cherry Moon* and have to say it was brilliant. Better than *Purple Rain*. The thing is, if I would have seen it back in the '80s, I would have hated it. In the '80s Prince was so hot that they had a Prince lookalike do a nude sex scene fantasy spread in *Penthouse*. (howard) ✿ Lest we forget that powerhouse of talent, Wendy and Lisa! Also, he had a much-publicized affair with Kim Basinger when they worked together on *Batman*, as well as with Sheena Easton when she sang his song "Sugar Walls." All of which were undoubtedly attracted by his lyrical claim that he could "fuck until the break of dawn." (nina) ✿ Hey, Sheila E. was inspirational, and today Vanity works for God, while the sexier Apollonia milks it selling her autograph at conventions. (darby)

Pringle's Potato Chips

As a definitive product of the '70s, Pringle's has always charmed the pants off me. The space-age-like canisters were all the rage and the saddle-shaped chips, all identical in shape and size, were mouth-watering fun. For the longest time, I couldn't figure out how they sliced potatoes so perfectly; that is, until I found out it's just a hearty mixture of potato flour, water, and salt. In other words, it's just mulch. Like I give a shit. I still love this synthetic, overprocessed junk, and if I feel like a king I get myself a tube. I just read in *Beer Frame* zine that in 1991, the product was officially renamed, "thenceforth to be known as potato *crisps*, rather that *chips*." On the down side, there are those awful Pringle's commercials that exploit hip-hop in the worst way, much worse than the Kriss Kross plugs for Sprite. On the up side, you can simulate a duck bill by placing two of these (one in the opposite direction) in your mouth. (noël)

Prog

Overcomplicated and overambitious, but glorious to those who practiced their instrument a lot and dreamed of transcendence, power, fantasylands, demons, and UFOs. Lots of people are buying into a revival of the really obscuro foreign stuff from Italy or Germany (Can, Faust, Neu, PFM), but the classic stoner albums of the '70s that everyone remembers by the likes of Rush, King Crimson, and Genesis are still amazing and revelatory today. Especially deserve respect for being so gosh-darned happy, positive, and goal-oriented. (brian)

Punk Translated to TV

One of the most exploitative TV episodes ever aired was the 1982 legendary "Battle of the Bands" *CHiPs* show. Designed to discredit anyone with the label "punk," and to glorify the safe, happy-go-lucky New Wavers lifestyle, it featured a similar aesthetic to one of those late '60s *Dragnet* episodes about the youth movements and LSD, while at the same time confirmed the concept (at least to any thinking and aware human) that the media could be your biggest enemy. Any doubts or fears adults had about their children's interests were not only confirmed but glorified.

Now an often joked about, highly revered classic, this historic episode offers scenes like cops simulating slam-dancing in the locker room, a Battle of the Bands (complete with bad Knack- and Romantics-type groups), and a singer whose name is Snow Pink (a stereotypical example of the harmless, New Wave, potential groupie scene-making chick). The so-called plot focuses on her shattered dreams brought about by the rival, dirty, no-future-bound punk rock band aptly titled Pain, who steal Ms. Pink's band gear and (in typical *CHiPs* slo-mo action!) mutilate her tour van. The Battle of the Bands includes our punk scumbags, the New Wave princess, and the mighty warrior of the highways Poncherello, who wants to enter the band contest. Being new to the wave, he recruits the ever-so-hip Snow Pink (who of course works at a New Wave clothing store) to dress him up for his big night on stage (complete with a gold lamé shirt!). For this he is persuaded to take special interest in retrieving her stolen equipment and generally spends most of the show hanging out with her and being macho rather than fighting crime.

The Battle of the Bands becomes just that when they take to the stage, with the club owner conveniently tied up and gagged in the rest room (after ignoring the pressure Ponch puts on him not to book punk acts). Pain inflicts itself on a normally well-behaved crowd, causes a riot, and gets kids to start beating each other up during their show (note Pain's punk rock lyrics: "Take a hunk of concrete and stick it in my face, I like to play with razor blades, I hate the human race"). Spotting the fuzz, Pain abandons the stage and hopefully the premises, but of course gets nabbed, 'cause *CHiPs* are the heroes! John (in off-duty plainclothes) gives the hyper kids in the audience a pep talk to calm them (in the middle of a fucking riot!), explaining that it's Pain's fault this all happened . . . and they stop! How simple! Who needs bouncers? The show concludes with Ponch singing Kool and the Gang's "Celebration," symbolically glorifying their victory against punk rock and showing sympathy for youth culture by awarding Snow Pink first place in the band competition. (mike v.) (See also *21 JUMP STREET* and check out the many other punk interpretations on TV shows like *Simon and Simon, Quincy, C.P.O. Sharkey,* and if we're going this far, *Punky Brewster!*)

Project U.F.O. The original concept the show *The X-Files* is based on. *Project U.F.O.* (itself based on Project Blue Book — a half-hearted government attempt to investigate UFOs during the '60s) was about two Air Force guys who went around investigating UFO sightings and related phenomena. A tamer version of *In Search Of* and one of the last shows produced by Jack Webb, which came in the wake of *Close Encounters*. The problem was, the *Project*'s files were inconclusive at best, and didn't combine too well with Jack's trademark wooden acting. (bruce)

Pssst! Dry-cleaning for your hair. Just spray it in and brush it out! From the bygone era of the '70s, when dirty hair was actually a fashion taboo. Unfortunately, it sometimes seemed to leave a dandrufflike residue, and dandruff was another big Me Generation no-no. Nowadays we have Mud, a product that makes clean hair appear grungy — for that "just shot up and vomited" look! (gwynne)

PTL Club It was shortly after midnight on a summer night in 1987. I was home from college, staying up late after *Saturday Night Live,* watching the tube. Jim Bakker, who grew up in a town about twenty minutes from mine in western Michigan, came on the *Praise the Lord Club*. I watched for kicks. He was good. By 1:30 AM my eyes were teary and I was considering the ministry. He somehow hit on every one of my insecurities, *bam! bam! bam!* Even Tammy Faye seemed nice. When he later fell from grace, I could understand why so many people had turned to his show. He had a soothing, friendly face in a sea of trouble — except for the thievin' part. (chip)

Puffy Stickers What kid didn't have a sticker collection? I for one was absolutely ruthless in my pursuit of sticker excellence. I was the Ivan Boesky of sticker trading. You could really fuck with someone if you had a puffy, changing, goggly eye that was in mint condition. (katy) ✿ There's been a lot of the old-school puffy *A-Team* ones going around lately. Don't know what that's about. (darby)

Pulltabs on Soda Cans 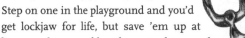 Step on one in the playground and you'd get lockjaw for life, but save 'em up at home and you could make vests, hammocks, hats, planters, and hot pants. Wear it to the Renaissance Pleasure Faire and you'd be a hit. (lisa aa.) (See also ARTS and CRAFTS)

Puppet Movies The *Thunderbirds* and *Stingray* movies were supposed to be live-action sci-fi, but the producers didn't spend money on creating sets and costumes or hiring actors, so they used wooden marionettes instead. The battle scenes are unbelievably drawn-out and uneventful in order to make the movies feature-length. In *Thunderbirds,* they film a puppet in a space ship cockpit for about ten minutes while he describes what's going on outside. Lengthy musical numbers are also a bonus. (wendy) ✿ These were part of a long tradition of puppet TV series: *Diver Dan, Supercar, Fireball XL-5, Thunderbirds Are Go!,* to name a few. (don) ✿ The creations of Sylvia and Gerry Anderson. They called their process of marionettes on "invisible" monofilaments "Supermarionation." These were produced in England and were originally made as daily segments for TV. When they are congealed into movies the plot seems bizarre, as it builds to a climax every fifteen minutes, with ten-minute segments showing nothing but rockets moving into firing position while heroic music plays! They later branched out into live action, producing the TV series *UFO* and *Space: 1999*. The folks who made puppets look like people turned out to be even better at making people seem like puppets. (bruce) ✿ Don't forget those holiday specials they'd show on TV every year. And Lamb Chop and Madame! (darby) (See also *DAVEY AND GOLIATH*)

P

Puttin' on the Hits Predated the karaoke phenomenon by a decade, it was the first and only lip-synch show, in which contestants pretended to sing songs while engaging in hilarious hijinks. The fact that the country could once support a lipsynch craze is, incidentally, a sign of both great wealth and spiritual lassitude. (nick)

Pyramid Money Schemes P.M.S.s were very popular during Carter, when with the tremendous inflation, people went totally out of control. It was an offshoot of the chain letter. It started where each person would send $5 to four people, and eventually they would get back hundreds or thousands of dollars. And then it became much more professional. People started to hire meeting halls, and it got to the point where people were putting in thousands and thousands of dollars and coming out with fifteen thousand dollars. Families were getting together and working the scheme, and for a while people were making good money. Then they couldn't bring in enough people to pay the people on the top, and the schemes folded after about a year or so and all but disappeared. There were laws against it; it's called the Ponzi scheme, and has been around since the early twentieth century. The people who put their money in may have known they were breaking the law, but they were just hoping they got in early enough to get out in time and take their money and run. That's how things were in the '70s. Inflation just kept going up so your money was almost worthless, so it was like a game everyone was playing. The price of gold skyrocketed, and cash money was like play money. (dad) ♣ Social Security, of course, is the world's most popular pyramid scheme. (brian) 🐑

Quaaludes These cost two or three bucks a *pop*, if my drug-addled memory serves me right, and were stronger than hell, kind of like a really good, non-speedy ecstasy. Rohrer 714 — ask for them by name! God, they were great. The first time I ever took one I was dancing to Bowie's "Suffragette City." I came on to the 'ludes and literally fell off my platforms on the dance floor. I spent the next four hours making out with people I'd always had crushes on. (pleasant) ✿ A later brand: Lemon 714. It was like achieving the perfect drunken state without the sick feeling or hangover with the mere pop of a $10 pill. (riley) ✿ Most of the local trade in these babies was controlled by speed-freak bikers, and these were dismissively known as Disco Biscuits. (bruce) ✿ I'm positive I read that Quaaludes were named for their effect of inducing a "quiet interlude." Recently, my friend Monster snidely informed me that he found out the name actually comes from their molecular chemistry. Okay, sure, but

what are the molecules named after? (nina) (See also DRUGS)

Quark A sci-fi comedy that aired from February to April 1978 (although the pilot episode with a different cast had aired the previous year). A very '70s Richard Benjamin starred as the captain of an interstellar garbage scow in A.D. 2222. Despite its short run, the show has always enjoyed a minor cult following. Other members of the crew included a cowardly robot, two clone gals, and Ficus, a highly intelligent plant being. About ten years ago, Benjamin was doing *Letterman*, and this show came up. Benjamin kidded about how the cast and crew knew the show would not last and began taking parts of the futuristic set home. Benjamin joked that if the show had been renewed, they would have had to film it in the director's living room. (bruce)

Suzi Quatro Part of the glam era of early '70s rock 'n' roll, a major influence on Joan Jett (and thus on the riot grrrls), and remembered by many as *Happy Days*'s

Suzi Quatro visits the Fonz

rebel rocker Leather Tuscadero, Suzi Quatro was actually more seriously talented than her packaging (leather jumpsuits, *Klute*-era shag hairstyle, power-chord bubble-gum AM radio tunes like "Can the Can" and "Daytona Demon") might have suggested. She began her music career in 1966 in her native Detroit, as sixteen-year-old Suzi Soul, guitarist for the all-girl Pleasure Seekers (her sister, Patti Quatro, was lead singer). Shortly after changing their name to the hipper-sounding Cradle, the band split up; Patti went on to form the hippie girl band Fanny; Suzi went solo. While still in Cradle, and on a tour of American military bases in the Pacific, Suzi was discovered by British record producer Mickey Most. In a move later repeated by Pretenders' leader Chrissie Hynde, Suzi relocated to England, where she began her rise to pop success. There, she hooked up with the songwriting/production team of Nicky Chinn and Michael Chapman (the team that also gave us Sweet, Nick Gilder's "Hot Child in the City," and the Knack's "My Sharona"), and by 1973 was riding the glitter wave to the top of the charts, recording a string of trashy, bouncy pure pop tunes and covers of such '50s hits as Elvis's "All Shook Up." After momentarily fading away, she reemerged at the end of the '70s, apparently energized by punk's back to basics, with both a recurring role on *Happy Days* and another hit song, "Rock Hard," significant as one of the earliest meetings of glam, punk, and the top 40. Finally, after TV success with Richie and Fonzie, and lite rock success with "Stumblin' In," Suzi went the way of fellow retired rockers Rex Smith and Tim Curry and found her way to performing in musicals (of the old-fashioned sort, not rock operas). Still living in England, she has been performing in London musicals since the mid-'80s. (thomas c.)

Queen Debuted in England July 6, 1973. Freddie Mercury (née Bulsara), a Persian art student and quasi deity, and Roger Taylor, a fun lovin' Kensington Market hipster, found Brian May, a guitarist with a degree in physics and a guitar made from an eighteenth-century fireplace, and they all joined forces to conquer the world. Along with bassist John Deacon, they went on to record twenty fabulous albums, be the first band to tour the Eastern Bloc, and become the most collectible band in England. Freddie died of AIDS in November of 1991. The Queen: Long may she reign. (skylaire) ❧ One of the bands whose music kept me from killing myself. The first concert I ever went to in my life (1978) also happened to be the first time Freddie Mercury was seen with a mustache. He was talking to the audience between songs and said, "What do you think of my new mustache? The girls think it makes me look a bit like Burt Reynolds," as if he would now be able to scam on all these girls. The audience didn't laugh at the joke

9

Freddie Mercury as lead Queen

attempt; instead, the Forum fell into this amazing hush with people there immediately whispering to each other, "He is so gay that his band is named Queen, does he really think we are buying this I'm-gonna-get-a-ton-of-chicks-now joke?" Besides, who thinks Burt Reynolds is good-looking anyway? (riley) (See also MUSTACHES)

Quiche Real men didn't eat it. (nina) (See also BESTSELLING BOOKS and SUSHI)

Quincy, M.E. I watched in pure awe as Quincy figured out all sorts of important things — like the bubonic plague in the water fountain at the stadium. *Wow!* Second only to my admiration of Sherlock Holmes. Unfortunately actor Jack Klugman was more in real life like the careless Oscar of *The Odd Couple* who smoked a lot, and for a while he had to talk through a voice machine since he damaged his voice box. I have more pity than awe for him now. (darby) (See also PUNK TRANSLATED TO TV)

q

Race-Across-the-World Movies
Cannonball, Cannonball Run, Gumball Rally, The Great Race, It's a Mad Mad Mad Mad World . . . The thrill of fast cars and paved roads, Penelope Pitstop suspense, and the pot at the end of the rainbow. (darby) ❖ For some reason, nobody at my grade school knew the proper number of "Mads" in *It's a Mad Mad Mad Mad World* except me, and I was always getting in arguments about it, like it actually *mattered* or something. (don) ❖ Part of *Gumball Rally* was filmed at my house in 1973. The East Coast guy calls up the West Coast guy, says, "Gumball," and West Coast guy is so excited that he leaps off our balcony into the pool onto some topless babe floating below. Everyone in the neighborhood came to see the topless babe and her big hooters. The director hated me because I would leave my teddy bear around on the set and yell while they were filming. Somebody working on the show taught me how to say "shit." (wendy) ❖ Also: CBS Saturday morning cartoon circa 1970 *Wacky Races, Speed Racer* (and its rip-offs); chase movies: *Smokey and the Bandit* (about the best) and *Convoy* (Smokey with a tractor trailer — about the worst). (ju-ji)

Rainbows How does one market a natural phenomenon like the rainbow? Put it on stationery, sheets, clothing, and jewelry. Rainbow shirts: the rainbow extended from one arm to the other and across the chest, with 3/4-length sleeves. Everybody wore them! Rainbow stickers: You may still see the faded remains of this once-popular sticker on the rear window (center and bottom) of old Datsuns — or at least the gummy residue that was left over after it was peeled off. Rainbow suspenders: Mork from Ork made these a big hit, and I always wondered why kids wanted to look like him. They pinned those oversized buttons on them too, and ended up looking more like doofus clowns. (winnie/bridget/darby)

Rap Yo! Although antecedents existed in black culture for ages, it really began in Jamaica with the dub "Toasters," such as U-Roy, Dillinger, and Tapper Zukie, then put down roots in N.Y. and was adopted to Afro-American rhythms. Who woulda thought it would still be around over a decade later? (mike s.) ❖ The granddaddy of it all, "Rapper's Delight" by Sugar Hill Gang. Also, Kurtis Blow, Public Enemy, Terminator X, Flava Flav, Ice Cube, Ice-T, De La Soul, Big Daddy Kane, Kool Moe Dee, Dr. Dre, L.L. Cool J, Stetsasonic, Fat Boys, KRS ONE, Choice, EPMD, BWA, NWA, A Tribe Called Quest, Jungle Brothers, Run-D.M.C., Beastie Boys, 3rd Bass, D.J. Jazzy Jeff and The Fresh Prince, Milky D, Schooly D, King T, Grandmaster Flash, Grandmaster Melle Mel, Salt-N-Pepa, Queen Latifah, JJ Fad. (howard)

Reagan Getting Shot This happened the same year that I lost my virginity. Hmmm . . . which is more important: the president getting shot at by a deranged gunman, or my having a big fourteen-year-old cock in my crotch? Needless to say, I don't remember much of the shooting except that I was at home with mono at the time and they interrupted *Guiding Light* to show the footage. (winnie) (See also SCANDALS)

Real People Besides being one of the most fascinating shows to document some of America's freaks and trailer trash, *Real People* had the mildly entertaining rapport between two of the hosts, Skip Stephenson and Sarah Purcell. In between features, Skip always found a way to profess his desire for Sarah through extremely bad innuendoes. She always blew him off with a laugh or two, but we didn't buy it. Skip was a bad role model for middle America, especially for sexually repressed, buck-toothed dweebs. (noël) ❀ Also had Byron Allen and Messy Marvin as hosts. Memorable episodes: The guy who could read things backward, and visiting Uriel of the UFO Church of the Unarians. (howard)

Recess Every day after lunch we got to go outside and fuck off for a while. We played four square, king of the mountain, freeze tag, kick the can, dodgeball, kickball, and football. You could also jump rope, play on the jungle gym (tar monsters), the swings, or the seesaw. You had your tires and your big cement tunnels. But the best was the daily reenactment of *Charlie's Angels* episodes or Barry Manilow ballads. "Copacabana" always lent itself to wonderful schoolyard interpretations. (jes) ❀ I always thought the metal rings (that only the girls played on) were an awesome invention. (darby) ❀ Tetherball, prison ball, smear the queer . . . (morgan and ferris) ❀ I always liked clubs with little outdoor areas because even when there were "no ins and outs" allowed, you could still have recess between bands. (gwynne)

Real People, Real Geeks

Record-Cleaning Products Back when vinyl still ruled the earth, audio buffs used a whole array of products that supposedly cleaned the dirt and fingerprints from the grooves and made records sound better. There were wiping cloths and brushes and cleaning fluids to go with them, plus a weird gadget called an anti-static gun that you zapped your records with so they wouldn't attract dust from the air. Some actual product names: D-Stat, Parastat, Zerostat, Disc Washer, Vac-o-Rec, and the Preener. (candi) ❀ These were all part of the Disc Washer system. I still have mine in its dark wood tray and clear smoke top. Now it's a potential antique, and I use the Zerostat to keep my socks from clinging. (bruce)

Rec Rooms I always felt underprivileged because we didn't have one. The ones with the game carpets were the best (mazes, hopscotch, checkers). (wendy) ❀ Unlucky souls without basements always referred to a cluttered corner of their house as the rec room. It was aptly named. (See also AIR HOCKEY)

Redd Kross Jeffrey and Steven McDonald formed the glitter-glam-pop-slinkster-punk-rock band Redd Kross in 1977 when Jeff was fourteen and Steve was eleven. They were the first L.A. kids to openly embrace the kitsch and the tacky, and they're largely to thank (blame) for bringing back hoards of would-be forgotten pop culture phenomena (musical and otherwise). These two bastions of retro have been busy making movies (*Desperate Teenage Lovedolls, Lovedolls Superstar, Spirit of '76*) and putting out albums (*Born Innocent, Teen Babes from Monsanto, Neurotica, Third Eye, Phaseshifter, Show World*) for two decades; I'm sure they'll be superstars any second. (lorraine)

Mason Reese Short, red, and cuddly, Mason began his career at age four (1969) with a commercial for Ivory Snow and won his first of seven Clios. In '72 he did a commercial for Underwood Deviled Ham in which he uttered the immortal phrase, "It's like having a borgasmord." From then on he was a household name, doing seventy-three other commercials, including another favorite for Dunkin' Donuts Munchkins,

Mason Reese

co-hosting (age eight and up) the *Mike Douglas Show* thirty-two times, shooting a television pilot (*Mason*) in '77, and doing his final national commercial in '79, for *Beatlemania*. Since then, he's made semiregular appearances on the *Howard Stern Show.* (jon r.)

Relax! (Don't Do It) Big bold gigantic lettering of "Frankie Goes to Hollywood" lyrics on T-shirts. All the rage at the down and out T-shirt shops during the later '80s (the Day-Glo period) — where I unfortunately worked at the time. (darby) (See also CHOOSE LIFE)

Religious Cults People could choose from a whole smorgasbord of religious options in the '70s. You could be a born-again Jesus freak hippie Christian, possibly finding your way into groups like Jews for Jesus, the Way, the Love Family, or the Children of God. Then there were the Eastern religious cults with their guru leaders and (seemingly hypnotized) followers selling flowers on street corners. Other psychology-heavy religious groups: est, Synanon, Silva Mind Control, Transactional Analysis, and some other groups who would mess with our minds if we mentioned their names in print. Nonjoiners dabbled in astrology, pyramid power, acupuncture, UFOs, and the occult. (candi) (See also EST and THE OCCULT)

Remote Control Don't you remember the day your parents brought this wondrous piece of technology to your living room? Think about how different the world would have been if they never figured out how to make these. This and video games were most instrumental in the initial speeding up of society. (darby) ✿ Our first one had a long wire that attached to the VCR and stretched to the couch. (lorraine) ✿ This board of buttons also created a whole new sport for men to impress the ladies with: channel surfing. The way they go at it, you'd think thumb dexterity was the ultimate turn-on. (nina)

Repo Man This funny, cynical 1984 cult classic with Emilio Estevez and Olivia Barash (and, let's not forget, the Circle Jerks!) was the nearest thing to a generation-defining movie for early punk rockers, and it uses a fairly accurate version of L.A.'s punk subculture as background. But there's much much more, including a government cover-up of dead aliens, brain-dead hippie parents (a cinema first?), and lessons on living by the Repo Code. Features two of my favorite character actors, Harry Dean Stanton and Tracey Walter (as burnout/mystic Miller, who explains the secret meaning of the "plate of shrimp" and points out the cardboard pine tree air freshener in every car). (candi) ❖ "What about our relationship?" "Fuck that!" "Let's go get sushi and not pay!" "John Wayne was a fag!" "No explanation. No point in looking for one." (howard) (See also *DECLINE OF WESTERN CIVILIZATION*)

Retarded Not very P.C., but I sure used to say it a lot (and still do). We had retard-sensitivity training in eighth grade when we watched a movie about Willie — this retarded boy who wanted to play baseball or some such nonsense. "Knuckleball, Willie!" his friend coached him. My friends and I still yell this at each other. (morgan and ferris) ❖ A steady kid-vid diet of P.S.A.s about the handicapped led to this misuse of the term. All those do-good messages ringing in our heads simply led to a heightened awareness, but not an understanding, of their plight. Calling someone retarded was searingly rude, even back then, which is why you said it! By age ten, we were all victims of media-induced compassion fatigue and needed to blow off steam. This is an early sign of the same crotchety ire that now makes people think Rush Is Right. I used to use this term on people and things until I started working with the retarded. Not only is it unkind, it's highly inaccurate. Retarded isn't stupid, it's bizarre! (bruce) ❖ The best TV movie of all time on the subject was *No Greater Love* ('79), starring Shaun Cassidy and Linda Purl as a retarded couple who try to make a go of marriage despite their "normal," yet idiotic, parents' protests. A particularly retarded scene had Linda's character coming home after a mandated hysterectomy and screeching in her over-the-top retard voice at Shaun's character, "No more babies, Rogerrr!" My friends and I said that so many times I'm sure we all sustained some form of brain damage. Another memorably mentally challenged moment had Roger asking his soon-to-be-wife in art therapy class if she was drawing a picture of Bugs Bunny. Her reply, "Noooo, it's Mrs. Bugs Bunnyyyyy!" was also gleefully imitated on schoolyards across America for months. (nina) (See also POLITICALLY CORRECT and SAYINGS/SLANG)

Mary Lou Retton Before there was Polly Klaas, Mary Lou Retton was America's daughter. In the 1984 Summer Olympics, devoid of any competition from the Communist Bloc, this stocky midget from hell (in sharp contrast to the talented twigs who make up most of the world of women's gymnastics) blazed in a number of gymnastic events, becoming an Olympic gold medalist and guaranteeing free Big Macs to lucky game-card holders across America. Her spunkiness tickled America's funny bone as her ubiquitous Jabba-like face was eventually plastered across millions of boxes of Wheaties. (noël) ❖ And let's not forget her brief career as a tampon-usin' no-leaks gal as demonstrated by her nonstained crotch during the backward walkover in those Tampax commercials. (bridget)

Burt Reynolds So maybe Burt's naked exposé in *Cosmopolitan* was the '70s equivalent to Madonna's *Sex* book, but I never understood how Burt Reynolds — with Dom DeLuise and friends — could serve as the '70s answer to Sinatra's Rat Pack. (jeff) ❖ Burt was the mustached hunk all the women swooned over and the young girls had daddy complexes about. He was most amicable as the people's hero, escaping the clutches of big bad smokey in big bad muscle cars, usually with the even more amicable Sally Field on his arm. His demise was best represented in the humorous flick *The End*, which would have been an honorable swan song. Instead he went on to scare us in *The Best Little Whorehouse in Texas*, and more recently in Demi Moore's *Striptease*. (darby) (See also QUEEN)

Mary Lou Retton

The Richard Pryor Show This short-lived network TV show was brilliant because it moved from skits to dramatic mini-plays seamlessly. I remember a pre–*Spinal Tap* ten-minute segment with no dialogue in which Pryor leads an Alice Cooper/Sabbath-y heavy metal band called Black Death in a mock concert in which he ends up machine-gunning the entire band and audience. It was actually a good song, too, if I remember, better even than Cheech and Chong's "Earache My Eye." (falling james)

Rinks Roller and ice. They used to be everywhere, and everyone used to go and do the Hokey Pokey. My favorite trip with my day camp was when we went to World on Wheels in Los Angeles (🍀), and we would skate to Billy Idol's "White Wedding," Wham!, Missing Persons, and Midnight Star. I could never skate backward, though, and felt a jealous rage consume me when my friends left me by the Zaxxon machine for the "Backward Only" skate. (bobby) 🍀 The rink was the place to score with some cute boy who lived in another neck of the woods, safely removed from you and, more important, your parents. Like the mall, the roller rink was the kind of place you could guilt or outright badger your folks to take you and your friends to without them feeling inclined to supervise. It was not a place grown-ups felt comfortable hanging out at, at all! "Drop the kids off and let's go!" This attitude made it the perfect set-up for make-out city. We would rush in, personal skates in hand, and find a locker. Then, free of parental objections, we'd head straight for the girls' room to try out all of those nifty cosmetics tips we had recently picked up from *Seventeen* magazine, using make-up lifted from either Mom's stash or the local Thrifty's market. Off came the jeans or skirts, replaced with Dove shorts or hot pants made to order. On went those legwarmers and up went those blouses, tied under the breasts to expose a nubile midriff. Out came the curling iron successfully smuggled from home in a book bag.

Rhinestones Forever a part of the white-trash and cowboy elegance, rhinestones come and go in the mainstream. From variety show–style gowns to Tony Alamo jackets to B-I-T-C-H spelled out in script across tiny lace tank tops. (ju-ji) 🍀 Remember that delightful Ronco machine that could transform the most mundane denim into a spangly showstopper? (bridget) (See also AIRBRUSH, RONCO, and SCANDALS)

Ribbons Super girly style: big hair bows, thick grosgrain multicolored ribbons hanging off barrettes, or just one thin strand around the hair, or even one tied around the neck under the collar of an oxford shirt. Ribbons are forever. (jaz) 🍀 Definitely not forever, just part of the whole early '80s preppie fashion fiasco that seemed interminable. (nina) (See also PREPPIE)

And, *look out!* Homegirls were dressed to kill and on the make. (karrin) ❧ Fewer and fewer of these all the time. Victims of too many injuries, too many lawyers, and the undeclared war on anywhere young people congregate without spending lots of money. (bruce) ❧ Every town had its own local roller rink which held many fond — and not so fond — memories. In Los Angeles, we had Flipper's Roller Boogie Palace. It was 1978 and disco was out but Flipper's was in. "Shooting the Duck" to the tunes of Michael Jackson's "Rock All Night" and the Bay City Rollers' "Saturday Night," though nothing got the rink going more than the Knack's "My Sharona" — talk about wild! Noteworthy Flipper items include Cher having a birthday party there for Chastity Bono; TV show *CHiPs* filming an episode there with special guest star Leif Garrett, who ended the show with a performance of "I Was Made for Loving You." It was like we had all made the big time, our local rink on national TV! (gihan) ❧ Sometimes they'd book punk and New Wave shows. I saw the Last, Eddie and the Subtitles, the Simpletones, the Falcons, and the Plimsouls there. Black Flag played once, and some of their entourage threw dirt and rocks all over the rink, which put an end to *that*. (gwynne)

Ripley's Believe It Or Not

The one show that never failed to creep me out and question our plush but narrow-minded (sub)urban realities. This show on ABC was hosted by the insidious Jack Palance, whose sinister voice lent the show that extra punk/death rock edge. Covering everything from Bigfoot sightings to UFOs to midget freaks to ghosts to shrunken heads, *Ripley's* exceeded the Cathy Lee Crosby coolness of *That's Incredible!*, which mostly documented more lighthearted subjects like Rubik's Cube champions. Jack Palance has since gone on to do one-handed push-ups on televised award shows and disgust zillions by gorging on a Taco Bell Texas Taco with lizardlike aplomb. (noël) (See also PHENOMENA, *REAL PEOPLE,* and *THAT'S INCREDIBLE!*)

Risky Business

Essential, if only for the Ray-Bans, the scary scene with Tom dancing in his undies to Bob Seger's "Old Time Rock 'n' Roll," the sex in the subway (with Rebecca DeMornay in her prime) to Phil Collins's echoing "I Remember" song, and, most important, because we want to go on the Rosie O'Donnell show. (darby/nina)

River's Edge

This 1986 movie perfectly cast with Keanu Reeves, Crispin Glover, Ione Skye, and Dennis Hopper was such a major downer that we all loved it. Disturbed the whole Generation X culture into a creepy death obsession — which we still haven't gotten over. (jaz)

Roach Clips

Originally, these were known as Jefferson Airplanes, due to the vaguely avian shape of the early models (the group named themselves after this, not the other way around). Sure, they were mostly decorated alligator clips, but it didn't matter — they were icons, a symbol of the enlightened life. Even if you didn't partake, stoner etiquette demanded that you have one. By the time I hit seventh grade, kids simply kept them as talismans of teenage cool. They came in a wide variety of shapes and designs. Look deep in the dresser drawer of many boomer age moralists, and you'll find them still. (bruce) ❧ We also wore them feathered and beaded in our hair or as earrings. Pheasant feathers were the best, longest, and coolest ones. (pleasant)

Rock'em-Sock'em Robots

I always thought people at Survival Research Laboratories played with these too much when they were kids. In the opening scene of Spike Lee's *Crooklyn*, which is set in the early '70s, two boys are shown playing with Rock'em-Sock'em Robots, and a large appreciative *"Yeah!"* came from the audience. (bruce) ❧ I can recall wanting Rock'em-Sock'em Robots so badly that they were the only thing I asked for that year for Christmas. I spent many hours attempting to "knock the block off" of my opponent, and causing that annoying head-popping-up noise that drove my folks crazy. The thing about the Rock'ems that was frustrating, though, was that you got to the point where you were too evenly matched with whomever you were playing against, and the charm faded pretty quickly. I guess they look cool at least. (creepy mike)

RETROLEXICON

These are a few of the current terms used to refer to the retro world and retro worldviews — which will help you gain a better understanding of the conspiracy, and help you communicate with all hip enough to use them.

Retrology — The study of retro.

Retrolectual — One who has the ability to argue everything with outdated logic.

Retrophobia — An obsessive anxiety over retro culture. When a person is retrophobic they don't watch TV for fear of seeing reruns; can't listen to the radio for fear of hearing the oldies; etc.

Retrobulimic — One who obsessively consumes mass quantities of retro and has to barf it up in order to stay human.

RetrObGyn — Someone who checks women for cameltoes.

Retroblivious — One who can somehow block out and ignore all retro culture.

Retrobot — One who acts and reacts to the world in a robotic, automatic pilot manner, content to maneuver through life only as others have done before.

Retroriental — David Carradine.

Retrobscene — Being forced to listen to Rick James while locked in a basement.

Retrobvious — When people recall memories of obvious retro culture and think they're being neat-o for remembering.

Retrocalifragilisticexpialidocious — Even though the sound of it is something quite atrocious.

Retrococo — The overdone decorating style of George Clinton.

Retrodor — The stink of retro.

RetrOedipus complex — To have an unhealthy obsession with Carol Brady.

Retrogress — To be so involved in retro culture that one actually becomes young again. Some even de-evolve to the point of reliving their birth.

Retroptimism — Being optimistic about the past.

Retrokay — "I'm O.K., you're O.K.." (Who the hell wants to be "O.K." anyway?)

Retrobituary — Some futuristic possibility we can only fantasize about today.

Retro phone home — Obsession with extraterrestrial E.T.

Retrostiltskin — Smurf (papa).

Retrow row row your boat . . .

Rock Flowers "A swinging, singing trio" of six-inch rubbery-limbed rock star fashion dolls by Mattel, circa 1971. Heather, Lilac, and token Afro (literally!) American Rosemary had outfits with names like Flares and Lace and Tie-Dye Maxi. Each came with her own seven-inch single on colored plastic (not vinyl). Wheel Records released two Rock Flowers albums featuring the Partridge Family/Fifth Dimension session crew (Wes Farrell, Hal Blaine, etcetera), but nowhere on the albums are the toys mentioned. Instead, maxiskirted models looking like a poor man's Carrie Nation (*Beyond the Valley of the Dolls* band) graced the covers. The albums and the plastic singles don't sound much like one another; the singles are far superior. (gwynne) ✿ The plastic records had three strange slots around the spindle hole. You were supposed to attach a transparent plastic cone to them and use it to position the dolls atop the record. As the disc played, the Rock Flowers would seem to dance! Of course if you were like most people, your turntable was dominated by a tall automatic spindle, and this wouldn't work. But I'll tell ya, if you ever saw that Lilac's long hair blowin' in the breeze, while she danced atop her magenta platter of "Good Friends," you would never respect that damn Barbie again. If you cranked it up to 78 rpm, she'd become a Berkeley speed freak, and sound like one too! (bruce)

Rocky Horror Picture Show

Sure, you guys were all having fun jumping to the left and being a Frankie fan. But I was one of the guys working in a floundering art house that survived only by its weekend *Rocky Horror* screenings. Hearing 300 amyl-scented freaks screaming bits of dialogue might be fun when it's voluntary, but imagine hearing it dozens of times, while you try to clean out a popcorn machine. Imagine having to unstop the toilet after some girl dressed like Columbia threw up in it, again. After a while, you'd find yourself wondering if you should sell a box of candy to this made-up drag queen, knowing she'll only throw it at the screen and leave you to clean it up. As if there were not enough crap on the floor after a midnight show, you had to add rice and spent lighters to the pile. Ever seen what 200 squirt guns and wet newspapers do to a vintage theater's upholstery? No, I imagine you haven't. You and your wacky friends fled when the lights came up, danced out the door, and went home to bed. I was left to deal with all the debris, and anticipate the next weekend, when you'd do the Time Warp again, all over my nice clean floor. (bruce) ✿ Glitter's finest moment on the silver screen. Somehow Tim Curry's career survived this, unlike John LaZar, who played a similar sexual freak in *Beyond the Valley of the Dolls*. Susan Sarandon must've been about nineteen when she was in this. (Don't forget the little-remembered sequel, *Shock Treatment*.) (mike s.) (See also MIDNIGHT MOVIES)

Rodney "On the Roq" Bingenheimer

Perhaps more recognized by us Angelinos, Rodney was responsible for enlightening the world to such local hits as the Go-Gos, Red Cross (later Redd Kross), Agent Orange, the Circle Jerks, Black Flag, UXA, the Pandoras, and out-of-towners like the Waitresses via his long-standing role as weirdo punk/New Wave deejay for L.A. "alternative" ("Rock of the '80s") station KROQ, his clubs like Rodney's English Disco, and his series of super Rodney on the Roq party albums (note: Brooke Shields does the intro for Volume 1). To this day a true purveyor of bubblegum pop, he's still starring on the air Sunday nights, though his radio time is dwindling. He can still be seen around Los Angeles — he's the skinny Davy Jones lookalike all dressed in black (a look not far off from the days when he actually played Davy's double on the Monkees TV show). (darby)

Roger Ramjet

"Roger Ramjet, he's our man. If he can't do it, no one can." Like Underdog, Popeye, and others, Roger Ramjet ingested some drug (Proton Energy Pills) to become ultrapowerful and save the day. Unlike most other cartoons, however, *Roger Ramjet* was actually funny. (don)

Roller Skates Precursor to the '90s ubiquitous roller blades with their in-line wheels, roller skates with out-of-line wheels had the same engineering dilemma: how do you stop? One of my most vivid skating memories involved watching my best friend fly down the hill of our street, out of control, over a parked car, and into the trunk of the huge pine tree in our front yard. My sister and I helped pull pine needles out of her lips as she slowly regained consciousness. An extreme sport for preteen girls, rollerskating ruled! (nina) ❖ After Vans tennis shoes, roller skates — the old kind — were the foot apparel of choice. God help you if you didn't know how to skate. (karrin) ❖ Also hellishly memorable, the roller-skating style: the shuffle. Only the cool kids could shuffle 'cause it took rhythm. (krista) (See also RINKS, VANS)

Roller Skate Shoes When my parents owned a clothing store, my sister and I would go with them each year to the clothing conventions in Los Angeles. I remember seeing this one booth with shoes and upon a more careful examination I saw to my utter joy and excitement that these sorta platform wooden-soled shoes actually hid inside of them wheels that popped out of the bottom and turned them into fancy roller skates. I dreamed of these things for years after — my parents wouldn't get them for me and I'm sure I cried over the tragedy. I started drawing my own design plans (just like the go-cart I never made). I always thought they should have been big then and that they should be on the top of the list of things that need to be brought back today, yet it hasn't happened. Actually the only person who recalls these says they were featured on a *CHiPs* episode where the bad guy makes a quick getaway because he has these shoe-skates on. James Bond functional fashions with an Emma Peel feel are always in with me. Also, a variation on the theme: tennis shoe roller skates. They were colorful Adidas-type sneakers on wheels: fashion winning over ankle support. In the end, though, their lack of functionality forced them out of style, especially as the sneaker thing was dying down. (darby)

Ronco, As Seen on TV! Two companies owned by Ron Popeil, the father of late-night-TV mail-order commercials. Remember "Popeil's Pocket Fisherman"? In the summer of 1978, I was working for Yul Brynner while he was appearing in a revival of *The King and I* on Broadway, and he used to stay up real late at night and order all kinds of crap (primarily Ginsu knives, if memory serves) and they would arrive C.O.D. at the office the next day, where I would have to pay for them. (allison) ❖ Part of the Useless TV Crap Trilogy, along with K-Tel and Dial Media. My personal favorite was the in-the-eggshell egg scrambler. I've successfully repressed memories of most of the other products, save for the motorized record cleaner. (jeff h.)

Venice Beach: Where roller-skating is always in

Gilda Radner

Roots It is undeniable that the '70s were a time of increased cultural awareness. So when the mini-series *Roots* was on television, people paid attention. Though we all dismounted our wheels to eat dinner in front of the TV, it's difficult to say what actual effect this epic saga had on us. At the time, my sister and I were living with our cousins in a beach house on Balboa Island in white-bread Orange County, so the world of *Roots* and its significance was for the most part, I think, lost on us. (karrin) ❧ I'll never forget the whipping. (darby) ❧ One aspect of the '70s nostalgia fad was a new interest in one's personal history. *Roots* conveyed the idea that everybody (not just the rich or elite) had an interesting personal background. Genealogy — researching one's ancestors — was a growing fad, and many grew interested in an easy, do-it-yourself kind of research, oral history (talking to oldsters with a tape recorder). Oral history served as a framing plot device in the '70s film *Little Big Man* and the '70s novel *Interview with the Vampire!* (candi) ❧ After I saw *Roots,* I was convinced I had been a slave in a former life. Little did my mind grasp at the time that it is actually *this* life in which I am a slave! (nina) (See also *SHOGUN*)

The Ropers The ultimate dysfunctional couple, the Ropers left their successful gig on *Three's Company* to do their very own loser of a show. Mrs. Roper is what happened to independently minded sexually active women when they got older. The Ropers played to the hilt the easy laugh of a man turning down his wife for sex. (ju-ji) ❧ Norman Fell dancing with the plunger was very funny. (howard) ❧ Norman Fell is an unsung comic genius! (bruce)

Roseanne Rosanna-Dana The real life prototype for this beloved character played by Gilda Radner on *SNL* was Roseanne Scaramanda, a "woman about town" commentator on New York's WNBC. She was as famous for her strange hairdos as for her commentaries. Not only did she really say things like "It's always something" and "You know, it makes me sick," but she really did read frequent letters from a genuine Mr. Richard Fader in Fort Lee, New Jersey. It was this imitation of life that gave a New York audience an instant laugh of recognition. (bruce) (See also *SATURDAY NIGHT LIVE*)

Johnny Rotten Terrifying hunchbacked lead singer of the greatest punk band of all time. Spent twenty years slagging his former bandmates and insisting the Sex Pistols would never regroup. Of course, we all know how *that* came out. When I saw the Pistols play the Hollywood Palladium in 1996, it was so weird and pathetic; there they were, resurrected from the dead and stinking like it. The place wasn't even that crowded, and most of the crowd were thirty-five-year-old yuppies and little punk kids who'd only come to see the opening acts. The Pistols sounded a lot like they did in 1977, but they reminded me of one of those *Beatlemania*-type revival bands that tour the country pretending to be someone else, and "Pretty Vacant" played without conviction is not a pretty thing at all. A few days later I heard one of their songs in a commercial, I think it was for Mountain Dew. The band had always joked about selling out — "sell the swindle" and all that stuff — but now here they were trying to sell their souls for real, and all they got for 'em was a gig doing a commercial for some stupid soda pop. The Kiss reunion had more dignity. When Rotten performs with his other band, Public Image Limited, he sings in this high, strangulated warble that makes me think of Yoko Ono. He lives in Venice, California, now, and allegedly you can get his phone number from directory assistance. I've called once or twice, but I always get this answering machine with a pissed-off voice that sounds a little like Johnny doing an American accent. (stymie) (See also MALCOLM McLAREN)

Rubik's Cube   Another fluke toy of a bygone time. A cube with a different color on each side which you mixed up and then tried, by rotating the different sections of the cube, to bring back together. There's a formula for completing the stupid thing, which I was never let in on, but people who knew it treated the knowledge as some gift from heaven and delighted in endlessly displaying to you their genius. Yes, even today. Where is *your* Rubik's Cube? (darby) ♣ You could also cheat and take it apart and put it back together correctly or you could buy "extra" Rubik's Cube stickers to put over the scrambled ones. I generated plenty of undeserving compliments this way, thank you. (jes) ♣ I mastered the snake, but hated Angie Neuman, who could solve any Rubik's Cube in a minute, no matter how messed up it was. On more than one occasion I peeled off the stickers to prevent any further grief and frustration. The Orb was retarded. The beads in it were pretty but the thing didn't turn very easily and seemed impossible to solve. (morgan and ferris) ♣ *The* mania of 1982. Created by an Eastern Bloc engineer named Eno Rubik. His

follow-up, Rubik's Snake, failed to catch on. The cube also served as the inspiration of a Saturday morning cartoon in 1983 — perhaps the worst one of the decade. However, it is notable for being the first network cartoon to feature Hispanic protagonists, who unfortunately ended up with white voices. (bruce)

Rub-On Tattoos   They're big again, but I can recall them getting really big in the late '60s when you could find them in vending machines, potato chips, Cracker Jacks, and various specially marked boxes. The ones for boys were okay; they were mostly tough-looking butch things like dogs and anchors. But the ones for girls were groovy! Lots of way mod designs that would make you look like one of the dancers on *Laugh-In*, or a genuine hippie gal! They were a "lick-'n'-stick" kinda thing, and the big rumor at the time was that licking them would give you a dose of LSD! The only ones who believed it were the same morons who would later be chewing on the covers of Cheech and Chong albums for the same effect. (bruce) 🐿

Rush   High school friends Alex Lifeson and Geddy Lee joined with John Rutsey in the late '60s to form Rush, a Toronto bar band. After three albums that brought them moderate success, Rutsey bailed, and the boys picked up a local farm equipment salesman and percussion god, Neil Peart. His obsession with Ayn Rand led to the conception of *2112*, a concept album about a futuristic planet without free will. Like, it's sci-fi! He's the sole lyricist and an absolute genius. This band had a tremendous impact on many outsider types, and for a lot of people it was a phase to go through. ("I was way into Rush in high school.") They were my first concert at age twelve, when I first started playing bass guitar. The appeal for me was seeing these absolutely amazing musicians banging out songs about the human struggle, intellectual alienation, philosophy, and so on. Recommended discs include *2112, Moving Pictures, Grace Under Pressure, Hold Your Fire, A Show of Hands;* and *Presto* was pretty good. (skylaire) ♣ The band played at my high school dance in 1972 or '73 in a suburb of Toronto. Also the name of common '70s and '80s club drug, amyl nitrate — which was also known as locker room. (patty)

Nipsey Russell Most people remember the name but have a problem figuring out just *what* Nipsey ever did. You can spot "Who's Nipsey?" posts appearing randomly on the alt.70s and alt.80s newsgroups on the Web. (juji) ❧ Guest on numerous game shows throughout the '70s. Nipsey was a regular on *Cross-Wits*, *$20,000 Pyramid*, *Match Game*, and others. His shtick: He would always come up with a pertinent rhyme. Presumed dead, possibly from embarrassment. (nick) ❧ A stand-up comic, a little dance . . . the thing I liked him best in was *The Wiz*. (dad) (See also GAME SHOWS and *THE WIZ*)

S

Saccharin Used in all the best soft drinks until those damn rats came along and ruined it. Now we have NutraSweet. (winnie) ♣ The savior to sugar and weight-loss junkies. A sugar substitute which has been proven to cause cancer in laboratory animals (so the warning label says). Tab, the first sugar-free cola to utilize this godsend, was *the* drink of the mature adult (especially women). Diabetics around the globe practically shot this stuff up. The late, great Gilda Radner sang a saccharine song that said it all. (darby) ♣ You should have seen the fat people stocking up when they pulled it from the shelves. "I'm gonna die without it." Ha ha. (dad) (See also ASPARTAME and TAB)

Sailor Pants With the double row of brass buttons holding in that teenage tummy of mine, in godawful neon colors. (rose) ♣ Also known regionally as "Cracker Jacks." (bruce) 🐷

San Francisco This was one of the first fonts ever invented for the Macintosh that wasn't just your basic serif or san serif style. Wacky! If ever a font was Retro Hell . . . (darby)

Sara T. — Portrait of a Teenage Alcoholic One of NBC's more "relevant" TV movies, starring problem child Linda Blair. The film plays like a lame American remake of *Christiane F.,* only without the needle tracks. Naturally all of us budding high school alkies watched it and laughed. For about a year afterward, any girl we knew who drank like a guy risked being called a Sara T. All she had to do was be seen at a party carrying an open beer, and the other girls would say, "So who does she think she is, Sara T.?" But they soon learned the boys kinda dug a Sara T., who could drink as much as they did and only throw up once. Word around was that Sara T.s were so alkie that they'd even chip in beer money. Such is the stuff of high school dream dates. Where are they now, those Sara T.s? Probably shacked up with Bad Ronald in some midwestern trailer park, throwing beer bottles at Ronald Jr. and his pregnant girlfriend. (bobby) (See also LINDA BLAIR)

Sasson, Ooh La La I guess Sasson jeans were well established before, but they first came to my attention with the supersexy late-'70s ad campaign featuring the more flamboyant players on the flashy-but-mediocre New York Rangers hockey team with an incredibly permed and poufy Ron Dugay. One of the pivotal events in thoroughly confusing my perception of the opposing yet similar ways of being jockish and being effeminate. (pete) ♣ I always got this confused with Vidal Sassoon of '60s-bob-haircut fame. But if you listened to the commercials, they pronounced it "Sass*on*" instead of "Sass*oon*" — actually making it sound more exotic. (riley) (See also DISCO CHIC)

Satan It used to be really shocking to even *joke* about the big red guy who's all on fire. A mere mention of the number 666 was enough to get you some weird looks and maybe even a gasp or two. Alas, all that changed over the years. First, the Church Lady on *Saturday Night Live,* then the Warlock Pinchers did their "Satan is cool" schtick, and by the time L.A.'s Hill of Beans did "Satan, Satan, Lend Me a Dollar," Satan humor as we knew it had gone to hell. (don)

Satan was a big cinematic draw. In *Rosemary's Baby* ('68) he merely mocked the Jesus story, but by *The Exorcist* ('73) he had become a full-fledged child molester. He conquered the world in *The Omen* ('76), but in *The Sentinel* ('77) he settled for a brownstone in Brooklyn. He was recently bumped to TV in the now-canceled *American Gothic,* with retro star Shaun Cassidy at the helm, but no comment from Anton LaVey about this. (lisa m.) Satan was also really influential in rock music. Some of the bands he supposedly sponsored: Ozzy and Black Sabbath, AC/DC, Led Zeppelin, Deep Purple, Ted Nugent, Alice Cooper, Mötley Crüe, and a whole slew of speed metal bands. (nina) (See also *THE NIGHT STALKER*)

Saturday Night Live

This late-night comedy show *live* from New York quickly transformed the young, naïve kid of the '70s into an aware, almost hip, young adult. The importance of sleepovers and staying up really late culminated to an extreme during this period. *Saturday Night Live was* an awesome television moment. (darby) Debuted in October 1975 with host George Carlin, the *Saturday Night Live* original cast of the Not Ready for Prime Time Players — Chevy Chase, John Belushi, Garrett Morris, Dan Aykroyd, Gilda Radner, Jane Curtin, Laraine Newman, and, from 1977, Bill Murray — had an enormous impact on American comedy. If you watched it, you will probably never forget the following sketches: "Mailman, ahh, pizza delivery, ahh, land shark"; Belushi's samurai; Chevy Chase as President Ford; Aykroyd as President Carter; Radner's Ba Ba Wawa and Emily Litella; the *60 Minutes* point-counterpoint parody, "Weekend Update,"

with Aykroyd's sardonic quip, "Jane, you ignorant slut"; and Belushi and Aykroyd as the Bee Brothers who later transformed into Jake and Elwood, the Blues Brothers. In the '80s, *SNL* featured the likes of Eddie Murphy (who was damn cute as Gumby!), Joe Piscopo, Martin Short, Julia Louis-Dreyfus (of *Seinfeld* fame), and Billy Crystal. (jaz) (See also THE LOUD FAMILY, STEVE MARTIN, MR. BILL, MUPPETS, NOOGIES, ROSANNE ROSANNA-DANA, *SCTV,* SITCOM CATCH PHRASES, and THE WHINERS)

Sayings/Slang

When a word gets stuck in our head, it also gets stuck in our mouth. Before we even realize, we no longer use the word as merely an adjective or a verb, but tweak it to fit into any part of speech on an as-needed basis (e.g., "It's so freaky, the freakin' freak freaked on me!"). Is this culturally inflicted brain damage or are we just born this way? Something to ponder as you go through this sample of '70s and '80s slang and figure out how many you still use (and in how many ways) when you're hangin' with your peers: Great — **far out, groovy, heavy, it's outta sight/killer, awesome, bitchin', it rules.** Good — **baaad, sweet, boss, solid/wicked, outrageous, intense, excellent, it's a rush.** Not so good — **sorry, bunk/lame, hurtin'.** Bad — **crappy/nappy.** Really bad

John Belushi

— shitty, downer/bogus, wack, ill, heinous, sucks. Absent-minded — flaky/spaced out, space cadet. To be glad — jazzed, stoked/psyched. To be mad — p.o.'d/majorly bummed. To really want or need — jones for/have a *thing* for. To not do — shine/blow off, bail on. To play well or win — whale, smoke/burn, slam, kick ass. To play poorly or lose — get creamed, brick/bite the big one, get spanked. To leave fast — book, split, boogie/blow (this Popsicle stand), haul ass. To relax — mellow out/jell, veg out, chill. To be tired — wiped, beat/ragged out, spent, burned out, fried. To pick on someone — bag /rag on, diss, go off on. To pick up on — put the make on, hit on/work it, scam. To have sex — ball, get down, get off, do the wild thing, do the nasty, boink, get busy, knock boots. Female breasts — knockers, jugs/boobage, bodacious ta-tas. Attractive female — stone fox, chick/rad babe, fly girl. Attractive male — happenin' guy/studmuffin, hunk. Nerd — cretin, dork, spazz, geek, doofus, feeb, dweeb, loser. Money — bread/bank. Car — wheels/ride. Cigarette — cigs/smokes, cancer sticks. To drink — get loaded/catch a buzz. Intoxicated (drunk or stoned) — faced, tanked, buzzed, ripped, blitzed, wasted, bombed, baked. To vomit — barf, ralph, hurl, blow chunks, lose your lunch, toss cookies. Marijuana — grass, weed, ganga, spleef. Marijuana cigarette — reefer, doobie, J. fatty. Hello — hey bro', what's happenin', what's cookin', how's it hangin', what's shakin', what's up, yo! Goodbye — see you on the rebound, catch you on the flip side, later, I'm outta here, I'm history. Other miscellaneous sayings — man, I can dig that; dude, I can relate; no duh (or doi); no shit, Sherlock; eat me; bite me; jive turkey; fuckin' dick; right on!; word up!; nu-uh! uh huh!; no way! way!; you wish; dream on; get with it!; get a clue! (or job, or life); go with the flow; take a chill pill; screw you; up yours; moated; psych!; on the same wavelength; been there, done that; boogie down; party hearty; rage on; dynamite!; fuckin' A!; what's your sign?; wanna do some lines?; peace, man; fuck off and die; mother-fuckin' titty-suckin' two-balled bitch. (nina/darby/amy) (See also BUMMERS, BUMPER STICKERS, "FACE," "MAN" TO "DUDE," RETARDED, SITCOM CATCH PHRASES, "SUPER," TURKEY, VALLEY GIRL/DUDE, WHERE'S THE BEEF?, and "YOU'RE SOOOO GAY")

Scared Straight Innovative juvenile-crime-prevention program in which youthful offenders were taken to actual prisons where prisoners would scare them with stories about homosexual rape. If nothing else, it pushed the envelope in terms of cursing on TV when PBS ran documentaries about the program, which was universally deemed a failure. Indeed, the one person I know who went through S.S. later attacked two cops with a crowbar while drunk. (nick) (See also OFFICER BIRD)

Scented Stickers This superior, and currently unappreciated, creation was invented in the '70s. Got popular in 1976 with stickers, kids' books, and in 1981 when John Waters utilized it as "Odorama" in his movie *Polyester*. (darby) ❧ Stickers that had scents with everything from pizza to sardines. If you kept them preserved they could retain their scent forever. Inspired the perfume/cologne samples found in magazines today. (howard) ❧ God knows what noxious chemicals they put in these things, but I'll be damned if popcorn didn't smell like popcorn, or cherry like cherry. Never quite understood bone-scented, which featured a dancing skeleton with a cane and top hat. Every now and then the scent of a cheap perfume wafts into me which is reminiscent of this tragic smell. Scratch-and-sniffs were sold in expensive bulk packs and ofttimes you didn't want 100 skunk-scented stickers. Recognizing this neglected niche in the sticker market, our friends began trading and selling them individually at school until Mr. Mershon, the principal, broke our little sticker-trading ring. (morgan and ferris) ❧ I always liked the skunk stickers best, as well as the vomit-scented ones. I even remember making someone puke since it smelled so real. Weak stomach, I guess. (e. c. cotterman) ❧ These were used by my grade-school teachers to liven up corrected homework assignments and spelling tests they deemed commendable. Chocolate ice cream smelled like chocolate crap. (noël)

Satanism

It was spring 1972, and the movie *The Exorcist* was scaring the hell out of Americans. My mother had always been interested in the occult (she currently makes a modest living as a psychic, tarot reader, and astrologer), and she was in her Wiccan phase at that time. Not that she was something any present-day Wiccan would be proud of: The occult scene in the early 1970s was more concerned with going through the motions than getting to the Source. Being a witch meant dipping candles in salt and vinegar and saying the proper incantations, not understanding *the Goddess*.

Anyway, *The Exorcist* was in theaters, and for a while satanism was cool in the occult community. One night at one of these Wiccan get-togethers, one of the women brought an incredibly tall, evil-looking bald man to her house and introduced him as a satanist. (I know, I know — I'm wondering myself if it was Anton LaVey!) I remember being literally petrified, unable to move when I heard that that man worshipped the Devil.

To make a long story short, the satanist guy was there to make some converts. As I understood it (and this is from the perspective of a terrified eight-year-old, so my facts might be screwed up), one of the rituals was to write Satan a note, asking him for something. You had to sign the note in your own blood, and then burn that paper in a candle flame. My mother's klatch wrote their notes, and I remember a lot of nervous giggling as Mr. Satanist pricked their fingers so they could sign. When it came my mother's turn, she balked, and asked Sam, a man in her group, to sign the note for her. Sam agreed. When the ritual was over and the papers burned, my mother stupidly/jokingly commented to the group that they all were going to hell, but she wasn't, because she didn't sign her note. Sam turned to her and said that she was condemned to hell with the rest of them; he had signed her note, but he had signed *her name!* The satanism guy said that was sufficient: My mother's intent had taken her far enough, and as long as the intent was there and the proper name was on the note, Satan wouldn't argue over trifles. "After all," the guy said, "it's not like we're dealing with God!"

I remember that night so clearly: I crawled into bed and cried and prayed nonstop, begging Jesus not to send my mother to hell. She was an irritable nervous wreck for about a month afterward.

Of such scenes are future comedy routines made. (anonymous)

Schleprock Famous guest star on *Flintstone's* spin-off, *Pebbles and Bamm Bamm*. What klutzes and jinxes have been called ever since. (ju-ji)

School Cafeteria Pizza Square with sausages, loved it, every Thursday. (jory) ❧ Ours was triangular and really greasy. There was a black kid in my class whose mother was a cook in the cafeteria, and he'd get really offended when people put down the pizza. "That's not grease," he'd protest, "it's cheese!" But he was really popular anyway because he was the only one in the school who could do a no-handed cartwheel, and he got to do gymnastics in a Coke commercial. (gwynne)

Schoolhouse Rock Number two in the book of "Oh my god do you remember . . . ?" right after Sid and Marty Krofft shows. People have rere-membered each and every episode of these between-Saturday-morning-cartoons short-form animations, from "Conjunction Junction" to "Interplanet Janet" to the lonely little "I'm Just a Bill" sitting on Capitol Hill. In the past few years there were actually a few Schoolhouse Rock "tribute" bands; they've started showing the episodes on TV again, and now they're offering the collection on video, and Rhino Records has released the whole collection on CD. These shorts came from a time when teaching children through TV was actually attempted. I passed one of my history tests specifically because I remembered "The Preamble Song" ("We the people . . ."), and lolly lolly lolly do I know where to get my adverbs! Learning through song is a great concept if you can keep a beat — just ask Potsie. (darby) ❧ "A noun's a special kinda word, it's any name you ever heard, I find it quite interesting, a noun is a person, place, or thing!" (bridget) ❧ I never learned my times tables in third grade because our teacher had huge charts with all of them staplegunned to the ceiling and you could just look up during tests and copy the answers. But I did finally learn my three-times tables from Multiplication Rock's "Three Is a Magic Number." It ruled; there was this funky groove with simply "3, 6, 9, 12, 15, 18, 21, 24, 27, 30." (riley) ❧ I remember the cartoons for "Hey Little Twelvetoes" and "Figure Eight" as being so dreamy and poignant; they always made me sad. (nina) ❧ Note: Keep an eye out for Bob "Three Is a Magic Number" Dorough, who's been touring the U.S. recently — sometimes with other old-school Schoolhouse folks — singing all your favorites. As well, try to catch *The Simpsons* parody of these shorts. Brilliant. (See also THE MUNCHIES and TIME FOR TIMER) ❧

Debralee Scott Showbiz can be so fickle, sitcoms doubly so. Case in point: Ms. Debralee Scott. A ubiquitous TV presence — for a while she virtually owned the role of ugly-duckling-tomboy-kid-sister-in-blue-collar-households. During the '70s she rose to become the poor man's Julie Kavner. Perhaps her best-known role was as Cathy Shumway, the kid sister on *Mary Hartman, Mary Hartman*. She also appeared on *Angie* (kid sister again), *Welcome Back, Kotter* (as Rosalie "Hotsy" Totzie), the failed '50s retro drama *Sons and Daughters*, and in the film *American Graffiti* (as one of Harrison Ford's groupies). However, I feel her greatest role was that of the sensitive woman on the airplane during the segments inserted into the network TV prints of *Earthquake*. (bruce)

SCTV It was almost like you'd tuned in to a pirate TV station! These people knew how to do parody right. The commercials, bumpers, and station IDs seemed so *real*, and since there was actually a basic premise involved (a low-budget, sleazy Canadian TV station and the characters responsible) the humor was a lot subtler, more surreal, and more often than not a heck of a lot funnier than the frat-house slapstick of *Saturday Night Live*. Some fave moments were the Count Floyd segments ("Monster Chiller Horror Theater") and the "movies" he showed, like *Doctor Tongue's 3-D House of Cats*, the ultraschmaltzy *Sammy Maudlin Show* with funnyman Bobby Bitman (no doubt one of comedian Neil Hamburger's major influences). And I'll never forget the image of John Candy as an evil, beef-hawking leprechaun, terrorizing a wholesome family with elfin magic and his shillelagh as they try to eat their breakfast. (don) ❧ Toronto's legendary comedy group the Old Firehall grew out of a production of *Godspell* that featured Gilda Radner, Paul Shaffer, John Candy, and Andrea Martin. Eventually, the group got Canadian rights to the name The Second City, Chicago's famous improv troop. After losing several members to *SNL,* they started their own TV show, calling it *Second City T.V.* Launched in 1978, it eventually became a success both on Canadian networks and in U.S. syndication. By the time NBC picked it up, the troop had honed many of its characters to the nerdy point of insularity. No wonder I loved it. Some of the most surreal parodies of celebrity culture and mass media ever produced came from this show. My favorite was Jerry Todd. Rick Moranis played this AM deejay who had his own TV video show. It was a witty parody of MTV, made before MTV ever existed! (bruce) ♣ For some reason, nearly every ex-*SCTV* and early *SNL* ensemble member went on to make scores of dreadfully unfunny movies. One of the only good ones is *Sesame Street's Follow That Bird.* (gwynne) (See also *SATURDAY NIGHT LIVE* and "TAKE OFF, HOSER")

Sea Monkeys When you were a kid and you saw those colorful ads in comic books with those happy marine fairies and it said that you could grow them yourself . . . what kid in his right mind wouldn't say, "Golly! That sounds swell!" Too bad real Sea Monkeys are just brine shrimp and look nothing like those pictures. Invented by Harold von Braunhut in 1960, these little fuckers are up there with ant farms as far as their Retro Cool Factor. Sea Monkey fact: The Super Growth Food you can send away for really does make them grow bigger. (howard) ♣ The only pet I ever had that could dry to a crust and be revived. Try that with a hamster! How many children forever lost their faith in advertising after buying these things? Such valuable lessons can last a lifetime. While some pets teach mere responsibility, Sea Monkeys teach real life. (bruce) ♣ I discovered that you can kill a whole colony of these ugly fuckers with a single Alka-Seltzer tablet, like a nice Jacuzzi death. (noël)

Self-Help Books The generation that needed "a little help from a friend" got it in more ways than one. Sex Help: *Everything You Always Wanted to Know About Sex* (David Reuben); *The Sensuous Woman* ("J"); *The Joy of Sex* (Alex Comfort); *Your Erroneous Zones* (Wayne Dyer); *Living, Loving and Learning* (Leo Buscaglia); *The Hite Report: A Nationwide Study of Female Sexuality* (Shere Hite); *Open Marriage* (Nena and George O'Neill); and all books by Masters and Johnson. Fitness Help: *Dr. Atkins' Diet Revolution* (Robert C. Atkins); *The Complete Scarsdale Diet Book* (Dr. Herman Tarnower); *The Complete Book of Running* (Jim Fixx); *Never-Say-Diet Book* (Richard Simmons); *Jane Fonda's Workout Book* (Jane Fonda); *Beauty and Exercise* (Linda Evans). Financial Help: *Crisis Investing: Opportunities and Profits in the Coming Great Depression* (Douglas Casey); *You Can Profit from a Monetary Crisis* (Harry Browne); *The Coming Currency Collapse and What to Do About It* (Jerome Smith); *How to Prosper During the Coming Bad Years* (Howard Ruff); *Paper Money* (Adam Smith). Pop Psychological/Spiritual Help: *I'm O.K., You're O.K.* (Thomas Harris); *How to Be Your Own Best Friend* (Mildred Newman); *TM: Discovering Energy and Overcoming Stress* (Harold Bloomfield); *The Relaxation Response* (Herbert Benson); *The Aquarian Conspiracy* (Marilyn Ferguson); *Passages: The Predictable Crises of Adult Life* (Gail Sheehy); *My Mother, My Self* (Nancy Friday); *When Bad Things Happen to Good People* (Harold Kushner); *Surrender to Love* (Rosemary Rogers); *Megatrends* (John Naisbitt); and of course, *Looking Out for #1* (Robert Ringer). (thomas c.) (See also MASTERS AND JOHNSON)

Sesame Street Long-running, liberal-oriented kids' show: who didn't watch it? This was almost as important as going to school — perhaps since we got just as much out of it. Their trips to the factories with that weird trippy bouncy Stereolab-ish music in the background. Mr. Hooper's death. Each episode was brought to you by a number and a letter. I loved the painter, played by the English neighbor on *The Jeffersons,* who while trying to paint the number on a door would inevitably goof up and paint it on some bald guy's head. Their fine line of fad LPs: *Sesame* disco, *Sesame Street* Fever, *Sesame* country, etc. Nobody ever should have ever seen the Snuffle-upagus but Big Bird! (darby) ♣ Bert and Ernie (I always wondered if they were TV's first gay couple) doin' the pigeon walk — we finally got to see Bert's legs! (bridget) ♣ And Oscar the Grouch who lived in a trash can, TV's first homeless puppet. (nina) (See also MUPPETS)

S

Scandals, Urban Legends, and Other Brouhaha

1972 ❖ Deep Throat Ordeal

What happens when a woman has a clitoris in the back of her throat? What happens when a porn star (the infamous Linda Lovelace) claims she was coerced into making the film? Simple, it becomes one of the greatest scandals of the decade — and one of the most popular porn movies ever.

1972 ❖ Jane Fonda Goes Hanoi

Once a sex idol (see *Barbarella*), Jane shocks many of her fans as she travels to Vietnam during the height of the war and poses in an anti-aircraft gun used to shoot down American pilots.

1974 ❖ Patty Hearst

Debutante Makes Waves as Mesmerized, Bank-Robbing Terrorist

Mid-'70s ❖ Candy Controversy

Urban myths abound as red M&Ms mysteriously disappear from candy store shelves, Pop Rocks are rumored to explode, and word hits the streets that a kind of bubble gum contains spider eggs. Looks like we never should have believed any of it anyway.

1977 ❖ Suicide of Freddie Prinze

Not heeding the advice of Jose Feliciano's title song to his sitcom, it seems Chico does get discouraged.

1977 ❖ Roman Polanski Splits

Roman becomes best known not for his movies, or for the fact that his wife, actress Sharon Tate, was slain by the Manson clan, but for having to steer clear of the U.S. because of his scandalous attraction to young girls

1978 ❖ Mommy Dearest

Joan Crawford's daughter, Christina, shocks with her controversial exposé detailing her mother's abuse of her.

Chico and the Man

Rare footage of Bigfoot?

1978 ❖ Larry Flynt Shot

1978 ❖ Jonestown: Who Spiked the Punch?

More than 900 commit mass suicide through cyanide-laced Kool-Aid.

Late '70s ❖ Toxic Shock Syndrome: Killer Tampons Attack Menstruating Women

1978/79 ❖ Death of Sid and Nancy

1979 ❖ Skylab Is Falling

NASA's space station, Skylab, comes crashing back to earth while the world waits breathlessly to see if it might fall on them.

1979–81 ❖ Iranian Hostages

Americans held in the former American Embassy in Iran are released the day Ronald Reagan is inaugurated as the new president.

'80s ❖ Big Foot/Sasquatch Sightings

That rare footage we all saw a million times of the Foot running in the forest, most of us trying to believe it's true — ha!

1980 ❖ Who Shot J.R.?

Eighty % of America watches to find out whodunit. Everyone in Dallas had a reason to knock him off, but Kristin Shepard was driven to it because she was pregnant with J.R.'s illegitimate baby, and he wanted her to split town. Kristin was actually J.R.'s wife and Sue Ellen's (played by the now chic again Linda Gray) trampy sister.

1981 ❖ Who Shot J.P. (John Paul) II?

1981 ❀ Why Shoot R.R.?

John Hinckley's reason? Was it that he blamed Reagan for the death of his idol, John Lennon? Or was it to win the affection of his obsession, Jodie Foster? Or was it that he thought that killing the president would bring him fame? Whatever. Instead, he wound up wounding the president, one cop, and crippling Reagan's press secretary, James Brady. Reagan survives, Lennon is still dead, and Jodie is unavailable for comment.

1981 ❀ Ozzy Osbourne Goes Batty

Ozzy bites the head off a bat and then denies he knew it was real ("I honestly thought it was one of those Halloween prank bats"). Why destroy the myth?! Ozzy did admit to chomping doves, though, which is, I suppose, a more satanic gesture anyway.

1982 ❀ Tylenol Scare

Somehow this tampering scare ruins Halloween and initiates the dawning of the safety seal.

1984 ❀ Vanessa Williams Takes Off Her Crown

She is the first black Miss America, and the first Miss America to resign after *Penthouse* publishes revealing photos of her with another female model. Leaving the crown behind, she goes on to a successful recording career.

1986 ❀ Traci Lords, Teen Porn Star

Her underage porn is pulled from the shelves.

Mid '80s ❀ Imelda Marcos: Shoe Fetishist

Our attention to the trial of Philippine dictator Marcos is eclipsed by his wife Imelda's enormous collection of shoes. When the American public finds out about those shoes, there is no end to it.

1987 ❀ R. Budd Dwyer's Televised Suicide

Following his conviction for financial improprieties as Pennsylvania State Treasurer, he holds a televised press conference before beginning his prison term. Budd surprises everyone by pulling a gun out, placing the muzzle in his mouth, and spraying gray matter all over the place.

1988–92 ❖ J. Danforth Quayle, Capturing the Essence of the Vice Presidency

"What a terrible thing it is to lose one's mind. Or to not have a mind. What a terrible waste that is."

1989 ❖ Milli Vanilli, You Know It's True

The Grammies award Best New Artist to a pair of twin rasta-headed Europeans who sold millions of records but never sang a note on them. When the truth is later revealed by their producer, the Grammy is revoked.

7-Eleven

When this convenience store opened its door in the early '60s (though its heavy growth occurred during the '70s and early '80s), the store's name confirmed their hours open — 7 A.M. to 11 P.M. By the late '70s, certain stores stayed open later and later, making bank on selling stuff like late-nite munchies and beer, and eventually 7-Eleven went twenty-four hours, catering to the new demands of the twenty-four-hour lifestyle. These disgusting little stores spread like wildfire. No lie, I have *four* within a one-mile radius of my own home. Though they were known mostly for their cherry and cola Slurpees, mini-arcades, and window washers, many now are also fax centers, Lotto suppliers, and even surrogate banks. People despise the place but can't help themselves from going there. (darby) (See also ATMs, JUNK FOOD, and THE MUNCHIES)

7-Up, the Un-Cola

7-Up was always a pale relation in the world of soft drinks, too light and clear to be much of anything; people always thought they'd gotten soda water by mistake. Things began to change with the '60s. Suddenly, it was okay to be hard to define, to be odd and original. Thus 7-Up became the Un-Cola. Psychedelic ads and inverted glasses added to a counterculture image. For a brief shining moment, 7-Up was the most countercultural thing you could buy at 7-Eleven. (bruce)

Sex Pistols in the '80s There was a friend of mine in my placement that called me into her room because she wanted to play me a song she knew I'd like. It was "Tainted Love," by Soft Cell, and she was right, I loved it. That weekend, on a pass, I went with my dad and sister to Westwood. I begged for a tape and he gave in and agreed to buy us both one. I wanted to buy the Soft Cell tape, but all I could remember at the time was the pink cover and that its name started with an *S*. So I asked my sister if she knew what it was and she handed me the Sex Pistols tape. Unsure what to do, I looked and found Tears for Fears, another tape I wanted. My sister kept egging me on to get the Sex Pistols one so I decided to take a chance that it was Soft Cell and bought it. Getting home I played the entire tape looking for "Tainted Love" and, boy, was I fucking mad. It sucked and I wished I had just got Tears for Fears. It took me about a month and finally I just forced myself to play it, figuring I had the damn tape anyway, and soon "Pretty Vacant" caught my ears and Tears for Fears was history after that. (selena) (See also JOHNNY ROTTEN)

Sgt. Pepper's Lonely Hearts Club Band Neutron bomb of a movie released in 1978 built around shitty Beatles songs and which rightly destroyed or disrupted the careers of all who participated, including Peter Frampton, the Bee Gees, Steve Martin, Aerosmith, and Alice Cooper. Proof that sometimes people get what they deserve. (nick) ✤ I liked George Burns singing "Fixing a Hole." (howard) ✤ I think I did too. (ju-ji) ✤ In a decade studded with nightmare musicals, this one is a stand-out. Not even *Xanadu* can approach this scrap of celluloid. That the original album's reputation survived this onslaught is the greatest testament to its worth. It's not even good stoned. (bruce) ✤ I saw it the day it opened in Westwood with my friend Greg. Greg was really hung over, and during the movie, he threw up. (gwynne)

Shaddap You Face "What's matter you, eh, gotta no respect..." Joe Dolce found himself a hit with this corny Italian tale. When Ween came to L.A. a few years back, I, in a drunken stupor, yelled, "Shaddap You Face" repeatedly to the point of almost being booted from the club. Finally they caved in and belted out a stunning impromptu rendition of this fabulous tune. (darby)

The Shag It's 1982. I'm sitting in some foofie, uptight hair salon with a bunch of rich housewives and their daughters, half of which I've fucked in my head a million times, in the missionary position, of course. I pull the picture out of my pocket but my palms are sweating and I'm having a hard time not tearing it and this is pissing me off 'cause I didn't want to fold it in the first place. I'm wondering if this is still a good idea and maybe I should've let my mom come with me, but then I remember she was behind that Dorothy Hamill conspiracy and that took at least a year to grow out. Then this perky, prom queen voice says, "So, how are we cutting your hair today?" and I wonder why they always say "we," 'cause it's not really a "we" thing, but then the voice in my head is saying who the fuck cares, just hand her the fucking picture. So I do, explaining the importance of the hair sticking up on top and could she do that, and please be careful 'cause it's my best picture of Rod, and this is when I hear the giggle, giggle, and I sort of giggle back not knowing what else to do and this is starting to remind me of when I was in seventh grade and I had to explain the difference between layered hair and feathered, that Scott Baio had layered hair and Kristy McNichol had feathered hair and that I didn't want feathered hair but I wanted it pefectly layered like Erik Estrada, and as I start reliving these emotions I realize that the prom queen has that really disgusted look on her face like she just thought of her parents having sex, but I think it's 'cause she can't deal with a chick wanting to look like Rod Stewart, so I try not to think about how humiliating this is and instead that soon I'll be home free, and this is true 'cause now I'm in front of my mirror, playing air guitar to "Maggie May." (nancy) (See also FARRAH'S FEATHERED HAIR, THE MULLET, and THE WEDGE)

Shampooʌ Prell (that green stuff in that clear toothpaste tube that you only needed a small dab of; in the '70s they'd drop a pearl in Liquid Prell to prove how rich and thick it was); Head shampoo ("is breezy, so clean and easy"); Lemon-Up (with the plastic yellow lemon for the top); Herbal Essence (very green and natural); Flex (the conditioner smells great); Body on Tap (it was common knowledge that putting beer in shampoo was good for your hair, but who didn't wonder if you could get buzzed by opening your mouth in the shower when rinsing it out of your hair?); Gee,

Your Hair Smells Terrific (it stunk); Head and Shoulders (made one wonder if one had dandruff); Fabergé with Milk and Honey ("Tell a friend, and she'll tell a friend, and she'll tell a friend, and so on, and so on . . ."). (riley/gwynne/jes) ♣ Nexus; Jerri Redding; Pert (another great scientific breakthrough, this was important when it came out. A shampoo and conditioner *in one!* Really caught on at first but most girls *like* having more bathroom/beauty supplies, opting for Vidal Sassoon, and later Sebastian, who offered shampoo, conditioner, deep conditioner, stay-in conditioner, finishing rinse, oil treatments, and so on. So Pert ended up more of a guy thing). (darby/jes) ♣ Very much a guy thing. So what if it left my hair flat and looking a little greasy. It was simple, unbreakable, and fit in my gym bag! (bruce) (See also FARRAH FAWCETT-MAJORS) 🐿

Sha Na Na As a kid I actually thought these goons were old guys from the '50s and I couldn't figure out why they were still trying to act like young hoodlums. (darby) ♣ '50s retro band — they even appeared at the "first" Woodstock. (don) ♣ The main gold-suited older guy became a cardiac surgeon and got a really bad hair transplant. (bridget) ♣ Bowzer and one of the other guys live in Studio City and do public school music-appreciation assemblies. (I heard them interviewed on a local NPR show recently.) (jeff)

Shark Tooth Necklaceʌ Supposedly these were big in '75 because of *Jaws.* Mostly worn by hesher and surfer boys on leather with beads. (ju-ji) (See also JAWS)

Shazam! The *Shazam!* show was a contemporary of *Isis* and was similar in that it had a mythological source for the superhero's power. In this case, it's the whole pantheon of Greek gods/goddesses, who choose Billy Batson to wield the power of Captain Marvel and fight against the evil forces of modern times (i.e., the decadent '70s). Along with the guid-

5

7-Up Popsicles

From third to sixth grade these were a good 50% of the fun at recess: sucking a frozen dripping Popsicle made from 7-Up while out on the hot black schoolyard asphalt. (darby)

ance of the gods (whom he has a confab with at the beginning of each episode), Billy also had a traveling companion/mentor that went around with him giving him advice while he kicked ass on the bad guys. As with *Isis*, there was always a moral lesson to be learned at the conclusion of the show. (creepy mike)

Shields and Yarnell Originally San Francisco street mimes. Today Shields designs Fimo jewelry with feathers and sells it in artsy gift shops. I ran across the items in Sedona. (laurel) ❖ Besides being guests on TV shows, they toured schools across the U.S. in the mid-'70s. I remember them in my elementary school auditorium — were they teaching us something? (darby) ❖ Spooked the shit out of me. Death to all mimes! (noël)

Shoelaces These are as froofy as it gets. Shoelaces with unicorns, rainbows, checkers, hearts, stars, teddy bears . . . Great for sneakers, skates, as hair ribbons, for tying around blouse collars, you name it. (darby) ❖ Extra fat laces were used for souping up breakdancing sneakers. (noël) ❖ They sold the big neon ones at roller-skating rinks during the early to mid-'80s. They came in many tasteless varieties, such as neon green plaid, solid neon orange, etcetera. Girls you picked up at the rink would give you a single lace to remember them by along with their phone number. (dave) (See also RAINBOWS and RIBBONS)

Shoes When Mom took me shoe shopping in those days I can remember dutifully trying on a pair of Keds or Buster Browns or Mary Jane dress shoes when all I really wanted to slip onto my feet were those sexy-mama Korkie shoes. They were the answer

to all of my fashion needs. I was wistful about them for a long time, until the '80s arrived and Jellie shoes were the rage. Never got a pair of those either. (wendy) ❖ Candies (🐾) were really hot. Those were the kind of shoes that you had to put in a bag, leave the house, and then put on later. They were really scandalous for kids or young adults, plastic-soled mules with that really gnarly high heel — they were total ho' shoes. (laurel) ❖ Buffaloes: Those ubiquitous tan leather wedge-heeled sandals with the two straps that crossed over the toes. For buying shoes after we graduated from Kinney's, Standard Shoes was pretty good at the tail end of the glitter era, then Leed's in the '80s for things like pink glitter granny boots, discounted thigh-hi stiletto heels, and even the rhinestone-studded *Desperately Seeking Susan* style! (gwynne) ❖ In fifth grade, it was Wallabies (🐾). They were these sort of '70s version of desert boots with rubber-cement-looking soles and camel-colored suede uppers that tied with only two pairs of eyelets. Cherokees were really high-heeled platforms made of beige rubbery stuff with leather uppers that were really really comfortable. We had all different styles but they were always in that camel-colored leather and rubber. (riley) ❖ In the mid-'70s, it was all about Famolares. They had that way stylin' wavy platform sole that kept you rockin' whether you wanted to be or not. I never understood why my sister opted for flat, white Indian moccasins with black and red beading on top. She still wears them to this day so she must really like them (and didn't just wear them to mess with my head). (nina) ❖ Also Espadrilles, Hush Puppies, Dr. Scholl Exercise Sandals, Frye boots, Chinese cloth slippers, Injun booties, Tatami (straw thongs with velvet strap), clogs, pointy-toed "roach killer" flats . . . (See also DR. MARTENS; KORK-

EASE, MOON BOOTS, PLATFORM SHOES, PREP-PIE, SURFER SANDALS, TENNIS SHOES AND SNEAKERS BECOME "ATHLETIC FOOTWEAR," and VANS) 🐢

Shogun James Clavell's meganovel of an English pirate loose in Samurai-era Japan caught the attention of many producers. One was a Japanese filmmaker, who wanted to do it as a feature film starring Sean Connery. Another was NBC, who wanted their own megahit miniseries starring that god of the genre, Richard Chamberlain. When things shook out between the two camps, NBC got their miniseries, the Japanese locations, and crew from the filmmaker. The filmmaker got to re-edit the whole thing for Japanese television and a later feature-film release. The miniseries began on NBC on September 15, 1980; U.S. audiences were treated to beheadings, group baths, courtly intrigue, and even some water sports. As the week progressed, they were treated to seminudity, confusing third-person subtitles, and more courtly intrigue. Still, the series caught on. A mini Japan-mania spread throughout the land. Within a year, sushi bars had opened coast to coast, the Vapors' "Turning Japanese" was a minor hit, and the term *pillowing* briefly entered the common lexicon. (bruce) ♣ After I watched *Shogun*, I was convinced I had been Japanese in a former life. I have yet to be proven wrong. (nina)

Shogun Warriors Big plastic replicas of the Japanese metal toys. Dragoon! Combata! Raydeen! Now very valuable collector's items. They shot off missiles and your hands. (howard)

Shoplifting Back before all the fancy magnetic and laser sensors and hidden cameras, all one had to do was dupe the pimply, semiretarded (or obese, semiretired) security guard on duty. In clothing stores, the only form of detection was that big, clunky white plastic clamp (still used at the Gap) that once in the dressing room could be pried off with keys. Now you might make it home believing you're in the clear, until the cops show up at your door with a photo taken of you exiting the store with pockets overflowing. Then they bust your ass. (winnie)

Short People (Got No Reason to Live) "They have little hands, and little eyes, they walk around telling great big lies. Short people got nobody to love." Being a short person in a big person's world, this song was my anthem. Thanks, Randy Newman. (jes) ♣ My mom is 4'10" and shrinking (my grandma might be under the 4' status by now). Anyway, when my parents were still together my dad

The '70s Preservation Society

These are the people who wake you up in the middle of the night, after you fall asleep with the TV on, with their hideously cheesy nostalgia commercials, mesmerizing you into drowsy purchases of their CDs or cassettes, under the title of *Freedom Rock* or *The Fabulous '70s* or whatever cockeyed name they've come up with. Started in 1990 by Craig Bolsam and Cliff Chenfeld, who realized it was about time for that '70s comeback and banked on the idea people were fed up with the bleak period of the late '80s to early '90s and wanted back some of the frivolous aspects of their decadent past; let's just say these boys now operate a *very* successful business. (jaz/jes)

5

747

Incredible! It's so big! Imagine: Ten seats across! 231.8 feet long! The wings span a distance of more than 195 feet! It weighs over 350 tons! There are 14 stewardesses on each flight, with 364 passengers! They show you movies! There are 30 ovens, 100 pounds of meat, 150 pounds of vegetables, 266 cans of soft drinks, 760 pats of butter, 728 sugar packets, 50 pies, and 20 pounds of dinner mints . . . all for one flight! There are two stories, and a spiral staircase leads to the first-class lounge and the cockpit! It's just like a James Bond movie! Ah, '70s decadence. (darby, with facts from *Dynamite* magazine) ❀ For three years before these planes went into service, Pan Am and Boeing spent lavishly on a series of ads telling of the new age of "Speed, Size, and Comfort" that the '70s would bring. They went so far as to tour the country with an inflatable dome, in which there was a mockup of what a 747's first-class cabin would look like. The dome, and its lovely ladies dressed like stewardesses, went to malls and state fairs, spreading the Gospel of Flight. Sometimes, as I pass through a metal detector and wait to board an airbus packed with harried business travelers, I pause to think of those lost Super '70s, and weep. (bruce)

bought this 7" and had much joy playing it to torture her. We all laughed and laughed even though we weren't too tall ourselves. I mentioned it to him the other day and he said, "Oh, the one we used to play whenever your mother walked into the room? . . . *Hahahahaha!*" (darby)

Shrinky Dinks One of my favorite toys as a kiddie. The set came with colored pencils and usually a theme (clowns, dogs, dolls, and so on) and you got to color in the outline any way you chose. Then you cut out the different characters, stuck 'em in the oven (*Warning: Shrinky Dinks may not be used without the supervision of an adult*), watched them shrink into thick pieces of plastic, and started again! (katy) Note: Great for making jewelry too!

Andy Sidaris The first time you start to watch an Andy Sidaris movie you may think you're just watching another stupid late-night cable titty movie. In actuality, Andy is a brilliant conceptual structural-

ist filmmaker. His movies, whose plots always involve female CIA agents in bikinis, are peppered with such clever lines as, "I'll give you the girl when you give me the attaché." *Hard Ticket to Hawaii, Malibu Express, Savage Beach, Guns,* and my favorite, *Seven.* He's sorta an '80s cross between Ed Wood and Russ Meyer, but not as artsy. (jon) ❀ Provides careers to Playboy Playmates after they shed their clothes for the centerfold. (mike s.)

Sign Language Remember the sign language lady who was on TV before school? Most girls do. Somewhere along the way we all learned the alphabet and we'd add to that the new words we learned each morning. Signing was mucho fun around people who didn't know what you were saying — namely cute boys and bitch girls. Other things like secret languages were also worthy talents and quite necessary. "Bye fah now." (darby) (See also PIG LATIN)

Silly Putty Very cool for copying pictures from the newspaper onto your wad o' putty. (katy) ❀ Also good to chew on as a gum substitute, but after a while saliva breaks it down. (jen g.) ✿ Invented by James Wright at General Electric's New Haven labs during World War II as an inexpensive rubber substitute to line gun barrels with. It never really worked well in guns but was lots of fun to mold and bounce around the lab. Eventually, someone thought to put it out as a toy, and sold it with the slogans: "Nothing else is Silly Putty!" and "It's a very very solid liquid." (bruce) ✿ It seemed very sexy to me and I have never figured out why. (patty) ✿ Maybe it's similar to the same abstract texture-related attraction I had for the Pillsbury Dough Boy. Maybe not. (nina) (See also PILLSBURY COOKIE DOUGH)

Siouxsie Sioux

Richard Simmons This shocking hyperactive fitness freak gained notoriety after an appearance on *General Hospital*. All self-help mavens must have a past they've escaped; it gives them credibility. In Richard's case, it was the fact that he once weighed more than three hundred pounds. No war story has ever given me so horrific an image as a three-hundred-pound Richard Simmons. One wacky note: During his fat phase, Richard visited Rome and caught the eye of none other than Federico Fellini. He was cast as one of the many bulbous eunuchs in the film *Satyricon*. Look for him there, if you dare. (bruce) (See also AEROBICS, SLIM GOODBODY, and TALENT SHOWS)

Simon This is a memory-testing battery-operated spherical game with four different large colored panels. The concept is similar to Simon Says. When the game is turned on Simon bleeps at you, flashing one of the red, yellow, blue, or green panels, while making an obnoxious variety of color-matching beep noises, to which you would then have to respond by pushing down on that panel. Then Simon would repeat that color while adding a new color, continuing to repeat and add new colors as the game continued until you picked the wrong color and lost. This game was most often played as solitaire but could be played by up to four people, each responsible for their color. I had one until I was nine, when my father, during one of his manic freakouts, threw it down the stairs because I'd left it on the floor. It never worked again; I guess he felt bad and he bought me a mini-version Simon to make up for it, but it wasn't the same. (selina) ✿ There was also a flashing-light electronic game sort of like Simon, called Merlin. Red and rectangular in shape, it had nine buttons that lit up with red lights. Merlin (the magic whiz that lived inside) blipped out codes and the player would repeat the sequence. My sister spoke to hers. (winnie) (See also ELECTRONIC HAND-HELD GAMES)

Siouxsie Clones Even before Siouxsie Sioux was in Siouxsie and the Banshees, she was a major fashion influence as a member of the Bromley Contingent, a group of Sex Pistols fans (that included Billy Idol) who were widely photographed. With her asymmetrical eye make-up, beautiful, slender body, classic features, and penchant for wearing kinky, revealing clothes that made her look like a Weimar Republic escapee crossed with a naughty punk dominatrix, she definitely had a distinctive look. When she formed the Banshees, she had a great sound, dark lyrics, and because she already looked so awesome, make-up artists and photographers went wild — as did record execs — and she became the dark, underworldly answer to Debbie Harry's all-American beauty. The phenomenon of Siouxsie Clones began before the Banshees' first single, "Hong Kong Garden," even came out. Basically, it was a mass copying of her trademark long, crimped, punky hair, pale white make-up with heavy dark-lidded eyes, and severe, Roaring '20s mouth drawn on. These main features seemed to flatter every possible facial type, and it was an exotic, alternative look that was still very sexy. Because Siouxsie's look was less angular and Cubist-inspired than, say, Sue Catwoman's or Jordan's (both punk icons in their own right, and members of the McLaren/Sex Pistols entourage), girls with day jobs could copy it and still get away with being subversive. More Siouxsie Clone attributes: China Doll wigs, black nails, torn net stockings, lacy black vintage dresses, layered black underwear, tank tops and leotards, small square black purses, kinky footwear, vinyl miniskirts with stockings and garters. Much of the Siouxsie look has now mutated into standard dress codes for Goth chicks, and her influences are still really strong after twenty years! (pleasant)

Sissy Vs. Macho Cartoons

Rainbow Brite, Smurfs, Care Bears, My Little Pony vs. *He-Man, Thundercats, G.I. Joe, Transformers* (more than meets the eye). Gender-specific/stereotypical children's shows of the '80s contrast pretty sharply with today's gender-neutral ones like *Power Rangers*. (wendy) (See also CARTOONS)

Sit-and-Spin

Looks like a lazy susan with a steering wheel attached at the middle. The idea is to sit on the spinning part with your legs wrapped around the steering wheel, which stays stationary. By pulling on the steering wheel, you spin on the lazy susan. It provided my little brother and me with our first motion sickness experience after we decided to set the Guinness record for the longest sit-and-spin session. We got the idea from Cindy and Bobby Brady when they decided to set the Guinness record for the longest teeter-totter ride. (bobby)

Sitcom Catch Phrases

In better times, whole TV programs were built around signature lines delivered with regularity by various characters. Viewers felt cheated if a show failed to include a couple of hits. Since the plague of so-called quality programming has settled upon the land, it is unlikely we'll ever thrill again to the likes of the following: "Whoaaaa!," "Sit on it" (*Happy Days*); "Up your nose wid a rubber hose," "Ooo, ooo, ooo, Mr. Kottah," "I got a note from my muddah," "I am Freddie Boom Boom Washington," "What, where, when, why . . . I'm sooo confused," "Did I ever tell you about my [choose one: Aunt XX, Uncle XX, Grandfather XX, Grandmother XX, Cousin XX, etc.]" (*Welcome Back, Kotter*); "Stifle yerself, dingbat!," "Shaddup, meathead!," "Meathead . . . dead from the neck up!" (*All in the Family*); "Nanoo, nanoo," "Mork calling Orson, Mork calling Orson, come in your fatness . . . ," "Shazzbot" (*Mork and Mindy*); "Looookin' good," "Stick out yer can, here come da garbage man!," "Eesss not my chob, man!" (*Chico and the Man*); "God will get you for this, Walter!" (*Maude*); "Here comes da judge, here comes da judge," "You bet your sweet bippy" (*Laugh-In*); "Dyn-o-mite!," "I knoooooow!" (*Good Times*); "This is the big one . . . I'm comin' to join ya, Elizabeth . . . ," "You big dummy!" (*Sanford and Son*); "Whajoo talkin' 'bout, Willis?" (*Diff'rent Strokes*). (nick)

Sitcoms, Low-End Late '80s

There exists a category of cheap sitcoms that were very '80s. You can tell these by their one-dimensional soap opera–esque approach, their sadly obvious low budgets (they were mainly shown on the smaller stations during the afterschool timeslot), the canned laugh tracks for their redundant cornball jokes, and often some sort of weirdness occurring in suburbia usually featuring robots or aliens. I think these were all somehow inspired by the success of *What's Happening!!* Some of our favorites include: *Small Wonder, Charles in Charge, Mr. Belvedere, Saved by the Bell, Alf,* and *Out of This World* (the one with Donna Pescow, from *Saturday Night Fever* and *Angie,* whose husband is an alien represented by a crystal box, and the daughter has alien powers). (darby)

Sitting Backward in a Chair Probably made famous by the Sweathogs on *Welcome Back, Kotter*. The "sittee" spins the chair around (most impressively with one hand) and straddles the seat, resting folded arms across the back. The necessity of sitting backward most likely arose when crazy combs got big and we had to avoid the embarrassment of the comb getting hooked on the chair and flipping clear across the classroom. But still it amazes me that something as simple as a way of sitting can go in and out of style. (winnie)

The Six Million Dollar Man Lee Majors (then husband of Farrah Fawcett-Majors) starred as Steve Austin, a U.S. astronaut who was critically injured in a test flight. The doctors decided he was the perfect guinea pig for their bionic experiment and wired into him a bunch of atomic-powered, electromagnetic doohickeys that made him better, stronger, faster. The rest is history. The only story I can remember is the one with that ominous tank machine that was trying to get him, which can still be re-enacted with a round laundry basket placed over my head. Not only does Marge Simpson dream about the Bionic Man, but a beer commercial did a parody of the spooky, mildly haunting introduction of the show. (noël)

Skateboards These have been around ever since roller skates. The first manufactured ones showed up in the early '60s, when a mania for them caused by the large number of paved entrance ramps to the still-unfinished freeways that girdled sprawling suburbia swept the U.S. The first steerable skateboards didn't come out until the mid-'70s, leading to the sport's golden age. Alas, like all things that attract adolescents in large numbers, skateboard parks were soon accused of being breeding grounds for trouble. This was compounded by the sport's punker rebel image. High insurance rates were the real culprit, forcing the parks to close as the Reagan era dawned. (bruce) ❁ The South Bay's one contribution to culture is the slogan "Skateboarding Is Not a Crime!" (jeff) ❁ My first was a small wood board with clay wheels. It wouldn't turn no matter how much you loosened the trucks. Then there was the plastic banana board with small plastic wheels — barely a step up. But my next board rarely left my sight. A thin fiberglass yellow board with a funky, gross guy (I think he was picking his nose), and the word *boogie*. I skateboarded everywhere on that thing — goofy-foot. When my friends invited me to go to the skate park (remember when those were *everywhere*?), I thought I would finally be able to show off my moves. My fiberglass board wasn't allowed though, so I borrowed one of their new big Black Night wood boards with the big Kryptonite wheels. Of course, per usual, I was the only girl there, and I nervously shot down the ramp and barely made the first turn when it hit me that (1) I didn't know what to do with this big crazy board with super-loose wheels; (2) I wasn't really a very good skateboarder (I was more of a utilitarian boarder); and (3) I should get out of there quick before I was completely trampled (physically, but also emotionally by my own embarrassment). This was after I'd already

Farrah as trendsetter

chair-lift traumas, breaking a leg, hangin' in the lodge, hot chocolate, *hot tubs!*, big boobies . . . oh yeah, and skiing. (ju-ji) ✿ Can't forget *Three's Company* and other sitcoms taking trips to the slopes; movies like *Ski Patrol, Hot Dog, Sunburst*, and all Warren Miller flicks. (bobby) ✿ Like golf, tennis, hockey, ice-skating, log-tossing, and water-skiing, skiing is pretty much a honky sport. (noël) ✿ Once you snowboard you never want to go back. (darby) ✿ To this day you can go into any après-ski bar in America and still hear the Eagles. (lisa aa.) (See also SUZI CHAPSTICK)

Slam Books There are arguably a few different ways to make a slam book. I prefer mine, which was confirmed in Judy Blume's *Otherwise Known as Sheila the Great:* "'Slam books are great fun. You'll see.' Mouse was busy writing something down in her notebook. In a minute she held up a piece of paper and said, 'This is a sample list. All of us fill it in about each other. It's the only way to find out what your friends really think of you!' I looked at the sample list. It said, Name, Hair, Face, Body, Brain, Best Thing, Worst Thing, and In General. 'You see,' Mouse explained, 'we'd never be brave enough to just sit around and tell each other the truth about ourselves. But since everybody wants to know . . . this is an easy way to find out.'" And the quickest way to turn your best friends into enemies. (darby)

Slappin' Five No jive, gimme five. This relaxed and casual hand slap was the precurser to today's spastic high five used by jocks and their girlfriends. (winnie) ✿ There was a bit on NPR, or one of those leftie radio programs, about the origins of the high five. Introduced by black players, it was injected into our culture in a big way in the '70s, when even white athletes started being more physically touchy (besides patting each other on the butt). When I asked my dad he said he didn't know any more specifics but went off on how black football players

gotten my membership card. (darby) P.S.: The new small wheels suck (fuck the tricks, how about riding around town), and using the thick old wheels is not only way retro, but very smart and cool of you — good luck finding them! (See also CHACHI)

Skiing The most important thing about skiing besides boy hunting was ski wear. Ski wear was high-fashion fun. There were a couple of things you had to have. Definitely those fucking bib things (for the girl that was used to wearing her tight-fitting Chic jeans, these were an insult to her neck); goggles or, better yet, mirrored ski glasses (with the colorful cords); Sea & Ski suntan lotion; and Bubble Gum Chapstick. Other skiing staples: Bunny slopes, ski bunnies,

also introduced the show-off touchdown dance. Anyway, a variety of the high five became extreme and perverse, and peaked about the time breakdancing did. Gimme five, on the side, up high, down low, you're too slow! (darby) (See also HAND GAMES)

Slime Awesome goopy green booger stuff that came in a mini green plastic garbage can. Must have been almost as popular as the pet rock in the '70s. I remember they even had a slime game in a super big box that none of my rich friends ever got so I never did get to see the thing, but a girl from our school was playing the game on that box cover so that was pretty neat. (darby) ❖ Warning label said to keep it away from carpeting — but when it dried out it became nothing. (lisa)

Slim Goodbody A scary guy with a 'fro who promoted health while sporting a bodysuit (literally). All of the organs were printed on his unitard and he would talk about nutrition, hygiene, and so on. He was a part of the *Captain Kangaroo* show. (krista scaredy-cat) ❖ He was also on the *Electric Company* and did segments for elementary-school health class viewing. My mom actually took me to see this Richard Simmons doppelganger perform at the mall. (lorraine) (See also RICHARD SIMMONS)

Slumber Parties All your friends together for a night of pizza, Atari, dirty movies on cable, crank calls, t.p.ing, light-as-a-feather, stiff-as-a-board, Bloody Mary, pretending to talk in your sleep, putting someone's hand in warm water while they're asleep to make them pee, putting bras in the freezer, making out with each other for practice, and, as we got older, quiffs (i.e., pussy farts), quarters, strip poker, Truth or Dare, Ouija, drinking and smoking (cigarettes, pot, banana peels, cloves, and so on). Raw teenage girl-dom! (jes) (See also *GIRLS JUST WANNA HAVE FUN* and THE OCCULT)

Smells What was it with the olfactory overload of the '70s? *Everything* was smelly: strawberry-scented shampoos, melon-scented deodorants, and even meadow-reminiscent douches. These were incredibly strong and overpowering smells. I wanted to devour every product I had in my possession. I think perfumes must've been a million times more potent than anything on the market today. Was this a backlash to the '60s rancid and offensive hippie body odor? It just wouldn't be right going around without my snatch smelling like a berry milkshake or a lemon tree! Yes, negative connotations still surround natural body odor/secretions/functions today, but there is a strong following of consumers who go for the unscented "natural" products. (jes) ❖ Everything that didn't reek of musk or lemons got the country touch of green apple. This smell obsession reached it's apotheosis in the early '80s, when Remington (the shaver people) introduced the Aroma Disc player. The discs were floppy rounds of pungent plastic with a sort of handiwipe in the middle. The player was a small black box with slots on the top, an On switch, and a computer-style slot to slide the discs into. Inside, it seemed about as sophisticated as a Mattel Thingmaker; the player simply heated up. The magic

S

Slime Recipe

It is 2 parts white glue, 2 parts water, food coloring, 1 part sodium borate solution (sodium borate solution is 1/3 cup powdered bleach mixed with one liter of water). Mix together water, glue, and food coloring. Mix the borate solution in with the other stuff, then knead it as it thickens. As smelly and good as homemade slime gets. (wendy)

lay inside the discs. Special oils in the plastic would warm up, travel along the cloths, and evaporate. You slipped your disc in the slot and soon noticed a perfumed mist drifting out the top. In a few minutes, the whole room was not-so-gently scented, and you put the disc away till next time. Remington put out several "titles," with names like Ocean Breeze (smelled like baby powder), Movie Time (popcorn), or Gourmet (I really don't know what). Later titles included Fireplace (Pine-Sol), Strawberry Field (not a Beatles rip-off), and my favorite, Man's World (I don't know either, but it was good). The market just wasn't ready for electric incense, and the players soon vanished. I still have mine, and crank it up when I forget to clean the fridge. (bruce) (See also PERFUME AND COLOGNE and SHAMPOOS)

Smurfs

Clearly from the hallucination of somebody on a bad acid trip, these gnomish troll miniatures were all the rage. They were sort of like the Seven Dwarfs shrunken and dipped in blue paint because they all had names from the following formula: "adjective" and "Smurf." Happy Smurf. Grumpy Smurf. Except, of course, Smurfette, the only girl Smurf, who was obviously nothing but a Smurf sperm receptacle. In retrospect she was sort of "blue trash," if you will, with her white pumps and bleached blond hair. I collected the miniatures, I admit it. I hated Gargamel and his cat, Azrael, with the nipped ear. Damn them for tormenting the Smurf village. Leave them alone, for Smurf's sake! (morgan and ferris)

Soccer Team Names

(from '75 to '82) Some of the soccer teams I played on and names of some opposing teams: The Bionic Women, The Bionic Girls, The Asteroids, The Rolling Stones, The Moon Zappers, Space Invaders, Solid Goaled. (darby)

Soda Cans on Feet

Important technique for obnoxious kids. You step on them in such a way that they flatten and the edges clamp onto your sneakers so you can very noisily stomp about. We recently dared Brian from Weezer to do this and walk into his hotel with it on if he wanted to join our gang. He went slippin' and sliding through the Mondrian lobby until an unhappy security guard yelled at him for scratching up the marble floors. Very cute. (darby)

Sodas

Shasta, RC Cola (in '70s switched from being Royal Crown to a hip "RC" and invented an ad campaign to push themselves as third choice: "What's good enough for other folks ain't good enough for me and my RC"), Bubble-up, Aspen (apple-flavored soda), Tab, Mountain Dew, Orange Crush, Cactus Coolers, Dr. Brown's Cream . . . most of these are still around today, it's just that their heyday is ultimately Retro Hell. (darby) Dr Pepper had the coolest ads during the early '70s — women looking like Carol Kane, sort of gothic and glam, running through fields. (patty) (See also "I'M A PEPPER," PEPSI LIGHT, 7-UP, FRESCA, and TAB)

Soft Toilet Seats

I always get a blast from the past, so to speak, whenever I sit on one of these. They're sorta gross for public use, but nice and comfy in the home and are just about ripe for a comeback. (jaz)

Son of Sam

The night of August 12, 1977, I asked my mother to let us camp out in the backyard, but she refused; she was terrified that we would become victims of the Son of Sam, the .44-caliber killer, who had been terrorizing the New York area for the past year. "Mommmmmmm," I said as I began to tick off points on my finger, "the Son of Sam only kills couples or single women, the Son of Sam only kills people in their twenties, and the Son of Sam is miles away — he's only ever struck in Queens and Brooklyn, not here in Yonkers." As I said this, the street and sky outside our house were filling with police cars, SWAT teams, helicopters, K9 units, and various media and political camp followers. We soon discovered that the Son of Sam, David Berkowitz, was being arrested in his apartment two blocks from our house. The next day, as we watched the replay of the arrest and arraignment of the Son of Sam on TV, my mother asked if David Berkowitz was on my paper route — he was. (patrick) (See also *THE NIGHT STALKER* and STUDIO 54)

Space Food Sticks The peanut butter were the best, a one-half-inch-thick cylindrical power bar without the icky sawdust texture; I think the astronauts were supposed to have eaten them in space. (riley) ❧ This is my second most missed food. There was original, peanut butter, and chocolate. I normally ate a few sticks a day, and liked to take one and squash it from each end into a small compact sphere and nibble the edges. I liked to mash different flavors together into a food-stick ball. They came in a brown wrapper that made them seem almost natural yet futuristic at the same time. (darby) (See also JUNK FOOD and STICKS)

Speak & Spell The ad told us that "thanks to microcomputer electronics, Speak & Spell, Speak & Read, and Speak & Math duplicate the human voice with outstanding clarity and fidelity. They entertain while giving youngsters extra motivation to practice and master the basic skills in reading, spelling, and math." You could never get the Speak & Spell to say "fuck" or anything dirty. E.T. used one to call his family. (noël)

Speed Reading As part of the plan to turn me into a worthwhile human being, my dad got me to go to speed-reading class after school once or twice a week. I went from reading a few words to *hundreds* of words per minute. You were supposed to read faster and have better comprehension and I just liked it cause I thought I was getting away with something. Riley says it was later discovered to be a scam, but I still use those techniques every once in a while. (darby) ❧ Remember the long, tedious commercials for the Evelyn Wood School of Reading Dynamics? Ms. Wood recently died. (bruce) ❧ Probably unre-

lated, but there was also a big deal around the same time made over people with photographic memory, who supposedly could remember everything on a page by just looking at it once. And who didn't try the "osmosis technique" of putting books under your pillow before a test to let the information seep into your brain while you slept? (jaz)

Spinal Tap Why does everyone I know find themselves using quotes from *Spinal Tap* in real life? I do this all the time. When I'm talking about someone I haven't seen in years, I say, "They are currently residing in the 'where are they now' file." When you're trashing someone behind their back, "What a wanker!" comes in handy. And "shit sandwich" is a good generic negative review for any song, movie, TV show, or music video. Others: "Kick this ass for a man!" (when apologizing), "Hello, Cleveland!" (when hopelessly lost), "Have a good time all the time" or "I believe virtually everything I read" (whenever anyone asks you what your philosophy of life is, or when giving advice). (joe) ❧ Also really handy is the line from the scene at Graceland when the band is looking at Elvis's grave and someone comments that "it puts a little perspective on things" and David retorts, "Too much, too much fuckin' perspective." This guy I used to live with punched that phrase out with one of those Dymo labelers and put it on our phone. (nina) ❧ More unforgettable *Spinal Tap* lines: "These go to 11"; "There's such a fine line between stupid and clever"; "What's wrong with being sexy?"; "No bones"; "You can't really dust for vomit"; "I'm just the way God made me"; "Money talks and bullshit walks"; "Fuck the napkin!"; "It's a complete catastrophe!"; "I told them a hundred times: put Spinal Tap first and puppet show last"; "We're not about to do a freeform jazz exploration in front of a festival crowd!" Side note: The three core members of Spinal Tap — David St. Hubbins, Nigel Tufnel, and Derek Smalls — had been performing together since December 1966. Today, their music is noted for its volume, as well as for the fact that the lyrics sometimes rhyme. Marty DiBergi's rockumentary *This Is Spinal Tap* ('84), about the band's 1982 U.S. tour, inspired widespread interest in the English rockers. To learn more about Spiñal Tap than you ever wanted to know, point your Web browser to http://thetransom.com/chip/tap. (chip)

Spinning/Hyperventilating Natural drug for kids (and they say we are only attracted to tripping because of society's evil influences). (darby)

Spirograph Clear (later tinted) plastic gears that you would stick your pen tips into to move and create geometric quasipsychedelic pseudo–Celtic knot designs. You could never tell when you were done, and then your pen would go through the paper. (noël) ❧ Mathematics meets mandalas! Kenner manufactured these in 1968. The equipment looked like daunting engineering instruments yet was easy to use. The drawbacks were the tiny pins needed to secure the rings, the drawing holes that were smaller than some pen tips, and the paper that tore just as your masterpiece was finished. For years, every loose scrap of paper in our house got adorned with precision doodles. They are still made this way and are still big fun. (bruce)

Spit Aggressive two-player card game which was very very big in elementary school. B.S. (bullshit) was the other good one. (darby) ❧ The cause of more fights between me and my sister than even Monopoly! (nina)

Splatter Films While Jason, Freddie Krueger, and even the lame likes of Chucky have become pop icons, and movies about serial killers now win awards, have multimillion-dollar budgets, and a modicum of critical respect, authentic splatter movies are recognized by their fans as having had an inauspicious start. They began in 1963 with *Blood Feast*, Herschell Gordon Lewis's schlock film about a crazed Egyptian caterer's special meal (made up of slaughtered young women's various body parts). Though wildly popular in drive-ins across the Bible Belt, the vividly detailed depictions of spilled blood and guts, as in such low-budget epics as *2,000 Maniacs, The Ghastly Ones*, and *The Flesh Eaters*, didn't fully catch on until about a decade later. Hence, it is the '70s and early '80s which represent the golden age of ultraviolent, low-budget horror, in a steady stream of films (most of which were made by independent filmmakers from such outposts as Spain, Italy, the Philippines, Mexico City, Pittsburgh, and Staten Island) about flesh-eating zombies, chainsaw-wielding cannibal families, toolbox murderers, satanic cults, hillbilly maniacs, hacked-up baby-sitters, and rampaging aquatic life. Audiences were lured to the theaters through advertising campaigns fully emphasizing the grotesqueries. There were even rumors that some such movies were really *snuff* films. Eventually, such films reached an apex during the "slasher" film era of the early '80s. Though writing, acting, and plot devices were often kept to a bare minimum (and were often completely beside the point), what remains compelling about low-budget splatter is how willing it was to push the envelope in providing shocking, surreal, nihilistic chills and thrills to its core audience, who ranged from ever more desensitized adolescents to even more hardened drive-in/Times Square/ghetto moviegoers. (thomas c.)

Rick Springfield Way back in the early '70s Rick Springfield was a struggling singer attempting to make it big outside his native Australia. He had a top-ten hit with "Speak to the Sky" in 1972 and a year later he starred in the Saturday morning cartoon *Mission: Magic!* I don't know who remembers this cartoon but it was really quite good, at least for Filmation (the studio most famous for *The Archies*). The show concerned a teacher named Miss Tickle and her cat Tut Tut and her adventures with her students beyond the Magic Blackboard. Rick was always on the other side of the blackboard, along with his owl Ptolemy (named after the Egyptian astronomer), and every week he would contact Miss Tickle saying he needed the help of her and her class. They would travel to some magical land or another (without the aid of hallucinogenics) and solve the problems of the people who lived there. At the end they would discuss their adventures and see what lesson could be learned.

(martin n.) ❧ He also did a record where he's the shoddily drawn cartoon superhero on the sleeve. Speaking of which, why *were* there always dogs on his record covers — that kinda disturbed me. (jaz) ❧ Rick was a *Teen Beat* hunk holding as high a rank as John Travolta — almost. I first saw him in the end of the '70s on *General Hospital*, but in Australia he was already a famous singer. Then in '81 he attempted the big screen with his hit teen movie *Hard to Hold*, which I and every other lusting girl went to see more than once. His hit song "Jessie's Girl," from the record *Working Class Dog*, played continuously on the airwaves. Then Rick got superpopular and left *G.H.*, and while we assumed it would lead to more music and movies, instead he faded from all formats. And so we silently waited. Then in the '90s we witnessed a superbrief comeback on the last episodes of *Knott's Landing*, where his aging but sexy hot self appeared to us again — until the cancellation of the show a couple of months later. His recent return (at forty-six) on the ignored *Baywatch*-style *High Tide* has already been canned. So I'm again left here patiently waiting. (selina) (See also *GENERAL HOSPITAL*)

Squirggle Totally cheesy kids' toy found in loot bags a lot. It looked like a pipe cleaner with frayed edges and had googly eyes pasted on (which usually fell right off). Attached to the end was an "invisible" string so when you pulled on the thing, some idiot adult had to pretend to be scared, like there was a bright orange fuzzy worm crawling across the floor. Duh. (katy)

SRA Reading Laboratories This is how we learned English. A color-based system that, as you advanced, had you move on to other, better colors. Totally asinine, but often the cards utilized decent reading material. I think it was really just for lazy teachers, and all the leftovers are probably still being used in poor school systems. When I was making up a failed high school English class at the community college, they actually made us use them. It was like third grade all over again. (darby)

Sssssss 1973 movie about a doctor who developed a serum to turn people into king cobras. The doctor found this cute young boy (Dirk Benedict) that he started injecting with the weird serum. But, of course, the man's daughter falls in love with the boy, whom the dad kept downstairs at their house. The dad comes home one day and sees this trail of the kids' clothes and underwear and knows they did it and grabs the daughter and tells her that one drop of the boy's blood could kill her! So then the boy turns into a snake and bites the dad and a mongoose kills the snake. A beautiful, tragic love story. (jes) ❧ But did she ever have a snake baby? Suppose that cliffhanger was for the possible sequel. (jaz)

Stadium Rock Around the time groups became bands, their shows became concerts, and the people attending these affairs fancied themselves concertgoers. Such delusions made stadium rock possible. Not since the Romans have spectacles been so large and lethal. Some promoting genius figured out that rockheads were the only fans who'd pay to be treated like cattle. After you waited for tickets, you were spat on, stamped, and stampeded into sports areas with the acoustic perfection of a men's room. Watching a band from affordable seats was like staring at a well-lit ant farm. The ordeal of murky sound, and even murkier merchandise, required the subject to be in an altered state. No sober person past the age of reason would choose to stew in traffic, bathe in flat beer, and slide on another man's vomit. You'd think that things would have changed once people started to die at these events, but no. These mass meetings had all the trappings of religion and were just as stupid. Not even retrospect can make a stadium show look good, but there are still fools and money parting to see middle-aged millionaire drug addicts hide behind smoke and screens. I know it's only rock and roll, but I hate it. (bruce) ❧ In the parking lot, smoking a joint and slamming back Jack Daniel's and Cokes inside your friend's TR7. "Day on the Green." On the bill: REO Speedwagon, .38 Special, Kansas, Journey, UFO. Backstage passes you won from a

5

radio station. Too stoned to make it out of the parking lot, too far gone to care. "Here, dude. Here's ten bucks. Buy me a UFO baseball jersey . . ." "Boom boom! Out go the lights!" (enrique marie) (See also HEAVY METALLERS)

Star Magazine This super little mag was put out by Petersen Publishing and was only out for a few issues. Kind of like *Sassy*, *Star* focused on how to be a teenage slut. It had interviews with groupies like Sable Starr and Lori Lightning, and articles like: "You First Always," "The Guys Who Won't Go Steady," and "Sunset Strip Groupies — Who, What, Where, and How: WOW!" Their fashion section had all sorts of wild make-up hints and featured hot pants and see-thru tops — no wonder it didn't last. (pleasant) ❖ I got every issue the day it made it to Scottsdale, Arizona, along with that coolest of music rags *Rock Scene*. There just wasn't much else for a kid in Arizona to read, if you were interested in the fabulous glitter rock world! So what if *Star* was for girls; I used all those groovy make-up tips too! And so did the one other guy in Scottsdale that was into glam. (don)

Star Trek-kies The irony of the Trekkie phenom was that it really didn't take off until after the show was canceled for declining viewership in '69. For a whole decade, *Star Trek* survived only in syndication and in the minds of its ardent propeller-head followers who lobbied to get the show brought back to network TV, formed an alarming numbers of clubs, and held annual conventions. If you asked "Why all the fuss?" they'd tell you their secret society was responsible for keeping alive the last gasp of '60s optimism for the future. So no one asked, let alone paid much attention to them. That is, until the shocking success of *Star Wars* ('77). After that, Hollywood was suddenly in the mood for a little outer-space exploration, as evidenced by *Battlestar Galactica*, *V* (short for "Visitors") — which was the first ever TV space-opera (sci-fi show with a soap opera format) — and, of course, the *Star Trek* motion pictures. There have been six T.O.S. movies (cast from The Original Series) to date; real Trekkies don't even bother to

count the two T.N.G. flicks (cast from *The Next Generation*). (bruce) ❖ *Beam me up!* The cult of *Star Trek* reached new heights with the '97 Heaven's Gate mass suicide in Rancho Santa Fe, California. Members of the cult who believed that a space craft traveling behind comet Hale-Bopp was going to transport their souls to the "next level above human" were avid *Star Trek* watchers. One of the castrated culties was even the brother of actress Nichelle Nichols, who played Lt. Uhura (*uhura* is Swahili for "freedom") in the original cast and who later worked for NASA doing promos for the first test space shuttle, named the *Enterprise*. I guess some other people took it all kinda seriously too. (nina) ✿

Starving Ethiopians We were forced to finish our meals because of these people. (darby) ❖ As recently as the 1950s, Ethiopia was one of the few countries in Africa that was able to export food. By 1984, the land was ravaged by famine. Sure, stories were around, but it wasn't until one BBC crew pushed to get their pictures seen that the world began to notice. Still, many avoided the fact that the government in Ethiopia caused the famine through forced collective farming. More and worse famines are going on at this very moment, but no camera crews are there. Bon appetit! (bruce) ❖ I still think it's funny every time someone suggests we go out for Ethiopian food. (lisa aa.) (See also HANDS ACROSS AMERICA)

Star Wars When *Star Wars* opened in the summer of 1977, it was like nothing else existed. In those days *Star Wars* was everywhere, in the movies, in Marvel comic books, on the radio with a sick disco version of the movie's theme song (complete with musical laser-gun interludes), even on TV in a couple of lame specials and *Donny and Marie* appearances. But even with all that nonsense, me and my friends still couldn't get enough of *Star Wars*. We used to run all over Long Beach making *ptchow!* laser-gun noises and pretending we were Darth Vader, Lord of the Sith (the coolest), Han Solo, Chewbacca (a close tie for second-coolest), or Luke Skywalker (just sort of average cool). There were always a lot of lame parts to play,

Princess Leia and Luke Skywalker

though, like Obi-Wan or the droids. . . . Nobody, of course, not even the girls, wanted to play Princess Leia, and being assigned the role was a sure sign that you were a royal geek. If you could recite Jawa or Greedo-speak, however (Oota tuta, Solo?) then you were definitely the coolest of the cool, and the best way to learn all that stuff was to see the movie over and over and over again. I lost count after my thirteenth time. But for the truly obsessive seven-year-old, the best way to relive the movie was with those fuckin' Kenner toys, the kind Christian Slater still can't get over. . . . The toys for the second movie were slightly better made than the ones from the first, and one of them was known far and wide as, bar none, the coolest thing in the universe: the Imperial All-Terrain Armored Transport, or AT-AT Walker for short. I begged, *begged* my parents to get me one, but my family was not rich and the damn thing cost $40! But weeks went by, then months, and when I still didn't relent about the damn toy, my folks showed some

mercy and bought me the thing. When the fine machine at last stood there in my living room, I looked at it lovingly for a long time, and then finally opened it up and looked inside. A strange numbness came over me. This, a voice in my mind said, is a toy. Toys are for babies. At that instant I lost all interest in toys and things *Star Wars* related. It was a nightmare. In an instant my most prized possessions in the world were transformed into cheap trinkets, nasty plastic shit. My parents had worked hard to pay for all of that stuff. . . . I was nauseated with guilt and self-disgust. A few years later I went to see the third film, *Return of the Jedi*, and I sat through it bored, disappointed, resentful. Had the other films been this bad? I couldn't believe it was possible. My childhood innocence suddenly seemed a remote and sad thing — a long time ago, a galaxy far, far away. (stymie) ♣ The Darth Vader Game: The boys in the band Jawbreaker created this game, good for bands to play when traveling across the country. The objective is to come up with what would have been the funniest character to be under Darth Vader's mask when it was removed. I think the best one they came up with was Lamb Chop. (darby) ♣ Star Wars was also the name of the strategic missile defense system. Republicans are pushing for its retro comeback. (winnie) (See also GEORGE LUCAS) 🐗 🐗 🐗

5

Static Cling How a form of electricity could be fashionable during a certain time period is beyond me. Flyaway hair and clothes that stuck to their owner seemed much more prominent years ago in the '70s. Why the hell is that? Was it a time before Bounce and Cling-Free? Could it have been from all that disco and polyester? Why, why, why? (jes)

Station Wagons The wood-paneled station wagon evolved from the kind of long wagon you took to the train station. They were open and had removable wooden walls. By the '30s, automotive versions were appearing, today known as Woodies. By mid-century, they were the icon of American domestic bliss, still paneled but in synthetic wood. Many fondly recall them and have obviously managed to blot out the rolling hell a car full of kids can be. In the far-back seat, no one can hear you scream. (bruce) 🍀 And they had maroon vinyl interiors that made cleaning up even the stickiest bodily secretions a cinch for the teenagers that eventually took them over. Of course, the minivan (or Euro–station wagon) replaced the station wagon in the late '80s when yuppie moms wanted a car that didn't look like the Bradys'. (wendy) 🍀 Comeback Status: Now in the late '90s, anyone extravagant enough to have babies that are not federally subsidized must also have a Volvo or Mercedes station wagon with a turbo engine, tinted windows, leather interior, built-in baby seat, and side airbags in the back seat to transport the little ones to their tennis lessons in safety! (nina) 🐢

Stick Hockey A less-stupid guy toy. A miniature hockey rink with metal players controlled by several sticks protruding from either end of the rink. Playing a game on it was rather like performing on a church organ; still, it gave one pretty good play. The only problem: the puck was hugely out of proportion, as if the NHL played with a truck tire. (bruce) (See also VIBRATING FOOTBALL GAME)

Sticks Styx, fire sticks, apple sticks, joysticks, spacesticks, chopsticks (for food and the piano), Chapstick, drumstick, stick 'em up, Jerky Stix, Space Food Sticks, stick-on decals, stickers, Pixie Stix, Fun Dip dip sticks, sticky buns, Big Sticks, Popsicle sticks, pogo sticks, Pick-up Sticks . . . (carla/darby/noël) (See also CHICK-O-STICKS and STICKY CRAWLERS)

Stickshift A hairdo which was supposed to look like one — made by making one big braid stick straight out on top of your head, or by wrapping whatever hair you had around something that would stand up straight. I did this until *way* past the time it was fashionable, and damn it, when my hair grows back from shaving and mohawking it for eight years, I'm gonna do it again. (rosenda) (See also PALM TREE)

Sticky Crawlers (and Wacky Wall Crawlers) A rubber octopus thing you'd get free in a cereal box. You'd throw it against the wall, and it would crawl slowly down, sort of tumbling over itself. (dave)

S.T.P. Cars All the boys in first grade had them. It was this car with a plastic rip cord that you pulled out really fast, then let the car go. When it rained, the boys brought their S.T.P. cars and the girls brought their Barbies to watch the S.T.P. car races. (riley) 🍀 Stood for Supersonic Turbo Power. These were cool. I gave myself so many friction burns with that T-strip, it's a wonder my folks were never turned in for abuse. Thanks to gyroscopic action, these flew forever as they sailed off my binder. I'd love an audio sample of the sound they made, it would be sonic crack to me. (bruce) 🍀 Weren't they called S.S.P. — Super Sonic Power? Or was it S.S.T. — Super Sonic Turbo? My confusion stems from the fact that I remember the name changed at some point in the late '70s. Anyway, whatever they were called, they were awesome. (bobby)

Straight Edge Fad of the nondrinking, non-drug-using punks and skins in the late '80s to early '90s as a backlash to their fucked-up counterparts listening to the same music but by association damaging their good, clean image. Inspired by the likes of 7 Seconds and Minor Threat (later Fugazi), these straight fans would brand themselves with Sharpies, scrawling big *X*s on the back of their hands, in case you weren't sure which were the punks at the show who weren't wasted. (darby)

Streaking One time I went with my already self-conscious girlfriends jogging (they were worried about their weight — I wanted to fit in). This was suburbia in the early '80s, a little behind in the times. It was the first time I saw a streaker. He was jogging too, in a trench coat. And it was very exciting. (darby) ♣ My older brother dared me to when I was five, so I went door-to-door naked, and enraged the neighbors. On my third or fourth streak (yes, it became a hobby), the mother of a cute girl down the street chased me back home with a broom, swatting my bare ass and forbidding me to play with her daughter again. (mike v.) ♣ It was considered a huge new fad when Robert Opel (thirty-eight-year-old ad exec) ran naked across the stage during the live broadcast of the Academy Awards on April 2, 1974, which was seen in living rooms across America. There was a song released (five days after) called "The Streak," by Ray Stevens. My Girl Scout troop went on a camping trip to some Girl Scout camp on Catalina Island, and we decided it was a really good idea to do a group streak from this one tent to the bathroom, then back. I was a major prude and would only take my top off and left my panties on, not that there were any boys around anyway. (riley) (See also MOONING)

Stretch and Sew There was some trick to sewing stretchy fabrics that was unveiled at this weekly class at the fabric store. My mother was the queen of craft, but to retain her crown in 1978 she had to be well-versed in velour. For a few years, Mom, Dad, and I were walking spokesmodels for the versatility of the new wonder fabric. It was so soft, cuddly, and warm,

too; for tops, slacks, pullovers, jackets, matching hats, even culottes. Velour's cool again now, but don't forget about the previous decade, where it was the sign of the plague, probably due to all those misfit and misshapen Stretch and Sew disasters. (lisa aa.) ♣

Stretch Armstrong Viscous action doll that could be stretched out to about three feet long. Typically met his demise when older brothers with driver's licenses would draw and quarter him by tying him between car bumpers and driving in opposite directions. By about the seven-foot mark, Stretch would finally explode, spraying a mysterious red liquid everywhere. He also faced death by microwave on a regular basis. Stretch is currently available in a nonlethal, no-cholesterol version, filled as he is with 100% vegetable oil. (nick) ♣ He's also evolved (or is that de-evolved) into a no-neck, shorter, jockish mutant-looking thing now. (darby) ♣

Studio 54 In the late '70s, walking into Max's in New York was like walking into a page from *Rock Scene* or *Creem*. It was all about Sid and Nancy, the Ramones, and the Dead Boys. Outside of the club, the threat of Son of Sam and New York's reputation for danger made every acid-drenched second climactic. It was two in the morning and I was sitting in the deejay booth upstairs at Max's. Paul Zone (of the Fast) was my only New York friend and was the deejay that night. It was my second time in town and I'd taken four hits of purple microdot. Kristian Hoffman (of the Mumps) came in and asked me if I wanted to go to Studio 54 with a bunch of people. He had borrowed the Dickies' van and wanted to take a drive. The chance to go dancing at a disco (one of my secret pleasures even during punk's heyday) and to get into Studio 54 with Halston, Bianca, and Liza sounded too fabulous to miss. I hopped into the crowded van. After a quick introduction to Lydia Lunch, Jim Sclavunos, and Bradley from Teenage Jesus and the Jerks, Howie Pyro from the Blessed, and Annine (Jim's girlfriend), we were off. "How are we going to get in?" was the question on everyone's mind. Just looking like a punk often meant getting yelled at or beaten up outside of the East Village. Kristian came up with a brilliant idea. "I think we should just walk up to Steve Rubel and introduce ourselves as Andy Warhol." It didn't work. (patty) (See also ANDY WARHOL)

Studs and Spikes Very important punk rock accessory. Spikes became so long and spiky, they were considered weapons and often people weren't allowed into shows with them. (ju-ji) ❀ The lasting legacy of the film *Rollerball*. (bruce) 🐑

Subliminal Messages Often used in images of ice cubes and fire, this technique had been around for decades. Paranoids of the post-Watergate age began to see them everywhere. When it came out that certain stores broadcast anti-theft slogans under their Muzak, they all said "Told ya so." There are a few drawbacks to these: (1) They're great for basic things like hunger or fear but can't convey complex messages pertaining to politics or money; (2) Repeated exposure to them voids the effect. Your mind is an amazing place. (bruce) (See also PARANOIA)

Sucking on Hair In my day, all the cool girls had scraggly hair and at least one strand in the front that was long enough to suck on. (darby) ❀ My mother told me a horror story about a girl who had to have an operation to remove a huge hairball from her stomach after doing this. That ended my hair-sucking career fast! (gwynne)

Donna Summer My parents liked a wide variety of music, mostly sucky, so I was very, very happy when my dad kept this tape in the bathroom. I'd suds up singing with disco Donna and even had the lyrics for "On the Radio" scrawled word for word on my Spanish class Pee-Chee folder. Her songs ("Hot Stuff" and "Bad Girls") are remembered for best expressing the world's transition from disco back to rock. (darby)

Summer Replacement Shows Back in the days when TV shows ran for whole seasons at a time, it was not uncommon for them to go off the air during the summer months, knowing they, and their viewers, would return in the fall. In their place, the networks would run summer replacements. These were often try-outs for new shows or new talents. And like summer stock theater, they were often bad. They were among the last of the variety shows, which gave Carol Burnett's dancers something to do till fall. Glen Campbell ("Witchita Lineman") had one; so did the Starland Vocal Band and the 5th Dimension ("Up, Up and Away"); and even Gladys Knight and the Pips. Like iron lungs, they are part of a lost age. (bruce)

Sun Day From the creators of Earth Day. This 1978 event was supposed to become an annual occasion to celebrate solar and alternative energy. It was very nicely packaged for the media, and even had its own logo showing a sun made of people joining hands. The hoopla got me to attend a rally. Alas, it all turned out to be an overblown libertarian tirade against the big oil companies. The reason we never learned from the Energy Crisis was because too many

Donna Summer

stayed married to the silly idea of going off the grid and hanging out at some solar-powered version of Walden Pond. Today the same fools have fled either to Idaho or to one of the cyber communities that clutter up the Internet. (bruce) (See also SOLAR PANELS)

Sunflower Seeds The best were by David. I ate these things with a vengeance, leaving one long trail of seed shells from kindergarten until I graduated from college. A total addiction. You'd find yourself unable to stop eating them, even though your lips and tongue were swollen from the salt, until you got that one last perfectly roasted, perfectly plump seed that you cracked between your teeth right down the middle — ahh, seed heaven! Now they make BBQ, salsa, and ranch-flavored ones; it verges on sacrilege. (nina) (See also THE MUNCHIES)

Sunlamps Obsessive-compulsive tanners would share their home-tanning or sun lamps and use them too long and make ugly blisters all over their faces or even fry their retinas. By the time twelfth grade came around, these poor girls were lookin' pretty haggard. Their search for the healthy tanned glow turned more into a crispy fried look. (darby) One night in 1974 I came home tripping on acid and turned on the sunlamp in the living room and stared for hours at the way my pupils would constrict and dilate like sea barnacles. The next day I was rushed to the hospital with burned corneas. (patty) Now used for seasonal depression. (lisa aa.) (See also TANNING)

The Sunshine Family Way cool, perfect Aryan family in the doll kingdom. Consisted of Mom, Dad, Sister, and Baby Bro. If you had the Sunshine Family Treehouse, you were bitchin'. (katy) By Mattel, makers of Barbie. Wow, you could get the whole dress-up nature-loving earth family and their four-room house with furniture and many clothes changes, including prairie dress for Mom, and rad earth sandals and matching backpacks and baby with clothes changes too! The ideal 1970s healthy, earthy, camping, post-hippie family and house, all in one box! (riley)

Sun Signs, Linda Goodman's (Also the author of *Love Signs*.) I recently picked up Linda Goodman's 550-page book at a thrift store and found out that it's actually really good. The late '60s/early '70s mood and references make it even more entertaining. Of course, if you read this you will know if the sign you are attracted to will be a good provider, how much money he'll spend on you, if he's romantic, if he has weak tendencies, how he'll treat the kids, if he will beat you, want to cheat on you, and what you need to do to keep him happy — even if that means completely changing to suit his needs. It does have advice for men but for the most part it is written for the domesticated woman. This was in the foreword and I think it's too important not to pass along: "It's fun to practice with famous people, politicians, fictional heroes and heroines. Try to guess their sign, or what sign they most represent. It sharpens your astrological wits. You can even try comic strip characters. Good old Charlie Brown is obviously a Libran, and Lucy could only be a Sagittarius with an Aries ascendant and her Moon in Virgo. As for Snoopy, well, anyone can easily see he's an Aquarian dog, the way he wears that crazy scarf and the World War I aviator's cap, while he chases an imaginary Red Baron from the roof of his dog house." This is certainly rare information you may never find anywhere else. (darby) (See also ASTROLOGY and NEW AGE)

Sun Tea Not just a recipe but a solar-energy-demonstration project. You put some tea bags into a pitcher with plain cold tap water, set the pitcher in the sun, and in a few hours you'd magically find — tea! Add ice and sip while feeling smug about not being a resource-squandering energy hog, though in fact this act made almost zero impact on national energy consumption. Americans are suckers for gimmicky products and concepts, so soon you could buy special Sun Tea jars, gallon containers printed with the phrase "Sun Tea." They were completely unnecessary to the process, but zillions were sold — and you can still find new ones for sale today. (candi) One summer my mom was in her sunshine eco-lady phase, and she discovered the concept of Sun Tea. No lemonade for us anymore. She got into mixing blends, and even bought one of those jars. One night, she set up her Sun Tea jar, left it on the windowsill, and went to bed. In the morning, she was crushed to find it already full of tea. She felt duped and swindled out of sunny goodness. We cheered her up by calling it Moon Tea. But thereafter she'd just stick the whole thing in the fridge and wait for the same results. (bruce)

"Super" Remember that word? Man, in the '70s it seemed as though everything was *super* something. Originally, a superstar was an artist who was a top singer/dancer/model/actor/writer/poet/director/communicator/athlete — someone so versatile that he or she was proficient in at least three noteworthy things. Although he knew needlepoint, Rosey Grier was not a superstar; because they could sing and dance and act, Diana Ross and Liza Minnelli were. But soon enough, with everything from supermarkets to supermachines, every blasted advertiser and publicist tried to make you think that the shit they were ramming down your throat wasn't as fuckin' banal as toothpaste by slapping the word "super" right in front of it. "Superbands" consisting of "superstars" were having "supersessions" while they snorted "superdrugs" over their "superdeals" before we all got hip to the rip. Or did we? (karrin) (See also SAYINGS/SLANG and ANDY WARHOL)

Super Elastic Bubble Plastic Wham-O's multicolored plastic goop that you'd blow into a big gigantic psychedelic balloon that you could play with like a light, sticky, fragile beach ball . . . until it shriveled up into a scary wad a few days later. No kid that played with this junk will ever forget the smell . . . ah! I've looked for it for more than ten years now — I think that's when it went off the market with no warning. People in toy stores who know what you're talking about will inevitably lead you to some tiny little tubes with inferior goop and wimpy straws. I want the real stuff! I've never asked a collector type, though I imagine any old tubes might have hardened by now. This needs to be reinvented for the '90s. (darby) (See also WHAM-O)

Super Jock This boy-toy came in different sports, but I only ever had the football one. It was a foot high, plastic with stickers that you put on. The point was to bash Super Jock's head down into his neck, making his leg kick. The more violently you bashed his head the more violently his leg would kick, sending the plastic football you'd set up in front of his foot farther down the plastic football field you'd rolled out and through the plastic goalposts. (pete)

Surf Clothing The perfect accoutrement for paltry wardrobes of suburban wannabes and midwestern ne'er-do-wells who have no idea what a beach is really like aside from movies and postcards. The world's fascination with buxom California blondes and the carefree lifestyles of beach cultures led to the surfing fashion craze. In the late '70s, stuff like Rags, Jams, Ocean Pacific, Pacific Coast Highway, and Hang Ten was the fly shit that made you popular in school. As the '80s rolled in, Town and Country Designs made a big splash with their iconic yin and yang logo, which was found on an assortment of stuff from T-shirts to sweatshirts and ultimately (gulp!) the dreaded painter's cap. By around 1984, the surf thing was really taking off with stuff from Quicksilver, Body Glove, Maui and Sons, Rip Curl, and most important, Gotcha. Gotcha was popular with the kids because they had all these groovy, multicolored stickers that came with their clothing and soon people just ripped those stickers off from the department stores. This sticker thing was similar to the stunt started by Rags and PCH clothing. All this eventually led to the development of neoprene bikinis and the short-lived publication of *Beach Culture,* which was David Carson's baby before *Ray Gun* magazine. As a side note, there was (still is) a product called Sex Wax, which is basically surf wax that smells really good. Stupid kids like myself used to chew it like it was candy. (noël) ❀ I grew up in Malibu and the first surf company to have T-shirts with their logo on it was Natural Progression. You had to actually go to their retail store to get 'em. It was way before O.P., and they actually made surfboards. The logo was a rainbow trapezoid and they had all kinds of different T-shirts. The coolest was a light blue long-sleeved T-shirt with cuffed sleeves with these little surfers surfing up and down the logo. You'd wear your shirt with Levi's light blue cords (long, not floods), light blue/dark blue two-toned lace-up Vans, and extremely long, straight, side-parted, no-bangs, naturally highlighted hair (just like Malibu Barbie's), and a serious beach-baked tan. Boys look the same but with hair a bit shorter. (riley)

Surfer Sandals Remember those rainbow-layered rubber Zorries, with the blue thong straps? And sometimes they even came in platform-stacks, with a lightning bolt on the side. They were really comfortable, and you could get 'em at Thrifty's. All the surfers and surfer chicks wore them, with long-sleeved pastel Hang Ten T-shirts, faded jeans, and either puka shells or turquoise and silver "liquid bead" necklaces, usually with a moon and star pendant. (pleasant) ❖ I heard someone say the other day that they used to take the bottom of one rainbow-soled thong and Superglue it to the bottom of another one for the superplatform look. They could have been lying though. (nina) ❖

Susan B. Anthony Dollar This was the first U.S. woman coin — of course it was fucked up! (darby) ❖ Some consolation prize for not getting the Equal Rights Amendment passed. (jeff) ❖ The Susan B. only lasted from '79 to '80 and was one of the shortest-lived coins in U.S. history. One of the fundamental leaders of the suffragette movement, 1870–1914, Susan B. is the only real woman to appear on a U.S. coin (though fictional female representations like Liberty and Freedom have graced our coins in the past). The chief reason the coin bombed was because it was so similar in size to a quarter. There is still talk of bringing back the Susan B. and making it out of distinctive bronze or copper. (bruce) (See also TWO-DOLLAR BILLS)

Jacqueline Susann (1918–1975)
This former Broadway actress married a top publicist and went on to become the best-selling novelist of all time, using tawdry tales of her personal brushes with show biz to help provide grist for her brilliantly trashy books. *Valley of the Dolls, The Love Machine,* and *Once Is Not Enough* were all made into equally high-camp trashy films. Her work is still adored by homosexuals and thrill-seeking twelve-year-old bookworms the world over. (gwynne)

Sushi Used repeatedly as sitcom fodder, sushi became a fad in the decadent '80s, and had a similar reputation to quiche's in the '70s. And just like star-bellied Sneetches and Sneetches with none on thars, there was a mini-war with the sushi eaters and the sushi haters. It's taken a while but there's not as many people around who will snicker at you for "going for sushi." (darby) 🐿

Swatch Watches These things were *huge!* At one point they even launched their own line of clothing. Everyone had at least one Swatch. And they even started accessorizing an accessory by offering changable wristbands and Swatch guards to protect your timepiece from scratches. These Swiss clocks for the hand are still around and surprisingly popular. (morgan and ferris) ❖ You were supposed to wear two or three at a time! (lorraine) 🐿

Sweaters The V-neck in a variety of colors. It was very trendy (around the same time as cut sweatshirts) to steal them out of your dad's closet and wear them backward. Of course, a few years before this, the beaded button-up '50s retro style came back — but most moms were so small that no one could fit into the things. Why were they so damn little back then? (darby)

Sweatsuits The designer variety are being bought up by the Japanese in their quest to own all of America's past. So be forewarned. Surely you'll still be able to find the non–brand names. Back then sweatsuits (otherwise known as jogging suits) were more often *not* sweated in, but worn as the ultimate casual wear. The satin and velour were especially cozy. Loads of stripes down the leg and arm and across the chest. And don't forget the long zip-up sweatshirt robes! (darby) ❖ Sweatsuits are still big with rappers and retired senior citizens. (nina) (See also JOGGING) 🐿

S

Sushi eater

Well, I was young enough to read through three Super Specials and all the way up to volume forty, I think. Once I discovered the teen books with sex in them, however, I abandoned the nonsmoking, virginal world of the Wakefield twins for books good enough to inform us eleven-year-old kids about blowjobs. (wendy)

Sybil Like most impressionable pre-teens, I was captivated by this book/TV movie about a multiple-personalitied psy-chotic who as a child was sexually and other-wise abused by her freaked-out mother but was trying to somehow lead a normal life. The story was shocking, horrific, yet for some reason, strangely erotic. Played beauti-fully by Sally Field in the two-part television special, Sybil had to manage all these various and varying people inside her who had different names. It wasn't easy, but such things rarely are. (nina) That whole thing about being strapped up and having to hold cold water in her urethra was pretty hard-core. Sally Field always took those daring roles. (darby)

Sweet Valley High Even my mom and my brother made fun of me mercilessly for reading the series. My mom hated taking me to buy the latest *Double Secrets* or *Little White Lies* or whatever, but sup-plied my demand for the tales of the "perfect size-six, blond sixteen-year-olds" probably 'cause she knew it was better than my sitting on my ass watching soaps.

5

t

Tab "Tab cola, for beautiful people." Mommys and (rich) teen girls drank this in cans and bottles with a cool populux logo. (allison) ❧ In high school, all I ate was No-Doz, a six-pack of Tab a day, and an occasional doughnut. I was perpetually, insanely wired, weighed 120 pounds, and of course I still thought I was fat. (gwynne) ❧ It was made by Coca-Cola before they created the actually good-tasting Diet Coke. Just like how Diet Rite is the sugar-free cola put out by RC Cola (Royal Crown Cola) and now RC has a really great tasting Diet RC. (riley) (See also POLO, SACCHARIN, and SODAS)

Taggin' "Taggin' was invented in the summer of 1970, when a young man in NYC began to print his name on ice cream trucks, and because he worked as a messenger, he had the opportunity to inflict his tag all over Manhattan. Eventually the tag caught the attention of a *New York Times* reporter. Impressed by the *Times* article, youngsters all over NY invented tags and took pride in spraying them often and in boastfully inaccessible places. Gradually — according to an RTD police handout — the hip-hop culture took up tagging, diffusing it nationwide through films, videos, magazines, and books" (from *Avenues,* the Automobile Club of California's magazine — so believe it, sucker). 🐿

Tails And a variety of Culture Club/Thompson Twins down-the-neck braids. Tails were the most hideous of hair looks that even Annabella (Bow Wow Wow) was barely able to pull off. Gwynne says Darby Crash (Germs) was the first, and I think Aimee Mann ('Til Tuesday) tried to be the last. (darby) (See also NEW ROMANTICS) 🐿

"Take Off, Hoser" The origins of Bob and Doug McKenzie are as telling an insight into the Canadian mind as any of their skits. When *SCTV* began its third season, the producers were informed that the show did not meet Canadian broadcasting requirements for uniquely Canadian content. The flabbergasted producers argued that they were Canadian, the cast and crew were Canadian, and that the show was produced in Canada! The bureaucrats were undaunted, and they eventually worked out a compromise. Since the episodes aired in Canada were three minutes longer (due to Canadian government restrictions on commercial time), this time gap could be filled with the required Canadian content. So the writers went off and created Bob and Doug McKenzie. To the horror of Canadian bureaucrats and intellectuals, the duo were soon embraced by the public as icons of genuinely Canadian pop culture, which is all a real beauty, eh? (bruce) ❧ For the record, I have never heard a fellow Canadian string together "take off" and "hoser" in one expression. Correct usage is the casually uttered "Take off, eh." (adam s.) (See also *SCTV*)

Talent Shows Very much a middle school phenomenon. In seventh grade we did a sketch comedy piece, "The Richard Simmons Show." We made fun of obese people, teased Richard about having an effeminate nature, and did makeovers à la Jenny Jones. Ha ha ha. We followed up this boisterous mirth with a lip-synch to Toni Basil's uno hit "Mickey." Ferris wore a cheerleader's outfit and the rest of us put on Styrofoam wigs and wore really long skirts so that it looked like we were seven feet tall, and we danced around like we were on crack. *Quel amusant!* (morgan and ferris) ❧ And then, of course, there was *Star Search.* (jaz)

Tanning "Gettin' the tan." People deep-fried themselves like KFC with oil straight from the cupboard and a tinfoil-covered board or album cover which they'd angle properly to make the sun reflect off it and onto them . . . and they've got the cancer to prove it. (darby) ❧ Tanned skin was not always fashionable. First came tanning lotions, then the tanning shields, then the silver-lined tanning lounge (rumored to fry sleeping housewives). Finally we got sunlamps, and then tanning booths. Even Malibu Barbie got a tan! In the post-ozone world, the whole tanning boom will take its place in the infamous halls of brutal beauty, right next to bustiers and bound feet. (bruce) ❧ At one time to have colored skin, either natural or sun-induced, indicated that you worked in the fields, i.e., were not one of the aristocracy. To be tanned now is an indication that one has the privilege and free lifestyle to be dabbling in cancerous sun activities. "Bain de Soleil for that Saint-Tropez tan . . ." (noël) ❧ I always thought people who went to tanning salons looked . . . wrong. You just cannot convince me that these, or microwaves, are completely safe. There's just no way. (ju-ji) (See also SUNLAMPS)

Tap-A-Snaps Seeing as I am the only person alive who remembers this little contraption that you attached to the bottom of your shoes with an elastic band to create a blissful tapping sound when you walked or danced around, I must pay homage. Actually if the truth be known, I even forgot about them until recently when my mother told me they were the only toy I ever pined for as a child, so much so that she felt compelled to pool her limited resources and buy me some. All of which I have no memory of whatsoever. How fleeting the longings of youth! (nina)

Teen-Diary Books *Go Ask Alice* and *Jay's Journal.* Though both can be found in the Fiction section of your local library, we kids believed they were taken from real-life diaries of druggie teenagers who died as the result of their lifestyles. In addition to being a druggie, Jay was heavily into witchcraft. His convincing accounts of the supernatural make me never want to dabble, even as a joke, in the occult. (dave) (See also GO ASK ALICE)

Televised Gays When it comes to television, one has to remember that we started so far back, being bashed was at least a step up from the well of loneliness. It was better to see you and your kind shown as nutty next-door neighbors than as predatory perverts. The first gay guys I remember seeing on TV were a silly couple on Norman Lear's silly sitcom *Hot L Baltimore.* Like blacks', our only good lines seemed to come in comedies. Televised tokenism shows us all as safely silly, for which we are supposed to be grateful. I know it's foolish to expect a realistic depiction of anyone's life to come out of some nineteen-inch glass screen, but that lack just makes it seem that much smaller. Which is all a shame, because if you've ever looked at a Tom of Finland sketch, you know it would make for some really funny TV. (bruce) ❧ The first time I ever noticed gays portrayed in a stupid way in the media was in sitcoms like *Three's Company* and, to a lesser extent, *Too Close for Comfort.* In the first episode of *Three's Company,* a drunk Jack Tripper (John Ritter) was found passed out in the bathtub of Janet (Joyce DeWitt) and Chrissy's (Suzanne Somers) leisure pad after a going-away party for a housemate. The three became instant friends and next thing you know, the two spunky chicks asked Jack to take over the vacant room. Match made in heaven, right? Wrong. They knew that landlord Mr. Roper (Norman Fell) would have some problem with the co-ed living arrangement. Solution? Tell 'em Jack's gay because that way he'd be less threatening! The Ropers were duped and it worked like a charm, even though it had Jack on his tippy-toes all the time. He continued to front homosexuality even when Mr. Furley (Don

Knotts) took over the building (whose patented kung fu maneuvers and overbloated machismo inadvertently led many to think that the old man Furley was gay too). Jack finally confessed his true heterosexual nature when he married this boring but sexy airline stewardess and moved on to a spin-off show called *Three's a Crowd* so he could run a restaurant with the sassy and infallible Felipe. Of course, Mr. Furley took credit for the change in Jack's sexual orientation and they lived happily ever after. *Too Close for Comfort* worked off of a similar premise, but the gay character, Monroe (J. J. Bullock), did not live with girls on the show, he was merely a neighbor. Even though the setting was in liberal-minded San Francisco, the producers always made it a point to spark some homophobic tension between Monroe and the girls' high-strung comic-artist father (Ted Knight). Those were both pretty stupid shows to begin with. (noël)

Tennis Wooden rackets anyone? *Everyone* played tennis. Even Wifey. The fact that it's a lost sport is evidenced by the volume of tennis rackets available at thrift stores and garage sales (not to mention the twenty-year-old cans of stale balls). (winnie) 🍀 Retro tennis players: Chris Evert, Tracey Austin, John McEnroe, Björn Borg, Jimmy Connors, Bobby Riggs, Billy Jean King, Arthur Ashe.

Tennis Shoes and Sneakers Become "Athletic Footwear" Back in the old days, only occasionally would adults wear *tennies* on the weekends, and only kids ever wore *sneakers* (mostly Keds)! All that changed after the Munich Olympics ('72) when Adidas pushed their wares to non-Olympiad adults. Before we knew it, there were more brands (K-Swiss, Tretron, Reebok, and New Balance among the first) than we could keep *track* of, and by the '80s jogging/fitness craze, no one young or old wore anything else ever. When kids started shooting each other for their $150-a-pair basketball shoes so tricked out with shock calibration that they looked more suited for moon exploration than hoops, who didn't give thanks for growing up in simpler footwear times? Maybe that's why old-school brands like Adidas, Converse, Puma, and Vans are coming back so strong. (nina/bruce) (See also TRAVELING BY JETPACK) 🐿️

That's Incredible! The thing to note about this show is that people always mix up its hosts with those of the similarly hosted show *Real People*: each had multiple hosts; both had ex-football players; Cathy Lee Crosby was kinda like Sarah Purcell; and John Davidson and Skip Stephenson are oddly familiar types, especially their names (John and Skip, Davids*on* and Stephens*on*) (darby) 🍀 Featured ordinary people doing extraordinary things. I liked this show because it often featured kids. One of the few shows I ever wrote to — I wanted to be on it for having the uncanny ability to whistle and do bird calls with my hands. Never heard from them — not even an autographed snap. (morgan and ferris) 🍀 This show featured memorable goings-on such as a man who catches bullets in his mouth (he used some wax block between his teeth), spontaneous combustion (this still fascinates me), and the most memorable show where they had a big round pool with some logger type doing log rolling with another logger. Somehow they convinced Cathy to get up there and she (of course) got dumped. When she came up she flipped her hair and her now-see-thru T-shirt was plastered to her chest. Man, what a time for puberty to kick in! (e. c. cotterman) (See also *REAL PEOPLE*)

Jack W. Thomas No wonder I hate Judy Blume. When I was twelve, I found *Heavy Number* in the Young Adult section of Doubleday, and literature has never been the same. Jack, no doubt influenced by the Manson slayings and his years of work as a social worker with delinquent teenage boys, wrote a baker's dozen of graphically violent and twisted tales of terror teens (1969–1984), including *Turn Me On!; The Fear Dealers; The Bikers; Girls' Farm; High School Pusher; Burnout;* and *Reds*. These classics absolutely have to be read to be believed. (gwynne)

t

Teen Idol Freakout

I guess loyalty wasn't part of my vocab while I was growing up. Here I am agreeing to explore the crushes I've had on boy celebrities throughout my early hormonal life, and I quickly realize I had been a *Teen Beat* slut. I would flit from one boy-toy to the next at the drop of a hat (or the appearance of a zit on my guy of the moment). Save for Leif Garrett (yucky yellow hair) and the DeFranco Family (bad Osmond wannabes), there wasn't a teen mag guy that didn't grab my attention. If my bedroom walls could talk . . .

Jeff and Joe Fithian

The first studs that caught my eye were the adorable Tracy and Trevor from *Please Don't Eat the Daisies* ('65–'67). Since I was born in 1968, I guess it was the magic of reruns that set my three-year-old heart aflutter. For those not in the know, *PDETD* focused on the misadventures of the Nash boys: Kyle, Joel, Tracy, and Trevor, along with loyal and lovable sheepdog, Ladadog. I *luved* Jeff and Joe, even if I couldn't tell them apart.

Trent Lehman

I crushed major on this little guy, the middle child of the Everett family on *Nanny and the Professor* ('70–'71). Trent played moody Butch, and my fave episode revolved around a school bully problem and an inflatable clown that served as a punching bag. Sadly, I have learned that Trent since committed suicide by hanging.

Brandon Cruz

The star of my favorite show, Brandon starred as Eddie Corbett on *The Courtship of Eddie's Father* ('69–'72). Besides starring a total boy-babe, *Courtship* also had a killer theme song ("People, let me tell you 'bout my best friend, baaaah, ba, ba, ba, ba, bum") and a neat episode ender, where Eddie would always ask his dad (Bill Bixby, R.I.P.) a series of "only a kid would ask" questions. After *Courtship*, Brandon sort of fell out of sight, only to turn up four years later as Joey Turner in the film *The Bad News Bears*. As a rival team pitcher who gets smacked by his pop (Vic Morrow, R.I.P.) for trying to bean Bears' pitcher Mike Engelbert, Brandon had obviously grown as an actor. Such drama when he held the ball so the Bears could score a run, then dropped it in spite at his dad's feet.

Tatum — checkin' out the Bad News Babes — learns about the spitball from drunk dad Matthau

Mike Lookinland

After *Courtship,* I got into *The Brady Bunch* ('69–'74) in a big way, and Bobby most of all. My favorite episode was when Bobby, the big loser, went on the *Kartoon King* show to prove he wasn't a spaz and lost the "hands-tied-behind-your-back-eat-all-the-ice-cream-from-your-dish" contest. Once Bobby stopped putting the black rinse in his hair and went orange, I was over him. And the braces didn't help either.

Brian Forster

The second Chris to drum for the family Partridge ('70–'74), Bri was way hipper than that dorky Chris #1, Jeremy Gelbwaks (a Jewish Partridge? C'mon), and he really looked as though he was beating those skins. Though Chris and his tambourine-playing sister Tracy never got to do much, I remember one show where they ran away to Reuben's house, which was one of my favorite episodes except for Laurie getting a radio transmission through her braces. You'd think with all the money the Partridges made touring, Shirley could've found her a better orthodontist.

The Bay City Rollers

The Rollers were all over the teen mags, so try as I might, I couldn't really avoid them. I didn't really like them either, but my seventh summer was spent at Pierce Day Camp, and my counselor was crazy about the boys from Bay City. She had our bunk singing "S.A.T.U.R.D.A.Y. Night!" at the top of our little lungs, and in an attempt to impress her, I "picked" Derek Longmuir as my favorite BCR.

John and Tom Keane

The forgotten *Keane Brothers Show* ('77) was a half-hour variety show hosted by twelve-year-old Tom and his thirteen-year-old brother John Keane. I can't really remember who was Tom and who was John, but one of them played the drums and had braces. Sigh.

The Boys of ABC Saturday Morning

Some smart TV exec of the mid-'70s realized that cartoons were getting lame and kids needed live action on Saturday morning. Quicker than you could say "*Teen Beat*," these were the fellows I looked forward to seeing on weekends. Fresh from *The Brady Bunch* came Robbie "Cousin Oliver the Jinx" Rist, who starred in *Big John, Little John* ('76–'77). *BJLJ* told the tale of a forty-five-year-old man (Herb Edelman, R.I.P.) who drank from the Fountain of Youth and thereafter changed into a twelve-year-old (Rob-er-roo) at inopportune times. Another fave was *Thunder* ('77–'78), about a horse that was stabled with future *Lambada* star Melora Hardin and her foxy brother Willie (Justin Randi). *Shazam* ('74–'77) starred long-locked Billy Gray as long-locked "Billy Batson," who could turn into Captain Marvel by uttering, "Shazam!" Most memorable was *The Red Hand Gang* ('77–'78), which revolved around young supersleuths led by Matthew Laborteaux. Laborteaux would later turn up as morphine-addicted raga-muffin Albert on *Little House on the Prairie* with his real-life brother Patrick.

Todd Turquand, Shane Sinutko, Rad Daly, and Paul King

I've lumped these guys together because they ended up as a crush for only a month or two. Todd was a regular on *The New Mickey Mouse Club*, which also starred a young Lisa Whelchel (who'd go on to great stardom as Blair on *The Facts of Life* and later marry a preacher and have a ton of kids!). Shane was actually a good actor, best known for his star turn in *My Mom's Having a Baby*. He would pop up on this sitcom and that family drama, and I even recall a *Love Boat* episode, but Shane seemed to fade from the limelight. Rad had a small role on the television version of *The Bad News Bears*, but was all over the teen mags. He was a total babe, and one of the neat secret facts about him was that his real name was Robert Anthony Daly, and Rad was just a nickname derived from his initials! Do you think his publicist thought of that? Paul, on the other hand, was only a guest star on such shows as *Archie Bunker's Place* (as Danielle Brisebois's boyfriend, natch!), but *Tiger Beat* et al. covered him like the Second Coming. Paul contributed nothing to the world of entertainment but paid his dues to teen idol-dom by looking very cute indeed in his variety of Izod shirts.

Meeno Peluce

Besides Rad, the TV show *The Bad News Bears* ('79–'80) showcased tough guy Meeno Peluce, who played tough guy Tanner Boyle. I really appreciated the way Meeno invited *Teen Beat* readers into his home for photo ops. I dug his leather wristbands, sleeveless tees, and sultry sneer. Meeno would later go on to star in *Voyagers* with Jon-Erik Hexum (R.I.P.), be a model big bro for real-life sister Soleil Moon Frye, *and* hang around with the future ex–Mrs. Michael Jackson (Lisa Marie, duh!) during Lisa's chubby stage. Way to go, Meeno!

Ricky Schroder

Or as I like to refer to him, my WASP phase. I got hooked on the Ricker when *The Champ* came out. After that day, it seemed my whole life revolved around the moptop from Staten Island. I *had* to see *The Earthling* (William Holden, R.I.P.) the day it opened. I *had* to have the same white baseball jersey with yellow sleeves that Ricky wore in *The Last Flight of Noah's Ark*. I *had* to be glued to the set for the television premiere of *Little Lord Fauntleroy*. So hot in those knickers and ruffled shirts. During my full-on Ricky stage, I found a pen pal from the back of *Tiger Beat* magazine who was as passionate for Ricky as I was. We corresponded for a while, traded stories, Ricky articles, fantasies, and even swapped photos. I sent my fifth-grade school picture, but there was something terribly off-putting about the photo of a thirty-seven-year-old woman I received in return. My days as a Ricky fan quickly came to an end.

Adam Rich

The first true love of my life. It still hurts to talk about our unrequited love. I chanted the theme song to *Eight Is Enough* as if it were my mantra (". . . and eight is enough to fill our lives with love"), had an *Eight Is Enough* T-shirt, and even wrote to Adam care of ABC so I could get a faux autographed picture of the cast. I even went so far as to ask the doctor who performed my tonsillectomy to make sure I was out of anesthesia by 8 P.M. the Wednesday night of my op. Unlike most youngest children on family shows, Adam was the focus of many episodes, my favorite being a two-parter where Nicholas went on the lam after he left the soldering tool plugged in and burnt down part of the Bradford home. Horrifically, my parents began to use my love of all things Adam as a method of punishment around the Krassner household, banning viewership of *Eight Is Enough* when I misbehaved or removing pictures of Adam from my wall when I really ticked them off. I mourned the day *Eight Is Enough* was canceled and blamed that creepy Ralph Macchio who played Abby's nephew Jeremy Andretti during the last season. When Ralph would later turn up in *The Outsiders* (stellar cast, by the way) I was perversely pleased when he died saving those kids in the fire. But did Pony Boy have to keep hearing his voice all the time ("Stay golden, Pony, stay golden")? *Annoying!* Adam would go on to star in the films *The Fish That Saved Pittsburgh* and *The Devil and Max Devlin*, plus the short-lived television show *Code Red* with Lorne Greene and Andrew Stevens.

Fickle little miss, wasn't I? Thank god I am over that stage of my life and can now spend my free time doing constructive things like watching Jonathan Taylor Thomas on *Home Improvement*. Talk about foxy . . . (katy)

The retro version of *Friends*

Three's Company Despite the comments of some philistines elsewhere in this issue, *Three's Company* was actually the most brilliant and satisfying TV show of the '70s. I think if this had been filmed in black and white rather than color (which oozed with the glaring oranges and browns typical of the '70s), critics would be hailing it as the best ensemble acting since *The Honeymooners*. *Three's Company* is just one of those overlooked, underrated gems that is a product of its times and that we'll never see again in this post-AIDS era. Not only did the show have better than expected acting and writing to go along with its generally silly and sex-related storylines, but *Three's Company* featured the most excessive and gratuitous use of tan pantyhose ever on TV. You'd have to be a nylon fetishist like me to appreciate and notice that actress Joyce DeWitt (who did ads for L'Eggs on the side) always wore them to bed or even just hanging around the house. (falling james) (See also TELEVISED GAYS)

Thrift Shops Are no longer thrifty! Yes, in the dried-up '90s, it's cheaper to shop at outlets and discount boutiques than at the Goodwill, and the selection is generally better. I pine for the days of the $2 '50s housedress, the 75¢ Day-Glo paisley muu-muu . . .

(gwynne) ❧ When I was little, I *never* got new clothes. After getting over the junior high mortification of not getting the latest designer trends until they were way over (my mom, the garage sale queen, didn't seem to give a hoot about the fact that I would never be popular), I eventually embraced thrift store fashion. This was the time right before vintage stores exploded and you could still buy bags full of cool clothes and jewelry for a buck apiece. Sadly, with each year the selection dwindles and the prices skyrocket. I still trek faithfully every week looking for that beaded sweater in a color that I don't have, or that perfect knickknack (just forget about trying to find old Barbies and toys), but I'm not sure how much longer I can keep up the façade. Supposedly the thrift stores in the Midwest are still all right, so there's *some* hope — for now. (lorraine) (See also *Thrift Score* zine in Resources section)

Thumb Sucking Much to the chagrin of my orthodontist, I sucked until age eighteen. True, there *are* more self-destructive bad habits, but none so satisfying, so soothing, so inviting, and so damn near impossible to quit. That thumb-suck/nail-bite paint they made was a joke; sure, it tasted horrible and burned your mouth, but after a few minutes of strenuous sucking, it was gone. (I suppose smarter children just stuck their thumb under the faucet.) Because I couldn't let eleven years of agonizing orthodontics be in vain, I somehow manage not to put my thumb in my mouth (which makes way for fingernails, pencils, little pieces of plastic, you name it). Giving in just once could get me hooked again, and all of you thumb suckers (you know who you are) know exactly what I mean. (lorraine) (See also JUNK FOOD and PENCILS)

Time In the '70s, people engaged in all kinds of time-consuming but fun stuff: baking their own bread from scratch, attending political protests, taking motorcycle trips across the country, doing laborious crafts like macramé and quilting, or attending personal growth seminars. These activities might not be cost-effective, but they provided personal satisfaction. Similarly, '70s health food not only took a long time to cook, it took a long time to chew; time-conscious '80s people gulped down fast food, frozen dinners, microwavable everything. (candi) ❧ I liked most all time-travel movies — and there were a lot of them when I was growing up. From *Time After Time* (with Malcolm McDowell) to *Time Bandits,* to *Back to the Future.* There was always something "wrong" with the sci-fi portion of the storyline that you had to ignore for it to make scientific sense. (darby)

Time for Timer "When your get-up-and-go has got up and went," do you still "hanker for a hunk of, a slab or slice or chunk of, hanker for a hunk of cheese?" (jaz) ❧ ABC first used this strange cane-twirling nutritionist in an Afterschool Special, where he took two kids on an animated tour of their fat uncle's body. Years later, his annoying voice surfaced on Saturday mornings, where he advised the latchkey generation that they should resort to such things as cold fried chicken rather than skipping breakfast. Truly, this was the death of educational TV. FYI: Timer, as well as Yuck Mouth ("They call me Yuck Mouth, 'cause I don't brush") were not part of Schoolhouse Rock! (bruce) (See also CAVITY CREEPS, THE MUNCHIES, and SCHOOLHOUSE ROCK)

Tinker Toys Tinker Toys are now plastic (though I think they still make the wood). Also note how really little these things are if you try to play with them today. (ju-ji) ❧ I had a friend who wanted to play doctor on me with those Tinker Toys — she was insane. She'd make me say that I was her best friend. She'd pull my hair and yell, "Say it! 'I'm your best friend!'" and I'm like, "O.K." (laurel) ❧ Also, Lincoln Logs had that wooden-toy thing going on. (jaz)

Su Tissue (Suburban Lawns) Most awesome '80s girl singer. Her offbeat cleverness still sends shivers down my spine. So, Su, where are you? (darby)

Tittie Twisters My dad told my sister and me that these would give you breast cancer so we wouldn't give them to each other when we were fighting. Yet I have this weird uncontrollable habit of giving them to boys now. (darby)

Toaster Foods Before microwaves, even before toaster ovens, every kitchen had a silver box that food occasionally popped out of; they were called toasters. These tabletop treasures are largely forgotten now, but in the early '70s, the food giants hit upon a way to nourish busy proto-yuppies' kids on the go and also feed the growing number of latchkey kids. First came Pop-Tarts, then Danish twirls, then pop-up French toast. Eventually pancakes, pastries, and even pizzas were popping up everywhere. Unfortunately, they also dripped goo into the works and started fires. Just how many happy families were made homeless by Junior's attempts to make breakfast, we may never know. (bruce)

Toe Socks I loved mine, rainbow with multicolored toes. So sad the elastic didn't last and they shrunk from knee-hi's to ankle length after a year. (ju-ji) 🐿

Tom Tom Club I always thought their *Close to the Bone* record was forever going to be obscured by the limelight of David Byrne and the Talking Heads. Strange to find that it's the hip-hop artists and stations who have brought their music back into focus, sampled regularly in their popular songs. (darby) (See also *MV3*)

"10"

The tasteless system of placing a numerical value on a woman's physicality — i.e., "She's a 10" — began before, but was made popular when, bimbo **Bo** () bounced her bountiful boobage on the beach in the movie of the same name. (jes) ❧ The film inspired the short-lived fad of cornrows on wealthy white women, until they eventually came to their senses. (bruce) (See also NADIA COMANECI)

Ugly Dudley Moore scores with the perfect Bo Derek

Tomy Pocket Games The appeal of these things was their size: pocket-sized fun for the kid on the go. You'd buy them, fooling yourself that because they were so small and you were so shifty, you could get away with playing them in class, but little balls and often motorized wind-up parts prevented such clever ruses. I had dozens: Blackjack, Space Invaders, a motorcycle race, a flippy one where you spun different parts of a body and when it stopped, the person would have, like, a cowboy hat, a ballerina dress, and chicken legs — ha! Hours of fun! (morgan and ferris)

Ton Sur Ton Clothing company which catered to cool kids and dance club geeks. They had the great bright puffy jackets that made you look fifty pounds heavier but it didn't matter. That was during my switch in loyalty from Molly Ringwald to Ally Sheedy in *The Breakfast Club*, and from Madonna and Boy George to Siouxsie and Soft Cell. (selina)

Toot-A-Loop "It's an *S*, it's an *O*, it's a crazy radio! It's Toot-a-loop!!" Panasonic's coolest consumer product ever. Part sculpture, part jewelry, part music machine. The hot-colored round radio with the hole in the middle was every kid's dream, until you tried to listen to the thing. Now found in trendy thrift shops, at trendy prices. (bruce) ❧ Along with its sister mechanism, the ball-and-chain transistor. (carla)

Toss-Across Tic tac toe with bean bags. They actually recently redid that insipid commercial with the dog winning the game. Fun to play for about three minutes until you realized that throwing the bags at each other was more fun. (bruce) 🍀

Toughskin Jeans Pants for boys and tomboys . . . from Sears! Strange color choices, like Incredibly Putrid Green. (jeff h.)

Trading Cards *Charlie's Angels; Star Wars; Starsky and Hutch; The Dukes of Hazzard; Dallas; CHiPs; Mork and Mindy; Grease; Saturday Night Fever; Pee-wee's Playhouse;* Garbage Pail Kids . . . ❧ *Star Wars* signified different series by the color of the border. (noël) (See also WACKY PACKAGES)

t

Trash as Art Big in the '70s, the concept of reusing your trash for recycling became an art form, and the most creative was the one utilizing the most unobvious throwaways. Schools and camps asked us to bring in things like empty coffee cans, shoeboxes, milk or egg cartons, and miscellaneous items found around the house so we could artistically transform them into something frameable or almost usable. This was around the same time people were building homes from old tires (which is a great concept considering how many used tires litter the countryside). Ten years later *Family Ties* liberal hippie parents Steve and Elyse Keaton would be appalled at daughter Mallory's boyfriend Nick, who was a punk trash artist. (darby) ✤ *Mad* magazine's Al Jaffe put out whole books of this stuff. (gwynne)

Trash Compactors As far as I was concerned, we moved into the upper-middle-class zone when we got one of these garbage-crunching babies. And I was grown-up enough to be able to use the thing. We squashed our mess into compact loads like a responsible eco-conscious family. It made up for the fact that we didn't recycle. (darby) ✤ I thought recycling was for poor people. (selina) ✤ When Whirlpool introduced these in 1970, they thought they'd be the next wave. After everyone got a dishwasher, you needed a trash compactor to complete your life. At the time, they were seen as very ecological. (bruce)

Traveling by Jetpack Aren't we supposed to be able to do this by now? (winnie) ✤ Not after several Air Force dupes died flying them, including one that was entertaining a crowd of children, but that's another story. The idea of the solo individual jetting away from it all was just too potent an idea for 1960s America to put down. Soon the jetpack was showing up in James Bond movies and on TV's *Lost in Space*. Keds sneakers thought up the character of Kolonel Ked, a Right Stuff kinda guy who flew his jetpack through a whole series of TV ads. The idea was that Keds sneakers would let you jump and fly just like Kolonel Ked did! The last hurrah for this wonder of science was during the opening ceremonies of the 1984 L.A. Olympics. Some brave soul was hired to add an extra ostentatious touch to the gaudy proceedings by flying his jetpack over the Coliseum. This blast from the past moved no one, and today the jetpack remains the technology of the future and will most likely stay that way. (bruce)

Tribes None of my friends remember this TV show, shot on video and set in a high school, that aired all the way back in the late '80s and early '90s. It starred a dark-eyed, handsome, pre–Dylan/Brandon hunk as he moped his way through high school. I am convinced that *Beverly Hills, 90210*, was heavily inspired by *Tribes*, even to the point of plucking Jennie Garth from the cast. On *Tribes*, Garth played a bitchy, gossipy cheerleader who runs the school newspaper. The overall mood was closer to *James at 15* than it was to *Saved by the Bell*, and unlike much of *90210*, most of the action on *Tribes* occurred on campus. (falling james) ✤ This is pushing Retro Hell a bit, but it is interesting how this and that other school show *Degrassi Junior High* are all but forgotten. And I always thought *90210* took more after the cartoon *Beverly Hills Teens*. (darby)

Tribute Albums Tribute albums were fun when they started getting popular in the early '90s. Lots of obscure songs from the '70s and '80s were being recreated by their fans, and recognition for the artists of the past by the musicians of today seemed a healthy homage. But as labels started noticing they were selling decently well, these so-called tributes became less creative and more about making a few bucks. By including lots of famous musicians to basically do cover songs we ended up with an influx of crappy CDs with regurgitated retro tunes. Led Zeppelin, Hüsker Dü, Richard Hell, Van Morrison, Kiss, Black Sabbath, Marc Bolan, John Fogerty, Devo, the Carpenters, Shonen Knife, the Residents, Joy Division, the Misfits, Tom Waits, the Germs, and the recently released Bee Gees tributes are the tip of the iceberg of the extent and variety of this phenomenon. (darby)

Tribute Bands Lately a few cream-of-the-crop cover bands (which previously might only find success at bat mitzvahs) have sprung up in the big cities, doing major tours and packing the local clubs. Among the groups most frequently covered are Abba (Bjorn Again); AC/DC (Dirty Deeds, Sin City); Van Halen (Atomic Punks, 5150, Fair Warning); Ozzy (Crazy Train); Rush (2112); Led Zeppelin (Dread Zeppelin, ZOSO); The Doors (Morrison Hotel, Soft Parade, Wild Child); Kiss (Destroyer, Strutter, SSIK); The Grateful Dead (Born Crosseyed); and Queen (Sheer Heart Attack) as well as any '70s band that had a few big disco hits. Also abounding are generic disco cover bands with names like "Boogie Knights." (darby)

Trivial Pursuit Invented by three Canadian guys (one unemployed at the time, all now rich), who used to bore their wives while shouting trivia at each other on long cold Canadian nights. This is why something like 58% of the Sports and Leisure questions concern ice hockey. The CBC even made a fictionalized movie about these guys and their struggle to market the game! (bruce)

Tron "Greetings, programs!" This is one of the all-time coolest movies *ever*, with a few notable credits: It was the first cyberspace movie, and even beat William Gibson to the punch as far as exploring the concept of physically entering a computer-generated space. It inspired two really cool video games: Tron and Tron Deadly Discs. It briefly revived Disneyland's antique Tomorrowland ride the People Mover by adding a journey into Tron's Game Grid, where a room-sized curved screen projected scenes from the movie all around you — a much fun (albeit bumpy) getaway for those who've forgotten how scary the Happiest Place on Earth can be on LSD. And finally it proved that Disney could do more than make cartoons about fairy tales and stupid mice. (howard) ❧ The cycle scene was especially boss, a retro version of virtual reality meets Intellevision's Snafu. First extensive use of computer animation and back then this must have taken a shitload of time to do. (noël)

Truckin' Movies *Duel; Road Games; Sorcerer* (with Roy Scheider); *Smokey and the Bandit; Convoy; Mother, Jugs and Speed* (Raquel Welch, Harvey Keitel, Bill Cosby, produced by Larry Hagman); *Breaker! Breaker!* (with Chuck Norris); *B.J. and the Bear; White Line Fever;* TV movie *The Great Smokey Road Block.* When I think of these, I see flashes of Dyan Cannon and Burt Reynolds, but who knows. They're from a time when kids had orgasms over making trucks blast their airhorn, and "10-4, good buddy" was a hip saying. (darby) (See also CBs)

T-Shirts Cropped with slogans, shredded, beaded, french-cut, or Daisy Duke–style (pulling the bottom part of your tee over through the neck hole). (wendy) ❧ Shirts designed to look like a skeleton, a yachting blazer, a tux, all made for easy sitcom laughs. Also, Kandinsky-inspired splatter-painted neon shirts were everywhere! (ju-ji)

T-Shirt Transfers Since my parents owned a T-shirt transfer shop when I was growing up, I got to press thousands of these things onto shirts after school and during summer when I worked there (mmm, that smell!). I remember the early days of Keep On Truckin', Marriage Encounter, the eggs on the boobs, Wet Paint, Foxy Lady, Dyn-O-Mite, Elton John . . . But my dad says the real beginning of the transfer business came with Farrah Fawcett and that infamous bathing suit photo, followed by Fonzie, and then *Star Wars.* After *Star Wars* everybody and everything came on transfers. Occasionally a movie would come out that was too high class, but basically every movie was on a transfer. That is, until *Batman* came out in '89, and they insisted that they screen their own shirts. Today there's been a definite resurgence, but many people are just into finding old transfer-printed tees at thrift stores. (darby) 🐾

Tube Amps Have never gone away, although Fender has moved out of Orange County, California, to Arizona. All were patterned after Fender; the Bassman was the original heavy rock guitar amp, and the Showman the first loud amp (designed by/for Dick Dale). Prior to the rise of Marshall in the '60s, almost every rock guitarist used either a Fender or Britain's Vox. The Vox AC series was the ideal amp for a Stratocaster. The British Invasion brought new brands, as well as bands, to America: HiWatt, Orange, etcetera, while in America, Fender manufactured Mesa Boogie and Music Man (also Sun, Custom, and Ampeg). Still the way to go for warm tones and rockin' sound. (mike s.) 🐿️

Tube Tops These were elasticized round bands worn over the chest area as a top. Faves with roller disco babes and high school chicks with mini tits in the late '70s. Worn often under Hawaiian shirts. (ju-ji) ☘️ Comeback status: In the late '90s, tube tops are haute again, with Calvin Klein and Gucci giving them their long-deserved fashion respect. (nina) 🐿️

Tube TVs In the old days you could actually hit things, like the TV, to make them work again. Taking aggression out on the boob tube made the relationship a healthier one. I liked goin' with Pop to Thrifty's to test the tubes on their futuristic machine that they kept in the front of the store. (darby)

Tucking In One's Shirt This is an A#1 retro phenom, which most kids today (even retro hogs) don't subscribe to (unless they aim to be big business geeks). (darby)

Tupperware Parties Edward Tupper came out with Tupperware in the '30s. Big since the '50s, Tupperware parties gave housewives a chance to invite over all the other housewives and neighbors to have tea and gossip and make a few bucks without leaving their home! Plastic containers for everything, especially leftovers, they came in fashion colors and you had to "burp" the lid to let out the excess air, as if this kept anything fresher. Yes, you can still host a Tupperware party! (riley)

Turkey As in "jive turkey." I like this derogatory label so much more than "motherfucker." Somebody please use it on me! (winnie) ☘️ In the white-guilt '70s, "hip" expressions like this were self-consciously integrated into the verbiage of many. The story is that all these terms descend from "cold turkey," used to describe kicking heroin. Folks going through this change of life tended to develop cold, clammy, goose-bumped skin, reminiscent of an actual cold turkey. As you can imagine, anyone in this state wasn't good for much. They'd just lie there like, well, a stupid turkey. And finally they would tell you anything to get what they wanted. No one can jive like a turkey. Thankfully, this term has gone the way of applejack hats. (bruce) ☘️ Don't let the turkeys get you down! (darby) (See also SAYINGS/SLANG)

Tina Turner Without a doubt the Comeback Queen of the '80s. Dumping partner/husband Ike, after years of abuse, she proved she was indeed a "Proud Mary" by throwing on a big ol' wig, slipping into a leg-barin' leather mini, and demanding to be told, "What's Love Got to Do with It?" ('84). Her duet with Bryan Adams, "It's Only Love" ('85), had us all wondering if maybe she was losing even more touch with reality than her fake British accent implied, but her role as Aunty Entity in *Mad Max 3: Beyond Thunderdome* ('85) more than made up for it. (nina) (See also MAD MAX)

TV-Movie-of-the-Week Women Nancy McKeon, Valerie Bertinelli, Jaclyn Smith, Cheryl Ladd, Elizabeth Montgomery, Farrah Fawcett, Lindsay Wagner, Loni Anderson, Jane Seymour, Ann Jillian, later Melissa Gilbert, and now Jennie Garth. (darby/mike s.)

TV Shows and Reruns That Stole My Life Away *Looney Tunes* and *I Love Lucy*. Hours and days, and who knows, maybe even years spent watching the same episodes, over and over and over again. It's so sad. I gave so much of my life away to this empty pit. I was too young and stupid to know. *Three's Company* also fits into this category, but I'm

21 Jump Street

It was a weekly TV drama that detailed the escapades of baby-faced undercover cops who went into high schools to save the students from themselves. This was the vehicle that set Johnny Depp's illustrious career in motion. The best thing about this show was when Johnny (Officer Tom Hanson) would have to dress up like a punk rocker to infiltrate the school's drug connection. This was TV Land's only regular acknowledgment of punk culture (except for the occasional *CHiPs* episode — on *Square Pegs* they were "New Wave, *not* punk!"), and let me tell you, I was in love. I had my Johnny Depp posters positioned so he was the perfect height to kiss good night (I found out years later that he's actually way shorter than I). After the show's run, he would only accept quirky, offbeat movie roles in an attempt to disillusion his prepubescent *Teen Beat* following. Guess what, Johnny, it didn't work. (lorraine) (See also PUNK TRANSLATED TO TV and JOHN WATERS)

barely able to put it down here without feeling sick in my heart. (ju-ji) ❧ *Gilligan's Island* and the *Flintstones*. (patty) ❧ Also occupying too many of our precious brain cells are *Addams Family; The A-Team; Benson; Bewitched; Bosom Buddies; The Brady Bunch; Cheers; Diff'rent Strokes; Dukes of Hazzard; Facts of Life; Family Ties; The Flying Nun; F Troop; Get Smart; Gidget; Gimme a Break; Gomer Pyle; Green Acres; The Andy Griffith Show; Happy Days; Hart to Hart; The Honeymooners; Hogan's Heroes; I Dream of Jeannie; It's a Living; The Jetsons; The Jeffersons; Knight Rider; Laverne and Shirley; Little House on the Prairie; Lost in Space; Love, American Style; Mary Tyler Moore; Munsters; My Three Sons; My Favorite Martian; The Bob Newhart Show; One Day at a Time; Partridge Family; Remington Steele; Silver Spoons; Taxi; That Girl!; Too Close for Comfort; What's Happening!!; WKRP in Cincinnati;* and *Who's the Boss.* (natalie/nina/darby) (See also FANTASY ISLAND, LOVE BOAT, and M*A*S*H)

TV Show Songs on Radio "Those Were the Days" from *All in the Family* (Carroll O'Connor/Jean Stapleton); "Chico, Don't Be Discouraged" from *Chico and the Man* (José Feliciano); "Rockford Files" (Mike Post); "The *SWAT* Theme" (Rhythm Heritage); "*Happy Days* Theme" (Pratt and McClain); "Makin' Our Dreams Come True" from *Laverne and Shirley* (Cyndi Grecco); "*Welcome Back, Kotter* Theme" (John Sebastian); "Keep Your Eye on the Sparrow" from *Baretta* (Rhythm Heritage); "*Charlie's Angels* Theme" (Henry Mancini); "*The Dukes of Hazzard* Theme" (Waylon Jennings; "*WKRP in Cincinnati* Theme"; "Believe It or Not" from *Greatest American Hero* (Joey Scarbury); "*Hill Street Blues* Theme" (Mike Post); "Theme from *Miami Vice*" (Jan Hammer).

t

'20s Chic, '70s Style Biba, 🐾 the originally London-based superstore, was absolutely synonymous with the whole fashion idea — from slinky square-necked T-shirts to rayon dresses copped from the '30s, eyeshadows with glitter in them, black and silver and burgundy lipsticks, all in black and gold art deco containers. Biba and faux–Roaring '20s ruled — thinly plucked eyebrows with Vaseline mixed with glitter for shadow, bee-stung purple lips, cloche hats, marabou, T-strap shoes with Louis heels — it was at its height just about the time Jodie Foster did *Bugsy Malone*. Personally, I was way influenced by the movie *Cabaret*. The deco/decadent look was in, darling. (pleasant)

Two-Dollar Bills Phased out in 1966, reintroduced in 1976. The picture on the back of the '76 version was different from the original. Instead of Jefferson's Monticello, the new bill showed the famous painting of the signing of the Declaration of Independence. After the bill had been on the streets a few weeks, someone noticed that four guys in the painting were missing! (bobby) 🍀 Everyone who worked the cash register was flustered — there was no bin for the new bills. (lisa aa.) 🍀 Just remember to tear the corner off or carrying it around is bad luck. (darby) (See also SUSAN B. ANTHONY DOLLAR)

Ty-D-Bol Your toilet wasn't clean unless the water was blue. It did seem like a cool thing — that is, until the 1971 earthquake (when people didn't keep bottled water at home) and the neighbors kept coming over to our house to borrow the water from the toilet tank 'cause they had contaminated blue water and we didn't. Of course in the midst of this disaster they just wanted to make coffee with it. I got my first real insight into the plight of a caffeine addict. (darby) 🍀 Ty-D-Bol Man led a miserable life of stinkiness. (noël) 🍀 The Ty-D-Bol man had been in ads since the '60s. Bored housewife opens her tank to find a little guy in a rowboat. In the '70s, he got a motorboat. Then he filled it with lemons. Then, in one of the decade's most infamous ads, he appeared on a raft, complete with a calypso band. For a toilet-dwelling illusion, that guy got around. (bruce)

t

U

Underoos These were basically comic book superhero underwear for kids. My friend Zach used to wear the same Spiderman Underoos top to school every day. I always wondered when his mom had a chance to wash it. (jon) ❧ Underwear that was fun to wear! Weird commercials with kids standing around in stupid long underwear, some of them too old to be wearing such underwear, and most looking like they'd never be seen in such an embarrassing situation if they weren't getting paid so much money. (darby/don) ❧ I can, and still do, squeeze into mine, which means they *really* stretch. (lorraine)

Underwater Births Weird hippie concepts like this were usually introduced to me via "daring" episodes of sitcom TV. I learned about this when the defiant rebel Julie (Mackenzie Phillips) of *One Day at a Time* wanted to have her baby in the tub. (darby)

Underwater Tea Parties The only tea parties in which Americans participate. Young girls underwater, sitting on the bottom of the pool; fake cups and saucers and pinkies extended. (ju-ji)

Underwear with Days of the Week Scrawled Across the Butt Seven treasures. Every day of the week had a different design or pattern. My "Sunday" panties were lacy — for church, you know. (jes)

Union '76 Seems like they would have changed the name and color scheme of this orange gas station after the Bicentennial. Instead, they continued to give away promotional gifts with a fill-up. Nothing beats those orange Styrofoam antenna balls though. (winnie) (See also ORANGE)

Unisex Clothes or hairstyles that fit members of either sex. Seldom heard these days, it was a very common term in the '70s, especially for hair salons that served both women and men (a radical new idea at the time). Of course, jeans were then, and remain now, the classic item of unisex clothing. (candi)

Unprotected Sex with Strangers If only someone in high school had told us that what we innocently did without a second thought, like unprotected sex with strangers, free-basing at slumber parties, or "borrowing" cars before we knew how to drive, would one day be considered extremely dangerous and prohibited by a will to survive, we might have enjoyed it more. But who could have known? (nina) (See also AIDS)

Urban Cowboy How did this happen? All of a sudden in the very midst of a disco uprising, cowboys became chic. Cowboy hats were everywhere. I had one made of a funny white flexistraw material with a wire running along the outside of the brim so

John Travolta and Debra Winger

superthick (usually white) cowboy-ish belts; conch shell belts; tacky and big silver jewelry; bolos; cowboy boots worn with jeans tucked into them. Ugh. Instead of the classic cowboy look, this was more white-trash. You can probably still find it all new at a swap meet near you. I think the whole thing traumatized me in a lot of ways I haven't yet dealt with. (darby) ♣ This whole fad happened just as Texas was enjoying its reputation as an island of prosperity in the nationwide recession. Many who hoped to move there for the good life began their journey by dressing the part. One legacy of those times is this fondly recalled joke: Why is a cowboy hat like a hemorrhoid? Because sooner or later every asshole gets one. (bruce)

it could be shaped in the style that went best with my feathered hair. Also, it had a brown feather band that matched the brown feather roach clip that hung off the back. I tried hard to join the urban cowboys in my tight Sergio Valente jeans, but never really got it. I wanted to ride the mechanical bull, but I was like thirteen or something, too young for the many Gilley's-style cowboy bars that dotted Ventura Boulevard. I ditched the hat in a month but kept the roach clip. I still long to ride the bull. (jory) ♣ I don't know how to best describe this tragic period. Perhaps it all started with the movie of the same name ('80), but I remember the aftereffects long after the movie disappeared. You may recall the long denim skirts with the ruffly bottom (or sometimes they were gathered at three different spots around the skirt); the white overly puffed sleeved and ruffly blouses; the often

U.S. Festival It was this sad attempt to recreate Woodstock in the early '80s, somewhere in northern California, with bands like Van Halen, maybe Foreigner or Pat Benatar, whoever was big in '82–'83. It mixed New Wave and pseudo hard rock and a *whole lot* of hype. Reasonable crowds showed up but not what promoters anticipated, so it was sort of a fiasco. Bloom County did a parody of it that went on and on and on for months. (stymie)

U

V

Fernando Valenzuela Oh, Fernando. Was he good or what! Pitcher for the L.A. Dodgers in the '80s, Fernando was just pure joy to watch; this fuzzy little round guy throwing screwballs and striking out these monster hitters. There was nothing better. And the fans that came out to see Valenzuela, all the excited Mexican fans, would just be cheering, yelling, screaming, especially in the bleachers. It's probably very similar to what people feel about Nomo, but it's harder to talk baseball with the Japanese. (dad)

Valley Girl/Dude When it happened, we can't say fer sure. Us valley chicks were totally like *not* in the know as to the scariness to come. All of a sudden everything we were, everything we did and said, was blown out of proportion by one New Wave hit, "Valley Girl" ('82) by ultra-hip, ultra-dog Zappa teen Moon Unit (with the help of her daddy, Frank). Being that I spent a great portion of my formidable years in, like, pre-valley-girl-phenomenon Encino, I know that the song affected the val culture more than val culture actually affected the song. After the tune exploded outta Los Angeles, vals united together in one grody JAP (Jewish American Princess) fest and proudly took on the terms they were branded with. Suddenly we were all hooked to the catch phrases: Barf me out, Gag me with a spoon, Bitchin', Tubular, Gnarly, Awesome, To the max, and, like, I'm

soooo sure! To this day I *totally* think that skanky gel-head Zappa chick has a lot to answer for! (darby) ❧ In Malibu we were trained to hate vals because they made our beaches crowded, looked dorky, drove lame val cars like Camaros, Firebirds, and pickup trucks, had center-parted blow-dried hair, got sunburned, made traffic on P.C.H. hell, and imitated us locals, especially the way we talked. A Malibu accent is a mild version of what you probably think a val accent sounds like, a really laid-back overenunciation, sort of like a stoner. After the evil record came out, a lot of Malibu kids tried to lose theirs. But, I mean, *whatever*, like, who cares anyway? (riley) ❧ Moon Unit Zappa was just imitating Laraine Newman on *Saturday Night Live.* (mike s.) ❧ The locus of all val activity was definitely The Galleria, a mall in Sherman Oaks, California. This is where they went to buy their white pumps, their bitchin' miniskirts, and their little ankle socks — all on Daddy's credit card, of course. (ju-ji) (Note: Like, check out the movie *Valley Girl.*)

Van Conversions *Do It in a Van!* Only in the '70s could the fading passions for big cars and promiscuity collide to transform a lowly utility vehicle into a rolling icon. Once, vans were for deliveries and suspicious urban gypsies. Somewhere during the Something Decade they became transformed into trysting transports. What often looked like Scooby Doo's Mystery Machine was in fact a Make-out Machine. As the station wagon died at the hands of OPEC, those who needed room were left with only utilitarian vans. There is something deep in the American soul that cannot tolerate an empty space, and soon van doors were sprouting trippy air-brushed murals depicting the artist's fascination with the covers of Yes albums. On the inside, even the plainest vans often were encrusted with floor-to-ceiling shag carpeting. These cushy caverns were augmented by the addition of two small windows high on the sides. These could be shaped like portholes, dice, or that sexual deity, the Playboy Bunny. Everything about the properly "converted" van gave off a swinging sleazy sexual air. However, for the most part they were simply Winnebago wannabes. Imagine Greg Brady's attic pad on wheels, and you have the idea. Imagine a dank rec room that smells of spilled bong water, and you have the reality. (bruce)

Vans "Man, I need Vans!" Vans shoes were the coolest shoes at my elementary school. It was a matter of prestige to own a pair and we would not be caught dead in "imos" (imitation Vans). (karrin) Checkered or Hawaiian pattern were cool for skater gals and guys. Weird Al still wears them. Then again, he's still singing "Eat It." (wendy) These also came in different color combinations, whether it was hi-top or low-top or slip-on, and are still custom made if you so desire. When Sean Penn was still a nobody, his retarded surf-punk character Jeff Spicoli in *Fast Times at Ridgemont High* catapulted him into the limelight. It wasn't long before every nimrod including myself mimicked his high school rebel antics, ordering pizza in class and saying stuff like, "Hey, bud, let's party!" His fashion sense was to die for and his checkered slip-on Vans were proof positive of that.

(noël) We used to wear the white ones and draw checkerboards and write band names on them — then a couple of years later they started making them with checkerboard denim; took the fun out of it. (riley)

Variety Shows Before *Saturday Night Live* sort of rendered the format obsolete, everyone who was anyone for the requisite fifteen minutes or made a bad novelty song (whichever came first) had one of these: Captain and Tennille, Sonny and Cher, Donny and Marie, Tom Jones, Tony Orlando and Dawn, Helen Reddy, Mac Davis, Jim "Spiders and Snakes" Stafford. I say, let's bring 'em back! I can see it now: *Kim and Thurston's Comedy Hour, Mojo Nixon's Hee-Haw, Beck and Friends!* (gwynne) (See also CHEST HAIR, *DONNY AND MARIE,* and *PINK LADY*)

Velcro George de Mestral, a Swiss engineer, utilized the bounty of nature when he returned from a walk one day in 1948 with cockleburs clinging to his coat. He peered at them under a microscope and over the course of eight years used the technology to develop the hook-and-loop fastener. We know it as Velcro. (skylaire) There was nearly a riot when this invention hit the suburbs. Velcromania in Super Yarn Mart! (polly) Everyone went crazy over Velcro because of its space shuttle use. In the early '80s, the impact of NASA was nothing to scoff at. (jaz)

Velcro Shoe Wallets They were named Zippers; you could attach one around your laces and it had a small pocket which was just big enough to keep money, a house key, and, later, a lipstick. These were actually more useful for girls/women, who have to suffer not having pockets in their clothing. If I ever designed clothes for women there'd be secret agent pockets in everything, especially dresses. No need to carry around pocketbooks or for boyfriends to carry your stuff. This is one of those ancient customs that is still in effect, and I can't understand why there are no feminist riots over it. Why do women designers

Video Games

Arcade gaming exploded in the '70s and was represented in movie culture by such flicks as *Tommy* ('75), *Bad News Bears* ('76), and *Tilt!* (with Brooke Shields as the sassy preteen pinball wizard — '78). As the years progressed the action moved more from classic pinball to the new high-tech video games as witnessed in *Tron* ('82) and *The Last Starfighter* ('84). Many TV sitcoms made references to them as well, as in *Square Pegs* (when the geek guy was addicted) and *Silver Spoons* (he had his own arcade and even let Menudo play in it in one episode). After the advent of **Pong** — the first video game most of us ever played — the world was getting prepped for an onslaught. As time progressed these games went from the simplicity of the black and white **football** game, with the players being represented by Xs and Os, **Tank** and **Break-out,** to the more interest-

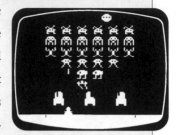

ing **Super Break-out,** the **Indy 500 car race,** and the amazing supernatural, super-intense **Space Invaders** (a lot of these were later made into those two-player sort of table versions as well). Space Invaders had lots of color, fast action, imagination, and some squirrely sound effects; a truly ground-breaking game. **Asteroids,** also in keeping with the prominent sci-fi theme, was a brisk challenging play. But somehow this slightly corny but cute game called **Pac-Man** (and its later counterpart **Ms. Pac-Man)** really became the king (and queen) of video games, standing the test of time beyond all others. Even today Ms. Pac-Man can hold her own against the modern kid's attention span, compared with most of the other old games, which are too flat, pixelated, and slow. It was a truly pivotal moment

where the doors seemed to explode open to the world of video games. When **Centipede** came out, I would leave early for school every single morning to play it at the 7-Eleven before the bus came to pick me up. And when **Tempest** emerged on the scene, its quick-paced manic frenzy thrilled me no end. Later, when I'd play it for free at Green Jelly's practice space, I realized how much more fun the game was when you had to pay for it. Around that time all those **Mario Brothers/Donkey Kong** type of games got real big, and I was moving on to more seedy afterschool play. **Marble Madness** (neat-o concept/great tunes), which I discovered with my pal Laura in a Berkeley pizza parlor on a crazy hit of L, was the last new video game I've really enjoyed, besides **Tetris** on the computer. When all the Street Fighter–type games eventually took over the arcades, I then found a real soft spot in my heart for all video games before them. (darby) ❧ My favorite old-school video game was called **Death Race,** where you were this little witch driving a car and had to run over people. When you got one, he/she would scream, turn into a tombstone, and the death song would play in moronic computer music. Some pathetic radical right winger probably had the game pulled off the market. (riley) ♣ **Q-bert,** a distant relative of Snorks, was one of the first really successful video arcade games where you could move around in 3-D space. (wendy) ♣ Other important games deserving a mention (some available on cartridge only): **Frogger, SNAFU, Bugertime, Defender, Berzerk, Pitfall, Demon Attack, Dragon's Lair, Adventure, Air and Sea Battle,** and **Zaxxon.** (See also ATARI, PAC-MAN FEVER, and *TRON*)

blindly follow the designs of men? Well, until the day it changes these have been brought back (by a company called Freestyle, outta Camarillo, California) — unfortunately they only really work well on sneakers and the like. (darby) ♣ There were also Kangaroos — shoes in the early '80s that featured a pouch for holding money and things. (dave) 🐾

Velcro Wallets The training-wheel version of the real-leather daddy wallet was this soft and thin Velcro variety. These were best with ugly brown-toned palm trees and suns or rainbows. The only cool brand was the aptly titled Ripper. (riley/jaz)

Vera Designer who made her way into every bathroom I ever visited. The orange, black, and brown prints on tissue boxes, picture prints, shower curtains, and scarves. (laurel) ♣ Don't forget those swirly-colored napkins. (bruce)

Vibrating Football Game (Coleco) It never ceases to amaze me that they actually marketed this thing and people bought it. Basically, you would spend enormous amounts of time setting up the player pieces and thinking up play strategies, and then you'd turn on the motor. The end result of most plays was that all the pieces would move wherever the hell the vibrations would take them (usually to the sidelines of the metal field), with one lucky individual in possession of the little metal football, which was attracted to the magnet in each figure's base. Just like the real game! It was pretty fun to watch the players move around in circles like they were possessed, but it lost its charm within minutes. My brother and I managed to break the spring-action throwing arm of one of the quarterbacks and lose both balls included with the set the first day we owned it. (creepy mike)

Videodrome David Cronenberg's 1983 thriller about a man's (James Woods) growing obsession with a bizarre cable TV interactive snuff show blew my mind! Debbie Harry, as his masochist lover, is divine! The special effects of the TV breathing and writhing are chilling! Watching it on video makes it all the more creepy, so rent it now to experience Cronenberg's insanely twisted mind. Also check out his freaky gyno-thriller *Dead Ringers* ('88) if you want to plunge into the depths of real sexual psychosis — and who doesn't? (nina)

Video Games Systems (Home Version) Atari, Pong/SuperPong (Atari), Bag-a-tel, Telestar (Coleco), Tele-pong, Conic, Nose t' Nose, Face-Off Hockey/Soccer (Executive Games), Fantasia 101, Video Sport, Heathkit, Odyssey (Magnavox — one of the earliest video game systems with screen overlays), Magnavox, Ricochet, Studio II (RCA), Tele-Match, Video Sport (Federal Transistor), TV Scoreboard (Radio Shack), Santron Gorilla Game (Santron), Video Action "Indy 500" (Universal Research Labs), Tournament (Unisonic), Video Sports (Venture Electronics), Superscore . . . (ju-ji)

V

Sample Viewmaster image

Viewmasters Soooo cool, but the fun was short-lived. I recently acquired an old one which I am rather proud of. They had reels for just about everything, although the real-life pictures were always superior to the cartoon ones. The precursor to virtual reality, I'm sure. I got to go places I had never been — Grand Canyon! New York! Disneyland! Jesus' birth! Yes, the good Christians got their soiled hands on this otherworldly toy and tried to inoculate us with not only the word of God, but his 3-D image as well. Those spikes through the hands of Jesus — Whew! Look out! You could put an eye out with one of them they were so lifelike! (morgan and ferris) ❀ Hunt around, and you will find 3-D Viewmaster reels for almost every '70s cartoon or kids' show. You haven't lived until you've seen *Scooby Doo, The Partridge Family,* or *S.W.A.T.* in 3-D! (bruce) ❀ I can't believe they still make these archaic toys! I have a *Pee-wee's Playhouse* disc. (riley) ❀ I always wanted to know, does Viewmaster porn exist? (adam s.)

Villa Alegre Early morning PBS kids' show with a multiculti, Spanish/English bilingual agenda. Very mid-'70s. The most memorable thing about it was its catchy song: Tra la la la la la la la la la la la Villa Alegre! (jon) (See also PBS)

Virginity I wanted to get rid of it, bad. I was only fourteen but figured I was already behind the rest of the world. I was worried about falling in love and obsessing over the guy, which seemed to accompany most first times. I was also slightly worried about being "good," so I figured I'd choose someone I would never want to talk to again, so neither of these things would matter. Properly lubed, I attended a popular/jock party one weekend and approached my victim, a grotesque senior. He was generally considered to be a stud. I don't remember what I said, but it didn't take long before we were out on the cliffs above the ocean, rolling around on a blanket under the stars. I sobered up awfully fast, but somehow my body went on auto pilot and he did the rest. I remember looking up at the stars and trying to remember each sensation as it happened. I filed every pain and pressure away to examine later, all the while fakely moaning and telling him how good it felt, like in all the books and movies. Afterward, we both wiped off, smoked a cigarette (me) and a doobie (him), and he drove me home. One step closer to freedom. (mikki) ❧ In the '70s, before we found out sex killed, there was nothing else to do, so everyone was losing their virginity at like fourteen or fifteen. (riley) ❧ I don't recall having mine, much less losing it. It's different with guys, you see. (bruce)

Vitamins *Flintstones* were ultimately the favorite of all kids. We also liked Spiderman, Choks (pillow-shaped), and Pals. My personal favorite was Monster vitamins. The usual brightly colored fruity-flavored children's vitamins, but shaped to look like rad monsters and they all had names. There was one called Screaming Mimi that was this girl pulling her own long hair straight up really hard while screaming in pain. (riley)

V.O. Visual orgasm. Said about a totally rad babe. "Hey bud, check out the major babage, V.O. to the max!" (jaz) (See also SAYINGS/SLANG)

V.P.L. Visible panty lines. This was once a major concern. (darby) ❧ Somebody told me that V.P.L. are very in now. (lisa aa.) ❧ No doubt fueled by modern women traumatized by thong panties, V.P.L. as a fashion statement also works with the whole '70s retro fashion idea. Wow, politically correct and fashion forward all at the same time! Low ridin', hip huggin' panties might look best for the straightforward V.P.L. statement, but why not try panties with ruffles over the bum to get the point across even more directly? (nina) (See also WEDGIES and XYZ)

V

W

Wacky Packages The ultimate bubble gum cards. Semi-gross, bitingly sarcastic parodies of the consumer society. Each card scoured some inane product whose ads cluttered the airwaves and our lives. Putting them on your binder was the boldest social statement a twelve-year-old could make. They gained my lasting respect when they put out a card parodying themselves. (bruce) ❧ Did you know that Mr. Hoity-toity Comic Art Man Art Speigelman did those Wacky Packs? I'm not altogether certain if he just did the art or the whole concept and execution or what. My brother and I plastered our bedroom doors and dresser drawers with those things. (ellen) ❧ Also had a rip-off: Krazy Labels. (howard)

Wait 'Til Your Father Gets Home

After the *Flintstones* and before *The Simpsons*, there was a syndicated cartoon that ran in prime time in many markets called *Wait 'Til Your Father Gets Home*. It featured the voices of Tom Bosley, Jack Burns, and several others. The dad was an Archie Bunker–type guy trying to deal with the wild and crazy times and with his hippie kid, and it was about as funny. The pilot episode appeared on *Love, American Style*. Later, this same pilot was done with a live cast, and starred Van Johnson: it didn't fly. (bruce) ♣ The humor was very similar in style to the early '90s animated series *The Critic* (ju-ji).

Walkman   Introduced in the U.S. in 1979 by Sony, the personal portable stereo truly changed the way people live their daily lives. Two things impressed people at the time: how tiny the main tape deck was and how good the stereo sound was from the coin-sized ear pieces. People were accustomed to the giant earmuff-style headphones popular up to that time. (candi) ♣ Portable tape decks that allowed fitness freaks to jog around town listening to Sheena Easton's "Morning Train" on foamy headphones. A significant jump from those ugly Radio Shack transistor radios that only pulled in AM. These were created and perfected by Sony around 1980. The first kid on the block that I knew to have one was Mark Eads, a spoiled brat who got everything — from pinball machines to nice BMX bikes to an endless supply of Pepsi and Totino's party pizza — all because his dad made bank working for Union Carbide. The first tape I heard on a Walkman was Mark's copy of REO Speedwagon, and boy, was it grand. Although hundreds of other companies have developed similar machines since, people still refer to any of these devices as a Walkman. (noël)

Wallpaper, "Fuck The . . ."   My dad had this in his bathroom. I spent a lot of time reading who should be fucked (tooth fairy, mailman, relatives, et cetera). (laurel)

Andy Warhol   Vapid, prolific albino from Pittsburgh. He became the father of pop art, a compulsive shopper, a media whore, and an enigma (and, thus, a good role model). He was a painter, a filmmaker, a scenester, a celebrity, an evil hag. Synonymous with all that is New York: emotionless, hip, and disposable. Shot in 1968 by Valerie Solanis, after which his artistic vision became a grotesque need for fame and wealth. (skylaire) ♣ I wrote my twelfth-grade term paper on Warhol. For precisely all the reasons listed so eloquently above, he was my patron saint. I scoured books of photos of the Factory days while aurally drowning in Velvet Underground — Nico, Viva, Ultra Violet, Joe Dallesandro, Lou Reed, and the divine Edie Sedgwick. The glitter off Warhol's twisted aesthetic shone on them all so brightly. Plus, it was brilliant the way he moved through the '60s, '70s, and '80s perversely embodying the basest American values of the times. I don't think anyone needs to dig too deep to find that part of themselves that wishes they had been Warhol — waved past lines of people into Studio 54 with Liza Minnelli, Bianca Jagger, and Halston in tow, coked out of his mind, looking fabulous and turning everything he touched into million-dollar works of art. Pure genius! (nina)

Andy Warhol and the glitterati

W

John Waters

John Waters invented punk rock, laying the foundation for the whole terminally parodic, wiseass cynical attitude attributed to the so-called X Generation. Straight outta Baltimore's Dreamland Studios festered the petri dish of talent responsible for still-outrageous films *Multiple Maniacs, Pink Flamingos* (among the most profitable movies ever released, alongside other retro favorites *Night of the Living Dead* and *Deep Throat*), *Female Trouble,* and *Desperate Living.* Waters took the upsy-downsy worldview of Andy Warhol and the low-budget sensationalist filmmaking techniques of Herschell Gordon Lewis and Russ Meyer, employed his sociopathic, screwball drug buddies Mink Stole, Mary Vivian Pierce, Cookie Mueller, David Lochary, Edie "the Egg Lady" Massey, and, most notoriously, three-hundred-pound drag queen Divine as the stars, and created some of the funniest, most irreverent comedies of our time.

He slaughtered the sacred cows of not only his parents' conservative generation but his own reactionary-liberal one as well. He ridiculed hippies, artists, sexual deviants, loadies, and experimental filmmakers right alongside God, country, and grandmothers. He cultivated the fashion-up-your-ass trash-chic of campy '50s leopard print, rhinestone cat glasses, overprocessed blue hair, and so on that would later set apart punk rock's style from its father "glitter" look. American pop-culture nihilism was defined by his film characters' rhetoric: crime is beauty, flaws and deformities are hip, filthiness is next to godliness, and everybody except you is an idiot. Though his characters were clearly parodic, their underlying message advocates shedding your shame and living your so-called flaws, making them your gimmick, your trademark, your shtick. Divine (née Glenn Milstead), for example, took the derogatory labels "fat" and "fag" and turned herself into an icon, the most garish, obese, yet glamorous and coolest drag queen in the world. This was no small feat in the early '70s, an era of rigid and judgmental conformity, where everyone was obsessed with fitting in by achieving an unrealistic standard of physical perfection dictated by sadistic, misogynist, old Hollywood–obsessed fashion designers.

Waters's films helped us face our fear of the gross. Maybe you had a visible booger last week, but Divine ate dogshit — on purpose, yet. Incest, shrimping, burglary, buggery, bestiality, puke-eating, cop-killing, and furniture-licking are blithely portrayed in the Dreamland films. Painful pop-psych taboos like child abuse, incest, teen pregnancy, anorexia, and dysfunctional marriage were bandied about like knock-knock jokes, demystifying and deflating them. Additionally, John Waters was a feminist filmmaker. All his films focus on female characters, with the exception of *Cry-Baby,* (coincidentally?) his artistic nadir. Influenced by the girl-delinquent and women's prison genres, Waters empowers his protagonists with the assertiveness, aggression, and violence that would only appear predictably boorish in men. A testament to Russ Meyer's influence, too, gender role reversal is a pet source of gags. Motherhood in general and neurotic mother-daughter relationships in particular are explored at great length in *Female Trouble, Desperate Living, Polyester,* and *Hairspray,* while fathers are either written out of the scripts early or reduced to one-joke afterthoughts. It is no coincidence that Waters also professes an early obsession with Disney's notorious animated psychodramas like *Snow White.*

As each successive film increased Waters's popularity, his later movies relied less on gross-outs. In 1988's *Hairspray,* which launched the career of prettier Ricki Lake, he proved his ability to make a hip and hilarious movie without the shock. I dare go so far as to call it an important film, as it is the first to equate racism with weightism. Unfortunately, it's the last memorable film he's made to date. Whether it was the demise of Divine a few weeks after its release, or the inner workings and outer gloss of big-time Hollywood not agreeing with his style, *Cry-Baby* and *Serial Mom* are virtually devoid of classic quotables. But then again, Fellini had his off days too. Other Waters flicks: *Roman Candles; Fag in a Black Leather Jacket; Eat Your Make-Up; The Diane Linkletter Story; Vintage Waters; Mondo Trash.* (gwynne) (See also SCENTED STICKERS)

The Warriors Walter Hill made a low-budget surreal film of urban gangs. It died at the box office but hipper critics whipped it into a cult film. Seen today, it is a wigged-out bit of '70s oddness. I for one screamed, "Warriors, come out and playyayy" into any echoey space for several months. Hollywood never understood why the cult film worked, so they just gave Walter $35 million to go make another one. The resulting *Streets of Fire* didn't even work as a cult object. (bruce)

Water Pics Another one of those technological advances that the world became enchanted with. Everyone bought one (they must have had good ads for it), but soon after, it was only the kids who really used the thing. I still admire the simple design. (darby) They just reminded me too much of all that gross stuff they do when you go to the dentist. I didn't even want to look at them. (gwynne)

Water Toys The Slip 'n' Slide was a long yellow rubbery sheet that attached to the hose and oozed water. Jump on it and slide like a wounded jet liner, wee! It killed the grass under it, leaving your lawn looking like a UFO had landed. The Water Wiggle, a squirming spermlike thing that attached to the hose and just flew around, getting you and everything else very wet. The goofy eye decals on it were scary. My favorite was the Water Weenie. Built like an industrial-sized condom, you filled it from the hose and were able to douse siblings and barbecues from a safe distance. (bruce)

The Wedge Awful hairdo popularized by hideous Olympic skater Dorothy Hamill. I got one of these before going to camp ('76) when I was thirteen and wondered why none of the boys who'd had crushes on me the summer before would speak to me. (allison) Seems to have made a huge comeback with '90s indie-rock boys. (gwynne) (See also THE SHAG)

Dorothy Hamill and the wedge

CDs, and tapes than any other person on this planet." (darby) ✿ Al is the chameleon of our time, a man who magically captures the essence of the songs and the singers he portrays. Oftentimes, as with his Nirvana "Smells Like Nirvana," his video parodies might get as much MTV play as the original. Besides being a staple in retro hell music and film, he's equally famous for his curly 'fro and his closet full of hundreds of various assortments of Vans sneakers and Hawaiian shirts. (ju-ji) ✿

Weird Science This movie was the embodiment of everything I had ever wished for as a teenager. Two boys make a perfect woman on their computer, and she helps them score with hot-looking popular girls that never gave them the time of day before. It was because of this movie, *Sixteen Candles,* and *The Breakfast Club* that Anthony Michael Hall developed a geek complex that ended with him doing bad action movies like *Johnny Be Good* and *Out of Bounds* (which did have a kind of cool Siouxsie and the Banshees performance scene) in an attempt to show us all how cool and manly he really was. (howard) (See also BRAT PACK)

The Wet Look A term coined by Sebastian hair company for their product Wet, this was the vogue hairstyle that moved '80s big hair into a more stylish sleak post-punky look. (jaz)

We've Got a Fuzzbox and We're Gonna Use It The greatest all-girl band *ever!* Magz, Jo, Tina, and Vix claimed they couldn't play, but they somehow had it all: great hooks, humor, clever lyrics, amazing four-part harmonies, a high-energy stage show, and green-and-pink mohawks. By their second album, however, they'd gone "house" (British euphemism for arty disco), dyed their hair back to normal colors, and tried to be the sex kittens they'd so adamantly mocked in the past. (gwynne)

Wedgies Sandals with solid, angled platform soles. Also, what someone gleefully gave you by yanking your pants up real high so that your undies went way up your butt. (nina) ✿ Wedgies can be perfected by strapping the waistband of the victim's underwear to a space shuttle that's about to blast off. Timing is of the essence. (noël) (See also KORK-EASE and V.P.L.) ✿

Weird Al Pop-music prankster who went from youngster accordion player to Dr. Demento Top 10 when he was just 16. Most famous for his re-creations of such songs as the Kinks' "Lola" (mutated into "Yoda"), Michael Jackson's "Beat It" (transformed into "Eat It"), and the parody of the Knack's "My Sharona" (becoming Al's first monster hit, "My Bologna"). The Knack were actually partly responsible for initiating the idea of Capitol's releasing the then demo-only release on their label. From there it's rock 'n' roll history. As the Doctor himself said in the liner notes for Al's boxed set (!): "Alfred Matthew Yankovic is rock music's greatest humorist. Since his first LP came out in 1983, he has sold more funny records,

Wham! Before George Michael became an obvious bore, he was in the two-boy group Wham! They had a manically popular tune, "Young Guns" ('83), with the lyrics "young guns havin' some fun, crazy ladies keep 'em on the run." Anyway, it was big MTV and *all* the girls knew the words back then. (darby) ❧ Don't forget "Careless Whispers." (wendy) ❧ "Wake me up before you go-go, I'm not planning on going solo." Which is, of course, exactly what George Michael did. Leaving his never-to-be-seen-dancing-in-white-pants-again partner Andrew Ridgeley in the dust, he went on to shake his butt all the way to a number-one record, *Faith* ('87), a slew of hit songs, and being one of the biggest sex symbols of the '80s. Well, at least he tried to be. (nina) (See also CHOOSE LIFE)

Wham-O Toys Sure, Mattel made all the stuff you wanted, but Wham-O made all the stuff you *needed.* They were a small toy company with really big ideas, always right there with the right fad at the right time. These were the geniuses behind the hula hoop, the superball, the Frisbee, monster bubble, and many many others. Wham-O's cheaply produced ads always showed mischievous kids exacting revenge on adults, big sisters, and other banes of existence. The exploding Wham-O logo was the very stamp of kid cool. And the exploding Wham-O wind gun was what every cool kid wanted. How harmful could a powered puff of air be? Very, it turned out. Especially if you shot it into an ear. Who else would market a toy like that, or like Disappear-O, an economy-sized bottle of disappearing blue ink that came with its own tiny squirt gun? In the TV ad, a gang of gun-toting kids ambush an unsuspecting mom, dousing her wind-dried bed sheets with streak after joyous streak of Disappear-O. TV mom laughed when the stuff came right off; my real mom did not. You just knew Wham-O stuff was cool when your parents refused to buy you any of it. They might try to pawn an action figure off on you, but Wham-O's incessant ads told you to yell, "*I want Wham-O!*" and ya know what? It worked! (bruce) ❧ Wheel-O's were *the* Wham-O must-have. I never did figure out how to use the damn thing, but then again, I could never get my Slinky to walk down the stairs either. (gwynne) (See also SUPER ELASTIC BUBBLE PLASTIC)

Where Did I Come From? "By this time, the man wants to get as close to the woman as he can, because he's feeling very loving to her. And to get really close the best thing he can do is lie on top of her and put his penis inside her, into her vagina." The means by which too large a majority of American youth learned about sex. It's how I learned. My parents handed me this thing — I was at least nine and still clueless — and I laughed and laughed in utter disbelief. I still can't believe they ever *did it.* (darby) ❧ Mine also got me the sequel about puberty, *What's Happening to Me?* I don't feel like either one helped much, especially since the penises in the cartoons looked nothing like real penises. The daddy didn't even have testicles. (gwynne)

Where's the Beef? Old lady Clara Peller made Wendy's stock go up for her repetitive inquiry commercial where she can't seem to find the shrunken beef patty in a giant hamburger bun. (howard) ❧ This crotchety old lady also had her own spaghetti sauce to boot, but I didn't bother to check its beef contents. Note: The phrase "Where's the beef?" was actually used in a debate between Democrats running in the 1984 presidential campaign. (noël) ❧ The first Democrat to start using it was Gary Hart, and we know where he put his beef. (bruce) ❧ Since he couldn't find *his* beef, Reagan also used this line to smooth over awkward moments of memory lapse. (ju-ji)(See also SCANDALS)

The Whiners Joe Piscopo and Robin Duke in *SNL* sketch about a depressive couple, Doug and Wendy Whiner, who had numerous health problems and would talk by whining. (howard) (See also *SATURDAY NIGHT LIVE*)

Wife-Swapping Unlike many adult things I couldn't wait to try, I've never wanted to go near this one. I'd probably get stuck with a friend's fat, hairy, or mustachioed spouse. This is still done, but has the more P.C.-hip term "swinging." (winnie)

Larry Wilcox I just saw him on public access selling some industrial sunscreen, and he still looks as cute as when he was pinned up in my locker. Screw Ponch, give me John! (bruce)

Paul Williams Short blond guy who wrote "We've Only Just Begun" and the *Love Boat* theme song (and appeared on the show like a million times . . . just like everyone else who appeared on the show). Recently my sister was dating his cousin, and Paul sang the *Love Boat* song on her answering machine. He was also brilliant as the devil in *Phantom of the Paradise*. (jon) ❀ In a video for the song "November Rain," Guns N' Roses singer Axl Rose looked very similar to Paul Williams during this one scene in which he is mourning the loss of his wife, Stephanie Seymour. Rose-tinted glasses intact. (noël)

Willy Wonka and the Chocolate Factory This movie was *super*. Everybody gets what they deserve, and the future is safe for a chocolate genius to blossom once more. (bridget) ❀ My favorite scene is when everyone is on a boat hurtling through a dark tunnel. They go past giant images of reptiles and insects crawling out of *skulls!* During all of this, Wonka recites an eerie rhyme that could be our generation's epitaph, "There's no *earthly* way of knowing which direction they are going! There's no knowing where they're rowing, or which way the river's flowing!" Only in the '70s would a kids' movie show so much greed and mayhem visited upon kids. I used to have my own Willy Wonka chocolate factory. I made little candy bars in the W molds and wrapped them up in their own wrappers, complete with golden tickets. (bruce) (See also ROALD DAHL)

Wings Long bangs worn flipped outward, wings were the halfway point between the generic long 'n' silky Greg Allman hairdo and the hard-to-maintain feathered Farrah shag. Also the name of Linda McCartney's tremendously popular band, as well as a mediocre '80s movie and today part of a '90s sanitary napkin. (gwynne)

Wispies Thin "wispy" bangs. My hair was too curly for 'em, but all the popular girls got the look and tied their heart-printed shoelaces around their heads to accent them . . . *and didn't they look sweet!* (darby) (See also SHOELACES)

Witch Movies Around the time of the feminist uprising there were a number of movies with psycho-female women with evil supernatural powers — and I was wondering if this was just a coincidence. (darby) (See also HYSTERICAL-WOMEN ROLES)

Katarina Witt Sure, Dorothy Hamill broke hearts everywhere and popularized that haircut, but for me, Katarina Witt is the most glamorous and distinctive figure skater of the century. Besides winning gold medals in the 1984 and 1988 Olympics (who can forget this East German's blatantly sexy interpretation of *Carmen?*), Witt took skating to another level beyond athletic jumps and spins. Unlike many of the narcissistic, upper-class skaters', Witt's performances revealed a conscience, whether it was as a German skating to the *Schindler's List* soundtrack or her anti-war dance that commented on the Bosnian civil war. Not only is she politically correct, but she is so gorgeous in her red lacy costumes that I am hopelessly in love with her. (falling james)

The Wiz The *Phantom of the Opera* of the '70s; *Cats* was *The Wiz* of the '80s. (winnie) A future midnight movie classic! (bruce) A movie totally ruined by what's her name, that woman from the Supremes. Imagine, in the Broadway play the girl was fourteen, fifteen, but they wouldn't take her, they had to take a hag who looked like she was just getting over a bout of bulimia. Then to top it off, in the end of that movie you see one of the greatest singers of all time, Lena Horne, singing next to Diana Ross. No, Diana Ross did not belong in that movie. (dad) Oh come on, it's like the black *Whatever Happened to Baby Jane?* (gwynne) Diana Ross was my patron diva by the time I could open my mouth to lip-synch "Touch Me in the Morning." Seeing her *and* Michael Jackson (though I can't remember which one actually played Dorothy) "easin' on down the road" rocked my pre-teen world! So let's get it straight, daddy-o, Miss Ross is always in the house! (nina) (See also *MAHOGANY* and NIPSEY RUSSELL)

Wonderama Flashback to the last scene of the show, where the special chosen child got to pick one of the fake nut containers that had those spring snakes which flew out if you were a loser and a bouquet of fake flowers connected to the lid if you were a winner. I always wondered why I wasn't special enough to be on this show, or *Romper Room,* or *Zoom,* or even *New Zoo Revue* for that matter — but I was too scared of the answer to ever ask. These types of old-style Bozo shows were still popular in the '70s. (darby) (See also BOB McALLISTER)

The Wonderful World of Disney One of the most important TV shows, which we watched every single Sunday night without fail and that I'm certain influenced us greatly, but what were they? Old Disney movies? Newer ones with animals? It's strange how something so essential just didn't stick at all. (ju-ji)

Wonder Twins Two teenage cartoon characters on *Super Friends* (ABC), a brother-and-sister team with special powers. When they wanted to change into their superhero selves they stuck out their fists, put their rings together, and shouted, "Wonder Twin powers, activate!" Then the sister would yell, "Shape of [any kind of animal]!" And the brother would say, "Form of [any form of water]!" For example, she'd end up a clutzy large bird carrying a bucket of her brother as water. They'd inevitably get caught by the bad guys or botch the job in some way. We, as millions of kids, would put on rings and act out their routine and pretend to turn ourselves into these sorry excuses for superheroes. (selina/darby) Asexual superheroes with Asian characteristics and lavender outfits. They had a blue monkey called Gleek (did they ever spank him?), who was a banana-munching nutcase. The term *gleek* is now used to describe the ability to expel a fine stream of saliva between one's front teeth. (noël) (See also CARTOONS)

Wonder Woman *"Wonder Woman!*
Wonder Woman! . . . In your satin tights, fighting for
your rights." I don't know if this TV show starring
Lynda Carter was intended, like *Charlie's Angels*, to
provide a positive role model for girls by making a
woman the superhero. As a boy, I just noticed that
Carter looked great in that satin costume. More
important, someone was being tied up in almost
every episode, thus introducing me to the sleazy,
seamy world of bondage and sadomasochism! (falling
james) ❀ Dads loved her. Lynda epitomized the full-
figured male fantasy at the time. (darby)

Woodsy Owl In about 1974
Smokey Bear (not Smokey *the* Bear)
introduced America to his pal Woodsy
Owl. Woodsy, with his large scary eyes
and green Robin Hood suit, had arrived
to help us all fight pollution. He left us
with nothing more insightful than the
jingle "Give a Hoot, Don't Pollute!,"
and a song that went, "Never be a dirty
bird in the city, or in the woods, help
keep America looking good [hoot
hoot]." The whole goal was to get
America clean in time for her 200th
birthday. (bruce)

World's Finest Chocolate The makers
of the chocolate that you schlepped for a buck a bar to
raise money for band, flag team, sports, key club, and
various other geeky organizations. There was usually
a coupon for Burger King or somewhere inside the
wrappers as an added incentive. We preferred the
overprocessed animal-byproduct pepperoni sticks.
(morgan and ferris)

Lynda Carter, superhero

X

X-Men Once the punk alternative to all the bloated old DC superhero comics. (dave) 🐿

XYZ eXamine Your Zipper. (noël) ♣ PDQ: Pretty Darn Quick. (lisa aa.) (See also V.P.L.)

4

Yellow Ribbons Precursor to the red ribbons worn by celebrities at awards ceremonies to show their sympathy for AIDS-related things, the yellow ribbons expressed sympathy for hostages and other victims of war and terrorism. The connection between trees and hostages remains a bit vague despite Tony Orlando and Dawn's frighteningly catchy love song on the subject. "Oh, tie a yellow ribbon 'round that old oak tree / It's been three long years, do you still love me?" (jaz) ♣ People started tying ribbons around trees in their front yards in honor of the Iranian hostages held during Carter's presidency. The news didn't give it that much coverage, probably because those people were like the ones who fly that M.I.A./P.O.W. flag in their yards today. (jeff)

Yes and Know Invisible Ink Game and Quiz Books Hours and hours of "by-yourself enjoyment" for ages 12–112. The answers are all in invisible ink, which you could make appear by running the Magic Pen over 'em. Some of the games include baseball, bingo, hangman, fleet, ultra-bowl, twenty-one, and a few mystery/clue things. These are still around — look on those dusty shelves in the back of bookstores. (ju-ji)

"You're Soooo Gay" This was an obligatory term used to refer to anyone being supremely retarded or geeky. I really understood the perversions of P.C. when I was visiting friends in S.F. in the late '80s and said it (as I had for the previous ten years) and was immediately chastised — the idea being that I was prejudiced and insensitive. Sheesh, I never thought about it before, and they had my utmost sympathy, for a few days, until I realized I never once thought of gay to mean homosexual. (darby) (See also RETARDED and SAYINGS/SLANG)

"You're So Vain" The big mystery was who Carly Simon was singing this song about — some say James Taylor, most say Mick Jagger. For men, the big mystery was who the song "Ruby Tuesday" was about. (ju-ji) ♣ The song features Mick Jagger on back-up vocals, that's why everyone thinks the song is about him. Supposedly it's actually about Warren Beatty. (falling james) ♣ Which I can believe from reading that book *You'll Never Make Love in This Town Again*. (darby)

You're Special We grew up being told that we were all special. People blamed society for any rotten apple. All these people being told since birth that they're okay and just as wonderful as anyone else, *regardless* of whether or not this was true. So today you see all these worthless idiots who are brainwashed into believing they're unique, and now they don't even need to prove it, least of all to themselves. (darby) ♣ In the mid '70s, *Captain Kangaroo* aired a series of five-minute cartoons called *The Most Important Person in the Whole Wide World*. Each episode always got around to informing us that this VIP was none other than "You, and you hardly even know you!" Anybody wondering where the self-contained and self-absorbed Generation X'ers come from would do well to blow the dust off this ditty. I'm sure it was a pioneering work in the field of self-esteem, but this kind of smug '70s niceness did us far more harm than good. The Aquarian journey of self-discovery may well have been fine for drop-outs and divorcées. However, children dragged down this path found it a long and lonely ride of disconnected relativism that led them nowhere. No developing latchkey kid should ever be told that they have to be "their own best friend." Today America is an amalgam of special

people and their special needs, a nation with issues that can feel anything but do nothing. Remember this, kids, feeling good is *not* the same as being good. Wake up before you grow up! (bruce) ☘ "God doesn't make junk." (bridget) (See also #1)

Yuck   Mighty Man's dog, Yuck, wore a doghouse on his head because he was so horrifically ugly. Whenever they got into a jam, Yuck would lift up his house, exposing his head, and everyone would run screaming. We never got to see his face, all we saw were a few strands of hair and the back of his balding head. (jaz) (See also CARTOONS)

Yuppies   What rich '80s ex-preppies were called. I think a lot of them sprouted out of the make-it-rich-quick stock-market whirl — but most are just the freeloaders/big-ego kids of the upper class. (ju-ji) ☘ *Yuppies* is short for "young urban professionals." Does that make successful punks of today Puppies (punk urban professionals)? (noël)

Z

The Z Channel One of the first cable all-movie channels, Z Channel was bitchin', being the only channel that showed things like *Myra Breckinridge, Ladies and Gentleman, the Fabulous Stains,* and *The Seventh Seal,* followed by its ten-minute parody *The Dove.* Also showed weird animated shorts between movies, like *The Big Snit.* (gwynne) ✿ A true movie lover's channel that could only have existed in L.A. When Z Channel went under, the guy behind it murdered his wife and shot himself in the head. Yet another true Hollywood tale of glamour, greed, and grief. (bruce) ✿ What the rich kids' houses had. It was long before music videos, so between feature films they would show short-subject movies and strange animation, including this cool animation short to the "Banana Boat Song" by Harry Belafonte and my favorite short ever: *Quasi at the Quackadero.* (riley)

Ziggy The wimpiest plebe of all time, Ziggy was your basic square (although he was quite amorphous), leading a life riddled with failure. Always one to evoke some kind of pity, he found his way into newspapers and greeting cards and into the hearts of millions of mushy people. I've actually heard people debate over whether or not Ziggy had genitals to begin with. Obviously had a profound effect on Morrissey's self-indulgent songwriting. (noël)

Zipper Wax/Hook For the time when jeans were too tight to put on without lying down. The zipper wax helped lube the zipper and the hook was to help get a grasp on it to pull the fucker up. My dad says he actually sold these fancy items in his clothing store. (darby)

Zips These shoes went by the very enticing slogan of Zips Big Z, promising that you could outrun anyone in these, especially if you drew a big Z in the dirt with your toe first. My husband swears I made this up, but maybe his mom didn't shop at Pic and Pay! (jessica a.) (See also SHOES)

Zoom! Between Fanny Doodle, "The Cat Came Back" song, and Miss Mary Mac, kids learned more than just the zip for Boston, Mass. (02134) (katy) ✿ I learned that it was possible to eat lemons, 'cause the littlest girl on the show did and shocked all the other kids. (ju-ji) ✿ *Zoom!* or *The Stepford Children?* Horrible Boston-based PBS kids' program in which child prisoners (all wore matching striped polo shirts) played boring games, acted nice around each other and kids with handicaps, and generally behaved themselves. (nick)

Zotz   "Carmella gusto uva frizzante." An innocent candy gem on the outside, but with explode-in-your-mouth jizz inside! Yum! (morgan and ferris) ❧ What a nice way to end. Zotz epitomized the fun in candy, and the intense fun in life kids looked for. They packed a punch that'd make your eyes water. You'd stick it in and the fizzle would ooze out harsh, yet nice and slow, or you'd crack it in half and let your tongue attack the fuzz foaming up in your mouth until you'd drool sweet sticky tart. Don't you dare compare them with the revamped version today. They're not the same, only one-third the fizz (I think they're still scared of the whole Mikey Pop Rocks propaganda). Or maybe they're just cheap. Or maybe my memory of them just supersedes the reality — which is probably the case for half the shit in this book. Anyway, whatever the reason, they're not worth your time, and the candy part tastes stale for some reason. Came in pops as well. Toodles. (darby)

Resource Material and Recommended Reading

Zines

Ben Is Dead magazine is available from P.O. Box 3166, Hollywood, CA 90028 (www.benisdead. com). Sample copies are $5 (send checks or m.o.s made out to *Ben Is Dead*), and a 32¢ stamp for full catalogue. Please specify issue you want or we'll send the most recent. You can get our whole darn retro series (three issues at 150 pages each!) — for just $15.

Bunnyhop: *Ben Is Dead*'s softer and fluffier little brother zine edited by *Retro Hell* contributor Noël Tolentino. Sample copies $6 to P.O. Box 423930, San Francisco, CA 94142-3930.

Chip's Closet Cleaner: *Playboy* editor Chip Rowe's intelligent, completely independent side project. Sample copies $4 to P.O. Box 11967, Chicago, IL 60611.

Cometbus: One of the longest-running zines around (since 1981 — and the editor isn't even thirty yet) and still totally inspirational. Sample copies $2.50 from BBT, P.O. Box 4279, Berkeley, CA 94704.

Creepy Mike's Omnibus of Fun: A rip-roarin' good time for all, including some fun oddball Retro Hell reminiscing. Sample copies $2 to Mike Raspantini/Clownhead Productions, P.O. Box 983, Buffalo, NY 14213-0983.

Funk N' Groove: One of zinedom's funnest contributions to the world of Retro Hell, written by '80s experts Morgan and Ferris. Sample copies $3 to P.O. Box 471881, San Francisco, CA 94147-1881.

Genetic Disorder: More punk rock satanic than retro but that's why we love it. Sample copies are $3 to P.O. Box 15237, San Diego, CA 92175.

It's a Wonderful Lifestyle: Candi Strecker writes extensively about the 1970s in her dedicated zine. Sample copies $4 to P.O. Box 515, Brisbane, CA 94005-0515.

Scaredy-Cat Stalker: Fun stalking stuff, from *E.T.*'s Henry Thomas to Mac Caulkin. Sample copies $2 c/o Krista Garcia, 5535 N.E. Gilsan #5, Portland, OR 97213.

Thrift Score zine: By thrift-store princess Al Hoff. Sample copies $2 to P.O. Box 90282, Pittsburgh, PA 15224.

Comics

Ellen Forney, *I Was Seven in '75*. Fab comics, direct from the source: $7 to P.O. Box 23368, Seattle, WA 98102.

Seth, *It's a Good Life, If You Don't Weaken* (Canada: Drawn & Quarterly, 1996)

Joe Matt, *Peep Show, the Cartoon Diary of Joe Matt* (Canada: Kitchen Sink Press, 1991)

A few other necessary comics read during this book's production: **Blue Hole, Cuckoo, Definition,**

Dirty Plotte, Eightball, Grit Bath, Hate, Johnny the Homicidal Maniac, Optic Nerve, and *Tart.*

Books

Steve Hagar, *Art After Midnite* (New York, St. Martin's Press, 1986)

Jonathan Price, *The Best Thing on TV, Commercials* (New York: Penguin, 1978)

David Thomson, *A Biographical Dictionary of Film,* third edition (New York: Alfred A. Knopf, 1996)

David Wallechinsky and Amy Wallace, *The Book of Lists* (Boston: Little, Brown and Company, 1993)

Connie Eble, *College Slang 101* (Connecticut: Spectacle Lane Press, 1989)

Tim Brooks and Earle Marsh, *The Complete Directory to Prime Time Network TV Shows,* third edition (New York: Ballantine Books, 1985)

Lisa Carver, *Dancing Queen: A Lusty Look at the American Dream* (New York: Owl Books/Henry Holt, 1996)

Jim Hougan, *Decadence: Radical Nostalgia, Narcissism, and Decline in the Seventies* (New York: William Morrow and Co., 1975)

George C. Kohn, *The Encyclopedia of American Scandal* (New York: Facts on File)

Douglas Brode, *The Films of the Eighties* (New York: Citadel Press/Carol Publishing, 1990)

Mark Frauenfelder and Carla Sinclair, ed., *The Happy Mutant Handbook* (New York: Riverhead Books, 1995)

Leonard Maltin, ed., *Leonard Maltin's 1997 Movie & Video Guide* (New York: Signet/Penguin Group, 1996)

Ira A. Robbins, ed., *The New Trouser Press Record Guide,* third edition (New York: Collier Books/Macmillan Publishing Co., 1989)

Pagan Kennedy, *Platforms: A Microwaved Cultural Chronicle of the 1970s* (New York, St. Martin's Press, 1994)

Theodore Modis, *Predictions: Society's Telltale Signature Reveals the Past and Forecasts the Future* (Simon & Shuster, 1992)

Lester Bangs, *Psychotic Reactions and Carburetor Dung* (New York: Vintage Books/Random House, 1987)

Frank Mankiewicz and Joel Swerdlow, *Remote Control: Television and the Manipulation of American Life* (New York: Times Books, 1978)

Norm N. Nite, *Rock On: The Illustrated Encyclopedia of Rock 'N' Roll* (New York: Thomas Y. Crowell Publishers, 1978)

Andrew J. Edelstein and Kevin McDonough, *The Seventies: From Hot Pants to Hot Tubs* (New York: Dutton/Penguin Group, 1990)

Matthew Rettenmund, *Totally Awesome '80s* (New York: St. Martin's Griffon Press, 1996)

Derek Elley, ed., *Variety Movie Guide '97* (Great Britain: Bath Press, 1996)

Fred Davis, *Yearning for Yesteryear: A Sociology of Nostalgia* (New York: Free Press/Macmillan Publishing, 1979)

Joanne Price, ed., *You'll Never Make Love in This Town Again* (Los Angeles: Dove Books, 1995)

8-Tracks

For more info, try http://pobox.com/~abbot/8track — or write for a year subscription to the paper version by sending $8 ($2 for a sample — checks made out to Russ Forster) to: 8-TM Publications, P.O. Box 14402, Chicago, IL 60614-0402. There's also a funny but long video entitled *So Wrong, They're Right* available on VHS, Beta, and PAL for $25.

Newsgroups

Alt.70s and Alt.80s are a good start. A consistent stream of "Oh my god, do you remember"s, which seem to replay themselves every six months. Great way to get your Retro Hell questions answered.

Record Labels

Ben Is Dead's "Kiddie Comp" is packed with recordings people made when they were fourteen years old or younger. Includes contributions from lots of talented-as-children unknowns plus some underground heroes, like Ms. Vaginal Cream Davis, Laura from Superchunk, Tracii Guns (L.A. Guns), Theo from the Lunachicks, Brad Laner from Medicine, and even an unreleased song by Brandon Cruz with his then–TV dad Bill Bixby, from the period when they both starred on *The Courtship of Eddie's Father*. $10 p.p.d. to *Ben Is Dead*, P.O. Box 3166, Hollywood, CA 90028.

Rhino Records: One of the leaders in Retro Hell reissues. Rhino not only re-releases oldies long lost or forgotten, they compile some of the more worthy retro CD compilations around. A few of our faves are the Golden Throats series (celebrities sing!), the Schoolhouse Rock Box Set (featuring all the original favorites, including all the material from the out-of-print 1973 Multiplication Rock LP, and making available for the first time music from the other Schoolhouse Rock subjects, including Grammar

Rock, America Rock, and Science Rock), "Dr. Demento's 25th Anniversary Collection," and "New Wave Hits of the '80s — Just Can't Get Enough." Call Rhino direct at 1-800-432-0020, or ask for them at your favorite record store.

K-Tel: Any of their packaged hits from the '70s or '80s. See your local thrift store.

Also check out a **TeeVee Toons** compilation CD that should be easy to find, called *Television's Greatest Hits '70s and '80s* with 65 TV theme songs.

For the Retro-Obsessed

Our ultimate listings of Retro Hell bands, movies, TV shows, websites, and e-zines are available for $3 plus two stamps from *Ben Is Dead* Retro Lists, P.O. Box 3166, Hollywood, CA 90028. We'll throw in our *Retro*

Top 20 Worst Retro Hell Songs

These are the top 20 worst songs of our Retro Hell, as deemed by the *Ben Is Dead* staff and our readers. Before you have a hissy fit 'cause you actually like some of these songs, please keep in mind we like some of them too (I mean, I *love* the "Devil Went Down to Georgia" song!) — but for the most part we like 'em cause they *were* so awful!

There are obviously an infinite number of bad songs. But while some bad songs and bands are good, in retrospect — like REO Speedwagon, Journey, Loverboy, maybe even Darryl Hall and John Oates — some leave the funny zone immediately and just hurt, like they were designed just to cause real pain. They put the *hell* in Retro Hell, you know. So we did our own little survey of the top worst songs, and these are our winners.

#20 "Werewolves of London" — Warren Zevon

#19 "Owner of a Lonely Heart" — Yes

#18 "Horse with No Name" — America

#17 "Don't Worry, Be Happy" — Bobby McFerrin

#16 "You Light Up My Life" — Debby Boone

#15 "Against the Odds (Take a Look at Me Now)" — Phil Collins

#14 "Lady" — Kenny Rogers

#13 "Take On Me" — Aha

#12 "Poetry Man" — Phoebe Snow

#11 "Boom Boom (Let's Go Back to My Room)" — Paul Lekakis

#10 "Party All the Time" — Eddie Murphy

#9 "We Are the World"

#8 "Bette Davis Eyes" — Kim Carnes

#7 "To All the Girls I've Loved Before" — Julio Iglesias and Willie Nelson

#6 "You've Got a Friend" — James Taylor

#5 "Physical" — Olyvia Newton-John

#4 "I Love L.A." — Randy Newman

#3 "Escape (The Piña Colada Song)" — Rupert Holmes

#2 "Morning Train" — Sheena Easton

#1 "Once, Twice, Three Times a Lady" — Commodores

Plus honorable mention to "Sometimes When We Touch," by Dan Hill, and anything by Rod Stewart and Sting. Check our website for the runners-up.

credits

EDITOR: Darby

ASSOCIATE EDITOR: Nina Blake

EDITORIAL ASSISTANT AND PHOTOGRAPHY: Lorraine Mahru

PHOTO EDITOR: Jocko Weyland

MR. MEMORY: Bruce Elliot

FACT-CHECKING FOOLS: Brian Doherty and Ayala Ben-Yehuda

THIS WORK IS A COLLABORATION OF:

Allison Novak, Amy Wallace, Brian Doherty, Bridget Miller, Bruce Elliot, Candi Strecker, Chip Rowe, Cliff Thurber, Darby Romeo, Dave Coban, Don Bolles, E. C. Cotterman, Enrique Marie Presley, Falling James, Frank Romeo (dad), Gwynne Kahn, Howard Hallis, Jazmine Yates, Jean Erhardt, Jeff Charreaux, Jessy Jones, Jon Salenger, Jory Felice, Ju-Ji Yamasuki, Karrin Vanderwal, Katy Krassner, Lisa Anne Auerbach, Lisa McElroy, Lorraine Mahru, Mark Fletcher, Mike Vague, Mikki Halpin, Morgan and Ferris, Nancy Nathan, Nick Gillespie, Nina Blake, Noël Tolentino, Patty Powers, Pleasant Gehman, Riley More, Rosenda Moore, Selina Romao, Skylaire Alfvegren, Stymie Baldwin, Thomas Conroy, Wendy Bryan, Winnie Weshinskey.

AND THANKS TO THE FOLLOWING FOR THEIR HELP AND PARTICIPATION, INCLUDING MANY OF OUR FRIENDS AND READERS WHO WROTE IN WITH ADDITIONS, CORRECTIONS, AND/OR ENCOURAGEMENT:

Adam Sobolak, Amok Books, Amra Brooks, Ann Greenberg, Arlene Mahru, Ashli Foshee, Ayala Ben-Yehuda, Becca Schemelin, Bob Mack, Brandon Spoons, Carla Bozulich, Chokebore (for the music), Clancy Amanda Cavnar, Clay, Cliff Chenfield, Corey Summers, Creepy Mike

Ruspantini, D'arcy West, Daevid Machen, Deborah Harry, Dorran Ragnarok, Ellen Forney, Ellen Levitt, Emma, Eric Reynolds at Fantagraphics, Eric Brown, Erich Orser, Evan Mack, Gloria Alvear, Golden Apple Comics, Guitargrrl, Heidi R. Post, Hollywood Book and Poster, Jeff Boggs, Jemiah Jefferson, Jen Dalton, Jen Garber, Jennifer Lehrer-Brannon, Jennifer Wasserman, Jessica Alexander, Jessica Gruner, Jimmy Callaway, Joe Blavin, Joe Maynard, John Lydon, John Marr, Johnny Masiulewicz, Jon Rosner, Jonathan Cronin, Judy Jade Miller, Kate Arthur, Kate Seros, Kenyata Sullivan, Kevin Chanel, Kim Gruenenfelder, Kris Haight, Krista Krol, Krista the Scaredy Cat Stalker, Laurel Sterns, Lindsey Anderson, Lisa Roth, Liz Alward, Liza Parelich, Magic Wanda, Malcolm McLaren, Mark Hill, Mark F. Stevens, Martin A. Nemeth, Matt Sweeny, Maureen Shields, Mike Snieder, Mitch Youts, Mondo Video, Natalie Blake, Nick Monahan, Paul Iannone, Pete Relic, Pollyanne Hornbeck, Princess Superstar, Ron Athey, Russ Forster, Sam Crawford, Sarah Zimmerman, Scott Saaveda, Sean Gaffney, Selene Gonzalez, Shannon T. Leonar, Sky "The Fly" Ryan, Stark, Stephanie Fidel, Steve Martin, Steve Moramarco, Steve Payne, Steven F. Sacharff, S. Cirelli, *The Simpsons*, Tom Jones, Tom Rogers, Tori Williams, Trevor Blake, V. Totire, Vince Cornelius, Weird Al Yankovic, Zoë Orgasma, plus any and all who sent their feedback.

AND FINALLY, THANKS TO Paul Harrington, Michael Pietsch, Madeleine Schachter, Susan Canavan, Becky Hemperly, Rachel Salzman, Michael Ian Kaye, Sarah Crichton, David J. High, Tracy Resnik, Julia Sedykh, Mary Reilly, Teresa LoConte, and all at Little, Brown and Co., for making this book possible.

IMAGE CREDITS: AP Wide World Photos (pp. 3, 13, 14, 16, 19, 32, 36, 37, 38, 44, 48, 52, 54, 55, 58, 59, 70, 72, 76, 81, 87, 94, 102, 113, 116, 121, 127, 128, 129, 133, 134, 135, 136, 142, 144, 154, 156, 159, 169, 170, 171, 173, 174, 176, 180, 181, 185, 190, 191, 199, 201, 202, 209, 212, 221, 224, 226, 233, 241, 244, 248); Courtesy of Columbia Pictures Publications (p. 4); Jory Felice (pp. 9, 73, 100, 108, 167); Ellen Forney, from *I Was Seven in '75* (pp. 103, 246); Lorraine Mahru (pp. 2, 42, 58, 64, 82, 95, 109, 117, 119, 147, 160, 204, 216, 234, 235); Joe Matt (p. 238); Tom Rogers (p. 110); Darby Romeo (p. 139); courtesy of Scholastic, Inc. (p. 62).

index

Boldface indicates pages with illustrations.

X

Y

Z